ISC2 Certified Cloud Security Professional (CCSP) Exam Guide

Essential strategies for compliance, governance, and risk management

Kim van Lavieren

www.bpbonline.com

First Edition 2024

Copyright © BPB Publications, India

ISBN: 978-93-55517-654

To View Complete
BPB Publications Catalogue
Scan the QR Code:

Dedicated to

My loving wife:

Sarah van Lavieren

&

My grandparents:

Fred *and* **Ada**

About the Author

Kim van Lavieren is currently a managing consultant at SimplifyNow. Throughout his career, he has helped many organizations bolster their security. His experience ranges from security engineering (at a FANG company) to architecture to the boardroom as a CISO. He holds an MSc in cybersecurity and a BSc in software engineering. Throughout his career, he has obtained a wide variety of (cloud) security certifications, including (but not limited to): CCSP, CISSP, CISM, CISSP-ISSEP, CISSP-ISSAP, CISSP-ISSMP, CSSLP, CGRC, Microsoft Certified: Cybersecurity Architect Expert, and the AWS Security Specialty.

About the Reviewers

❖ **Thomas** has a wealth of experience architecting and delivering cloud-native solutions to global organizations of all sizes. Being recognized as a 'leader who coaches', Thomas is proficient at leading teams as part of larger solution delivery projects or working independently within a virtual team to deliver on specific solution areas.

He has experience of working in the Microsoft channel and recently in a well-regarded Cyber Risk organization. Tom was responsible for the overall platform architecture of solutions delivered across several SIEM, EDR, NDR, and EASM vendors.

Tom has earned a mix of vendor certifications from Microsoft, Swimlane, and Armis and holds the ISC2 Certified Cloud Security Professional qualification, demonstrating expertise in multiple domains covering compliance, governance, and cloud security.

❖ **Fouad** is a seasoned Lead Consultant and Cloud Security Architect with 15 years of professional experience in the digital and software industry at global corporations. Fouad excels in designing and implementing comprehensive cloud solutions across multi-cloud platforms. He has assisted numerous businesses in effectively governing and safeguarding their information, proactively identifying cybersecurity risks, and enabling them to make informed and strategic business decisions. Fouad is CISSP, CISM, CASP+ certified.

❖ **Dwayne Natwick** is the CEO of Captain Hyperscaler, LLC, a technical cloud and cybersecurity training company. Dwayne was previously the Global Principal Cloud Security Lead at Atos, a multi-cloud GSI. He has been in IT, security design, and architecture for over 30 years. His love for teaching led him to become a Microsoft Certified Trainer (MCT) Regional Lead and a Microsoft Most Valuable Professional (MVP) for Security and Azure.

Dwayne has a master's degree in Business IT from Walsh College, the CISSP, CGRC, SSCP, and CCSP from ISC2, CRISC from ISACA, and 18 Microsoft certifications, including Identity and Access Administrator, Azure Security Engineer, and Microsoft 365 Security Administrator. Dwayne can be found providing and sharing information on social media, industry conferences, his blog site, and his YouTube channel.

Originally from Maryland, Dwayne currently resides in Michigan with his wife and three children.

❖ **Pushkar Nagle** is an InfoSec professional with 13 years of experience, holding professional IT certifications, including CCSP, CISSP, CISM, CEH, and CCNA. Pushkar attained a Licentiate Diploma in Electronics from VJTI, a B.Engg. in Electronics from Mumbai University. Pushkar has held several positions, including penetration tester, vulnerability manager, risk management advisor, and application security consultant. Pushkar has experience in handling large and complex penetration testing projects, providing risk advisory to businesses, and assisting organizations in vulnerability remediation.

Pushkar has managed 500+ onsite/offsite Web Application pentests, Mobile applications, Infrastructure, Build & Code reviews, and other risk-based security testing projects.

❖ **Andy Pantelli** is CISSP, CCSP, ACIIS, CCNP Security, CCNP Ent, CCDP, CCNA Cyber Ops, CCNA Security, JNCIP-E, VMware VCP, AWS Cloud Practitioner and Mimecast Secure Email Gateway certified. Previously serving in the Armed Forces, he completed 2 operational tours of duty before settling in the North West of England. He has over 20 years experience in Information Security across the Aviation, Financial, Legal, & Global Media sectors. He is currently a Cyber Security Architect consulting for the UK Central Government.

Acknowledgement

There are a few people I want to thank for their continued and ongoing support, both concerning this book and my cybersecurity career in general.

Firstly, I want to thank my wife for her tireless encouragement and support while writing my first book. I also want to thank my father for his extensive review work throughout the writing process.

Secondly, I want to thank my long-time mentors, "Coach Ron" Woerner and Ralph de Graaf. They have played a vital role in my security journey and have helped me get to where I am now.

Additionally, I want to thank my employer, SimplifyNow, for always supporting my professional growth and allowing me time to dedicate to this book. Together, we are building a safer world.

Lastly, I want to thank the publishing team at BPB for their extensive support, guidance, and assistance in making this book a reality.

Preface

The book will teach you the contrasts and similarities between cloud and on-premises computing. Show you reliable mechanisms to create a secure cloud environment, from the strategic to the operational level. It highlights what security controls help you create a secure cloud from the start and guides you into setting up security processes to keep your cloud secure over time.

The (ISC)2 CCSP is the industry's most sought-after vendor-agnostic cloud security certification. This book prepares you to pass the exam and excel within your business by providing tangible and concrete mechanisms to secure your organization's cloud environment.

The book takes you on a journey throughout all facets of secure cloud computing, from the policies an organization should have to the technical nitty-gritty of securing security groups. The book uses real-life examples, experiences, and tips and tricks from one of the industry's most broadly certified ISC2 professionals.

The book is divided into 24 chapters that cover the domains of the ISC2 CCSP exam. The details are listed below:

Chapter 1: Understanding Cloud Computing Concepts - Cloud computing is different from on-premise computing in many aspects. This chapter highlights definitions related to cloud computing and examines the shared responsibility model between Cloud Service Providers and customers. The chapter reviews cloud computing characteristics and common technologies in the cloud domain and explores the different levels and models for cloud computing

Chapter 2: Concepts and Design Principles of Cloud Security - Security in the cloud relies on foundational concepts and design principles. This chapter explores how cryptography, **Identity and Access Management (IAM)**, network security, and other concepts form the building blocks of cloud security.

Chapter 3: Evaluating Cloud Service Providers - In a world with a wide variety of Cloud Service Providers, it is challenging to pick a provider that meets your requirements. This chapter helps you pick a CSP by providing methods to evaluate different vendors against your business requirements

Chapter 4: Discover, Classify, and Manage Cloud Data - Storing data in the cloud may sound scary, however, implementing good mechanisms to discover, classify, and manage data in the cloud will offer you unprecedented data security.

Chapter 5: Cloud Storage Architectures and their Security Technologies - Now that you know how data "lives" in the cloud, it is time to explore how different architectures support data types. This chapter explores different architectures for data storage, the threats they face, and what security technologies should be implemented for them.

Chapter 6: Cloud Infrastructure and Components - Cloud infrastructure relies on similar components as on-premise computing. However, how cloud computing is managed is very different from on-premise computing. This chapter explores how cloud infrastructure is set up, used, and managed securely.

Chapter 7: Datacenter Security - You might have heard, "The cloud is just someone else's computer". In this chapter, we explore how data center security is a vital part of cloud computing, regardless of the service model.

Chapter 8: Risk Management in the Cloud - The cloud comes with new and familiar risks, this chapter examines how you can effectively manage and analyze risks within a cloud platform or cloud infrastructure.

Chapter 9: Cloud Security Controls - Understanding and managing risks is extremely important. However, picking the correct controls to (cost) effectively mitigate risk can be extra challenging in the cloud. This chapter covers how you can implement security controls within your cloud environment.

Chapter 10: Business Continuity and Disaster Recovery - While we design for systems and applications to be resilient, things go wrong sometimes. This chapter dives into ensuring your business continuity is ensured, even when things go wrong. The chapter also explains strategies on how to recover from disasters if they do occur.

Chapter 11: Secure Deployment, Awareness, and Training - The cloud offers new perspectives and tools for security, however, developing insecurely is as dangerous in the cloud as it is on-premise. This chapter explores common pitfalls, cloud-based vulnerabilities, and development tactics to ensure the software is developed securely within or outside of the cloud.

Chapter 12: Security Testing and Software Verification - Secure development is essential in creating a secure (cloud) ecosystem. However, while we always aim to develop securely, we must verify that we did so. This chapter explores the role of security testing methods such as static and dynamic code analysis, code review, penetration testing, and functional and non-functional testing. The chapter also sheds light on how APIs can be secured, and vulnerabilities within dependencies or open-source software can be detected.

Chapter 13: Specifics of Cloud Security Architecture - Cloud computing allows us to look at security from a different perspective. This means that we also have to use security tooling in different places and in different ways. This chapter explores supplemental cloud security components such as web applications firewalls, API gateways, and database activity monitoring. Moreover, the chapter dives into encryption in the cloud, security of virtualization through containers, microservices, and sandboxing

Chapter 14: Identity and Access Management - Broad access is one of the characteristics of the cloud. However, to have broad access and be secure, we must manage identities effectively and securely. This chapter explores how SSO (single sign-on), IdP (identity providers), user federation, secrets management, multi-factor authentication, and **cloud access security brokers (CASB)** form the puzzle pieces of secure access in the cloud.

Chapter 15: Infrastructure Security - While **cloud service providers (CSPs)** take over a lot of security responsibilities, it is essential to understand the underlying technologies that enable the security functions. This chapter explores how hardware security

models, trusted platform modules, and hypervisor security allow CSPs to create a secure computing environment for their customers.

Chapter 16: Secure Configuration - Security tooling and complex cloud architectures can improve security, however, the configuration powering the tools and systems is what ultimately decides if an ecosystem is secure. This chapter explores the different security policies that must be in place to create a secure environment. It dives into secure network configuration, network security controls, OS Hardening, patch management, Infrastructure as Code, High Availability, Monitoring of performance and hardware, backup, and restore.

Chapter 17: Security Operations - Policies and configuration are essential to create a secure baseline within your environment. However, security processes ensure your environment stays secure over time and adapts to emerging threats. This chapter further expands on security policies, digital forensics, security operations like SOC, SIEM, incident management, and how to communicate with customers, vendors, partners, and others if all our controls prove to be ineffective.

Chapter 18: Legal and Regulatory Requirements in the Cloud - Cloud computing has many benefits, it offers better availability, for example. Some of these characteristics have drawbacks. When talking about legal requirements, the dispersion of data can complicate the scope of regulations your organization must adhere to. This chapter explores various legal requirements and risks associated with computing in the cloud.

Chapter 19: Privacy - Similar to legal requirements, privacy issues can become more complicated in the cloud. It is essential to approach privacy with a well-thought out approach. This chapter zooms in on country-specific legislation, data categories, jurisdictions for privacy, standard privacy requirements, and privacy impact assessments.

Chapter 20: Cloud Auditing and Enterprise Risk Management - The work of developers, system admins, and security engineers is not the only work that changes when switching to cloud computing. Auditors have had to change their approach as well. In an environment with shared responsibilities, auditing can be challenging. This chapter equips you with tactics, tips, and tricks on auditing processes within the cloud, the types of audit reports you might require of a CSP, how you plan audits, and how you can provide auditors with the data they need before they ask for it.

Chapter 21: Contracts and the Cloud - When you decide to use cloud computing within your ecosystem, how you purchase services changes significantly. You will have to ensure the services you purchase live up to your organization's expectations. This chapter explores how you can use service-level agreements, master service agreements, and statements of work to ensure you get the services you need. While vendor, contract, and supply chain management ensure you can prevent issues now and in the future.

Chapter 22: Duties of a CCSP - Passing the CCSP exam allows you to join a select group of cloud security experts. However, being a CCSP or associate of ISC2 also bears Responsibilities. In this chapter, the responsibilities of a CCSP are highlighted based on the ISC2 code of ethics.

Chapter 23: Exam Tips - The exam tips section highlights a breakdown of the exam process and provides tips and tricks to approach the exam most effectively.

Chapter 24: Exam Questions - The exam prep section contains a CCSP practice exam to test your knowledge across the six different domains.

Code Bundle and Coloured Images

Please follow the link to download the
Code Bundle and the *Coloured Images* of the book:

https://rebrand.ly/kj3cv76

The code bundle for the book is also hosted on GitHub at
https://github.com/bpbpublications/ISC2-Certified-Cloud-Security-Professional-Exam-Guide
In case there's an update to the code, it will be updated on the existing GitHub repository.

We have code bundles from our rich catalogue of books and videos available at **https://github.com/bpbpublications**. Check them out!

Errata

We take immense pride in our work at BPB Publications and follow best practices to ensure the accuracy of our content to provide with an indulging reading experience to our subscribers. Our readers are our mirrors, and we use their inputs to reflect and improve upon human errors, if any, that may have occurred during the publishing processes involved. To let us maintain the quality and help us reach out to any readers who might be having difficulties due to any unforeseen errors, please write to us at :

errata@bpbonline.com

Your support, suggestions and feedbacks are highly appreciated by the BPB Publications' Family.

Piracy

If you come across any illegal copies of our works in any form on the internet, we would be grateful if you would provide us with the location address or website name. Please contact us at **business@bpbonline.com** with a link to the material.

If you are interested in becoming an author

If there is a topic that you have expertise in, and you are interested in either writing or contributing to a book, please visit **www.bpbonline.com**. We have worked with thousands of developers and tech professionals, just like you, to help them share their insights with the global tech community. You can make a general application, apply for a specific hot topic that we are recruiting an author for, or submit your own idea.

Reviews

Please leave a review. Once you have read and used this book, why not leave a review on the site that you purchased it from? Potential readers can then see and use your unbiased opinion to make purchase decisions. We at BPB can understand what you think about our products, and our authors can see your feedback on their book. Thank you!

For more information about BPB, please visit **www.bpbonline.com**.

Join our book's Discord space

Join the book's Discord Workspace for Latest updates, Offers, Tech happenings around the world, New Release and Sessions with the Authors:

https://discord.bpbonline.com

Table of Contents

\|⌐

145

CHAPTER 1
Understanding Cloud Computing Concepts

Introduction

Cloud computing is different from on-premise computing in many ways. This chapter helps you understand the various forms of cloud computing. This chapter will introduce you to the characteristics of cloud computing and standard technologies found in the cloud. It also examines the cloud reference architecture, which outlines responsibilities between **Cloud Service Providers (CSPs)**, cloud consumers, brokers, and auditors.

Structure

This chapter covers the following topics:

- Cloud computing characteristics
- Public cloud, private cloud, hybrid cloud, community, and multi-cloud
- Cloud operating models (IaaS, PaaS, and SaaS)
- Shared responsibility model
- Cloud reference architecture
- Building block technologies (virtualization, storage, networking, databases, and orchestration)

- Cloud computing characteristics
- The impact of cloud technology

Objectives

In this chapter, you will be able to understand the concepts of cloud computing. You will gain an understanding of the different shapes of cloud computing, the related service models, and the characteristics of cloud computing overall. The chapter will outline how cloud computing environments can integrate with an organization's IT landscape. It will also cover the strengths and weaknesses every cloud computing service model presents and help you determine which model is suitable in what situation. The chapter covers all building block technologies you will see in cloud computing environments while also helping you outline the responsibilities within the cloud.

Essence of cloud computing

Cloud computing. Many people do not know what to expect when they hear this term. However, the essence of cloud computing is simple. Cloud computing is using someone else's computing resources for your computation needs.

Throughout the past decades, we have already been working with forms of cloud computing. Think of web applications offered by third-party providers (**Software as a Service**) or even companies like **Azure** that allow you to rent servers and infrastructure (**Infrastructure as a Service**).

The main difference between current-day cloud computing and the examples above is that companies have branded themselves as **cloud service providers** (**CSPs**). These CSPs have adopted a business model of providing computing services to their customers through on-demand self-service in a scalable fashion. A web hosting company allows you to rent a pre-defined number of servers. But a CSP lets you (automatically) start and create new servers to accommodate more traffic or stop servers or instances when you no longer need them. We call this rapid concept elasticity.

Cloud computing has more benefits than past-day hosting models. One of them is called **measured service**. Measured service means that your usage of the CSPs services is continuously measured, and you only pay for what you use. Combined with rapid elasticity, this offers some attractive benefits.

For example, if your company uses an internal application only during work hours, you can shut down the servers that support the application after work hours. Meaning you would only pay for the hours that the servers were running. If you have a workday from 9 am until 5 pm, you would only pay for 8 hours of operation.

Of course, you could do this in your data center, but you would have to shut down an entire server to save on energy costs. Since you already paid for the servers, turning them off does not save as much money. If you use virtualization within your data center, shutting down a server might also impact other applications. In short, rapid elasticity can be challenging to achieve in **on-premise computing.**

CSPs use an operating model called **resource pooling** to facilitate rapid elasticity and measured service. Resource pooling means the provider has a pool of computing resources. For example, storage is assigned to a specific customer **on-demand**. On-demand assignment of resources means the following;

In the example above, your company only uses a server during work hours. Once the server shuts down, the available computing resources return to the pool. Similarly, if another CSP customer requires more resources, the compute capacity you just released becomes available to another customer.

EXAM TIP: Resource pooling is a significant risk of cloud computing as it involves sharing hardware resources with other organizations.

The effect of resource pooling is significant to CSPs as it allows them to serve multiple customers without having dedicated hardware for every customer. Limiting the amount of required hardware lets the CSPs control costs. However, it can also bring risks to the table. If customers demand more service than is available, the CSP might not have enough resources to satisfy demand, leading to service outages. On the flip side of this coin, when a CSP overprovisions its resources, and there is little demand, the CSP is incurring high costs for no returns. Many CSPs will offer customers reduced rates if they commit to a minimal pre-determined usage level. Such commitments allow the CSP to determine better how much hardware should be available, preventing the resources from being over - or under-leveraged.

The last characteristic of cloud computing is called **broad network access**. Broad network access means cloud computing resources are available to customers online. Most CSPs (like **AWS**, **Microsoft Azure**, and **GCP**) offers an online portal that allows you to log in and provision your resources on demand over the internet. Contrary to on-premise computing, where the need for new resources requires the purchase of new servers and access to the physical site of the devices. Broad network access makes cloud computing easy.

To summarize, NIST defines the five characteristics of cloud computing: on-demand self-service, broad network access, rapid elasticity, measured service, and resource pooling. These characteristics will be the red line throughout this book, presenting many significant strengths and specific security challenges.

Cloud comes in many shapes

Cloud computing is applicable in different ways. An organization might use cloud computing for all or some of its workloads. A computing cloud environment is creatable at different scopes as well. Some clouds serve a single company, while others might help a whole community of companies. Regardless of the shape of cloud computing used, every model has its benefits and drawbacks. Lets us explore the different forms of cloud computing that exist.

Public cloud is probably one of the most well-known shapes of cloud computing. In a public cloud, a CSP provides cloud computing services to virtually anyone wanting to purchase them. The CSP wants to make it easy for customers to consume their services. Because a public cloud provides services to a broad audience, they usually are very good at self-service provisioning. However, a public cloud also means many customers share the available resources. When you share resources with other organizations, you must realize that this creates security risks.

An attacker on a completely unrelated company could cause service outages (or worse) to your organization. For example, if another customer is hosting a virtual machine on the same server your virtual machine is running, and an attacker can break out of the virtual machine of the other company, they can potentially disrupt the availability of the underlying server. Of course, cloud providers take measures to prevent such events from occurring, and we will examine those measures throughout the book.

Private cloud is a form of cloud computing where the hardware (and infrastructure) used is exclusive to a single customer, or the company itself owns and manages the hardware. A private cloud is generally more secure but almost always more costly. If the organization operates the private cloud, it also involves more effort and knowledge of secure design and operations. Many CSPs provide private cloud services to the customer by allowing them to reserve hardware for their organization only. Other large parties, like governmental agencies, even build their cloud computing environments in their data centers. When a company or governmental agency creates its cloud, they act as the CSP and the consumer. The consumer can then still benefit from the characteristics of cloud computing without having to share underlying infrastructure with other organizations.

Hybrid Cloud is a form of cloud computing where private and public clouds are combined. A hybrid cloud allows an organization to pick and choose where they want to process specific workloads. Determining where you process a workload will enable you to separate sensitive workloads. You might not want to process in a public cloud from everyday computing that does not require dedicated infrastructure. Public and private cloud environments are often connected using dedicated connections such as VPNs or even leased lines. The following table shows examples of the composition of different cloud shapes:

Public cloud	Private cloud	Hybrid cloud	Multi cloud
Microsoft Azure	on-premise data center	on-premise data center	Microsoft Azure
OR		AND	AND

Public cloud	Private cloud	Hybrid cloud	Multi cloud
Amazon Web Services (AWS)		Amazon Web Services (AWS)	Amazon Web Services (AWS)
OR			AND
Google Cloud Platform (GCP)			Google Cloud Platform (GCP)

Table 1.1: Examples of public, private, hybrid, and multi-cloud setups

Community cloud is a form of cloud computing where multiple organizations share the same computing environment. Community clouds are common for organizations that collaborate. For example, universities that perform research projects can benefit from using a shared cloud environment to process and share research results. Sharing a computing environment with other organizations can pose security risks, as every organization must ensure its internal security practices are in line.

For example, if university A uses usernames and passwords to authenticate and University B uses **Multi-Factor Authentication (MFA)**. Attackers would be far more likely to gain access to the environment through a compromised university A user. Therefore, it is essential to create a standard set of controls that establishes a security baseline of how the community cloud should be secured, configured, and operated between all organizations.

Multi-cloud is the last form of cloud computing to cover. A multi-cloud environment is an environment that exists out of multiple cloud environments. For example, a multi-cloud environment might have a **Microsoft Azure environment** and an **Amazon Web Services (AWS) environment**. Separating your computation needs over multiple clouds allows you to leverage specific tools that a CSP has to offer. Those tools might work better at one CSP than the other, or costs might be lower at one CSP than the other. However, many organizations also choose a multi-cloud environment to fight the risk of vendor lock-in. Vendor lock-ins are not specific to cloud computing and mean that you establish a dependency on a single vendor that might force you to keep doing business with them as your operations are highly dependent on the vendor.

In some cases, this dependency on a vendor can be dangerous. For example, a vendor promises to perform security patches daily per their **service level agreement (SLA)**. But it turns out your vendor does not do this. Your organization confronts the vendor, but the vendor refuses to fix the issue. Your organization might choose to pull out of the contract, but if all your online services are hosted at this vendor, pulling out might mean you have to shut down your services. Shutting down the services for a prolonged period can significantly damage an organization. Multi-cloud attempts to solve this, allowing you to build the same online services at two vendors. If you properly sync data between the environments, you can shut down the environment at the vendor you no longer want to work with and continue with the other vendor. Remember that not every multi-cloud environment solves vendor lock-in and that the effectiveness of preventing vendor lock-in depends on the setup of the cloud environments.

You might have realized that private, public, hybrid, community, and multi-cloud cloud computing are not mutually exclusive. For example, you can create a hybrid community multi-cloud. Such a cloud might consist of an on-premise data center at a university, a cloud environment in AWS, and a cloud environment in Azure accessible to multiple universities. The following figure provides an example of a hybrid multi-cloud:

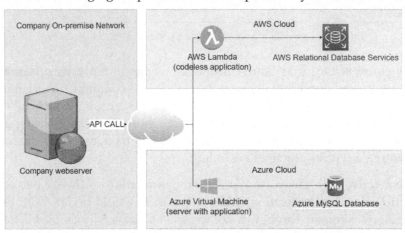

Figure 1.1: Example of a hybrid multi-cloud infrastructure where an on-premise web server makes API calls to Microsoft Azure and AWS

EXAM-TIP When taking the CCSP exam, it is essential to understand the different forms of cloud computing. The exam will always consider a private cloud more secure than a public cloud, and you should consider multi-cloud as a control to prevent vendor lock-in

Operating (in) the cloud

Now that you know what shapes cloud computing comes in, it is time to examine how you can operate (in) the cloud. A significant benefit of cloud computing is that you can choose how you consume services. These options are called **cloud service models** and consist of the three following major categories:

Infrastructure as a Service (IaaS) is a service model that allows you to purchase cloud services as computing infrastructure. This infrastructure consists of virtual networks, virtual machines, storage devices, and other related services, such as logging services. IaaS as a service allows you to create a virtual data center in which you have control of the way the virtual overlay network is set up and can completely configure the operating systems of your virtual machines. IaaS offers you the most considerable amount of customization options but also the most significant amount of responsibility.

Platform as a Service (PaaS) is a service model that allows you to purchase cloud services in the shape of a platform that enables you to do specific things. For example, a PaaS service often offered is a database service (think of **DynamoDB** in AWS or **Azure SQL Database** in Microsoft Azure) or a service to run code directly (**AWS Lambda** in AWS). PaaS provides a managed solution you can leverage to execute the workloads you need without setting up the underlying infrastructure. PaaS has limited customization options but also transfers much responsibility from the consumer to the CSP.

Software as a Service (SaaS) is a service model allowing you to purchase full-fledged applications for a specific business need. For example, **GitHub** is a SaaS offering for code repositories and version management. So, how is SaaS different from a regular desktop application? SaaS applications are still cloud-based and, when properly designed, benefit from cloud computing characteristics. For example, you should only pay for your usage, and the application can be very scalable while being reachable over the internet. SaaS offerings usually only offer customization within the software you are purchasing. You will likely not have any control over the underlying infrastructure.

X as a Service, if you have been around cloud computing, you might have noticed many other terms, such as **Identity as a Service**, **Security as a Service**, **Security Operations Center (SOC) as a Service**. Dozens of service models outline specific functions *as a service*. In most cases, these service models are SaaS models that offer applications to satisfy a particular need. For example, Identity as a Service can come as an identity provider such as **Keycloak** or **Okta**.

EXAM TIP: IaaS, PaaS, and SaaS are the only "official" service models the CCSP exam considers. You must understand these service models throughout to pass the CCSP exam.

Following the service models and their responsibilities are explained:

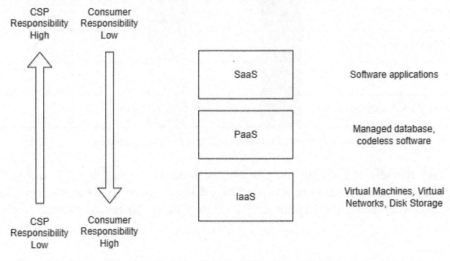

Figure 1.2: Service models, their responsibilities, and common examples

Shared responsibility

Now that you have a basic understanding of the service models, examining how they affect the responsibilities of the cloud consumer, CSP, and cloud auditor is essential. Understanding how responsibility sharing takes place in every service model will allow you to determine where your organization must focus its effort to implement security controls.

Let us start with what shared responsibility means. We have already examined that cloud computing comes in many forms and operating models. The shape and operating model have consequences for who manages what.

It is time to look at the following table to understand how responsibilities align in the different operating models:

Controls / Responsible party	IaaS		PaaS		SaaS	
	CSP	Consumer	CSP	Consumer	CSP	Consumer
Data						
Accounts and Access						
IAM Infrastructure Security						
Application Security						
Overlay Network Security[1]						
Operating System Security						
Hypervisor Security						
Underlay Network Security						
Physical Device Security						
Physical Data Center Security						

Table 1.2: Shared Responsibilities within cloud computing

EXAM TIP: Review the shared responsibility models created by the large CSPs to gain a good understanding of this topic Shared Responsibility Model - Amazon Web Services (AWS) and Shared responsibility in the Cloud - Microsoft Azure | Microsoft Learn

---

[1] *Overlay networks are networks that are propagated on top of the network underlay (the physical network). An example of an overlay network is a VPN.*

You might have noticed these interesting patterns in the table above:

- The cloud service provider is always responsible for the physical data center security, physical device security, underlay network security, and hypervisor security.

- The cloud consumer is always responsible for the data. It is essential to realize that controlling access to data and ensuring your data is stored and handled securely within your applications is solely your organization's responsibility.

- You might have noticed that some service models show overlap in some responsibilities. Some responsibilities are shared. For example, in a PaaS model, the CSP and cloud consumer are responsible for overlay network security, application security, and IAM infrastructure security. The CSP provides the base level controls for network security, application security, and IAM infrastructure security, while the cloud consumer can evaluate these controls and turn on additional controls based on the requirements.

First, examine why the CSP is always responsible for so many controls. The reason behind this is simple. The CSP provides computing infrastructure to its customers through its data centers. However, the CSP does not give customers access to their physical data centers. The fact that the CSP is responsible for the security of everything data center can be very beneficial from a security perspective. Small organizations cannot often maintain data centers and all the required security. Additionally, purchasing, maintaining, and replacing hardware requires significant up-front investment and technical knowledge not required of the customer in cloud computing.

Secondly, why is the customer always responsible for data? Customer responsibility for data is primarily due to security considerations. An organization does not want the vendor to be able to access, read, and modify their data. Therefore, CSPs organize their cloud offerings so that direct access to data is often impossible (or very limited). For example, a CSP might offer encryption with a **Customer Managed Key (CMK)** or **Customer Provided Key (CPK)**. Such keys are unknown to the CSP, meaning they cannot decrypt the data without the customer providing the key. A CSP can, of course, not be responsible for something they cannot access. Security of data in the cloud involves a variety of controls. For example, the customer is responsible for enabling encryption (where needed), making back-ups, and, most importantly, access control to the data.

Lastly, shared responsibilities are also part of the nature of the different service models. For example, in a PaaS service model, the CSP and cloud consumer are responsible for overlay network security. You might wonder why this is the case.

Let us look at the following example. If a CSP provides a PaaS database, the database is a service. The customer does not have to manage the underlying network or the database server. However, the customer is responsible for ensuring that only authorized applications can access the database over the network. Similarly, the CSP is responsible for ensuring your service is always available. Thus, the CSP must protect against network-based attacks such as **Denial of Service (DoS)** that disrupt service availability by causing excessive traffic to a particular server or network.

Similarly, suppose you are running a codeless application (an application for which you do not set up the runtime environment). In that case, the CSP ensures the application's secure environment. However, the customer is responsible for writing secure code. Meaning both parties are responsible for a part of the application security.

EXAM TIP: To pass the CCSP exam, you must understand which party is responsible for which security controls—practice by picking a random CSP cloud offering and modeling who is responsible for which control. Verify by referencing the CSP's shared responsibility model

Cloud reference architecture

An essential part of the CCSP exam is understanding the cloud reference architecture as defined by the NIST[2]. To understand the cloud reference architecture, we must first examine which parties can be involved in cloud computing. NIST identifies four distance parties; The **Cloud Consumer**, the cloud service provider, the cloud auditor, and the cloud broker. We have already examined the cloud consumer and the cloud service provider. However, not the terms of cloud auditor and cloud broker.

Many organizations have concerns about hosting their data and applications in the cloud. These concerns center around data confidentiality and (local) laws and regulations. A **Cloud Auditor** is, simply put, an auditor that performs audits on the cloud itself and its use. Cloud auditors play a critical role in ensuring cloud service providers provide the security they claim to provide. Likewise, cloud auditors can help cloud consumers determine if they are properly executing their responsibilities within the cloud. After all, in cloud computing, responsibilities are shared.

A **Cloud Broker** is a party that provides services that help a cloud consumer pick and purchase the right cloud computing services for their business and security needs. You can view a cloud broker as an intermediary between a cloud service provider and a cloud consumer. The cloud broker often resells cloud services to a cloud consumer and can help the cloud consumer implement or even operate the cloud services within their ecosystem.

In the cloud reference architecture, NIST provides a conceptual model of cloud architecture and what roles the different parties play, let us take a look at it:

---

[2] *NIST Cloud Computing Reference Architecture | NIST*

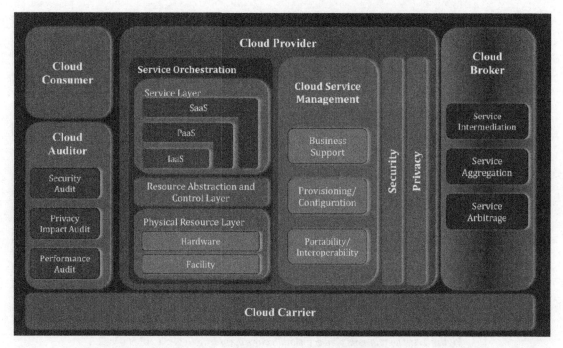

Figure 1.3: *The cloud reference architecture as defined by NIST in NIST SP 500-292*

When you examine the cloud reference architecture, you will notice that the cloud consumer is, in essence, the customer of the other parties involved. Cloud consumers can use a cloud broker to procure services from a cloud provider. Alternatively, a cloud consumer can purchase services directly from the cloud provider.

Cloud auditors play an exciting role. On one side, the cloud service providers hire cloud auditors to audit their cloud services. But cloud consumers can also utilize cloud auditors to audit their private clouds or how they use public cloud services. Of course, cloud auditors also interact with cloud brokers, as they often resell cloud services.

Audits are essential for cloud service providers to gain certifications for (international) standards such as ISO27001 and to obtain audit reports they can share with their customers. A CSP must have evidence to provide to its customers that its security controls are in place and effective. After all, the cloud consumer cannot access the data center or underlying infrastructure to verify the controls themselves. Cloud consumers cannot audit the hardware and infrastructure their data resides on, which is a significant difference from on-premise computing. The following figure displays the relationships in the cloud environment:

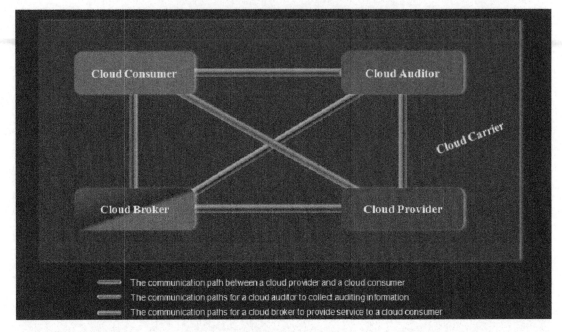

Figure 1.4: *The relations between cloud actors according to NIST SP 500-292*

EXAM TIP: During the CCSP exam, you will likely get questions about the challenges of auditing in the Cloud. You must understand that the cloud consumer has limited abilities to audit the services the CSP provides.

EXAM TIP: Review NIST 500-292. It contains valuable examples of interaction between the different parties in a cloud computing environment.

Building block technologies

Up to this point, we have examined the characteristics of cloud computing, what forms exist, the usage of service models, how responsibilities differentiate based on the previous, and what actors you will find in the cloud computing landscape. Now, it is time to examine how CSPs build cloud computing services.

Any cloud computing environment consists of the following foundational building block technologies: networking, storage, virtualization, databases, and orchestration. In the following section, we will examine every building block technology and provide examples.

Networking

Networking is essential to cloud computing in many ways. Firstly, the CSP must ensure they can provide services to multiple customers (multi-tenancy) over the internet (broad access) at any time (on-demand self-service). To do so, CSPs use networking to facilitate the ability to use services in conjunction and over the internet. The CSPs manage the physical underlay and networking hardware while providing the cloud consumer with a network overlay or virtual network.

Virtual networks form the core of cloud computing services. Virtual networks allow customers to segregate their traffic from other customers virtually. The network overlays enable the CSP to create multiple private networks on top of one physical infrastructure. Virtual networks prevent data leakage to other customers on the same physical network.

For example, imagine if the CSP had a single physical network for all its customers. If you place a machine in that network and configure its networking adapter to promiscuous mode, another customer could easily listen in on the communications of another. Such a network would be terrible for data confidentiality.

However, by creating overlay networks, every virtual network acts like its own physical network. Customers cannot intercept each other's communication, and the CSPs' maintenance traffic on the main network does not interfere with customer traffic.

Another aspect of networking is cloud computing surrounds high availability. CSPs offer **service level agreements (SLAs)** that allow minimal downtime. To facilitate this, CSPs have to be able to host your services in different zones (often called **Availability Zones**). Zones are geographically dispersed to ensure that power grid disruptions or other disasters do not affect multiple zones simultaneously. Networking allows the CSPs to connect different machines and equipment in these zones to act as a single entity to enable fail-over.

In general, most cloud service providers make the following networking resources available to their customers:

- Virtual networks (subnets)
- Virtual firewalls or access control lists
- Security groups
- Virtual **web application firewalls (WAFs)**
- Virtual network interfaces
- Direct connections to on-premise networks
- Virtual network peering

Virtual networks interconnect customer systems and services. These networks act like *normal* physical network. You can assign virtual network adapters to these networks to give virtual machines access or directly allow certain PaaS and SaaS services to access other devices and services within the network.

Virtual firewalls or **access control lists (ACLs)** allow you to determine who is or is not permitted to access a virtual network. ACLs can usually allow or deny incoming and outgoing traffic. Virtual firewalls or ACLs are based on IP addresses or other device-related information.

Security groups usually also act as a firewall and deny by default construction. Security groups do not allow traffic unless the specified traffic is permitted (in contrast to ACLs). Security groups often work with identities, network adapters, and services. A security group can allow a specific service to access another service or from a device to another. Security groups are usually attached to an instance, while an ACL ties to a virtual network (subnet).

Virtual web application firewalls are a specialized type of firewall capable of reading the content of requests and are usually (somewhat) context aware. Since a WAF can understand requests and place them into context, it can recognize attacks in the contents of an attack. For example, a WAF might detect SQL injection in a request and block this.

Virtual network interface is a virtualized form of a physical network adapter. A virtual adapter can be assigned to a virtual device of service. The benefit of virtual adapters is that you can implement security controls on the adapter. While ensuring the adapter stays assigned to the correct device even though your application might run on servers in entirely different data centers every time youuse it.

Many CSPs offer **direct connections to on-premise networks**. Direct connections allow you to connect your virtual cloud network to your on-premise data center network, usually by creating a **virtual private network (VPN)** tunnel of the internet to connect both networks. Sometimes, a CSP might offer a direct connection that consists of a leased line that connects your data center directly with the CSP data center. Direct connections are commonplace in hybrid clouds.

Virtual network peering allows you to join multiple virtual networks (or subnets). By doing so, you can combine virtual networks within an organization or even combine virtual networks across organizations. Let us examine the implementation of the network building blocks at different CSPs, please refer to following table:

Service	AWS	Azure
Virtual Network	**Virtual Private Cloud (VPC)**	vNet
WAFs	**AWS WAF**	**Azure WAF**
VNI	**Elastic Network Interface (ENI)**	**vNIC**
Direct connections to on-premise networks	**Virtual Private Gateway / Direct Connect**	**ExpressRoute**
Virtual network peering	**VPC Peering**	**vNet Peering**

Table 1.3: Most CSPs offer the same building blocks but use different names

Storage

The networking alone is not enough to create a usable cloud. One of the significant components of cloud computing is storage. Storage comes in different forms in the cloud.

The first type is **block storage**. Block storage is, in essence, a hard drive. As a cloud consumer, you can configure how much storage you want and store data like on a computer hard drive. Block storage is primarily helpful for usage with virtual machines as it will hold the operating system. The main benefit of block storage is that it offers low latency.

The second type is file storage. **File storage** is a way to store files. You might have worked with your organization's file storage solutions such as **Google Drive**, **DropBox**, **SFTP servers**, or a network drive. File storage is usually available to network users and is not necessarily associated with a single machine or service. File storage offers good performance while allowing files.

The last type of storage is **object storage**. Object storage allows you to store objects such as files. Object storage is often available online and is accessible through **application programmable interfaces** (**APIs**) and allows ultra-granular access control. In an object storage instance, the CSP handles all underlying mechanisms, meaning you can store unlimited files without reserving more storage space. Let us review some examples of storage implementations at different CSPs, please refer to following table:

Service	AWS	Azure
Block Storage	Amazon Elastic Block Store (EBS)	Azure Disk Storage
File Storage	Amazon Elastic File System (EFS)	Azure Files
Object Storage	S3	Azure blob storage

Table 1.4: Most CSPs offer the same storage building blocks but use different names

Virtualization

Virtualization is another essential building block of cloud computing. Virtualization allows CSPs to create huge workloads on a single physical server. Without virtualization, the CSP must purchase dedicated machines for every workload. Not only would this be hugely unaffordable, but it would also be highly inefficient. By virtualization, the CSP can serve many customers from that single device and provide or de-provision computing quickly and on demand. Without virtualization, rapid elasticity and on-demand self-service are not possible.

When discussing virtualization, it is essential to understand what types are applied. We have already covered virtual networks in which a virtual instance of a network is used as an overlay to carry over the physical underlay network. However, for the CSSP exam, you must also understand how compute capacity is virtualized.

The first form of virtualization used by CSPs is called **type-1 virtualization**. A dedicated physical device runs a dedicated hypervisor in type 1 or hardware/bare metal virtualization. The hypervisor is a light and specialized version of an operating system specially developed to create virtual machines efficiently using the hardware of the physical device. The hypervisor uses logical isolation to prevent the different virtual machines from communicating with each other. It is important to note that the hypervisor controls every virtual machine and that a breach of a hypervisor puts all virtual machines at risk.

The second form is called **type-2 virtualization** or hosted virtualization. The virtualization software creates and manages virtual machines. In type 2 virtualization, a regular operating system is installed on the hardware. In essence, you install a hypervisor on top of the operating system instead of the operating system being the hypervisor. As a general rule of thumb, type 2 virtualization is less efficient than type 2 virtualization as the operating system requires resources in addition to the hypervisor. Additionally, in type 2 virtualization, the operating system is not built to protect against attacks against the hypervisor optimally.

EXAM TIP: (ISC)2 considers Type 1 virtualization more secure and efficient than Type 2 virtualization.

Databases

Databases are essential to cloud computing. Cloud service providers allow cloud consumers to use various databases on their platforms. For example, customers can host their database on a virtual machine. In that case, the customer performs the maintenance on the database application, ensures backup creation, and is responsible for database server security. However, many CSPs also offer managed databases. The CSP manages all the underlying infrastructure and the database server for these databases. The CSP ensures the database is highly available, and the customer can schedule backups at the required frequency. CSPs often allow the customer to activate database encryption with a single click. Managed databases are expensive but offer swift provisioning and excellent security and allow the customer to focus on creating the database model and storing/using the data.

EXAM TIP: (ISC)2 considers managed databases to be more secure than self-hosted databases

Orchestration

The last essential building block of cloud computing is orchestration. Orchestration refers to the mechanisms used to create new instances, storage, servers, databases, networks, and applications in the cloud. After all, all these services need provisioning through self-service in an on-demand fashion. All CSPs use **Infrastucture as Code (IaC)** to quickly orchestrate new services. IaC means that new infrastructure is provisioned through pre-defined templates. These templates contain the instructions to create the necessary services.

For example, if you use a managed database, the demand for your database increases quickly. The CSP must ensure the availability of your database is not affected. Therefore, the CSP has defined an orchestration mechanism that automatically creates new database instances if the usage of your database exceeds a specific limit. At the same time, the CSP orchestrates adding additional storage capacity when you suddenly try to import gigabytes of data from an on-premise database.

Orchestration allows CSPs (and cloud consumers) to act quickly and predictably. Manual provisioning of resources would be far too time-consuming. Another facet we will explore later in this book is that IaC increases security as administrators no longer have to manually log in to production environments to create new virtual machines or change network settings. More about this later.

Impact of cloud computing on other technologies

Great, you now understand what technologies support cloud computing and ensure we can benefit from the cloud characteristics. For the CCSP exam, knowing what the cloud has enabled organizations worldwide to achieve is vital.

Before cloud computing, every company had a finite amount of computing resources. After all, computing resources are expensive, and scaling up data centers requires high upfront costs that must be recouped over the years. In many cases, these costs meant that organizations invested in compute resources based on average usage.

However, we can provision vast amounts of compute resources on-demand with cloud computing. Suddenly, it has become much easier to run large computations, collect endless amounts of data, and collaborate with other organizations worldwide.

The main influence cloud computing has had is that it has made impossible computation possible.

For example, cloud services analyze sports games in real-time. Processing extreme amounts of live data streams and enabling smart decision-making is only possible with vast computing resources.

By now, you might have guessed where this is going. Cloud computing has paved the road for heavy computation applications such as **Artificial Intelligence** (**AI**). Especially since many CSPs have released services that allow organizations to develop machine learning algorithms or train AI directly.

Data science has also been accelerated by the cloud, as cloud computing allows the storage and collection of such vast amounts of data that organizations can more efficiently use and process the data they gather.

For the CCSP exam, you should also be familiar with the fact that cloud computing plays a role in developing quantum computing. Quantum computing is a form of computing that allows a quantum bit to contain both 0 and 1 binary values. A bit with two states might not sound exciting, but the implications of quantum computing are enormous. It will usher in a new timeframe in which computation speeds will grow to unprecedented rates. Many security experts even worry that quantum computing will crack current-day encryption within minutes.

Another technology that has developed quickly with the introduction of the cloud is the **Internet-of-Things** (**IoT**). Cloud computing allows small networked devices to store their data in the cloud for processing. Small IoT devices no longer need ample storage or processing capacity but merely the ability to send data to the cloud. The reduced hardware demand (and cost) allows technology integration into small everyday products. They result in smart watches, smart cars, and other intelligent technologies.

The last two critical technologies to understand are **DevSecOps** and containers. DevSecOps is a variation of DevOps, a software development philosophy that embeds operations and software development within the same team. DevSecOps has introduced security in this mix as cloud computing allows development teams to create entire infrastructures and applications as code. Since no dedicated system administrators or security personnel are needed to deploy IaC, it is essential to cover these facets in the development teams.

Container technology has also taken flight with the rise of cloud computing. Containers are small virtual machines that only include the software they need to run a particular application. The beauty of containers is that they are portable, meaning they can run on any supporting system. Through a container, you can run software for Linux on a Windows system and vice versa.

EXAM TIP: Review the technologies mentioned in the section above if you are unfamiliar. The exam will likely cover all of these topics.

Cloud shared considerations

Whenever your organization is considering or implementing cloud computing, there are some critical considerations to consider.

The first one is **interoperability**. When researching cloud technologies, it is essential to review if the services you are interested in are interoperable. Ergo, if the services can interact with your existing IT landscape. Sometimes, an organization might choose to stand up a brand new environment, but most of the time, cloud migrations are a long process that goes step-by-step. Picking a CSP that supports good interoperability will enable you to use your existing landscape and connect other services from other vendors later on.

The second factor to consider is **portability**. Portability focuses on transferring your cloud platform elsewhere. Portability ensures that you can move your environment to another CSP or even on-premise if your organization should so choose. Portability is usually enhanced by using services that support open standards and limit proprietary technology. Sometimes, CSPs will even over functionality to export your existing environment to a format used by another CSP. At the beginning of the chapter, we briefly talked about vendor-lockin.

The third one is **reversibility**, or simply how easy it would be to return to the previous state. Sometimes, an organization might want to try out cloud computing to evaluate if the cloud characteristics provide enough benefit. You might want to consider how easy it would be to return to on-premise computing if your organization is not satisfied with cloud computing.

The next one is **availability**, performance, and resiliency. Of course, these factors are important considerations. Different CSPs offer different availability and performance. But even within services, you will find a lot of availability, performance, and resiliency differences. Generally, you should regard managed services as more available, performant, and resilient. The responsibility for these factors lies in the hands of the CSP, which contractual agreements or SLAs often bind to provide these parameters. While cloud consumers managed environment can be available, performant, and resilient, it requires significant knowledge and expertise with non-managed services.

Service level agreements refer to the agreements between two parties on how a service must perform. For example, SLAs between a CSP and a cloud consumer might dictate how often an application is allowed not to be available. Many large CSPs do not allow you to create custom SLAs. You must agree to their standard SLAs to do business with them. In some cases, working with smaller CSPs might be helpful if you have specific requirements that large CSPs are unwilling to put into a contract. Nevertheless, establishing SLAs that support your business needs is essential before engaging in cloud computing.

The last aspect to consider is **audibility and regulatory compliance**. Auditability and regulatory compliance are of vital importance when considering cloud computing. Auditability dictates what the cloud consumer is allowed to audit the CSP on or what a cloud auditor audits on the CSP. Often, regulatory requirements require that you provide audit reports about your applications and infrastructure. Therefore, working with a CSP willing to subject themselves to a level of audibility acceptable to your organization is essential.

Similarly, you must ensure that your CSP complies with all regulations that apply to your organization. While it is the CSPs responsibility to perform specific tasks, your organization will ultimately be accountable for losing your customer data through a mistake of the CSP. So, ensure you are aware of the regulations that apply to your organization and pick a CSP that is compliant with these regulations.

Conclusion

In chapter one, we examined that the cloud comes in different forms: private cloud, public cloud, hybrid cloud, community cloud, and multi-cloud. These various forms can be combined and allow for other service models. The main service models are Infrastructure as a Service, Platform as a Service, and Software as a Service. The cloud consumer and service provider have different roles and responsibilities in every operating model. IaaS has the most consumer responsibility, while SaaS has the most CSP responsibility. The cloud consumer and cloud service provider are not the only parties involved in cloud computing. We explored how cloud auditors and brokers interact with the cloud service provider and the cloud consumer through the cloud reference architecture.

We discovered the building blocks that allow cloud computing to boast its characteristics, on-demand self-service, rapid elasticity, measured service, broad access, and resource pooling. The primary building blocks are storage, virtualization, networking, orchestration, and databases, which build highly performant and complicated infrastructures.

Our journey also took us through the evolution of new technologies like quantum computing, DevSecOps, containerization, IoT, and AI, among others. You now understand how cloud computing has significantly contributed to the development of these technologies.

However, when considering cloud computing, you must consider how performant, interoperable, portable, and available your environment has to be. Without factoring in these items, your cloud computing journey will not yield the results your organization seeks.

In the next chapter, concepts and design principles of Cloud security, you will learn about the foundational concepts and principles that affect the security of Cloud environments.

Learning goals

This chapter addresses the following CCSP exam outline [3] learning goals:

Domain 1: Cloud concepts, architecture, and design

      1.1 Understand cloud computing concepts

      1.2 Describe cloud reference architecture

---

[3] *CCSP Exam Outline (isc2.org)*

CHAPTER 2

Concepts and Design Principles of Cloud Security

Introduction

Security in the cloud relies on foundational concepts and design principles. This chapter explores how cryptography, identity management, access control, network security, and other concepts form the building blocks of cloud security. These building blocks play a vital role in the overall security of your Cloud environment and the data that resides within it.

Structure

This chapter covers the following topics:

- Common threats
- Cloud design patterns
- Business impact analysis, business continuity, and disaster recovery
- Cloud secure data lifecycle
- Identity management, access control, and authorization
- Cryptography and key management
- Data and media sanitization

- Network security

- Virtualization security

- Security hygiene

- DevOps security

Objectives

This chapter will teach you how common cloud design patterns can help you create secure cloud environments based on tried and proven designs. At the same time, learning threat modeling will enable you and your organization to identify threats specific to your organization. Security hygiene, access control, key management, and identity management will be discussed as essential building blocks for cloud security. This chapter will also examine the data lifecycle and challenges surrounding data and media sanitization in the cloud. As icing on the cake, you will understand how virtualization and network security are essential to security in the cloud and what role BIA, BC, and DRP play in determining what controls your environment needs.

Common threats

The first step to protecting something is knowing what can go wrong. Any IT system nowadays faces threats, both human and environmental. However, cloud environments are subject to threats that might not affect regular on-premise data center environments. After all, the cloud characteristic of broad access allows us to access our cloud environment from anywhere (by default). While broad access is fantastic from a maintenance and developer perspective, attackers can exploit this characteristic. Let us look at some examples of hijacking accounts and unauthorized access.

For example, many organizations use a CSP portal (like the **Azure** or **AWS web portal**) to manage their cloud environments. Unfortunately, many organizations also forget to take measures to secure these cloud consoles properly. Attackers often target administrative users to obtain passwords through phishing or other social engineering attacks[1]. Alternatively, attackers might even abuse weak passwords to gain access directly.

When an attacker gets the administrator's credentials, they can modify your entire cloud environment, destroy it, or spin up new servers for malicious purposes such as DoS attacks or crypto mining[2]. Sometimes, an attacker wants to cause financial damage by consuming large amounts of unnecessary resources.

However, unauthorized access is not the only threat cloud computing environments face. Similar to on-premise environments, misconfiguration is a massive problem in the

---

[1] *Attacks on Google Cloud Platform instances (kaspersky.com)*
[2] *Crypto Hacking And Power Outages: Buyers Beware On AWS Cloud (forbes.com)*

cloud. As we have seen in the shared responsibility matrix, the cloud consumer is almost always responsible for configuring applications that run in the cloud. In the SaaS model, an organization must ensure appropriate privileges within the application. Suppose an organization neglects to configure permissions or application-level settings securely. In that case, an attacker might be able to directly access more content than they should or even edit the data in the underlying databases. Misconfiguration can quickly affect any cloud environment's confidentiality, integrity, and availability.

For example, a common mistake is making object-storage solutions such as **AWS Simple Storage Service (S3)** publicly readable. If you do so, any person who can guess or enumerate the URL of your S3 bucket will be able to retrieve (or sometimes even write files). Many large companies and even government issues have fallen prey to this already[3][4].

Misconfiguration goes hand in hand with insecure design and vulnerable and outdated components. If an organization does not design a cloud environment securely, attackers can exploit vulnerabilities introduced by poor design choices.

For example, design a cloud environment that allows public access to all ports of the virtual machines in your virtual subnet. Attackers will be able to attack services directly within your subnet.

However, the insecure design also involves security hygiene (we will cover this extensively later in this chapter). Part of security hygiene is ensuring your systems do not use vulnerable and outdated components, or at least that your system has controls to prevent them from being exploited.

A threat that is not exclusive to the cloud but might be more prevalent is the lack of visibility. Especially in the PaaS and SaaS service models, a cloud consumer has limited visibility into what takes place on the underlying infrastructure and services. It is essential to ensure you implement logging and monitoring to the extent your service model allows. For example, you will want to log application-level user activity in a SaaS application. In contrast, you might want to log database access requests in a PaaS service model and any administrative action taken on an IaaS VM host.

EXAM TIP: The more responsibility the cloud consumer has, the more places you must ensure logging and monitoring are in place.

If you have been working in IT, you are likely familiar with denial-of-service attacks. The attacks seek to disrupt the availability of an application or network by overloading it with traffic. DoS attacks are prevalent in cloud computing environments as well. Especially since broad network access allows attackers to access the CSP services directly from the internet,

---

[3] *Data on 123 Million US Households Exposed Due to Misconfigured AWS S3 Bucket - Wiadomości bezpieczeństwa (trendmicro.com)*

[4]*https://portswigger.net/daily-swig/insecure-amazon-s3-bucket-exposed-personal-data-on-500-000-ghanaian-graduates*

another factor to consider is that public clouds support multiple tenants. Multi-tenancy means that the infrastructure is shared between customers, meaning that an attack on the underlying infrastructure of a cloud service will likely target numerous customers at once. So, simply put, you can become the target of a DoS attack without the attacker even knowing that you are leveraging the infrastructure. Of course, by the shared responsibility matrix, it is the responsibility of the CSP to ensure your infrastructure remains available. However, the items you are responsible for are available to protect.

For example, suppose you have an IaaS environment that runs multiple VMs. In that case, you are responsible for protecting these VMs against DoS attacks that target the applications running on the VMs. So, suppose you are running web servers on the VMs. In that case, you will be responsible for implementing controls against DoS attacks that target that server (if you want your services to have high availability).

In short, DoS in a public cloud environment is more complex than in on-premise environments due to multi-tenancy. Depending on your service model, you will have to implement DoS protection mechanisms in addition to the measures the CSP provides by default.

Some threats to the cloud are not technical. For example, a significant threat to cloud computing is **data loss** or **leakage** (due to malicious internal actors). Cloud environments make data easily accessible to highly authorized individuals (such as administrators and developers). Malicious inside actors or disgruntled employees can easily extract data from a cloud environment and either exfiltrate this data or even delete it entirely.

Cloud computing makes it easy to store data dispersed over many geographic locations. However, doing so might cause you to be incompliant with local, state, or federal laws and regulations. Your organization must give special consideration to regulatory compliance and data protection requirements.

For example, suppose you are storing data on EU data subjects (people who are residents of the EU), and you store this data on a cloud environment that duplicates data between an availability zone in the EU and one in the US. In that case, you might breach **General Data Protection Regulation (GDPR)**. Such a breach can result in stiff fines and reputational damage to your organization.

While some threats are more prevalent or challenging to protect against in the cloud, you might notice that many of the dangers a cloud computing environment faces are similar to the OWASP top 10[5]. Broken access control, insecure design, security misconfiguration, vulnerable and outdated components, identification and authentication failures, and security logging and monitoring failures are all threats we reviewed above. In general, you can say that the OWASP top 10 gives a solid overview of the main threats against cloud environments (after all, many cloud environments serve web applications).

---

[5] *OWASP Top Ten | OWASP Foundation*

EXAM TIP: Broad access and shared responsibility are the major contributors to the uniqueness of the cloud threat landscape. Broad access makes it easier to attack systems, and shared responsibility means you might not have access to all systems or logs you need.

While not specific to cloud environments, your organization must perform threat modeling of your cloud environment. Threat modeling lets you understand threats that are specific to your organization. For example, owning a small candy store with a retail website makes you less likely to attract attention from nation-state actors. However, if your organization works in the defense industry, you will undoubtedly face attacks from nation-states or other **Advanced Persistent Threat (ATP)** actors.

These ATP actors have significant resources and time to breach a system and require much more protection than attacks by script kiddies (people who use pre-built hacking tools without extensive hacking knowledge). Similarly, if your organization is an activist group or involved in sensitive (political) themes, your organization might face threats from (h) activist groups. In short, it is essential to understand both the threats your organization faces and who the threat actors are, as different threat actors have more or fewer resources, time, and motivation, please refer to the following table:

Actor	Available Resources	Time available to breach	Motivation to breach	Common targets
Nation-state or APT	Unlimited	Unlimited	Influence, warfare	Other nation-states, defense contractors, SCADA systems, large corporations
Hacktivist	Limited	Long	Political change	Governmental agencies, political groups, and organizations dealing with sensitive political subjects (fossil fuels, animal health, equal rights, and so on.).
Script Kiddie	Very limited	Limited	Monetary gain, fun	Low-hanging fruit targets, smaller businesses, and organizations that are publicly identifiable as vulnerable
Criminal Organizations	Significant	Long	Monetary gain	Companies with sellable data, companies with poor security, companies without proper disaster recovery capabilities

Table 2.1: Examples of threat actors and their means, time, and motivation to breach

EXAM Tip: For the CCSP exam, you have to understand the different types of threat actors and determine what poses the most significant risk to an organization.

Cloud design patterns

Now that you understand some of the most significant threats to cloud computing environments. It is essential to discuss designing your cloud environment to lower the likelihood of a threat actor being able to breach your environment. Many cloud service providers (such as Azure[6] and AWS) offer cloud design patterns. These patterns are designs for cloud computing architectures that will help you solve technical problems. However, these patterns have another significant benefit. CSPs design these patterns with security in mind.

For example, AWS CDPs align with AWS's Well-Architected Framework[7]. One of the pillars of this framework is the security pillar. Another is the reliability pillar. These two pillars help the solution protect the confidentiality, integrity, and availability of your applications, services, and data.

When architecting your cloud environment, leveraging these existing design patterns is smart. After all, CSPs that have significant knowledge of all the cloud services they offer have designed these patterns. Most of the time, you can even use existing design patterns and apply them to private cloud instances by modeling the tools used by the CSP to the equivalent tool within your environment.

Suppose you cannot find an existing cloud design pattern for the solution your organization needs. In that case, reference the cloud architecture frameworks created by various institutes and CSPs. Some of the most commonly used frameworks are the **Cloud Security Alliance (CSA)** enterprise architecture, the SANS security principles, and the AWS Well-Architected Framework.

> **EXAM Tip: For the CCSP exam, you do not have to know all these frameworks in and out. However, ensure you understand their purpose and when organizations should leverage them.**

Business impact analysis

Every organization has different processes, data, and value they provide to customers. Using existing design patterns can help us protect our cloud architectures without reinventing the wheel. However, another essential factor in determining what security controls your environment should contain is what we are trying to protect. So, it is crucial to understand what makes your organization work and what parts require what level of security.

An organization's first step to gaining this understanding is conducting a **business impact analysis (BIA)**. Gartner describes a BIA as *the process of determining the criticality of business activities and associated resource requirements to ensure operational resilience and continuity*

---

[6] *Design and implementation patterns - Cloud Design Patterns | Microsoft Learn*
[7] *AWS Well-Architected - Build secure, efficient cloud applications (amazon.com)*

of operating during and after a business disruption[8] A BIA lets you understand what your organization needs to function and what you require to keep it working if something goes wrong.

A BIA starts by conducting surveys to understand what parts of the business are critical to the organization. For example, let us assume a candy store has the following processes, ordering candy, stocking candy, selling candy, and registering sales in a digital system. The goal of a candy store is to sell enough candy to make a profit.

Ordering candy allows the shop to ensure they have enough candy to sell in the future. Disruption of this process means the store can only sell its current stock. However, if the inventory is large enough, a disruption of this process will not critically damage the shop if resolved quickly enough.

Stocking candy is essential to ensure customers can pick up items from the racks and purchase them. If the stocking process stops, the store cannot sell its inventory in the back of the shop. So, a disruption of the stocking process before a disruption of the ordering process will lead to critical damage to the shop.

Disruption of the selling candy processes prevents the organization from selling any products. Without selling products, the shop cannot pay its bills. If a disruption of this process persists (even with the stocking and ordering processes still in place), it will cause critical damage to the shop very quickly.

Now, let us look at registering sales in a digital system. Disruption of this process is not critical. The organization can fall back to recording sales on paper. After restoring the process, entering paper receipts into the system is not a problem.

You might have noticed the purpose of this process already. Now that the candy store understands that the disruption of selling candy is the most critical, followed by the stocking, ordering, and digital administration, it can investigate what situations would cause process disruption.

We already established that time is a factor in process criticality. For example, a fire could easily disrupt the sale of candy, so now the organization knows it should take measures to prevent fires. However, it should also take steps to stop a fire when it does occur. If the candy store has to stop sales for a week, it might be able to continue the business. However, the same might not be accurate if a fire causes damages that prevent the shop from selling for a month.

Organizations must weigh the proportionality and cost of control versus the criticality of what it protects. The candy store could open its own fire department next to it to ensure any fire is quenched quickly. However, the costs would be high. Instead, the shop could choose to implement a sprinkler system that can promptly react to fires. The damage the water causes will likely cause the shop to close for a week or two, but it will not result in a disruption that causes the shop to go out of business.

---

[8] *Definition of Business Impact Analysis (BIA) - IT Glossary | Gartner*

While the scenario above might seem silly, this is precisely how a business impact analysis works for your organization's IT (and cloud) processes. During a BIA, your organization will determine what IT processes and resources are vital to its continued existence.

However, it will also have to decide how long disruptions may last until they cause the organizations to fail and what events could occur that cause disruptions. These events might include scenarios you identified based on threat modeling but can also include environmental factors such as storms, earthquakes, flooding, power outages, and so on.

While not explicitly covered in the CCSP exam outline, it is crucial to understand the meaning of **Recovery Point Objective (RPO)**, **Recovery Time Objective (RTO)**, and **Maximum Tolerable Downtime (MTD)**. RPO, RTO, and MTD are metrics that outline how the duration of disruption affects business operations.

RPO is a measure that defines the maximum acceptable amount of time for data loss. For example, if you sell items on a webshop, your RPO is the maximum permissible amount of time for you to lose existing orders from your system. So, if your organization receives 100 orders per four weeks and can only afford to lose the data of the last 50 orders (because they are delivered every two weeks), your RPO should be two weeks.

You must implement controls to ensure you never lose more data than the data from two weeks ago. You could achieve this by taking daily backups and duplicating two weeks old backups to another cloud availability zone.

That way, if the facility storing your data is damaged and your data is lost, you can restore your two weeks-old data from the backup at the offsite facility or alternative cloud availability zone. Of course, you could also create backups daily and duplicate them to multiple availability zones. Doing so ensures you always be well within your RPO, but it will also create extra costs to store backups in two availability zones. It will be up to your organization to determine if the additional expenses are worth it. Controls to meet your RPO must be in place before a disruption occurs.

For example, in the candy store scenario, the RPO might be the last time you ordered candy inventory. If the store burns down and, your candy is lost, and ordering new candy takes two might, you might want to ensure a 2-week candy supply is stored in an offsite warehouse.

RTO is a measure of time that defines the expected amount of time until the restoration of operations. For example, the RTO for a fire at the candy store might be two weeks. However, if the shop cannot sell candy after a month, it cannot continue. Therefore, the MTD is one month after the events occur. It is essential to ensure the RTO is shorter than the MTD because if you cannot **restore operations (RTO)** within the MTD, your organization will not recover.

Some sources also include something called **Work Recovery Time (WRT)**. WRT is the time it would take you to verify all systems are operational and secure after restoration. (ISC)2 will not cover this term in the CCSP exam, please refer to the following figure:

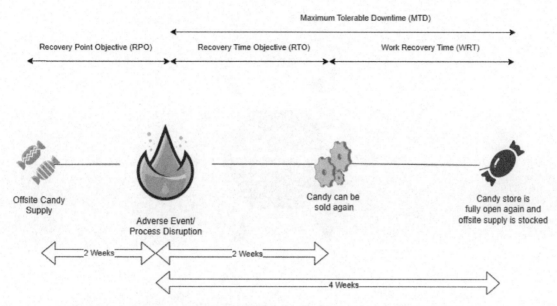

Figure 2.1: *Diagram outlining RPO, RTO, and MTD based on the candy store example*

In summary, your organization should always conduct a BIA as one of the first steps when considering security controls. BIAs usually start with surveys within an organization to identify critical processes. Risk assessments, cost-benefit analysis, RPO, RTO, and MTD are the deciding factors in determining what controls your organization should implement.

EXAM Tip: If the CCSP exam includes a question asking what step an organization should take to determine controls (ISC)2 almost always wants to hear "conduct a BIA."

The determinations of a BIA will form the basis for your disaster recovery and business continuity plans. We will examine these in *Chapter 10, Business Continuity and Disaster Recovery*.

Cloud secure data lifecycle

Before we dive into technical security controls, we must examine the lifecycle of arguably the most significant asset in the cloud, data. Data allows organizations to create new business offerings, support processes, and improve customer experience. However, securely handling data is one of the biggest challenges for organizations.

To be able to protect data, we must first understand the lifecycle of data in the cloud. While there is no industry-wide standard for this lifecycle, most organizations agree that the lifecycle contains six steps. Namely, **Create**, **Store**, **Use**, **Share**, **Archive**, and **Destroy**. Every data lifecycle phase has specific concerns we need to address. Please refer to the following figure:

Figure 2.2: *Cloud secure data lifecycle*

When we create data, we must ensure that we create data purposefully. Many data protection laws and regulations state that we should only use data necessary to protect the data privacy of the data subject (people the data is about). So, during the creation phase of the data lifecycle, we should ask ourselves, do we need to collect this data (necessity), what are we going to use it for (purpose), and is the collection of this data proportionate for the collection (proportionality)?

Similar to the creation phase, many laws and regulations restrict where and how you must store data. For example, credit card information requires encryption per the **Payment Card Industry Data Security Standard (PCI-DSS)**. When we store data, we have to ask ourselves how and where we are keeping this data. Other regulations like the **General Data Protection Regulation (GDPR)** can restrict in what geographical location data persistence is allowed.

Now, the use phase is of vital importance as well. During the use phase, an organization must determine how, why, and when data is used by whom. During the use phase, an organization must ensure that the data is only accessible by users, processes, and services who are authorized to view the data. At the same time, it is essential to ensure that the data is transported securely to where it is processed. In this phase, some of the main controls your organization will have to look at are authentication, authorization, encryption in transit, and monitoring. Monitoring is essential because you want to establish traceability of what is happening with your data and who is accessing, modifying, or deleting it.

The sharing phase is special within the cloud context. In on-premise computing, whom you share data with is usually pretty straightforward. However, you always share data with a cloud service provider in cloud environments. It is vital to remember that cloud service providers can almost always gain insight into your data through administrative backdoors (we will review controls against this later in the book). The sharing phase also includes sharing data with other parties.

Ensuring you create an overview of what information sharing per party is highly advisable. Additionally, you should ensure that the parties you share data with have appropriate controls to protect the data you share with them. For example, your organization might exchange data about user sessions with marketing platforms or other data with related organizations. After authenticating, you might even have your own **Identity Provider (IdP)** that shares user information with other organizations. Especially since your organization will be responsible for complying with legal or regulatory requirements, the GDPR might require you to remove user data you have collected under the *right to be forgotten* clause. In those cases, you must be able to trace whom you shared data with and have procedures to remove that data.

Data archival is an essential step of the cloud-secure data lifecycle. Often, data only has a limited useable lifespan. However, you might have the information you want to analyze later. It is a good practice to archive such data so that it might not be directly available but can be accessed when necessary. Data archival allows you to retain more records while lowering the chance of unauthorized parties accessing the data (if done correctly). In other cases, laws and regulations might require you to retain data for a certain period. Keeping data in fast and readily available storage might be costly (especially within the cloud). For archival in the cloud, you can use cheaper storage solutions (often called cold storage) to archive the data. While the data might not be accessible as fast as hot storage data, it usually costs less and is good enough to comply with legal requirements. Your organization should develop a strategy for identifying data that requires archival and procedures for archiving and restoring such data.

The last phase, destruction, is challenging in cloud environments. Data remanence is the main problem you will see in this step. This means that data remains on storage devices and is potentially recoverable by other parties. Your organization usually has access to physical storage devices in an on-premise environment. These devices are erasable using degaussing (for magnetic drives), zero-wipe operations, or even physical destruction. However, in a cloud environment, the CSP manages the physical devices (per the shared responsibility model). Thus, as the organization using (public) cloud services, you do not have the option to degauss or destroy devices. Unfortunately, this also means you cannot guarantee that your files will not be recoverable by the CSP or other malicious actors.

You might not even have access to the underlying storage device when using services like object storage, which means that standard methods of erasure, like zero wiping, are also not available to you. Luckily, there are reasonable solutions to ensure total data erasure. Whether you are relying on object, file, or disk-level storage, you always have the option to encrypt the data with a strong encryption algorithm and sufficient key length and then destroy the key used for encryption. Afterward, you can delete the data from disk, file, or object storage. Even if someone attempts to reconstruct the deleted files, they will only be able to restore encrypted files that they are unlikely to be able to decrypt. The process above is called **cryptographic erasure**[9].

> **EXAM Tip: Consider cryptographic erasure the most secure form of data erasure when using cloud services as a cloud consumer.**

In short, your organization needs to consider all phases of the cloud secure data lifecycle and determine which controls are necessary for your organization to handle data securely through every step.

Identity management, access control, and authorization

We have examined how you determine what threat and threat actors your organization faces. You understand how to use BIAs to decide which assets most require protection. Plus, you know how the lifecycle of data affects the ways we have to protect data. Now, the time has come to examine what technical control building blocks we have in cloud computing.

Arguably, the most crucial building block is identity management. Identities are persons, systems, services, or organizations requiring access to your cloud's resources or data. Identities allow us to define who will need access to our systems and data. Often, when we think of identities, we might think of users or employees within an organization. However, an identity can be a service (like a database) that interacts with another service (like a codeless application). As we examined in the data lifecycle, we must ensure that only those who should have access get access to systems, data, and services. Maintaining identities is the first step in the process.

Thus, one of the first things you will want to do is examine your processes to determine what identities you might need. Another factor to consider is the association of these. Are the identities you need only employees within your organization, or do you have a community cloud where identities could consist of employees from multiple organizations? Perhaps you have a hybrid cloud environment where you might have identities within a directory system that is not accessible to your cloud environment.

For example, suppose you consider the community cloud environment. In that case, you are likely to want to consider a model where employees from different organizations can log in with the credentials of their employer. Alternatively, you could create a new directory of identities to create new credentials for every employee that is valid within the community cloud environment.

Regardless of your situation, you must devise a robust way to onboard and offboard identities when access is (no longer) required. We call this a joiners, movers, and leavers

---

[9] *cryptographic erase - Glossary | CSRC (nist.gov)*

process that outlines onboarding new identities, handling job scope changes, and removing employees or services leaving the organization is setup. A vital part of these processes is how you register identities.

Overall, you can discern two main methods of storing identities—either **centralized** or **decentralized** identity management. In centralized identity management, all identities reside in a single repository (often called a **directory**). If you want to access a local system, your identity registration occurs in the central repository only once. In decentralized identity management, storage of identities is necessary for the different systems and applications that use the identities. Employees might have several identities (with the same information) spread out over different applications. Let us look at some of the benefits and drawbacks of the forms of identity management:

	Benefits	Drawbacks
Centralized	Easy to provision, modify or revoke access. One source of truth about the attributes (or information) associated with identities. A single place to manage authorizations assigned to a user.	A central identity directory must be available for any system to be reachable.
Decentralized	Software using local identities might be more straightforward. No dependencies on a central directory.	Data might differentiate between application or system-level identities. Providing, modifying, or revoking access is complicated and error-prone. Authorizations must be managed per identity per system or service

Table 2.2: *Overview of the main benefits and drawbacks of centralized and decentralized identities*

Many organizations prefer to use centralized identity management due to the ease of creating a more robust joiners/movers/leavers process and the benefit of having central storage of information (attributes) about the identity.

Now that we understand the difference between centralized and decentralized identity management, evaluating what this means in the cloud is essential. All large CSPs offer centralized identity management tooling within their cloud services.

However, sometimes organizations already have a central identity management platform within their on-premise or other cloud environments. In those cases, an organization can import or sync existing directories to the cloud. Alternatively, you can maintain an on-premise and cloud-based identity directory. However, this poses similar drawbacks to decentralized identity management.

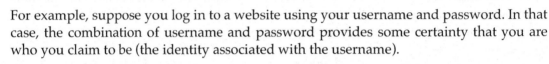

EXAM Tip: For the CCSP exam, you must understand the benefits and drawbacks of centralized and decentralized identity management.

When an organization has established what identities they need and how they are stored, it is time to look at **authentication** and **authorization**. Authentication means that you verify the ownership of your identity.

For example, suppose you log in to a website using your username and password. In that case, the combination of username and password provides some certainty that you are who you claim to be (the identity associated with the username).

Authorization determines what someone can do (after they have authenticated themselves).

For example, authorization might allow you to read a file but not delete it.

Exam Tip: For the CCSP exam, you must know the difference between authentication and authorization

Similar to identities, authentication can also take place centrally or decentralized. In centralized authentication, a central service is used to authenticate users. If you use a central service to authenticate and you use a centralized identity storage, you can combine these for identity and access management through federation. Federation means that you can use the centrally stored identities to authenticate with the central authentication service, after which your identity information is shared with the application you are trying to access. **Security Assertion Markup Language** (**SAML**) and **Open Identity Connect** (**OIDC**) are commonly used protocols to achieve this. One of the major benefits of the federation is that you can use the same identity across organizations.

For example, have you ever seen those websites that allow you to log in with **Google**, **Facebook**, or **Instagram**? If so, have you used identity federation before! In these cases, Google, Facebook, or Instagram maintain a centralized directory of identities and a central authentication service. When you click the link to log in, you redirect to the external service and type in your username and password (and MFA code) to assert your identity. After which, you return to the website you visited initially. At that time, Facebook, Google, or Instagram asserted for the other website that you are who you say you are, and they have provided some information about you (such as your e-mail address) required by the website. You did not have to create an account on the website using federation. Instead, the website only gets access to the information you approved to be shared.

As you might understand, the federation has some significant benefits. You do not have to share a username and password with every service you try to use. Secondly, you do not have to re-enter your information every time. The federation often allows **single sign on** (**SSO**), meaning you might not have to type in your username or password. You might be able to use an already-established authenticated session.

However, the federation has a significant downside, similar to centralized identities. What happens if the provider you use to federate your identity is unavailable? We saw a great example in October of 2021 when Facebook employees could not access data centers when issues on their internal network rendered their centralized federated user management system unavailable[10]. In short, if you use centralized or federate identities and the centralized identities or the authentication mechanism is unavailable, you cannot access the systems you use those identities for.

Let us take a deeper look at authorization as well. Authorization can also be centralized or decentralized. When it is decentralized, the determination of permissions is done by the application itself.

For example, you can use a centralized identity and attach a role to it. A function like a technician might provide access to the web server but might not give the authorization to use the HR system.

In a centralized authorization system, the identity directory provides granular information about what users can do within the network, systems, and applications. However, this authorization form is usually difficult to implement because not every application uses the same way to administrate permissions.

For example, the permissions within a web server might have different options than the HR system. If both systems do not use a standard representation for their permissions, administering privileges would be tedious and error-prone.

Now that you know how identities work, how you can authenticate users, and you have a basic understanding of what authorization is, it is time to examine different access control models. The most common access control methods are role-based access control, rule-based access control, discretionary access control, mandatory access control, and attribute-based access control.

Role-Based Access Control (RBAC) defines roles (often tied to job functions). Every identity with this role can perform the same actions and view the same data. This method is handy when you have clear-cut organizational job functions requiring differentiated authorization levels. You can even combine roles to provide easier provisioning of users.

Rule-Based Access Control is relatively similar to RBAC. However, the main difference is that rules do not tie to job functions. For example, multiple employees with different job titles might have the same rules because they work in the same department. Rule-based access is usually less restrictive/granular than role-based access control.

Discretionary Access Control (DAC) is a model where people can extend their permissions to others. For example, if we are allowed to read a file, we can also allow another identity to read that file. File storage systems such as you have available to you within Windows explorer use DAC.

---

[10] *Facebook blames major outage on maintenance work "effectively disconnecting Facebook data centers globally" - DCD (datacenterdynamics.com)*

Mandatory Access Control (MAC) is often used within organizations where data confidentiality is essential (governmental agencies, defense contractors). However, it always means access is restricted based on its sensitivity. This means that if you are authorized to view confidential data but not highly confidential data, you will not be able to access highly confidential data.

Attribute-based Access Control (ABAC) uses the attributes assigned to a user to determine if and what access they can have. For example, an attribute can be the country in which you work, the IP address you connect from, or even the time you connect. Since the cloud offers broad access, ABAC offers us new ways to validate if the usage of a resource is valid.

For example, if your organization only allows access to the HR system during work hours from corporate devices (and the application is reachable from the internet). You can use ABAC to block authentication requests made outside of work hours or from a device that your organization does not manage (based on IP or a certificate).

Exam Tip: All CSPs offer ABAC capabilities. ABAC will provide the best control to detect and prevent authentication-based attacks.

Another important facet to access control in the cloud is the usage of **Multi-Factor Authentication (MFA)**. In the example above, you already saw that broad access has implications for how you might want to detect malicious authentication requests.

However, what do you do if someone has captured valid credentials? They can authenticate within the typical pattern of a user with their credentials. Meaning your ABAC controls might not detect that the person stole credentials. Well, a solution to this is MFA. MFA is a mechanism through which a user has to attest to their identity using multiple mechanisms. Usually, the first mechanism is entering a username and password. The second mechanism can be using a one-time token app, an SMS, badge, biometrics, an E-mail code, or a physical token. MFA relies on the assumption that if an attacker compromises one of the mechanisms to prove their identity, it is unlikely they have also compromised another method.

For example, if an attacker can get your password using a phishing attack, they likely do not have direct access to your phone. If both methods are required to authenticate, the attacker will still not be able to show with just your password.

In general, you can distinguish three different factors: something you know, something you have, and something you are. When implementing MFA, it is crucial to ensure that you use multiple elements. That is, something you know (like a password) and something you have (a smartcard or phone) rather than the same factor twice. Using the same factor twice will potentially negate the added security. The following table outlines common factors and their implementations:

Factor	Example
Something you know	Password or Pincode
Something you have	Phone, keycard, token
Something you are	Fingerprint, voice, retina scan, palm scan

Table 2.3: Overview of common factors used in MFA

Exam Tip: The CCSP exam highly prefers MFA in access-control-related questions.

Now that we have covered the different access control models, you might realize the enormous role identities, authentication, and authorization will play in your cloud environment. When we reviewed the OWASP top 10 and threats to cloud computing, we saw that many of the most common attacks target authentication. Your organization must develop a program to manage identities, define the useable access control methods, establish processes to accommodate joiners/movers/leavers, and ensure the organization's best authentication and authorization model is applied.

Cryptography and key management

You will notice that cryptography and key management are essential to building a secure cloud environment. Earlier in this chapter, we covered that you must encrypt data in the cloud secure data lifecycle. Remember that you usually share physical servers and networks with other cloud consumers. While the CSPs are responsible for providing you with secure infrastructure, you, as the cloud consumer, are responsible for data protection.

Data security means you should try to encrypt data at rest and in transit within your cloud environment. Encryption in transit is vital to ensure that others who might access your virtual subnet cannot sniff network communications within your virtual subnet or even the underlying infrastructure. In the future, it might even be possible to encrypt data during processing. A technology called **homomorphic** encryption is paving the way for this.

It is crucial to be aware of the necessity of encryption due to the shared responsibilities within cloud computing. Luckily, CSPs provide many native encryption tools, especially for the PaaS and SaaS offerings. Many managed databases and file or object storage solutions can offer encryption with the click of a button. **Transparent data encryption (TDE)**, for example, is used by many CSPs to encrypt and decrypt databases dynamically to ensure the decryption of only actively used tables. That way, your data is always safe when at rest. Now, if you are using IaaS solutions, you might have to put in more effort to ensure your databases hosted on a VM are encrypted.

EXAM Tip: The CSSP exam considers managed services more secure because they often offer native encryption using public encryption algorithms.

EXAM Tip: A focal point of the CCSP exam is the implementation of encryption in transit. Answers using SSL or TLS < 1.2 are always insecure.

EXAM Tip: Never create your cryptographic algorithms. Many have tried and failed to develop crypto algorithms securely.

However, ensuring your data is encrypted is not the only challenge within a cloud environment. Another critical factor is the key management of the user to encrypt data. If a CSP can access your encryption keys, they can decrypt your data and view its contents. As mentioned in this chapter, a CSP can access your data as they own the devices. Most CSPs offer various models to manage keys within their platforms without them having access to your keys.

Customer Managed Encryption Keys (CMEKs or **CMKs)** are a method for managing keys in the cloud. CMEK means that you, as the cloud consumer create keys to use within your cloud platform stored in a specialized service. The service makes the keys available to services that encrypt or decrypt data. Alternatively, CMEK can also mean using your private (or third-party managed) key store. The key material on a **Hardware Security Module (HSM)**is a physical device created to store key materials using a tamperproof physical safe design.

Most vendors also offer a **Transparent Data Encryption (KMS)** that fully manages your encryption keys. Through such a service, you do not have to create keys manually, but you will also not have access to the underlying HSM. In many cases, you will even share one HSM with other cloud consumers.

Some CSPs also offer managed HSMs (in combination with **Bring Your Own Key (BYOK)**). Managed HSMs are dedicated to a single tenant as required by FIPS 140-3, while BYOK means that your organization creates the key material itself and provides it to the CSP. BYOK means your organization must put more effort into managing key materials as you must create keys to rotate them. While a CMEK environment can usually generate and revoke keys on the fly. However, some organizations might require keys that the CSP cannot provide.

In short, in addition to encrypting your data at rest and in transit, your organization must understand which requirements it has to comply with regarding key management. Governmental organizations (or subcontractors) might require BYOK with a Managed HSM.

EXAM Tip: You must understand the FIPS 140 Level 2 and Level 3 requirements for the CCSP exam.

Data and media sanitization

Earlier in this chapter, we discussed some of the challenges of the cloud-secure data lifecycle. The last phase of the lifecycle, destruction, is the main subject of this section. In a cloud computing environment, we might not be able to access the underlying storage devices of our services to perform degaussing or even physical destruction. However, data security is still the responsibility of the customer. Cryptographic erasure is the best way to ensure that the data stored at the cloud provider is not recoverable. This process means encrypting your data before deleting it from the cloud service.

The reason behind this is simple. When deleting data, data remanence takes place. Data remanence means that the data is recoverable using (specialized) tools. While we cannot solve data remanence, we can limit its impact. By encryption files before deleting them, any data that remains recoverable is encrypted. Also, destroy the encryption key, so the original data is only recoverable through cryptanalysis attacks. If we pick a robust encryption algorithm with a sufficient key length, the likelihood that our data leaks through data remanence is negligible.

Nevertheless, ensuring that the CSP has proper storage device disposal procedures is crucial. After all, if you do not intend to delete your data, you cannot prevent data remanence if the vendor misplaces a storage device. Thus, it would be best to verify that the CSP has processes set up to ensure encryption of storage devices at rest and physical destruction takes place per industry best practices and applicable laws and regulations. We will examine this subject more in the next chapter of this book.

EXAM Tip: As a cloud consumer, you cannot prevent data remanence but limit its consequences through cryptographic erasure.

Tip: If you are disposing of or re-purposing your storage devices, cryptographic erasure can be a cheap and safe way to prevent others from accessing remnant data. Cryptographic erasure is helpful for Solid State Disks (SSDs), as they might fail when zero-wiped (overwriting data with zeros).

Network security

When we examined the shared responsibility matrix, it became clear that the CSP has a lot of responsibility concerning the underlay network. However, the cloud consumer can be responsible for the overlay network of the virtual subnet that the CSP provides to the consumer. Especially in the IaaS model, the consumer will have to implement various security (and resilience) controls. Let us examine the primary building blocks that are available.

Regions

First, we must examine the concept of regions within cloud computing. Regions are large geographic areas, such as Europe or America, where a cloud service provider offers services. Frequently, every region has its virtual network and its resources. You may be unable to access services from one region to another. If your organization offers services in different parts of the world, you might benefit from providing services to customers in a specific area from the region closest to them. Not only will this increase speeds, but it can be helpful to ensure compliance with local laws and regulations.

For example, if you were to store data about your European customers in the US region, you might breach the GDPR. Similarly, you may want to take additional security measures for customers in a specific region that might not be required in another area.

Of course, you can replicate services and data between regions, so you do not have to build your infrastructure and applications multiple times. Also, remember that cloud services can be cheaper in one region than in the next. Depending on these costs, your organization can run specific workloads for a particular reason.

When creating a secure cloud environment, you must create a region suitable to your and your customer's needs while complying with local laws and regulations.

Availability zones: AVs

The second element to network security (and resilience) you should consider is availability zones. We covered this topic briefly in chapter one. Availability zones are the cloud version of a multi-datacenter setup in which you use geographically dispersed data centers. Availability zones are, in essence, clusters of data centers. The purpose of these availability zones is to spread compute capacity, so disasters generally do not affect multiple zones.

If you want your cloud environment to be highly available, you must leverage multiple availability zones to store your data and run your services. Most managed services will do this for you automatically. However, in an IaaS environment, the CSP will not automatically duplicate your services and data over multiple AVs. So, when you design your cloud network, you must consider that you back up critical data and replicate services to other availability zones. Doing so can ensure your services are still available, even in one availability zone's physical destruction of data centers.

EXAM Tip: Using three AVs is more secure than using two AVs but also more costly. AVs also play a considerable role in disaster recovery and business continuity.

Load Balancers

Even if you duplicate services, sync data, and store backups in other availability zones, your services do not magically switch over. However, you can use the concept of load balancing to direct traffic to available servers. Many CSPs offer global load balancing, a managed service that can direct traffic to servers or services throughout multiple availability zones. That way, if one availability zone is unavailable, a load balancer can automatically switch your user traffic to the still available zones.

Another load balancing usage is to prevent degrading user experience or even complete denial of service. Load balancers can direct traffic between your servers based on the load they experience.

For example, if you have two web servers, you might want to ensure that traffic is split over these servers to ensure neither of them gets overloaded.

Load balancing is essential to enable rapid elasticity. Imagine you have a situation where you run two web servers, and your organization just released a massive discount on online purchases. Many users navigate to your webshop to use the deal. Suppose your two servers cannot handle the traffic. Rapid elasticity allows us to create new instances of these servers automatically to handle the considerable load increase. Without load balancers, your users could not reach these new servers. Most cloud providers allow you to load balance based on *resource pools* dynamically. A resource pool can contain a pre-defined set of servers but can also scale dynamically based on the settings you provide. The following figure shows how load balancing can be used across availability zones:

EXAM Tip: Load balancing is a vital tool to protect the availability of your cloud environment.

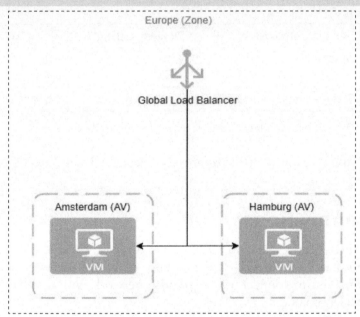

Figure 2.3: Sample of how a load balancer can direct traffic between availability zones

Access control lists: ACLs

ACLs function as firewalls in the cloud. ACLs allow you to define permitted incoming and outgoing network access to and from your virtual subnet. You can allow or block traffic at the IP range or protocol level through ACLs. It is essential to understand that ACLs allow all traffic by default.

Security groups: SGs

SGs are similar to ACLs. However, they are assignable to specific resources. They are useable at the subnet level like ACLs but also to restrict virtual network adapters of a virtual machine of services within your network. Security groups are more granular than ACLs and apply easily to a group of resources within a subnet.

For example, if you have a cluster of VMs, you can assign the security groups to the virtual NICs of the VMs. By doing so, you apply the same rule set to all adapters at once without having to put subnet-level restrictions through an ACL.

An essential difference between security groups and ACLs is that security groups work with the concept of **deny by default**. Ergo, SGs do not allow any traffic unless you allow it. Thereby, SGs are perfect for restricting traffic to and from IaaS components like containers and VMs because you should only expose the necessary services on the container or VM. The following table outlines the difference between ACLs and SGs please refer to the following:

Control	Applied to	Default setting	Can configure
ACL	subnets	Allow All	Allowed and Denied traffic
SG	Services, hosts, subnets	Deny All	Allowed traffic

Table 2.4: Outlining the difference between ACLs and SGs

EXAM Tip: Ensure you know the difference between ACLs and SGs during the CCSP exam.

Private connections

We covered private connections briefly in the previous chapter. However, private connections are essential when implementing network security controls. Private connections allow you to connect an on-premise network with a cloud-based network using a VPN or a leased line.

Instead, you allow the establishment of a VPN between the CSP and your on-premise network. For example, you can create an API management tool that exposes all your webservice endpoints in the cloud. By doing so, you can leverage CSP protections like DoS protection while closing your on-premise environment from direct incoming internet connections. Instead, you only allow the VPN connection from the cloud to your on-premise network. Effectively, you can use private connections to transfer part of the risk and attack surface to the CSP from your on-premise network.

Private connections connect the cloud network and the on-premise network so that, for example, a cloud-based API can interact with an on-premise database. Private connections are extremely useful if local laws and regulations prevent you from sharing certain data in the cloud, but your organization still wants to leverage the characteristics.

Web application firewalls: WAFs

Web application firewalls are **Open System Interconnection** (**OSI**) layer seven firewalls that inspect the contents of requests sent to your cloud environment. WAFs are a great way to scan for malware, malformed requests, and other application-specific abuse and attacks. WAFs are extremely useful for detecting application-level attacks like **Cross Site Scripting** (**XSS**) and injection attacks like **Sequential Query Language Injection** (**SQLi**). Remember that configuring a WAF requires a good understanding of the applications you are trying to protect. If your organization has multiple WAFs, you will likely want to configure them differently per API or web application.

EXAM Tip: WAFs protect specific web applications or APIs and do not serve as a generic network firewall.

Virtualization security

We have spent significant time discussing the building blocks of network security. However, virtualization security plays an essential part in cloud security as well. If you are using IaaS and PaaS components, you will have some responsibility for virtualization security. However, virtualization security is all up to the CSP in the SaaS model. Let us look at virtualization security for the CSP and the cloud consumer.

Firstly, the CSP must ensure that the security of the hypervisor is up to par. *Chapter 1, Understanding cloud computing concepts, and the cloud Reference architecture*, already discussed the difference between type-1 and type-2 hypervisors. Most CSPs only use type-1 hypervisors because they are more efficient and offer better security. Nevertheless, the CSP must ensure that the created virtual machines are not useable to escalate privileges to the hypervisor. After all, if an attacker gains access to a hypervisor, all virtual machines running on it would be compromised. The main useable controls to prevent privilege escalation are logical isolation, patching, and configuration (we will cover this under security hygiene later in this chapter).

Logical isolation means that the different virtual machines cannot connect directly. VMs must be separated and should not be allowed to communicate directly with each other. Similarly, logical isolation must be in place to prevent the usage of the hypervisor storage by the VMs. Of course, isolation also applies at the network level. VMs should never be able to communicate directly with the management interface of a hypervisor.

Patching and configuration are essential to prevent exploitation from known vulnerabilities or misconfigurations. CSPs must ensure they patch their systems upon discovery of new vulnerabilities. Similarly, they must harden their systems using tested and tried secure configurations.

Interestingly enough, the cloud consumer has very similar obligations as the CSP. However, the responsibilities apply to the VM or container running on the hypervisor or container platform. Cloud consumers must isolate the services running on the VM where possible. They must patch the operating system and securely configure it and its services.

Organizations should use pre-hardened virtual machine images or container images. Many organizations do not have the knowledge or capacity to test and verify configurations and patches. Luckily, organizations like CIS publish (paid) images and benchmarks[11] you can leverage. Most virtual machine/ container libraries in the CSPs stores offer pre-hardened images.

Keep in mind that government agencies (in the US) might be required to harden their VMs and containers per the NIST STIGs. STIGs are application security baselines that are mandatory for US government organizations.

EXAM Tip: For the CCSP exam, you must understand CIS benchmarks and NIST STIGs and their use. You do NOT need to know the individual controls they outline.

EXAM Tip: Review the CIS benchmarks and NIST STIGs (for a specific application) to gain insight into how they outline controls.

You might have noticed how we mixed in the term **containers**. Containers are virtual machines that only contain the bare necessary applications and configuration. Containers run on any platform that provides software to run containers. One of the most popular terms you have heard for containers is likely Docker containers. However, containers come in many shapes and sizes. Most CSPs offer PaaS services that allow you to *orchestrate* containers. You can deploy and scale containers without worrying about the underlying infrastructure. In general, containers are more secure than VMs because they contain fewer unnecessary packages (when configured correctly). Docker containers are also more efficient than virtual machines. While the CCSP exam does not require you to be a container expert, you must understand that many security controls apply to VMs.

EXAM Tip: The CCSP exam will consider containers more secure than VMs. Containers, when used correctly, only contain a minimal set of packages, software, and configuration. Thus, they have a smaller attack surface.

Security hygiene

Hygiene for security? Security hygiene is essential to security computing (in the cloud or elsewhere). The concept refers to ensuring you take the proper steps to incorporate security throughout your applications, systems, networks, and data lifecycle.

For example, security hygiene means monitoring vulnerabilities within your applications and systems and patching them when necessary.

However, security hygiene goes beyond patching and configuring. Hygiene means you need to incorporate security throughout the lifecycle of everything you do. This means

---

[11] *CIS Benchmarks (cisecurity.org)*

you must consider security before you build something. However, you must also test if your security controls are adequate. Another vital factor is organization. Ensure you remove deprecated resources, vulnerable systems, unused identities, rotate credentials in a timely fashion, and so on.

An essential part of security hygiene is implementing logging and monitoring within your environment. We will examine logging and monitoring throughout this book.

DevOps security

Technical controls are great, but we need more than just technical controls. With the rise of cloud computing, development and operations, DevOps has become more common. Development teams can create software and spin up databases, servers, and entire networks with the click of a button using cloud consoles. Many organizations have shifted to an approach in which teams can create a solution end-to-end, meaning development teams now include operations/infrastructure knowledge and specialists.

While DevOps can significantly improve the time to market of new developments and fixes, it also poses some security risks. The *old* way of developing systems and clear boundaries exist between developers and operations teams deploying software. Developers would write code, test code, and get approval, and the operations teams with production server access would develop it. In most cases, developers did not get any production server/network access. Access is restricted because separation of duties ensures that a developer cannot go ahead, write malicious code and deploy it to production without checks from other parties.

As you might understand, DevOps almost always eliminates the separation of duties. They hold all the power if a team can develop software, deploy infrastructure, and deploy code.

Any software and infrastructure that teams design must consider security requirements. Luckily, we can take steps to increase security within DevOps teams. The first factor we must discuss is secure coding practices. These practices prescribe the inclusion of security throughout the entire **software/system development lifecycle (SDLC)**.

Code quality is essential to prevent accidental security issues within code. Secondly, DevOps teams should use practices like peer coding (where two or more developers work on producing code simultaneously) and code review. Code review can help detect the introduction of malicious code by a developer. During code review, another developer validates the code for bugs, vulnerabilities, and functional defects. While manual code review is helpful, static code analysis, **Static Application Security Testing (SAST)**, can be used to detect vulnerabilities and bugs programmatically.

But SAST can also help improve code quality by reducing items like cyclic complexity, especially regarding cyclic complexity, which measures code nesting. The more code nesting takes place. The more complicated code becomes to understand, the higher the chances of introducing security flaws. At the same time, high cyclic complexity decreases the likelihood of manual code review detecting deliberate attacks.

Let us look at an example of the impact of cyclic complexity. The first example has high cyclic complexity. The developer used complexity to hide her wiring all non-**UK** customer transactions to her bank account:

```
var transaction = new object();

for (var i = 0; i < customers.length; i++) {

    transaction.bankaccount = 'MYACCOUNTNR'; // test value


    if (customer[i].active === true) {
        if (customer[i].phone_number !== null) {
            if (customer[i].address !== null) {
                if (customer[i].address.country === 'uk') {
                    if (customer[i].address.street !== null) {
                        if (customer[i].address.city !== null) {
                            if (customer[i].address.zipcode !== null) {
                                if (customer[i].bankaccount !== null) {


                                console.log('provide some logging about
what is going on');

                                transaction.bankaccount = 'prefix' +
transaction.bankaccount;

                                sendTranasctionUK(transaction);
                                }
                            }
                        }
                    }
                }
                else {
                    if (customer[i.address.street] !== null) {
                        if (customer[i].address.city !== null) {
                            if (customer[i].address.zipcode !== null) {
                                if (customer[i].bankaccount !== null) {
                                console.log('provide some logging about what
is going on');

                                sendTranasctionOther(transaction);
                                }
```

```
                    }
                }
            }
        }
    }
}
}
}
```

In the following example, the developer is trying to do the same thing in code with much lower cyclic complexity. Compare the code samples and determine where the malicious action is easier to detect:

```
var transaction = new object();

customers.forEach(
    (customer) => {
        transaction.amount = 500;
        transaction.bankaccount = 'MYACCOUNTNR'; // test value

        if (!isAllDataThere(customer)) {
            next;
        }

        console.log('provide some logging about what is going on');

        if (isUKAddress(customer)) {
            transaction.bankaccount = 'prefix' + transaction.bankaccount;
            sendTranasctionUK(transaction);
        } else {
            sendTranasctionOther(transaction);
        }
    }
);

function isAllDataThere(customer) {
    var outcome = true;
    if (customer.phone_number === null) return false;
```

```
    if (customer.address === null) return false;
    if (customer.address.street === null) return false;
    if (customer.address.city === null) return false;
    if (customer.address.zipcode === null) return false;
    if (customer.bankaccount === null) return false;
    return outcome;
}


function isUKAddress(customer) {
    if (customer.address.country === 'UK') return true;
    return false;
}
```

While the code is comparable in length, the second sample with lower cyclic complexity far more clearly shows that only the bank account is set for **UK** customers. For other customers, the bank account remains **MYACCOUNTNR**, the fictive number of the developer. Even if this was not a deliberate action but simply a bug, it would be much easier to detect with low code complexity.

SAST is not the only thing that can help us out here. Linting, a process of applying a set of coding rules, can also increase security by preventing developers from creating challenging-to-read code and standardizing how to write code in an organization for easier code review.

After we are sure the code is written securely and without bugs, it is time to perform testing on the software. Unit tests, dynamic application security testing, regression testing, vulnerability scanning, and penetration testing are all essential tools for this, which we will cover in-depth in *Chapter 12, Security testing and verification.*

The secure deployment code and infrastructure are vital DevOps security mechanisms to understand for the exam. We already covered that DevOps challenges the separation of duties we used to expect. However, we can use something can pipelines to re-introduce a form of SoD. Pipelines reproducibly deploy software (and infrastructure) without providing developers direct access to production systems. Pipeline software usually runs within the administrative part of your network or cloud. It has access to deploy software to test, accept, and produce environments. Instead of logging into production servers and manually deploying software, a DevOps engineer can use the pipeline tool to deploy the software directly to the environment. Because we have reviewed and tested the code, this limits how much damage an engineer can cause to the environment. After all, without direct production access, it becomes much more difficult to tamper with code, systems, and underlying databases.

Pipelines integrate with SAST tools to ensure code review has taken place before possible deployments. Keep in mind that someone has to set up these pipelines. This means the person that administrates them still needs to be able to connect to the production environment. If your organization uses DevOps engineers to set up pipelines, it is smart only to provide limited access for a limited time while performing work on pipelines. Also, you must ensure monitoring and altering actions performed during work.

EXAM Tip: If you are unfamiliar with development pipelines or software development in general, you should invest some time into understanding the basic process.

As briefly mentioned above, we can do more than deploy code. **Infrastructure as Code (IaC)** allows us to create code or configuration useable by pipeline tooling to provision or modify infrastructure automatically. If you search the internet, you will find many in-depth articles about IaC. For the CCSP exam, you must understand that IaC is essentially (a collection of) configuration files that describe how to create specific infrastructure. The beauty of IaC is that we can deploy IaC through pipelines, allowing us to deploy production infrastructure without direct production access for DevOps engineers. IaC is also an essential enabler of rapid elasticity. After all, CSPs need a quick way to deploy new instances or scale instances down for their customers. They do this using IaC because manual creation and configuration of VMs and other infrastructure would be time-consuming and error-prone.

EXAM Tip: IaC is considered a secure way of deploying infrastructure. The CCSP exam always considers it more secure to deploy new instances through IaC and shut down older ones rather than making configuration changes on an existing infrastructure element. IaC is also more efficient and less error-prone than manual configuration.

Conclusion

This chapter has taken you on a journey through the basic building blocks of security in the cloud. We have examined how determining threats to your organization is an essential first step in the security journey. However, we also realized we do not have to reinvent the wheel. We evaluated how a business impact analysis or BIA is necessary to determine what assets need the most protection. Common cloud design patterns can help us identify secure solutions that might apply to our organizations.

During our journey, we saw that data is at the core of any computing application. Understanding the lifecycle of data in the cloud and what security mechanisms to apply are of vital importance to a secure cloud environment.

Of course, understanding threats, data, and the patterns at our disposal is only one part of the puzzle. Throughout the chapter, we reviewed the building blocks of secure cloud computing. We visited identity management, access control, and authorization. We delved into cryptography and key management. We learned how to sanitize media in the cloud, even though we have limited access. As icing on the cake, we reviewed what security tools are available to secure networks, virtualization, and DevOps hygienically.

Throughout the rest of the book, we will dive deep into the concepts introduced in this chapter. Before you continue, it is essential to understand the basic security building blocks and the overall building blocks outlined in this chapter and *Chapter 1, Understanding cloud computing concepts, and the cloud Reference architecture.*

Learning goals

This chapter addresses the following CCSP exam outline[12] learning goals:

Domain 1: Cloud concepts, architecture, and design

> 1.3 Understanding security concepts relevant to cloud computing

> 1.4 Understand the design principles of secure cloud computing

---

[12] *CCSP Exam Outline (isc2.org)*

CHAPTER 3
Evaluating Cloud Service Providers

Introduction

Whenever your organization chooses to migrate (some of) its environment to the cloud, it is essential to work with CSPs that suit your organization's needs. This will explore what factors are crucial when selecting a CSP. This chapter will provide real-life tips and tricks to apply within your organization.

Structure

This chapter covers the following topics:

- Portability
- Interoperability
- Availability
- Security
- Privacy
- Auditability
- Costs

- Service level agreements

- Legal and regulatory compliance

  o ISO Standards

  o PCI-DSS

- Product certifications

  o Common Criteria

  o Federal Information Processing Standards (FIPS 140-2 and 140-3)

Objectives

At the end of this chapter, you will be able to understand the factors that influence the choice between CPSs. You will be able to determine the need for SLAs as a critical component of cloud computing. At the end of the chapter, you will also understand what certifications in the cloud context mean, and how they can be used to verify CSP legal and regulatory compliance.

Portability

In *Chapter 1, Understanding Cloud Computing Concepts*, and the cloud reference architecture, we briefly touched on some general considerations for cloud computing. One of the items we discussed was portability. Let us dive deeper into this subject. Many organizations have prevented *vendor lock-in* within their IT landscape. Vendor lock-in, in essence, is a situation where you build a dependency on a vendor that can threaten business continuity when the collaboration halts.

For example, let us say an organization has a vendor that leases data center equipment to an organization. At the same time, customers and employees cannot access the services you provide through that data center. Due to financial hardship, the vendor goes out of business and shuts down their data centers instantly. At that time, your services will go offline entirely, and you might be unable to regain access to the devices storing your data.

Another example is an organization that uses proprietary networking equipment. The support organization builds software to manage the devices. They have invested countless hours in building a fast and efficient support structure. However, the software only works with the proprietary software provided by one vendor. If your organization decided to switch to another vendor, the entire support system would no longer function. A simple networking equipment migration would cause huge downstream effects and costs on other parts of the organization.

In both examples, stopping or being forced to stop working with a vendor risks the business's continuity. Either by directly rendering services unavailable or causing costs that may not be affordable to an organization (for example, rebuilding the support software), an organization can take measures against these problems.

For example, the organization could contract another data center vendor and duplicate their setup to that vendor. So that if either of these vendors cannot provide service, you can move over to the other. However, those measures might be too expensive for an organization to take. After all, in this example, you would likely double your costs.

A better way to fight vendor lock-in is by ensuring your vendor offers high portability. Portability means that your services and data are transferable to another vendor. Portability is achieved by using open (industry) standards and preventing proprietary technologies were possible.

For example, if your organization is creating a PaaS environment in the cloud to run databases, selecting a database schema that other vendors support is wise. If your relationship with the vendor sours or they cannot provide services, you can restore a database backup at another vendor. While it might take you time, you can use the results from your BIA to determine if the restore operations fit your MTD (*Chapter 2, Concepts and Design Principles of Secure Cloud Security*). If they do, you can save money by not having to run duplicate environments, but you can still ensure one vendor does not lock you in.

So, what does portability mean for selecting a cloud service provider? Always check if a CSP provides services that leverage open standards. You might want to choose a CSP that uses SAML for authentication over a CSP that uses a proprietary protocol for authentication. Similarly, verify if the vendor allows you to export data and service definitions easily. Doing so will help your organization switch to another vendor more quickly and easily.

Later in this chapter, we will cover **service level agreements** (**SLAs**). N These can also be essential in contractually ensuring portability by enforcing portability requirements.

Interoperability

Cloud computing almost always takes place in a hybrid environment. Many organizations already have on-premise computing that has to be connected to the new environments in the cloud (even if it is only temporary). However, connecting to on-premise environments is not the only factor to consider. Often organizations spread their computing capabilities over multiple CSPs and service models. The spread of computing capabilities is why it is essential to consider the interoperability of a CSP.

Interoperability means the CSP's capacity to integrate with other environments on-premise or in the cloud. If your CSP does not offer high interoperability, you may not be able to integrate with existing environments or other applications, APIs, or cloud environments.

Similar to portability, interoperability relies on the usage of open standards. When a CSP leverages open standards for databases, API communication, and networking, it becomes much simpler to integrate the environment. However, open standards alone are not enough. A CSP must allow you to create integrations where you need them.

Let us look a some of the items you should evaluate:

Firstly, does your CSP offer private connections? Can you connect your on-premise environment through a leased line or VPN? If not, the CSP is likely not the best choice if you are trying to move only part of your computing capabilities to the cloud and need interaction between the cloud and your on-premise environment.

Secondly, does the CSP support your existing software packages and standards? In *Chapter 2, Concepts and Design Principles of Secure Cloud Security*, we covered federation. You would be wise to verify your vendor supports your directory services unless you want to duplicate identities to the cloud or maintain a separate identity store for the cloud. The same applies to logging. If you are gathering logs internally, you should ensure you can import records from your cloud environment or vice versa. Another critical factor to consider is APIs. Figure out if the CSP offers services using protocols other CSPs use (JSON, SOAP, SAML, OIDC, and so on.) rather than proprietary or rarely used protocols.

In short, interoperability is about ensuring the CSPs' services integrate with your environment, whether other CSPs, on-premises data centers, or other external APIs and services. Neglecting to consider interoperability will lead to high costs, postponed deadlines, and sometimes even the need for another CSP.

Availability

While interoperability and portability can be challenging topics, availability is where your organization will start to see value quickly. It is essential to look closely at availability at the level of the CSP and the level of the services you are using. When you select a CSP, you should consider what availability guarantees the CSP offers. As a general rule of thumb, the more responsibility a CSP takes, the higher the availability guarantee is from the CSP. So, in some cases, you might opt for a more expensive managed service instead of using IaaS, which comes with much more responsibility for the consumer to ensure the availability of the services.

You might be surprised about the availability of your organization's needs. SLAs cover availability, and most vendors will provide you with details on their availability promises. An excellent way to determine if a CSP offers the availability your organization needs is by mapping out your architecture and determining the availability of every component to ensure your MTD (*Chapter 2, Concepts and Design Principles of Secure Cloud Security*).) is never reached in case issues arise. Once you have established these values, refer to the SLA catalogs[1] provided by a CSP to pick services that can meet your demands, refer to the following table:

---

[1] *AWS Service Level Agreements (amazon.com)*

Availability percentage	Maximum downtime per year
99.9999	31S
99.9	8H 41M 38S
98	1D 19H 28M 8.8S
95	18D 2H 41M 28S

Table 3.1: Outline of availability and the resulting max downtime[2]

As you can see in the table above, 99.9999% availability means your services can only be offline for 31 seconds per year. If your MTD is two weeks, you are likely paying too much if your services all have 99.9999% availability. After all, your organization can be offline for two weeks before it cannot resume.

EXAM Tip: Security is an enabler of the business. The CCSP exam expects you to understand that more is not always better. While having the best availability is better from a security perspective, your organization must balance the trade-offs.

When you determine the availability you need, remember that availability of a single component affects the availability of a chain. For example, if you have a load balancer with 99.9% availability, a front-end application with 99% availability, and a database with 99.5% availability, you can calculate the chain availability like this;

0.999 (load balancer availability) * 0.99 (frontend availability) * 0.995 (db availability) * 100 = 98.4%

Many people think chain availability equals the lowest availability percentage in the chain. However, this is false. It would be best to calculate availability based on every item being unavailable at different times. Make sure you calculate clusters of services as a single availability percentage in your calculations, refer to the following figure:

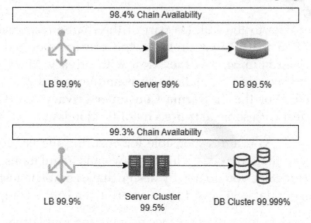

Figure 3.1: Chain availability examples

---

[2]*SLA and Uptime calculator: Uptime and downtime with 99.9 % SLA*

Security

Definitely, security is an essential factor when you consider a CSP. Some CSPs offer various security tooling as part of their cloud services. For example, some CSPs might offer integrated logging or **security incident and event monitoring** (**SIEM**) services within their platform. Other offerings include vulnerability scanning, DoS protection, and so on.

Determining what responsibilities your organization wants to take in the security domain is essential. If you have an organization with limited security capacity or capabilities, it might be wise to use managed (security) services provided by the CSP. For example, your organization could work with a CSP that offers **Security Operations Center as a Service** (**SOCaaS**). SOCaaS would alleviate your organization from the task of creating, maintaining, and staffing its own SOC.

In any case, every CSP dedicates to providing a secure environment. After all, they carry a large portion of the responsibility for security. It is up to your organization to determine what tools should be provided by the CSP. The same applies to documentation, as your organization will have (varying) levels of responsibility for security. It is helpful if your CSP has proper documentation on how you can create secure environments and configurations.

In short, look for a CSP that offers easy-to-configure, well-documented security tooling that fits your organization's needs. While finding a CSP that provides many security tools is excellent, you must establish if they present a use case for you. If you intend to use SaaS solutions, you might need far less tooling than IaaS solutions. The key is not to overwhelm the internal staff with 20 different tools but to cherry-pick what you need.

Privacy

Since we hand over data to the CSP (as part of the shared responsibility model), your organization must find a CSP that provides the privacy required. An essential part of choosing a CSP is examining how they deal with privacy. Many organizations have to comply with local laws and regulations surrounding privacy, like the **General Data Protection Act** (**GDPR**) or the **California Consumer Privacy Act** (**CCPA**). Virtually all organizations also deal with some data breach notification law.

When you select a CSP, you are responsible for ensuring the vendor handles the data you provide in a way that complies with the laws and regulations that apply to your organization. Unfortunately, you do not, by design, have complete insight into how a CSP handles and stores your data. So how do you assert that a CSP is compliant?

Well, most CSPs offer documentation on specific laws and regulations. For example, AWS and Azure allow addendums to contracts that define how they will and must comply with said laws and regulations.

Nevertheless, your organization is responsible for ensuring compliance. Using available documentation to examine how you store data and offer services through a CSP can be helpful. To vet CSPs, you can use the GDPR **checklistor** similar tools for your applicable laws and regulations.

Auditability

The main concern surrounding privacy also applies to audibility. How can you audit an organization that limits resource access by design? You can use the external audit reports, trust marks, and certifications they provide.

The **Cloud Security Alliance (CSA) Security, Trust, Assurance, and Risk Registry (STAR)** is an excellent place to start. CSA STAR has information on various controls a CSP has implemented. Depending on the level (one or two), the data is a self-assessment or a third-party audit. Level two STAR registrations are very useful, providing externally verified in-depth insight into a vendor's controls.

Other standard reports to check are SOC 2 type II reports. These reports provide valuable externally verified information about control implementation. Most CSPs make their SOC 2 type II reports available through their website.

The ISO 27001 control framework certification is a good baseline starting point. It simply means that the organization has implemented the controls required by the framework. Similarly, many CSPs might have an ISO 27001 certification on their website. However, an ISO certification is not synonymous with a secure organization. While an ISO 27001 certification verifies the controls from ISO 27002 have been implemented, it does not mean an organization is not vulnerable to attacks or might miss essential controls. The ISO 27001 certification process focuses on an organization's **Information Security Management System (ISMS)**. Meaning it looks mainly at the policy's existence and is likely to overlook application-level security controls.

Real-Life Tip: Never mistake an ISO 27001 certification for being synonymous with a perfectly secure organization

While a CSA STAR registration, ISO 27001 certification, or SOC 2 type II report does not indicate that a CSP offers the controls your organization needs. It does give way to audit the CSP to determine if they meet your needs.

Another essential part of audibility is what you define in your contracts. For example, do you require the vendor to provide you with a (summary of) an external pentest report or vulnerability scan? The more information you ask the CSP to offer you, the better your organization can audit the CSP. Remember that many CSPs offer these documents publicly to all their customers and that some CSPs might be unwilling to provide contractual terms specific to your organization.

The last facet of auditability in the cloud pertains to your services and data. It is essential to procure cloud services to access application-level logs and other evidence that internal or external auditors can examine during an audit of your organization. After all, auditors will also want to examine your side of the cloud environment. Make sure you understand audited data within your organization. A suitable CSP allows you to access this data to provide it to internal or external audits.

EXAM Tip: For the CCSP exam, you must understand how to use CSA STAR, SOC 2 type II, and ISO certifications for auditing and vendor selection purposes.

Costs

Costs will play a huge role in selecting a CSP. An organization has limited resources and should strive to spend effectively. In cloud, computing costs are different per CSP, but they are primarily different between service models. IaaS solutions are generally cheaper than SaaS solutions (if appropriately architected).

However, the basic costs of services are not the whole picture. If you use a SaaS solution, you will likely have far fewer administrative and maintenance tasks. They result in a different need for capacity and knowledge of underlying services in an organization. Especially with the shortage of IT and, specifically, security professionals, some organizations might elect to use higher service models to limit the capacity and knowledge required internally.

Nevertheless, when helping your organization decide on a CSP, you must weigh costs. Figure out the business needs, determine your availability using the BIA, examine your knowledge and capacity within your organization, and pick a suitable CSP.

Sometimes, you might even elect to use multiple CSPs and place specific workloads at the CSP where the services are the cheapest. On the opposite side of the spectrum, you might want to use a cloud broker that can configure and maintain your entire cloud environment for you if your organization has limited internal expertise.

It is essential to realize that cloud computing is not always cheaper than on-premises. Instead, it depends on your organization. Knowledge, capacity, and the ability to spend money upfront are deciding factors in the cost-effectiveness of cloud computing.

EXAM Tip: The main cost consideration is not which CSP you pick but what services you will use.

Service level agreements

Service level agreements define the level, quality, and availability of the services a vendor will provide to the customer. SLAs are where all the factors above come together. A vendor can be motivated to meet SLAs by incorporating fines for breaching an SLA. Most large CSPs offer standardized SLAs only and have even defined the penalties for breaching them.

SLAs should be part of a contract to make them enforceable. You will notice that SLAs in cloud computing vary significantly per service model and even by service. When you select a CSP, you must review the different SLAs in place for every product and service you intend to use.

Suppose your organization has particular requirements that are not satisfied by standard SLAs CSPs provide. In that case, it might be beneficial to seek out a smaller party that allows custom SLA creation as part of a contract. However, especially smaller CSPs might be open to negotiating SLAs.

When you define an SLA, it is essential to determine what the vendor must provide and who the customer can contact in case of an SLA breach. Even more importantly, an SLA must outline how the performance of the vendor is approved and monitored

EXAM Tip: An SLA should contain an expectation, a penalty for breaching, a point/ method of contact, and how it is monitored and evaluated.

Let us look at a sample of an SLA:

Expectation: Linux-based virtual machines are available 99.5% per 365 days.

Penalty: For every percentage point under 99.5%, the vendor will provide a 10% discount over the yearly costs.

Monitoring: Availability monitoring takes place using a health check system that pings the machine every 5 seconds. Downtime is registered if the machine is unavailable for two consecutive pings (10 seconds).

Evaluation: Availability evaluation takes place over 365 days from the first start of the machine or the last review.

You must be extremely careful reading SLAs. For example, let us say your VM is unavailable four times every hour for 9 seconds consecutively:

*4 * 9 * 24 * 365 = 315260 seconds = 87.6 hours*

Your SLA only allows 1d 19h 28m and 8.8s of downtime. However, the vendor does not breach SLA since recording downtime requires more than 9 seconds of downtime.

The example above illustrates that you should be careful about how SLA terms are phrased and thoroughly evaluate if they meet your requirements. Even though the scenario above might seem far-fetched, these situations happen frequently.

EXAM Tip: Carefully read SLA-related questions to ensure you fully understand the context and scope of the SLA.

Legal and regulatory compliance

Earlier in this chapter, we touched on GDPR and CCPA. However, your organization likely deals with other laws and regulations as well.

An excellent example of this could be the **Payment Card Industry Data Security Standard (PCI-DSS)**. PCI-DSS is an example of a standard that applies to all organizations that handle credit card information. If your organization handles such data, you must comply with PCI-DSS regardless of processing data in the cloud or on-premise.

Another example can be that your customers (such as government agencies) require you to have an ISO 27001 certification. You must ensure that your partner organizations (such as a CSP) also have one. Or, if you are dealing with US governmental organizations, you will have to comply with the NIST SPs

When you select a CSP, it is of the utmost importance that you ensure your CSP meets all applicable legal and regulatory requirements to your organization. The challenge is determining what conditions are imposed on your organizations and how CSP controls map back to them. Luckily, CSA has developed the cloud controls matrix[34]. The matrix maps different laws and regulations and the controls a vendor has implemented. While this matrix covers many important laws and regulations:

- ISO/IEC 27001/27002/27017/27018

- CCM V3.0.1

- AICPA TSC (2017)

- CIS Controls V8

- NIST 800-53r5

- PCI DSSv3.2.1

The CCM is a beneficial tool to determine if a CSP can comply with your requirements. However, to use it, your organization must first map out what all laws and regulations are essential to comply with. Based on this list, you must add mapping for controls required by laws and regulations that the CCM does not cover.

EXAM Tip: Review the CCM to see how it can help procure a CSP

EXAM Tip: Briefly review ISO 27002 and PCI-DSS, as you might face fundamental questions about controls in these standards.

Ensure you understand your legal and regulatory framework first. Then, use tools like the CCM to examine if the CSP meets your requirements.

---

[3] *CSA (cloudsecurityalliance.org)*

[4] *Cloud Controls Matrix and CAIQ v4 | CSA (cloudsecurityalliance.org)*

Product certifications

Aside from legal and regulatory compliance, your organization might have to use products with specific certifications or develop products requiring them. Either way, examining if a CSP has the correct product certifications you might require is essential. Even if you do not require product certifications, they can deliver valuable insights into the security and reliability of a product.

Let us examine some of the most common product certifications you will deal with in the cloud.

Common Criteria

The **Common Criteria** (**CC**) for information technology security evaluation is used to evaluate products by independent entities to verify and provide assurance on the level of security[5].

The CC knows seven different levels EAL-1 to EAL-7. Every level examines the requirements, functional specification, high-level design, low-level design, and product implementation. The higher the level, the more confident you can be of a product's security design and implementation.

Let us take a look at the different levels please refer to the following table:

EAL (Evaluation Assurance Level)	Description
1	Functionally tester
2	Structurally tested
3	Methodically tested and checked
4	Methodically designed, tested, and reviewed
5	Semi-formally designed and tested
6	Semi-formally verified design and tested
7	Formally verified design and tested

Table 3.2: The CC levels

When you look at this table, you can directly see how assurance ties to the product. In level 7, there has been formal verification of the design and the tests, while an EAL-1 product only has functional testing. It stands to reason that a product that only required functional testing might contain more deficiencies than a formally verified and tested product.

Let us examine the table a bit more closely. Testing a product is a requirement for every level. However, levels 1-3 do not require a design to exist. Instead, they focus on the testing

[5] *Common Criteria : New CC Portal (commoncriteriaportal.org)*

of a product. As you can see in the table, the higher the level will be, the more preparation and thought are put into the testing.

At EAL 4, a design must be in place. However, the requirements for the design are not as stringent as they are on the higher levels. Levels 6 and 7 require significant documentation around the design.

EXAM Tip: While you do not need to understand the ins and outs of every level, you must know the table above by heart for the CCSP exam.

Real-life Tip: If your organization builds products requiring CC, ensure you fully understand the certification level requirements before designing cloud solutions.

Federal Information Processing Standards (FIPS 140-2 and 140-3)

The FIPS requirements apply to non-military, American government agencies and contractors. So, if your organization operates in those categories, you must comply with the FIPS. FIPS 140-2[6] (superseded by FIPS 140-3[7]) has specific requirements for cryptographic modules. We have already examined that cryptography and key management are essential elements of cloud security. If you are an American government organization or contractor, you must evaluate your CSP against (especially) FIPS 140-3.

One of the requirements in this document surrounds the usage of **hardware security modules** (**HSMs**). As we examined in *Chapter 2, Concept and Design Principles of Secure Cloud Security*, these HSMs store encryption keys and certificates securely. Many CSPs offer key management solutions explicitly compliant with FIPS 140-2 or FIPS 140-3[8]. Let us examine the different requirements you might face, refer to the following table:

Level	Requirements
L1	1approved algorithm. No physical component required
L2	Level 1 requirements + evidence of tampering attempts
L3	Level 2 requirements + physical security mechanisms to prevent tampering
L4	Level 3 requirements + with automatic destruction of all keys upon tampering detection.

Table 3.3: FIPS 140-2 requirements for key storage

As shown above, L1 and L2 compliance does not require a physical HSM. However, L3 and L4 do. You must know what level to comply with and if your CSP can offer those services. In most cases, CSPs will offer these services (against increased costs).

---

[6] *FIPS 140-2, Security Requirements for Cryptographic Modules | CSRC (nist.gov)*
[7] *FIPS 140-3, Security Requirements for Cryptographic Modules | CSRC (nist.gov)*
[8] *FIPS validation - AWS CloudHSM (amazon.com)*

EXAM Tip: While FIPS 140-3 supersedes FIPS 140-2, the CCSP exam will likely reference 140-2.

EXAM Tip: For FIPS 140-2 L3 or L4 compliance, you require a physical HSM.

Conclusion

In this chapter, we explored the different factors you should weigh when selecting a CSP. It is essential to weigh the trade-offs your organization faces when selecting a CSP or even specific services. Sometimes, lower availability can be sufficient to prevent reaching the MTD in case of a disaster, which will likely save costs. In other instances, you might elect to choose a more expensive service with high availability to compensate for lack of internal engineering knowledge or capacity.

Regardless of our requirements, we must ensure capturing them in SLAs. Penalties and accurate descriptions of measurement, validation, and the nature of the expectations will help us solidify agreements with the CSP. We cannot hold a CSP accountable for the level of service they promise without SLAs.

Tools like the CSA STAR registry, ISO 27001 certifications, and SOC 2 type II reports can help us understand the controls a CSP has implemented. The knowledge gained from these resources allows your organization to determine if they provide the required controls. Nevertheless, you must first understand which laws and regulations are applicable to your organization. A tool like the CCM can help determine if the required controls are present at the CSP.

In addition to laws and regulations, product certifications might be a requirement to sell or use products. The CC plays an essential role in the level of assurance we have about a product's security.

Lastly, we covered the FIPS. While only applicable to US governments and contractors, adherence to the requirements created by the FIPS is essential for any party dealing with these parties.

In the next chapter, discover, classify, and manage Cloud data you will learn about the vital practices that allow you to understand the data your organization has and what measures must be taken to protect that data.

Learning goals

This chapter addresses the following CCSP exam outline[9] learning goals:

Domain 1: Cloud concepts, architecture, and design

      1.2 Describe cloud reference architecture

      1.5 Evaluate cloud service providers

---

[9] *CCSP Exam Outline (isc2.org)*

Join our book's Discord space

Join the book's Discord Workspace for Latest updates, Offers, Tech happenings around the world, New Release and Sessions with the Authors:

https://discord.bpbonline.com

CHAPTER 4
Discover, Classify, and Manage Cloud Data

Introduction

Storing and handling data in the cloud may sound scary. By implementing suitable mechanisms to discover, classify, and manage data in the cloud, you will find out the cloud is often more secure. This chapter will review data types, classification practices, data flow diagrams, and other data practices. Throughout the chapter, we will also review how these practices must be secured in policies, standards, and procedures to ensure they are consistently and correctly executed throughout the organization.

Structure

This chapter covers the following topics:

- Data types
- Data classification
- Data data flows
- Data mapping
- Data labeling
- Data dispersion

- Policies
- Data retention and storage
- Data deletion and archival
- Legal holds
- Information Rights Management

Objectives

In this chapter, you will learn to understand the different types of data you will store and process. The data type will serve as a determining factor of how it will be stored and processed. You will discover the significance of classification, mapping, and labeling for developing adequate security controls. At the same time, you will learn how retention and storage are affected by data dispersion and complex data flows.

At the end of the chapter, you will fully understand the cloud secure data lifecycle phases and how policies ensure correct storage, deletion, and archival. You will also gain an understanding of information rights management and how legal proceedings, like legal holds, affect your data.

Data types

In *Chapter 2, Concepts and Design Principles of Secure Cloud Computing*, we explored the different types of storage solutions most CSPs offer. Disk storage, file storage, object storage, and databases are all examples of these storage solutions. While we examined some of the technical benefits of these solutions, we did not discuss how the type of data affects your preferred storage solution.

Let us examine the data types you must know for the CCSP exam. (ISC)2 wants you to understand structured, unstructured, and semi-structured data. Unfortunately, these terms are somewhat non-descriptive, so we must dive deeper to understand them.

Structured data, in essence, follows a formatted and structured data model. This type of data is easy to interpret for humans and software alike because the structured data model makes it easy to understand what the data represents. Standardized formatting ensures that the data is easily readable as well. Let us look at an example please refer to the following table:

Name	Date of Birth	Place of Birth
Margo	1990-08-01	Amsterdam, The Netherlands
Eliot	1991-12-12	Berlin, Germany
Quinten	1988-05-03	Paris, France

Name	Date of Birth	Place of Birth
Julia	1992-03-05	Brussels, Belgium
Alice	1987-01-03	Luxembourg, Luxembourg
Penny	1987-02-08	Vienna, Austria

Table 4.1: *Example of structured data*

As you can see in the table above, a data model is applied. Every entry contains a name, date of birth, and birthplace. However, the data in every entry follows the same formatting. The name column only contains first names, the date of birth is formatted (yyyy-mm-dd), and the place of birth is (city, country). Because we know that every entry contains the same formatted fields, it is easy to write software to use this data programmatically. For example, if you wanted to see the birth country of every entry, you could split the value on "" to get the country. Another benefit is that structured data clearly shows you what you are storing. In this case, it would take seconds to understand you are storing three different data fields.

Rigid data models are not suitable for every purpose, sometimes we require some flexibility in the data modeling. Nevertheless, we still want to be able to interpret the data quickly. Semi-structured data can help us there. While structured data follows a rigid model, semi-structured data is data that describes its model.

Self-describing data is prevalent; you will have encountered it if you have worked in the IT industry. **JavaScript Object Notation (JSON)** and **Extensible Markup Language (XML)** are likely terms you have heard before. XML and JSON allow you to dynamically define the data model by describing the data stored in the model. Let us take a look at how this works please refer to the following code:

```
01.  [
02.      {
03.          "name": "Julia",
04.          "date_of_birth": "1992-03-05",
05.          "place_of_birth": "Brussels, Belgium",
06.          "hometown": "Antwerp"
07.      },
08.      {
09.          "name": "JuEliotlia",
10.          "date_of_birth": "1991-12-12",
11.          "place_of_birth": "Berlin, Germany",
12.          "hometown": "Antwerp",
13.          "eye_color": "brown"
14.      },
15.      {
16.          "list_name": "shopping list",
17.          "items": [
18.              "rhubarb",
19.              "yoghurt"
20.          ]
21.      }
22.  ]
```

Figure 4.1: *Semi-structured JSON data*

Above, you can see some of the data from the structured data example. However, this time, the data is formatted as a JSON array (a list of items). The array contains data about **Julia** and **Eliot**. The data about **Eliot** and **Julia** follows the same format but has a different structure. You can see a field with **Eliot**'s **eye_color** but not one for **Julia**. You might have noticed that the list also contains an entirely different object, a **shopping list**. The list clearly describes its structure. The first field is the **list_name**, while the second is an array of **items**.

As you can see, semi-structured data can contain various entries that do not follow the same structure. Nevertheless, they do describe their structure and can use strictly formatted data. It is still reasonably easy to process and understand this data programmatically.

EXAM TIP: Common forms of semi-structured data are XML and JSON. Both are used in web API communication.

If you understand relational databases well, you have already realized that most databases contain structured data. Non-relational databases are great for semi-structured and unstructured data.

EXAM TIP: Relational databases are generally better for structured data than non-relational databases.

Not every dataset has a pre-defined data model. If data does not have such a model, we call it **unstructured data**. Unfortunately, most data you deal with daily fits this category. For example, this data is unstructured if you create a text file with a word processor.

Now, you might say, but what about the data structure within the document itself? That is a good point. After all, you can structure a document in chapters, and so on. However, your document does not have a data model to adhere to. Meaning it is not enforceable. If you are writing a text document on customer experiences, what will keep you from including your shopping list somewhere in the document? Because unstructured data can be widely variable, it is often difficult to process it in an automated fashion. Other common examples of unstructured data are spreadsheets, presentations, and so on.

EXAM TIP: Unstructured data is not suitable for relational databases

In the next section, we will examine the influence of the data type on how we classify data.

Data classification

Reviewing the cloud secure data lifecycle in *Chapter 2, Concepts and Design Principles of Secure Cloud Computing*, we discussed creating, storing, using, sharing, archiving, and destroying data. Every phase has specific requirements based on the classification of our data. Thus, before you create any data, you should classify it. After all, public data requires different security controls than highly confidential company secrets.

Let us look at data classification, its place, and how the data type plays a role in this process. In short, data classification is a process through which you group data. The grouping of data is done based on the properties of the data. For example, how sensitive the data is, what regulations apply, how difficult or expensive it would be to replace or lose the data, or even how damaging a data breach would be on the organization.

In essence, your organization must understand the value of data. An organization should develop a data classification model based on the data's value. While a uniform data classification tiering system does not exist, many organizations use a system along the lines of the example, refer to the following table:

Commercial	US Government
Restricted	Top Secret (severe damage)
Confidential	Secret (serious damage)
Internal	Confidential
Internal	Sensitive but unclassified (some damage)
Public	Unclassified

Table 4.2: Examples of data classification tiers

EXAM TIP: For the CCSP exam, review the definitions of the US government data classifications.

Most organizations use 3-5 data classification tiers; you will find many variations online. The tiers represent the value of data to the organization and are expressable in many different ways. For example, an organization could define the following;

Restricted data results in a severe financial loss (>1M USD) to the organization or irreparable damage to the organization's reputation or market position.

An organization might consider its trade secrets restricted data based on the definition above. After all, if the organization loses its trade secrets, it might suffer irreparable damage to its market position. Another type of data that might be considered restricted could be the personal data of EU residents. The GDPR protects their data, and leakage of their data could lead to fines by an EU privacy authority of more than 1M USD.

However, data from customers outside a regulated market (privacy) might not result in such fines. The lack of regulations might allow a lower data classification if leakage would not cause irreparable damage to the organization's reputation or market position. The example above showcases precisely why an organization should create its data classifications. The same data is not worth the same to every organization.

Now that you understand what data classification is and how every organization must classify data itself, let us take a quick look at how you can perform it.

Data flows

A common way to classify data is based on data flows. Data flows are a way to map out which people, processes, and technology process or store certain data elements. By creating data flows using **data flow diagrams (DFDs)**, your organization can map out what data is used where. Data flows are essential in creating an inventory of your organization's data and, thus, classification. After all, it must understand what data it handles before your organization can classify its data based on its defined classification tiers. The easiest way to create DFDs is by interviewing various organizational stakeholders.

> **EXAM TIP: You must understand that DFDs are an essential tool in the data classification process.**

Try to work your way down from the strategic to the operational level. The interviews with stakeholders will reveal what systems are in use and what data goes through them. By interviewing stakeholders from different organizational levels, you will find that no one has the complete picture. However, combining feedback from various entities will likely give you a relatively holistic overview of data processing and storage in the organization.

> **REAL-LIFE TIP: Start interviews with a blank piece of paper. Going into interviews with too many assumptions will limit your ability to identify all data processed. Ensure you cross-check if you find discrepancies between stakeholders.**

Once you have interviewed enough stakeholders, and identified the processes and technology in the organization, ensure you follow up with process and technology stakeholders to confirm what you have learned is correct.

Now that you have gathered information from all organization levels and technical stakeholders, you can use your knowledge to model data flow diagrams and create a data catalog. Such a data catalog describes what data is handled by the organization, where, and why.

> **REAL-LIFE TIP: Many companies do not have a comprehensive data catalog. Ensure your organization implements data cataloging for new initiatives and then try to work backward to map out the existing landscape.**

Data mapping

A data catalog and DFDs will also allow you to start data mapping. The process of data mapping allows you to connect data from different systems or sources. For example, your DFDs might reveal that two systems maintain a database with customer names. Both databases likely contain data that is contradictory to each other or even missing entirely. Data mapping seeks to identify these types of problems.

Data mapping is an essential tool to ensure the integrity of your data is assured. In the example above, your organization should consider creating a single database that contains only the most up-to-date records from both data sets. That way, you can deduplicate data and prevent data discrepancies within your environment. These actions increase data integrity but can also reduce costs (especially in the cloud). After all, storing data once means you only pay for storing it once.

Let us look at an example where data mapping is important, refer to the following figure:

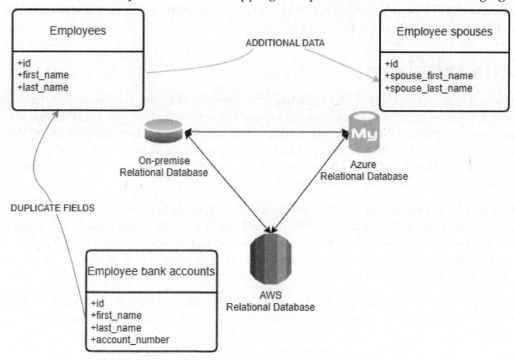

Figure 4.2: Data mapping in a hybrid cloud environment

The figure above shows that the sample organization uses three relational databases. Each database resides at a different location. The first DB containing the **Employee** table lives on-premise, while the second and third DB run in the cloud. Each database includes a single table. However, you can see that the **Employees** and the **Employee bank accounts** table have duplicate fields. Duplication means syncing would be required every time the duplicated fields are changed in either database. Such syncing causes the need for extra technical controls and can be challenging to scale. It is also possible that values change to contradicting new values in both tables simultaneously. If this happens, you must create logic to determine which value you should store.

Another thing you can see in this example is that the **Employee spouses** table stores data that is relevant for the applications using the **Employees** table. It is worthwhile to examine if merging the **Employee spouses** table with the **Employees** table (or even just the database) would make sense. Since the data in both tables are stored in separate databases, loose coupling is in place, making it more difficult to query the data effectively.

The content of the example above is not very relevant. You will encounter many different situations at different organizations. However, the model does illustrate how important it is to perform data mapping activities. Data integrity will suffer without them, while extra technological effort is needed to make systems work correctly.

At the time of writing, many organizations are releasing tooling to perform data mapping automatically. If your organization has little documentation or many datasets, such solutions can be worthwhile to consider.

Data labeling

Once you understand how your organization wants to classify data, how the data flow through your environment, and how data maps between datasets, you should ensure you label your data. Data labeling means marking the data according to its classification. When you perform data labeling, you can label the data itself or choose to label the systems and processes that handle it. The benefit of this practice is that you can easily see data classification and apply the correct security controls.

For example, if you have a system that processes payment and public website data, you should base its security controls on the highest classified data it processes. The payment data will likely be classified as *Restricted*, while the public website data might be *Public*. If you configured the system to meet the security controls for public data, it would not sufficiently protect the payment data.

If you label the system as *Restricted*, you know to apply that level of security controls. While these controls are likely overkill for public data, the system must protect its most sensitive data. In these cases, your organization might even consider splitting an extensive application (or monolithic) into smaller applications with a limited scope (micro-services). That way, you could process the public data in a separate system requiring only security controls appropriate for that level.

Remember, security is about trade-offs. Creating, maintaining, and monitoring security controls costs time and money. As security budgets are limited, you should put your efforts where they are most needed.

In any case, it is a good practice to ensure you label all your data and systems. Once you determine the appropriate controls for each data classification tier, it will be easy to decide what controls should be applied and monitored for new and existing use cases.

Policies

We discussed how important it is to classify, map, and label data. However, doing these things by itself will not make your organization more secure. You will have to create policies (high-level strategical documents), standards (mandatory technical requirements), and guidelines (optional guidance and best practices) on what to do with those, as mentioned above.

Firstly, you must establish your data classification tiering using a data classification policy or standard, which is a policy or standard that defines which classification is applicable in what scenario. A data classification policy allows your organization to easily classify new or existing data. Many organizations even include a data catalog in the policy or standard. The catalog outlines common data fields used within your organization and the classification level that applies to them.

After creating a data classification policy, your organization can work on creating data handling or data security standards. These standards outline appropriate security controls per classification level. For example, your organization might require that *Restricted* data be stored encrypted at rest and in transit. However, public data might only require in-transit encryption. Let us look at a sample policy below please refer to the following table:

Classification	Description
Public	Any data that does not cause harm to the organization's reputation or finances when accessed by external entities.
Internal	Any data that cause harm to the organization's reputation or finances impact confidentiality or availability. The damage is unlikely to exceed 1M USD.
Restricted	Any data that cause harm to the organization's reputation or finances impact confidentiality or availability. The damage is likely to exceed 1M USD.

Table 4.3: Sample of a data classification descriptions

In the next table, Sample of a data classification policy control requirements matrix is showcase please refer the following table:

Control/ Data classification	Public	Internal	Restricted
Encryption at rest		X	X
Encryption in transit		X	X
Cloud storage allowed	X	X	
Access Control Required		X	X

Table 4.4: Sample of a data classification policy control requirements matrix

In the following table, Sample pf data catalog is depicted please refer to the following table:

Data Field	Public	Internal	Restricted
Customer name	X		
Credit card			X
Customer address		X	
Customer e-mail address		X	

Table 4.5: Sample of a data catalog

Based on the sample policy above, your organization has much information about how it should deal with data security. The organization in the example feels that credit card information would likely cause more than 1M USD in damages to the finances or reputation when breached or unavailable. Based on this assumption, the organization requires encryption at rest and in transit for credit card data but not for the customer's name. At the same time, leakage of customer names is perceived not to cause any harm to the organization. Another interesting facet of this example is the *cloud storage allowed* control. The sample company does not allow storing restricted data in the cloud. While you should wonder if this makes sense, you will encounter many organizations that define such policies as they deem on-premise storage more secure.

As you can see in the sample policy above, the data handling standard only tells you that data requires encryption at rest and in transit for certain classifications. It does not define how one should do this. Your organization should utilize guidelines to guide how to control implementation. Or, if your organization has strict requirements, outline the implementation in a specific standard. For example, let us take a look at a data encryption example please refer the following table:

Implementation	Requirement
Encryption in transit	Usage of TLS v1.2 or v1.3
Encryption at rest	Usage of the AES algorithm with a minimum key length of 256 bits.

Table 4.6: Example of a data encryption standard

EXAM TIP: For the CCSP exam, you must understand the need for a data classification policy and data handling or data security standards.

Your organization must create a data classification policy, data handling standards, and other policies and standards based on its needs. Creating these policies and standards from the ground up can be challenging. The NIST has developed several documents that can guide your organization. The NIST cyber framework contains five categories (**Identify**, **Protect**, **Detect**, **Respond**, and **Recover**). The identify and protect category contains valuable documents when creating these policies and standards.

Remember, policies and standards are evolving documents. They do not have to be perfect. Try to re-use best practices and guidance that is in existence and tailor it to the needs of your organization. Also, when you create new policies, try to aim for future goals but do not alienate your policy too far from the current state. If you require encryption in transit for all data, while you know your data transmission takes place over serial connections, you are not focusing your efforts correctly.

Data dispersion

One of the items you will want to think about is data dispersion. So far, we have talked about data confidentiality. Availability of data is of equal importance. During your BIA, you have learned what systems and processes are critical to your organization. If systems are unavailable, they can harm your business, and if the downtime exceeds the MTD, it can ruin the organization. A significant part of ensuring systems are available during a disaster and in typical operating situations is the dispersion of your data. Data dispersion pertains to how and where your data spreads throughout your computing environment. Data dispersion occurs between on-premise and cloud environments in a hybrid cloud environment. However, data dispersion is also relevant within on-premise or cloud environments.

For example, in *Chapter 2* , concepts and design principles of Cloud security, we discussed the usage of availability zones. These availability zones represent separate data center locations that are spread out geographically. By dispersing your data over multiple availability zones, you can ensure your data is accessible when one of the available zones is unavailable.

So, how do you do this? Your organization can generally use **backups** or **syncing** (or mirroring) data to achieve data dispersion for availability purposes. Backups allow you to store a copy of your data in a different AZ or on-premise data center. A drawback of backups is that they usually require recovery to be usable. After all, a tape containing a backup is not useable unless it is accessible to your computing environment. **Mirroring** or syncing data allows you to duplicate your data (in real-time) between different environments.

CSPs use mirroring to provide highly available services like managed databases. The CSP must be able to scale your databases on demand. But, if only a single database instance exists, you can scale vertically (more hardware for the service) but not horizontally (more of the same services). Similarly, CSPs use mirroring to disperse data over different availability zones to ensure the managed service is still reachable in case an AZ is down.

Mirroring also has limitations, for example, real-time mirroring causes a lot of traffic as all data updates communicate between nodes. Real-time syncing is also seldom fully real-time. You are likely to experience delays (of seconds). These delays can cause problems when simultaneously altering the same record in two instances. In most cases, the last change to a record will override a previous change. Hence, mirroring would require coordination between the different nodes to prevent nodes from overriding each other's data.

Whichever request completes last will override the first (sometimes a race condition might also apply the other way around). For example, if your syncing occurs every 5 seconds and change one is made at 2 seconds, and change two at 4 seconds, change two will override change one.

In reality, most organizations use both backups and data syncing. Backups are used for disaster recovery efforts, while data syncing ensures availability and business continuity. While these concepts allow us to use data dispersion for good, it has some challenges, especially in the cloud.

The more data dispersion occurs, the more difficult it becomes to correctly classify, map, label, archive, and delete data properly. Data dispersion makes data flow far more complicated and must be applied carefully. If you do not know where your data resides, following the cloud secure data lifecycle will be near impossible. Documentation of data dispersion efforts is essential.

EXAM TIP: Backups and data syncing/mirroring use data dispersion to improve disaster recovery capacity and availability.

In cloud computing, we might use managed services that disperse data over different AZs without awareness. That dispersion of data can be tricky. Sometimes, data dispersion even leads to incompliance with local laws and regulations. For example, if you use a managed database service that spreads data over an AZ in Europe and the US, you could run into GDPR compliance issues. Luckily, data mirroring usually occurs within a single region and not across regions, you can see an example of such a setup as follows:

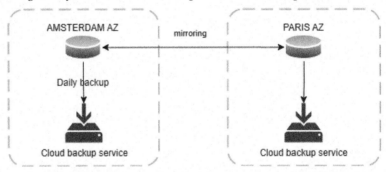

Figure 4.3: Combination of database mirroring with daily backups

Nevertheless, we can create solutions that disperse data across regions. If you choose to do so, ensure you leverage your legal teams to ensure you are not causing compliance issues.

EXAM TIP: Documenting how, when, and where data dispersion is allowed in a policy is essential to avoid compliance issues and data remanence.

Data retention and storage

We just talked about the dispersion of data. But we also have to think about how we store data in general. Earlier in this chapter, we covered the different data types and how we store them. Whenever you determine the lifecycle of your data, it is essential to pick a storage solution that works for that data. The storage platform should offer a suitable storage type for your data.

For example, if you have structured data, storing it on a file server that does not allow automated querying of the data makes no sense. Conversely, storing excel sheets in a database is also not likely to make sense.

So, when you determine the lifecycle of your data, figure out how you are going to use the data. Your data usage will ultimately decide whether you should store the data in a database, fileserver, or object storage solution. Sometimes, you will even conclude that you should turn unstructured data into a structured format for automatic processing.

For example, you might want to parse the content of text files to blobs that you store in a relational database for easy programmatic processing.

Another factor you should consider when thinking about storage is data dispersion, as we discussed previously. Determine how available your data has to be. Is it sufficient to only create backups stored in a cold-storage facility that take weeks to restore? Or do you need your data mirrored in real-time over multiple AZs because downtime is unacceptable?

Regardless of your conclusion, a factor you must consider is data retention. Meaning how long you will store the data. As a good practice, you should never store data any longer than you need for usage, sharing, or legal requirements. It will be up to your organization to determine the appropriate storage term, but remember that the longer you store data, the higher the breach chances.

For example, if HIPAA applies to your data, you might have to retain health records for 20 years. If you store your data for 20 years, attackers can access enormous data.

Your organization must establish standards and guidelines that define and outline the data retention period and what storage solutions are permitted. Such a policy is usually called a **data retention policy**. The data retention policy is often a legal requirement, but just a vital asset to your organization to ensure data is stored appropriately.

Another item your organization should investigate is access to stored data. Does data require authentication and authorization to access? Is data stored in an encrypted fashion at rest? Do the systems that process your data have security controls that match your data's labeling? As discussed earlier in this chapter, these facets belong to a data-handling policy.

Deletion and archival

As you saw in the cloud secure data lifecycle, archival and deletion are critical lifecycle phases. Most of the time, an organization might want to hold on to data after processing even though it does not require it to be quickly accessible. For example, retaining financial records for a set time might be required. We call this principle archival. Archival refers to the temporary retention of data for compliance purposes, evidentiary necessity, or future processing.

Data archival is possible in many ways (which we will explore in *Chapter 5, Cloud Storage Architecture and their security technologies*). Usually, archived data does not require fast and frequent access, which allows us to use different (and cheaper) storage solutions for archived data. For example, archived data is storable on backup tapes or blu-ray disks held in off-site storage.

Nevertheless, the data is still vital to the organization. So, when we archive data, we must implement the proper security controls, as required by the data label and the associated data classification. For example, some records will require encryption when they are archived. They might even need data dispersion in the form of backups in multiple AZs.

In any case, when an organization is defining its archival data process, it must evaluate the following:

- Do we need to archive this data, or should we delete it?
- How do we archive the data?
- How often must the data be accessed?
- How quickly must the data be accessible?
- What are the security measures required? (encryption, access controls, and so on.)
- Does archived data have legal retention requirements?
- Might archived data require deletion actions under applicable laws and regulations (like GDPR)?
- What are we willing/capable of paying for archival?

The questions above will help your organization determine which archival strategies fit their needs without wasting unnecessary time and resources. Especially in cloud environments, where you pay for your usage, it is essential to properly evaluate the conditions for archival and the frequency and speed of access.

Once data is no longer required or data subjects request data removal, the last phase of the cloud secure data lifecycle becomes relevant—namely, the deletion of data. As we covered earlier in this book, data deletion in the cloud is challenging.

For example, if you wanted to destroy archived data stored on tape, you could incinerate the tape or degauss and zero-wipe a hard drive. In the cloud, we do not have these options as a CSP has the responsibility for the physical devices. While on-premise networks, we have complete control of the storage devices.

We reviewed that (the only) suitable mechanism to destroy data in the cloud is cryptographic erasure. Cryptographic erasure is the process of encrypting data with a robust algorithm and considerable key length and subsequently destroying the encryption key.

Firstly, the rise of quantum computing. Quantum computing was briefly covered in *Chapter 1, Understanding Computing Concepts,* and poses a massive threat to cryptographic erasure.

If you apply cryptographic erasure, you must be aware of this development. However, cloud computing has more challenges when it comes to data deletion. As discussed, cryptographic erasure should occur with a robust algorithm and considerable key length. Unfortunately, the increase in computing power brought to the table by quantum computing is predicted to render many of the current-day encryption algorithms and key lengths breakable.

While quantum computing is hardly mainstream, at the time of writing, it is crucial to consider these developments. Luckily, NIST and industry partners have been investigating **quantum-safe encryption**[1]. These new encryption algorithms require shorter key lengths but are much more challenging to crack. When your organization creates standards and guidelines for implementing cryptographic erasure, ensure they consider these developments and utilize encryption algorithms and key sizes that will be resilient in the future. After all, your organization might have to store data for 20 years. Meaning you must design your security measures with the future in mind.

Another facet of data deletion that is incredibly challenging in the cloud is by lack of data mapping and the vast dispersion of data. When deleting data, an organization must ensure it deletes all instances of it. Cloud environments often depend on different services, providers, and environments, leading to significant data dispersion. Without creating data flows and no data mapping, data remanence is likely. Such remanence can be dangerous to an organization.

If your organization did not create data flows or perform data mapping, you might not thoroughly remove that subject's data. A breach occurs after the removal request and remnant data about the data subject leaks. For example, if your organization stores data from EU residents (which is protected by GDPR), a data subject can request the removal of their data. Your organization will be subject to severe fines and penalties.

In short, data deletion in the cloud requires correct data flow diagrams, extensive data mapping, and cryptographic erasure with quantum-safe encryption.

EXAM TIP: For the CCSP exam, you must understand how quantum computing threatens cryptographic erasure and how quantum-safe encryption can help protect your organization.

Legal holds

Sometimes, an organization might encounter situations where data deletion is legally prohibited. An example of this is a legal hold. Such a hold means a specific data set cannot be destroyed or altered. An organization's leg usually issues a legal hold when a legal case is started (against or by the company). Legal holds can be issued for any duration and generally depend on the local laws and regulations regarding evidence handling in legal cases. The hold can affect electronic and physical data alike. However, it is usually easier

---

[1] *NIST Announces First Four Quantum-Resistant Cryptographic Algorithms | NIST*

to prevent the destruction of physical documents. After all, this usually requires shredding or incinerating, while deleting digital files is very simple.

When your organization is creating (cloud) environments, it is essential to anticipate the event of a legal hold. Doing so allows you to create controls that logically prevent data from being deleted. After all, a legal hold cannot prevent people from destroying data. It would be best if you incorporated technical controls to prevent it. For example, when a legal hold is issued, you might use a mechanism restricting all access to a data set to read-only rights.

While legal holds, hopefully, do not frequently occur in your organization. It is essential to prepare for them. Incorporating procedures for legal holds in a standard or policy and providing employee training is highly advisable.

Remember that for the correct execution of a legal hold, data flows, data mapping and data classification are essential. Failure to do so can lead to mistrials, lost legal cases, and significant reputational and financial damage to your organization. For example, if you have multiple databases with employee information, but you only block access to one of them, it is likely that you are not executing the legal hold properly.

EXAM TIP: For the CCSP exam, you must understand legal holds and how to ensure they are executed correctly.

Information Rights Management

The last subject of this chapter is called **Information Rights Management** (**IRM**). IRM is generally considered a subset of **Digital Rights Management** (**DRM**). A common implementation of DRM is to protect against copying (or ripping) of DVDs and software. You might have encountered DRM when installing software from a disk or watching a movie from a DVD.

In *Chapter 2, Concepts and Design Principles of Cloud Security*, we covered the basic building blocks of cloud security. You will remember that we covered access control, authorization, identity management, and encryption as some of these building blocks. DRM and IRM use these technologies to ensure that only authorized entities can use information. In any case, both technologies protect who can access data.

IRM almost always uses authentication to ensure the identity is legitimate, while it uses authorization to determine the data access level. In IRM, encryption is also used as an access control mechanism. After all, encryption prevents you from reading data that you cannot decrypt. In the case of DRM, encryption of video files might prevent straight-up copying of the video file content.

However, IRM also seeks to prevent data from being dispersed through channels that could cause compromise. For example, your organization might use an internal file share for classified documents. If someone posts these documents on a public **Google Drive**, unauthorized entities will likely access the data. Hence, your organization might want to block the usage of Google Drive on machines that can access classified documents.

You might have noticed that the scope of IRM is comprehensive, from access controls to encryption. Remember, IRM is usually not a single tool. Instead, it is a goal that uses a collection of tools within your organization to ensure only authorized users can access data. The tools can include encryption, **Data Loss Prevention** (DLP) tools, identity and access management, single sign-on, MFA, and so on. Thus, it is up to your organization to decide how you ensure IRM is effective.

EXAM TIP: IRM is not a tool but an achievable goal with your organization's tools (access control, encryption, data loss prevention).

Conclusion

This chapter covered the many facets of discovering, classifying, and managing data in the cloud. We covered how data types (structured, semi-structured, and unstructured) affect how we store and use data. We learned how essential it is for organizations to classify their data based on their needs, how BIAs are vital to data classification, and that classifications are wholly dependent on the context of an organization.

We discussed the power of creating data flow (diagrams) to ensure we understand how data is processed, stored, and deleted throughout the organization, at how they, at the same time, allow us to map data between different systems and environments correctly. We examined the power of data labeling, its effects on applying the proper security controls, and how data dispersion is essential to ensure availability in the cloud. However, it has some inherent drawbacks for data deletion, archival, and data integrity.

After reading this chapter, you know that policies are crucial to managing data in the cloud. Without policies, standards, and guidelines, we cannot assert that the correct controls apply to our data and systems.

We also examined the importance of thinking about data retention, archival, and deletion in the cloud. You learned that Quantum-safe encryption is essential for cryptographic erasure and, thus, data deletion in the future of the cloud. But you now also know that legal holds can prevent an organization from being allowed to delete data. The application of technical measures is essential to enforce these legal holds.

Lastly, we covered the subject of **Information Rights Management** (IRM), which is not a single tool but an achievable goal with the tools throughout the organization.

In the next chapter, Cloud storage architectures and their security technologies, you will learn how data can be stored in the Cloud. You will also learn how different storage architectures allow for varying security controls.

Learning goals

This chapter addresses the following CCSP exam outline learning goals:

Domain 2: Cloud data security

> 2.1 Describe cloud data concepts
>
> 2.4 Implement data discovery
>
> 2.5 Plan and implement data classification
>
> 2.6 Design and implement **Information Rights Management (IRM)**
>
> 2.7 Plan and implement data retention, deletion, and archiving policies

Join our book's Discord space

Join the book's Discord Workspace for Latest updates, Offers, Tech happenings around the world, New Release and Sessions with the Authors:

https://discord.bpbonline.com

CHAPTER 5

Cloud Storage Architectures and their Security Technologies

Introduction

Now that you know how data *live* in the cloud. It is time to explore how different architectures support data types. This chapter explores different architectures for data storage, the threats they face, and the implementation of technologies to secure data handling. The chapter will cover items like the different storage types and the threats that they face. However, it will also delve into security measures you can take to fight these threats. For example, we will cover encryption, hashing, key management, and even more complicated techniques like data loss prevention and data backups.

Structure

This chapter covers the following topics:

- Storage types
- Threats to storage types
- Encryption and key
- Hashing
- Applications of encryption

- Key, secrets, and certificate management

- Data obfuscation, tokenization, masking, and anonymization

- Data loss prevention

- Tiering, CDNs, replication, and backups

- Sample architecture

Objectives

In this chapter, you will learn about different storage types and the threats they face. We will examine how encryption and key management are vital to ensuring the confidentiality of your data. We will dive into masking, data obfuscation, and tokenization as methods of anonymizing data. Moreover, we will explore how DLP can help your organization maintain data confidentiality through automated means. Lastly, we will examine the secure management of secrets and certificates in the cloud.

Storage types

The previous chapter covered the data types we encountered (structured, semi-structured, and unstructured). We also covered how different data types need other storage solutions. However, we have not covered the types of storage you will encounter.

Let us start with **ephemeral storage**. Ephemeral storage is short-lasting storage. The most common place you will encounter this storage is in **Random Access Memory (RAM)**. You likely know that RAM stores data that your computer's processor uses. Once you power down the system, it erases the data in RAM. Ephemeral storage is often called **non-persistent** or **volatile storage**. However, we encounter non-persistent storage in other forms as well.

For example, session cookies (data stored about a user or browser session) are non-persistent. Closing the browser erases the cookies. Cookies are also retainable for more extended periods. Nevertheless, realizing that non-persistent storage applies to more than RAM is essential. Following, you see a figure summarizing typical applications of **VOLATILE** and **NON-VOLATILE STORAGE**:

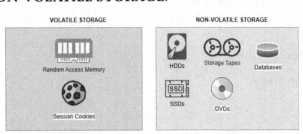

Figure 5.1: *Common types of volatile and non-volatile storage*

EXAM TIP: RAM and session data (cookies) are the most common forms of non-persistent data.

On the other hand, we also have long-term or non-volatile storage. This storage type persists data for long periods. **Hard drives**, **Solid State Disks**, **Blu-rays**, and **tapes** commonly store this data. Non-volatile data remains, even when power to the storage device is disconnected.

For example, contrary to RAM, **Read-only Memory (ROM)** is non-volatile. ROM storage stores the **Basic Input Output System (BIOS)** or **Unified Extensible Firmware Interface (UEFI)** on a motherboard. Imagine if ROM was volatile. That would mean every team you powered off a computer would no longer function (because of the erasure of the BIOS or UEFI).

It is crucial to understand the difference between **VOLATILE** and **NON-VOLATILE STORAGE**. Using volatile storage solutions for long-term data storage will have detrimental consequences for the data, but more than the usage of the storage types is relevant to a CCSP. Every storage type requires different security measures. Let us zoom in on the threats to every storage type encounter.

Threats to storage types

The nature of the way storage types function exposes them to a varying set of threats. For example, let us look at the following scenario:

A medical company has laptop computers they distribute to employees. Alice is the **chief information officer (CIO)** of the organization. She is writing a proposal to implement a new internally developed technology to analyze vaccine effectiveness. Marissa is typing this proposal in her word processor. She decides to go for lunch, locks her screen, and leaves her computer on her desk. Handyman Bob walks by her office, sees her laptop sitting there, swoops into the office, and steals the computer.

In the scenario above, Bob has multiple ways to access the data. He can access the data directly if he can figure out Alice's password. However, let us assume the organization has proper password requirements and lock-out policies. If Bob wants to access the data, he could attempt to power down the machine, reboot it with a USB-based operating system, and read the data from the hard drive. If the organization were smart enough to implement full-disk encryption, the data Bob could retrieve would be unreadable.

As mentioned in the first section of this chapter, cutting power to non-volatile memory erases the data. If Bob shut down the computer, he would not only be prevented access to the data on the hard drive because of encryption but also erasure of the data stored in the RAM.

As you can see, volatile storage faces the threat of being read outside its typical operating system. Reading can occur by extracting and plugging the device elsewhere or using a bootable operating system. However, removing RAM from the laptop would cut the power and lead to data loss.

If you have experience with computer forensics, you might know that methods exist to persist data in RAM (briefly), even without power. That process is called a **cold boot** (attack). During a cold boot, the RAM chips are cooled well below the freezing point, which can extend the time it takes for the data to be lost. Computer criminals, hackers, and data forensics might use a cold boot attack to compromise or save data stored in RAM.

The essence of the examples above is simple. Compromise of volatile storage and non-volatile storage requires different methods. Volatile storage is likely to require encryption to ensure data confidentiality, while encrypting data in RAM offers little benefit but would lead to significant performance and functional problems. After all, CPUs would require technology to decrypt the data in RAM before its usable.

Another threat that impacts both storage types is theft, physical destruction, or side-channel attacks. **Side channel attacks** use secondary factors like timing, noise, vibrations, and so on, to extrapolate the storage media's content.

EXAM TIP: For the CCSP exam, you should understand that side-channel attacks use secondary factors to breach systems or extrapolate data—the exam does not cover the technical details of these attacks.

Encryption and key management

In the last section, we covered that non-volatile storage media and data in transit require encryption. However, encryption is applicable in many different ways. The correct encryption algorithm and key lengths are essential to ensure data confidentiality. Let us look at how we encrypt data and the role of key management in secure encryption.

Firstly, it is essential to understand what encryption is. **Encryption** is a method to obfuscate data from people that should not be able to view data. Encrypted data becomes only readable to people and systems with the correct keys to decrypt the data. Encryption (and decryption) methods are either—**symmetric** or **asymmetric**.

Symmetric encryption

A symmetric encryption algorithm uses the data that should be encrypted (**plaintext**) and an **Encryption key** (often called a **secret key**) to create a **non-readable text** (**Ciphertext**). The **Encryption Algorithm** uses the plaintext and the key to generate the ciphertext. Let us look at this process, refer to the following figure:

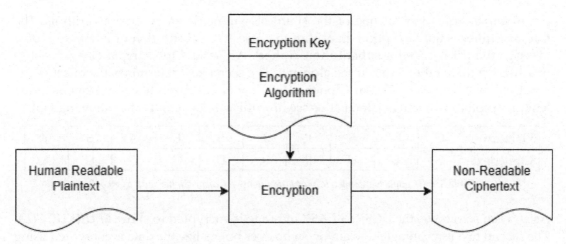

Figure 5.2: *Basic schematic overview of (symmetric) encryption*

While symmetric encryption transforms the plaintext into ciphertext, symmetric decryption reverses this process. It takes the non-readable ciphertext and uses the **Encryption Key** and **Decryption Algorithm** as shown:

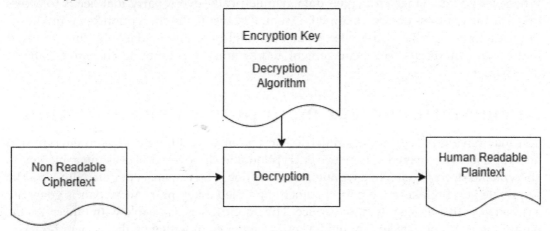

Figure 5.3: *Basic schematic overview of symmetric decryption*

So, why is this method of encryption called symmetric encryption? Well, that is because the algorithm uses the same key to encrypt and decrypt data (as you can see in *Figure 5.2* and *Figure 5.3*). When using symmetric encryption, you use one secret key. Anyone with this key can decrypt any data encrypted with that key (when encrypted with the same algorithm).

EXAM TIP: You must understand what role the plaintext, ciphertext, encryption algorithm, decryption algorithm, and (secret) key play in symmetric encryption.

For example, let us look at one of the simplest symmetric encryption algorithms. The **Caesar Cipher** is an encryption algorithm that uses the substitution of letters to hide a message (which is called a **substitution cipher**). A Caesar Cipher replaces every letter in a string with another letter in the alphabet. The secret key determines the offset of the substitution. If you use a Caesar Cipher with a key of 2, substitute every letter with the letter that comes two letters later. Let us see how this works, refer to the following table:

Plaintext	C	C	S	P	I	S	E	A	S	Y
Ciphertext	E	E	U	R	K	U	G	C	U	A

Table 5.1: Example of symmetric encryption using a Caesar Cipher with a key of 2

As you can see above, the *CCSP IS EASY* message is encrypted to show *EEURKUGCUA*. The second text is meaningless to anyone who does not realize the data is encrypted using a Caesar Cipher. However, if you know the Caesar Cipher was used for encryption using a key of 2, you could quickly decrypt the data. The decryption algorithm for a Caesar Cipher does the opposite action of the encryption algorithm. Ergo, it replaces every ciphertext letter with the letter that comes with N spaces before it (the key defines N).

Whenever you exchange encrypted data symmetrically, every party that needs to access the data must possess the secret key. It is essential to ensure the encryption key is unknown to unauthorized parties. Otherwise, your data might become readable by unauthorized parties. We will discuss key management and symmetric encryption challenges later in this chapter.

Asymmetric encryption or public key encryption

You may have guessed that asymmetric encryption uses different keys to encrypt and decrypt data. We covered symmetric encryption and discovered it uses the same key to encrypt and decrypt data. In asymmetric encryption, you can encrypt data with a **public** or **private** key. Both keys are part of something called a **key pair**. A key pair is generally associated with a user, system, or service. The public key is shareable with others. As the names suggest, a private key should be kept secret or confidential by the owner of the key.

If you use a **Private Key** to encrypt data, the **Public Key** from the same key pair is required to decrypt the data. However, if you encrypt data with the **Public Key**, the **Private Key** of the same key pair is needed to decrypt the data.

For example, **Alice** wants to send an encrypted message to **Elliot**. Suppose she decides to use her private key to encrypt the message; **Elliot** must use her public key to decrypt the message.

Let us take a look at how this works, refer to the following figure:

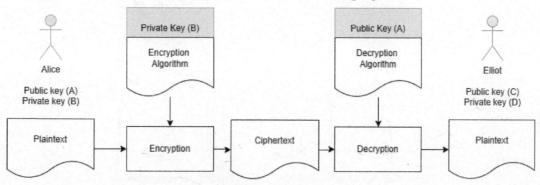

Figure 5.4: Alice sends Elliot a message encrypted with her private key

Because **Alice** can share her **public key** with **Elliot**, he can decrypt the **Ciphertext** that **Alice** sent. However, what would happen if **Alice** encrypts the message with her **public key**? Let us take a look, refer to the following figure:

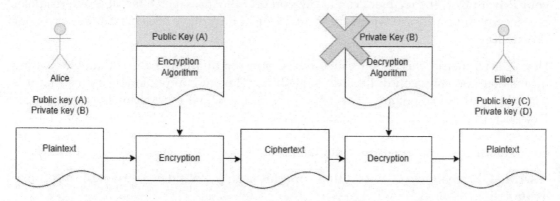

Figure 5.5: Alice sends Elliot a message encrypted with her public key

If you paid close attention earlier in this section, you remember that we should not share a **Private Key** with others. Because **Alice** cannot (or instead should not) share her **Private Key** with **Elliot**, he cannot decrypt the message. After all, if you encrypt with a **Public Key**, you need the **Private Key** from the same key pair to decrypt the message. In short, you cannot encrypt a message with your **Public Key** and expect another to decrypt it. However, since the other person can share their **Public Key** with you, you can encrypt a message with their **Public Key**, as depicted:

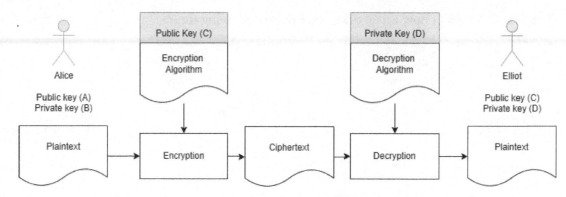

Figure 5.6: Alice sends Elliot a message encrypted with his public key

In the figure above, you can see that **Alice** does not use any keys of her key pair to send **Elliot** the encrypted message. Instead, she uses his **Public Key** to encrypt, and he uses his **Private Key** to decrypt the message.

Now, this is where asymmetric encryption becomes interesting. If you encrypt data with your **Private Key**, the recipient can know you sent the message. After all, if the recipient can decrypt your message with your **Public Key**, it must have been encrypted with your **Private Key**.

Hence, asymmetric encryption can provide **non-repudiation**. To repudiate something means that you state you did not do something. Thus, non-repudiation means that it is verifiable you did something. This concept is instrumental to security. By using **Public Key** encryption, you can establish (if the **Private Key** is secure) that the owner of a key pair sent a message. If we can verify that the key pair's owner is who we think they are, we know we are communicating with them.

EXAM TIP: Symmetric encryption provides only confidentiality and not non-repudiation.

You might not realize it, but non-repudiation is everywhere—for example, the encrypted connection when you visit a website over HTTPS. The server encrypts the data it sends you with its **Private Key**, and your computer decrypts it with the website's **Public Key**. Doing so lets you know you are communicating with the website you intend to use. We will dive deeper into this concept later in this chapter.

Unfortunately, using your **Private Key** to encrypt data has a colossal downside. Everyone that has your **Public Key** can now decrypt your data. As you can see below, if **Alice** wants to send an encrypted secret message to **Elliot** with her **Private Key**, the other day, she also sent an encrypted message to **Margo**, **Elliot**, and **Margo** could decrypt either message, refer to the following figure:

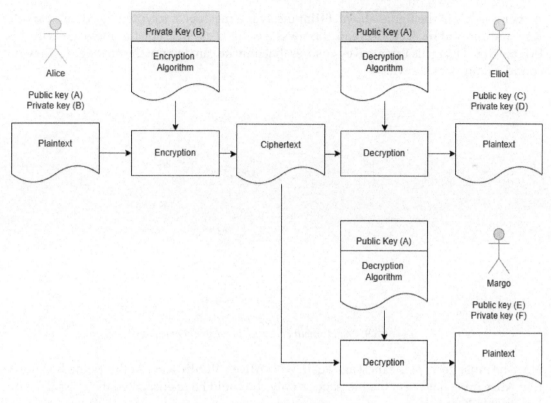

Figure 5.7: Everyone possessing your public key can decrypt data encrypted with your private key

In the figure above, you can see that you might not get the data confidentiality you need while non-repudiation is in place. After all, **Margo** could read the message sent to **Elliot** and vice versa. Luckily, there is a way to use asymmetric encryption that creates both confidentiality and non-repudiation.

When we encrypt a message with the recipient's **Public Key**, we know only that person can decrypt the message. However, if we encrypt the transmission with our **Private Key**, they are assured we sent it. Let us combine these methods as shown:

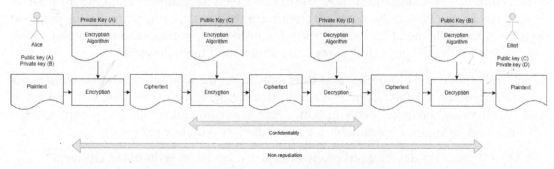

Figure 5.8: Achieving confidentiality and non-repudiation with asymmetric encryption

As you can see in the figure above, **Elliot** receives a message encrypted by **Alice**'s **Private Key** and his **Public Key**. To read the message, he must decrypt the message with his **Private Key**. Using his **Private Key** ensures that only he can decrypt the message (achieving confidentiality), as shown:

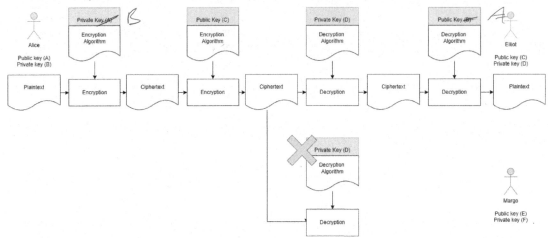

Figure 5.9: *Confidentiality achieved by combining methods*

Now, he must decrypt the message again with **Alice**'s **Public Key**. At this point, he knows that **Alice** must have sent the message as only she could have encrypted the message with her **Private Key**.

EXAM TIP: You must understand how asymmetric encryption achieves confidentiality and non-repudiation.

Block and Stream Ciphers

Aside from asymmetrical and symmetrical encryption, there is another significant difference we need to understand in how you can encrypt data. Encryption algorithms have two different ways of processing plaintext into ciphertext. The first method is called **block ciphers**. These algorithms take chunks of the entire plaintext and encrypt them in blocks. Alternatively, you can also use a **stream cipher**. Stream ciphers process the plaintext byte by byte. While the CCSP exam does not require you to understand the cryptographic procedures for these ciphers fully, you must understand the following:

Block ciphers are more complex and thus slower. At the same time, stream ciphers are more straightforward and faster. In general, stream ciphers are easier to reverse and crack. Block ciphers are the more secure option. Because stream ciphers are less complex, more efficient, and faster, they are suitable for using devices with few resources.

EXAM TIP: Storage device encryption should always occur with block ciphers.

Common algorithms

As discussed, you need an algorithm to encrypt and decrypt messages. This section will discuss some of the most commonly used algorithms. While you do not need to know how these work (in detail). You must know which algorithms are safe to apply in which scenario. Let us take a look at them in the table:

Stream Ciphers (algorithms)	Block Ciphers (algorithms)
RC4 (symmetric, insecure)	DES (symmetric, insecure)
SEAL (symmetric, insecure)	3DES (symmetric, insecure)
Salsa20 (symmetric, secure)	Twofish (symmetric, secure)
	Blowfish (symmetric, secure)
	RSA (asymmetric, secure)
	AES (symmetric, secure)
	ECDSA (asymmetric, secure)
	RC5 (symmetric, insecure)
	Kyber (asymmetric, secure, quantum-safe)

Table 5.2: Common encryption algorithms

As you can see above, there are many block and stream ciphers. Some ciphers are symmetric, while others are asymmetric. You probably recognize some of these encryption algorithms if you have been active in IT. **AES** is commonly used to encrypt hard drives and databases. At the same time, you have likely encountered **RSA** or **ECDSA** if you have worked with public key infrastructure, for example, in scenarios where you use public key authentication to get access to servers or version control software (like **Github**).

It is important to note that only **Kyber** is considered quantum-safe of all the listed algorithms. Some CSPs already offer Kyber (or other quantum-safe algorithms) in some of their services[1].

> **EXAM TIP:** For the CCSP exam, you must understand which ciphers are symmetric or asymmetric and which are still secure.

> **EXAM TIP:** For the CCSP exam, you must understand typical applications of different algorithms. Questions about hard drives or storage encryption almost always refer to AES.

Common attacks

The process of cryptanalysis is to understand cryptographic algorithms. It often results in either improving or cracking an algorithm. Like anything in IT, encryption algorithms are prone to attacks as well.

---

[1] *AWS KMS and ACM now support the latest hybrid post-quantum TLS ciphers (amazon.com)*

Mathematicians usually develop highly complex encryption algorithms. Many IT professionals have attempted to create their encryption algorithms or custom implementations. Unfortunately, they almost always create insecure algorithms. It would be best to never implement self-made encryption algorithms in your hardware or software.

Reliable encryption algorithms must be public, be based on correct mathematics, and have undergone rigorous cryptanalysis to ensure the algorithm is robust.

EXAM TIP: The CCSP exam will test you on the dangers of implementing self-made encryption algorithms.

As discussed previously, encryption algorithms use plaintext, a key, and an algorithm to create cipher text. If an attacker knows the algorithm used, has the key, and the ciphertext, the plaintext is easily retrievable. Even without all the puzzle pieces, attackers can use cryptanalysis to decipher your encrypted data. Let us look at some of the methods attackers can use.

Firstly, an attacker might attempt to use brute force to guess the key used to encrypt the data. To do so, the attacker must know the ciphertext and the algorithm. We call this type of attack a known **ciphertext attack**.

EXAM TIP: Other (mathematical) methods exist to conduct known ciphertext attacks, but you do not need to know these for the CCSP exam.

The second type of attack is a known **plaintext attack**. Contrary to a known-ciphertext attack, both the ciphertext and the plaintext are known to the attacker. If the attacker knows both values, she might be able to uncover the key used to encrypt and decrypt the data.

The last type of attack is called a chosen plaintext attack. This attack relies on encrypted data using the same key and algorithm, producing the same outcome. During this attack, the attacker provides plaintext (of her choice) to the encryption algorithm and observes the result. In essence, the attacker can attempt to guess the plaintext by creating an identical ciphertext to the ciphertext the attacker wants to crack.

All three attacks we examined above are dangerous. Luckily, methods exist to thwart these attacks.

Key size

Firstly, we can attempt to make known-plaintext attacks more difficult. We can do so by choosing a large key size. By using a larger/longer key, an attacker would have to perform far more attempts to find the matching key. The challenge here is to pick a key size that is big enough to keep attackers from cracking the data but not so big that it slows down our encryption/decryption speed too much. You should pick a key size that makes the effort needed to decrypt your data outweigh the value of the data.

An important consideration to take here is that computers become faster quickly. Especially with the rise of quantum computing, some of the most commonly used key sizes will be insecure in a matter of years. So, a key size that takes five years to crack today might be crackable in days five years from now. Nobody knows what the future holds, but as a security professional, it is wise to air on the side of caution.

EXAM TIP: For the sake of the CCSP exam, longer key lengths are always better than shorter key lengths

It is important to note that different algorithms require different key sizes to be secure. Every algorithm uses other operations. As you can see below, an RSA key must be much longer than an AES key to be secure, refer to the following table:

Algorithm	Key size
AES	>= 128
RSA	>= 2048
ECDSA	>= 224

Table 5.3: *Examples of commonly used currently secure algorithms and key sizes*

If you want extensive information on what key sizes you should use with the future in mind, look at keylength.com[2].

Hashing

Encryption is a powerful way to hide data from unauthorized parties. However, a key characteristic of encryption is that it is reversible through decryption. Sometimes, we need to store data without it being readable to anybody.

For example, when an organization stores passwords, they should not be readable to anybody who can access the database storing them. Otherwise, database administrators (and others) could easily use the accounts of customers or other employees.

The challenge is that we still need to verify if a user provides the correct password. How can we do this without storing the password in a readable format? The answer is through hashing. **Hashing** is a process similar to encryption, but it is not reversible, let us see how this works:

---

[2] *Keylength - NIST Report on Cryptographic Key Length and Cryptoperiod (2020)*

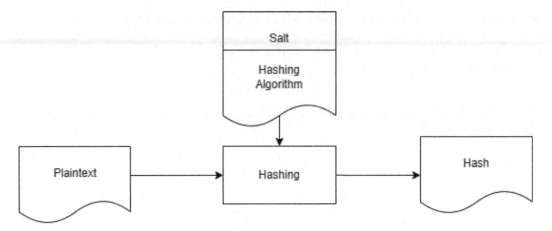

Figure 5.10: Schematic overview of hashing

As you can see in the figure above, hashing requires plaintext (similar to encryption). The plaintext is then *hashed* using a hashing algorithm and (optionally) a salt. The result of the hashing operation is a non-reversible ciphertext called a **hash**. Salt is a pseudo-random string added to the plaintext (which we will discuss more in-depth later). Let us see how this would work in practice:

Plaintext (without salt)
THISISAPASSWORD
SHA3 Hash
a5d032db9f5039c1c9db593527f823fb5e98118d9742f892ba7eedfb

Table 5.4: Example of a value hashed with the SHA3 hashing algorithm

As you can see above, hashing the value *THISISAPASSWORD* using the SHA3 algorithm results in a *meaningless* hash. If a database admin accessed the database storing this value, she would not know the plaintext.

Contrary to encryption, hashing does not use a key. The lack of key material gives hashing an exciting property. Namely, if you hash the same plaintext with the same algorithm, you always get the same result. That property is what allows us to use hashes to store passwords and still verify if the user enters the correct password.

EXAM TIP: You must understand the difference between encryption and hashing

If an organization stores passwords as hashes, the authentication system will take the password you type in, hash it using their algorithm of choice, and compare it to the password hash stored in the database. If the hashes match, you typed in the correct password. After all, hashing the same value always generates the same hash. Thus, by verifying the hashing operation created the same hash as previously stored, the correct value is used.

So, not only is hashing a secure way to store passwords, but it is also simple to verify if a user provided the correct password, there is a catch. What happens if multiple users have the same password? Every user that shares a password would have the same hash stored in the database. If a user gets access to the password databases and notices any users with the same password, she would automatically know their password by looking at the hashes.

While the situation above might seem likely, it is a genuine problem. On the Internet, you can find something called a **rainbow table**. Rainbow tables contain lists of hashes and the plaintexts that made them. Some of these hashes are discovered using brute-force attacks, and others because hashing algorithms have been found insecure over time. Nevertheless, suppose attackers get a hold of your organization's password database. In that case, attackers can quickly look up the plaintext password if your users use the same passwords in the rainbow table and your organization uses the same hashing algorithm.

EXAM TIP: Rainbow tables are a common threat to (insecure) hashing algorithms

It is essential to ensure your organization uses secure hashing algorithms, but it can employ another tactic to prevent rainbow tables from being used. Earlier, we reviewed how hashing can use salt. Salts are pseudo-random values added to the plaintext. They function similarly to a key in encryption. However, for salt to be most effective, every hash action should use a unique salt. Let us see the effect of salting:

Plaintext	Salt	Resulting SHA3 Hash
THISISAPASSWORD	SECRETSALT1	236abed8520bb514b2ddefe228bf144919799a7d-ce37f72d88e318da320b7f93db0010f70b1f4c-cb4ae98008db3ba96c55971ff9714dae0f17daa-302833c8a69
THISISAPASSWORD	SECRETSALT2	7424667b5dfbdd1d64e523413534606144ff067d-bc2294f98b31f618df05f21bd4414aa42ffdb-d347e1692fc39e253e165ddd45ada5ef5ef48e6a6e-899cf083e

Table 5.5: Example of the effect of salting on a hash

As you can see above, adding different salts to the plaintexts changes the hash significantly. It would be challenging to tell both hashes from the same plaintext. When you use salting, you must add salt to the plaintext provided by the user when you verify hashes. If you do not, the user-provided value will never match the hash, adding salt means that you have to store it somewhere. It is best practice to try and store your salts at a different place than your password hashes.

EXAM TIP: Salting is essential to create secure password hashes

While hashing is an excellent way to store passwords, secrets, and other credentials that should never be readable, hashing has other applications. For example, hashing can be used to prove authenticity and integrity as well.

Since a hash produces the same value with the same input, we can use hashing to create a signature or imprint of a file. Such a signature can prove that a file is unaltered or that a message originates from a specific identity or service.

The integrity of a file is provable by taking the file's content and creating a hash. The hash represents the exact content of the file. If the file changed, it would produce a different hash afterward. You commonly see this principle when you are downloading files. When you have downloaded the file, you should run the specified hashing algorithm on the contents of the file. The website might provide a downlink link with a hash. If the hash you produced matches the hash on the website, your file has not changed in transit. If they do not match, you can be certain that file loss or tampering has occurred. We can process this **checksum verification** or **hash verification**. We will cover checksums in *Chapter 11, Secure Development (SSDLC), awareness, and training*.

Checksums also apply in messaging settings, like e-mails. The sender can create a message digest by creating a hash of the e-mail. If the recipient hashes the message, they can verify that someone else has not altered the e-mail.

EXAM TIP: Checksums and digests are essential to verifying the integrity of files and messages. At the same time, hashing and salting passwords are critical for secure authentication.

Similar to encryption, your organization should rely on tried and proven hashing algorithms. Luckily, because hashing is irreversible, quantum computing is not rendering most hashing algorithms insecure. However, many existing hashing algorithms are insecure. During the CCSP exam, you must be able to identify secure and insecure hashing algorithms and determine which one you should use. Let us look at a list of secure and insecure algorithms:

Secure	Insecure
SHA-2	SHA-0
SHA-3	SHA-1
	MD4
	MD5
	RIPEMD-160
	NTLM (v2)

Table 5.6: Examples of secure and insecure hashing algorithms

As you can see above, many hashing algorithms are insecure. You might even be familiar with some of these. Many organizations still store passwords using MD5 hashes or NTLM hashes (Windows passwords, for example). Rainbow tables exist for these algorithms, making it easier for attackers to find the plaintext passwords after a breach. Organizations like NIST publish standards for governmental agencies on hashing algorithms (FIPS 180-4). In March 2023, NIST announced that SHA-1 would be removed from FIPS 180-4 as a permitted hashing algorithm. If your organization is looking to pick a hashing algorithm, you should refer to this documentation and monitor it over the team. Like encryption, hashing algorithms are constantly tested even if they are secure now. They might not be in the future.

EXAM TIP: The CCSP exam expects you to know which are secure and insecure algorithms. However, it does not expect you to understand why. The CISSP exam will require an understanding of factors that make hashing algorithms strong or weak.

EXAM TIP: The CCSP exam might still consider SHA-1 secure. If you do not see any other reasonable options, be aware.

Applications of encryption

Now that you understand encryption, we can quickly investigate what we will use it for. Encryption is used to secure data in transit and at rest. Data in transit is data that is being transported over a network, while data at rest is data stored on a storage device. Research is also conducted on encrypting data during processing (we call this homomorphic encryption). However, homomorphic encryption is not yet a focus point of the CCSP exam.

So, what can we do to encrypt data in transit? Well, the most common forms of encryption in transit are **Virtual Private Networks (VPNs)**, **Secure Sockets Layer (SSL)**, and **Transport Layer Security (TLS)**. VPNs can create an encrypted tunnel between computers, networks, and even clouds. A VPN tunnel encrypts the transmitted data between the sender and receiver, allowing you to send sensitive information through a VPN tunnel, even using an insecure network like the Internet. If a third party intercepts the packets you send, they cannot read their contents.

You can connect a cloud network to the on-premise network using a VPN in hybrid clouds. The CSP will allow you to configure a VPN tunnel that ties your corporate network to the cloud network. By creating route tables (addressing information in networking), machines in your corporate network can directly communicate with cloud services without traversing the Internet. As we covered earlier in this book, some organizations might require that specific data is only transferred over a VPN connection or even a direct connection. Remember that you do not need to use the VPN solution the CSP provides. If your organization has VPN-capable hardware, you can virtualize a similar piece of hardware in the cloud and create your own VPN tunnel that way.

Suppose you use a direct connection (or leased line). In that case, you might not need a VPN as the data will not be viewable to others (the network is logically isolated from other companies and organizations). Your organization should decide if it requires data encryption on trusted networks (corporate networks) and untrusted networks (the Internet, for example). Most security professionals advise encrypting data in transit, even if transported on a *trusted* network. Doing so is in line with the **Zero Trust** approach. We will examine Zero Trust and VPNs more in-depth in chapter six.

SSL/TLS can add encryption to various protocols, including the **Secure Socket Shell** and **Hyper Text Transfer Protocol (HTTP)**. SSH is often used for remote management of servers, while HTTP (in its encrypted form), and HTTPS, are used for web traffic. Both use public key encryption to ensure the confidentiality and integrity of the transmitted data.

The public key is registered on the remote server as an allowed key for a specific user. At the same time, the server proves its identity to you by using its private key. For example, you might authenticate with a remote server using your public key through SSH. We call this process a handshake process.

EXAM TIP: The CCSP exam does not expect you to know details surrounding the functioning of SSL/TLS. For that reason, the explanation above is not in-depth.

While the technical details of VPNs and SSL/TLS are not tested on the CCSP exam, you must understand that they are used to encrypt data in transit. It would help to memorize the following: Only TLS versions 1.2 and up are considered secure. SSL is always regarded as insecure.

EXAM TIP: Only TLS 1.2 and up are considered secure for in-transit encryption

In addition to encryption in transit, we must also encrypt data at rest. The CCSP exam expects you to understand that devices should be fitted with full-disk encryption (usually utilizing AES-256 and up). Object and file-storage solutions should use either cloud native encryption solutions (as offered by the CSP) or rely on encryption before uploading to the cloud.

Databases should utilize another form of encryption at rest, called Transparent Data Encryption (TDE). TDE is used to encrypt databases at the column level. The benefit of this is that only columns that are being used in a query will be decrypted. If, at any time, an attacker is able to access the database, they will not be able to view the contents of the whole database. Most CSPs offer TDE as a cloud-native feature for managed databases.

However, if you use self-hosted databases on virtual machines, you will have to take measures to encrypt the database yourself. Some database engines offer TDE, while others might only offer full database encryption, or even no encryption at all. In any case, your organization must ensure that the database engine of choice, offers the encryption you need.

EXAM TIP: The CCSP exam considers TDE the best encryption approach for databases.

EXAM TIP: Full-disk encryption for a self-hosted database is not enough. If the virtual machine or container is breached, attackers can still gain access to the database contents.

Key, secrets, and certificate management

You might have wondered why we have not discussed cloud computing much in this chapter. It does not matter. Encryption and hashing are the same everywhere, whether applied on-premises or in the cloud. However, managing encryption keys, secrets, and certificates for hashing and encryption is very different in the cloud versus on-premises.

First, you must realize that a CSP dramatically influences how you will perform encryption, and hashing in the cloud is essential. Depending on your service model, the CSP might perform many encryption and hashing-related tasks. However, even if you use cloud-native tools, you will be limited by the algorithms and settings your CSP allows. Some CSPs might not offer the algorithms you legally require or want to use. Some of the PaaS, and SaaS solutions a CSP has, might not provide algorithms that comply with your internal policies. You must consider this when selecting the CSP and the service model you will use.

Secondly, we must realize that giving a CSP control of encryption and hashing tasks, or even the keys, secrets, and certificates we use to do it ourselves, creates risks. What happens if a CSP stores encryption keys used to encrypt your data? In theory, the CSP could use these keys to decrypt your data and gain access to the plaintext. Or, what happens if a CSP uses an insecure encryption or hashing algorithm and hackers can decrypt your data after a breach?

The following section will examine how to encrypt and hash data in the cloud securely.

Secure key generation

We discussed how essential keys are for encryption. When you use short keys, the chances of an attacker being able to crack your encryption are larger than with long keys. However, the length of the key is not the only relevant factor. Key material should be unique. Without unique keys, someone might be able to decrypt data they should not have authorization for. Unfortunately, creating unique and entirely random values is computationally intensive and time-consuming. That is why the key generation is pseudo-random. While these values are not truly random, they are random enough to limit the possibility of repeated keys to a meager chance.

When you work in the cloud, you might have the option for the CSP to generate your keys. Alternatively, you might be able to generate your keys, upload these in the CSPs tooling, and use them for encryption (we will examine this later).

Whenever you generate a key, ensure that the key is generated using a reliable pseudo-random key generator. Similarly, ensure the keys are generated with a sufficient key length for your security needs. Most CSPs will limit the key lengths you are allowed to use. So, make sure you use a CSP that offers encryption that can withstand the test of time. Using key lengths that are resistant (enough) against quantum computing is highly beneficial.

EXAM TIP: For the CCSP exam, you must know keys are generated pseudo-randomly.

Key, secret, and certificate storage

As mentioned earlier, when you work in the cloud, you will (likely) have to share keys, secrets, and certificates with the CSP. If you choose not to, you cannot utilize native encryption technologies.

For example, if an object storage solution offers native encryption, it must have access to the keys used to encrypt and decrypt data. If you do not want this, you could encrypt the data before uploading it to the cloud and decrypt it once you have retrieved it through an API or download functionality. This makes object storage much more complicated and probably also slower.

Nevertheless, you might encrypt some data before uploading it to the cloud. You can even still utilize the encryption the CSP offers. However, by adding your encryption, others still cannot read the file content if they gain access to the key used by the CSP. Solutions like this are, generally, not very scaleable. However, they might provide a solution in cases where it is legally required or desirable that the CSP cannot decrypt your data.

In any case, if you elect to store data in the cloud using encryption provided by the CSP. They will always have some form of access to your keys. All CSPs ensure separation of duties, monitoring, and access controls are in place. However, if multiple entities within the CSP work together, they could access your data. While the likelihood of this is not very high, it must be considered.

Another issue that could occur is that the CSP (or another customer of the CSP) gets hacked. If a breach of the shared infrastructure happens, attackers might be able to obtain your key material or other secrets. Likewise, a physical breach of a data center might allow attackers to physically steal devices (such as HSMs) that store the keys. You must pick a tamperproof key, secret, and certificate storage solution.

In the data classification policy, you must establish what data is allowed in the cloud. What algorithms do you allow, what lengths do you require, where are the keys stored? and the requirements around encryption.

The same concepts apply to secrets (like service tokens) and certificates. For example, many CSPs allow you to create certificates within the cloud environment. The CSP can indirectly gain access to these certificates. If the certificates fall into the wrong hands, attackers could impersonate applications or identities using your certificates. Similarly, if you store API tokens for external services in the cloud, breaches could cause the secrets to end up in the hands of attackers.

CSPs offer different methods to protect your keys, secrets, and certificates in the cloud. Let us take a look at some of the solutions they provide.

Bring Your Own Key

Bring Your Own Key (BYOK) is an offering where the CSP allows you to generate your key material. The key material is then uploaded to the CSP platform and stored following your requirements. BYOK enables you to ensure key generation is in line with your needs.

While BYOK is excellent, if your organization is required to use specific algorithms or key lengths not supported by the CSP (or if you do not trust the CSP to generate keys), it will increase the load on your IT organization. However, it does make key management more complicated in the cloud. After all, BYOK does not allow you to rotate keys automatically. You must generate, invalidate, and replace keys manually (or programmatically).

Your organization should carefully weigh if the extra efforts around BYOK weigh up against the potential gain in security. Most small organizations or organizations with a limited security staff are likely better off using the key generation on the CSP side.

> **EXAM TIP: Governmental agencies or organizations with specific legal requirements often use BYOK.**

Key Management System

A **Key Management System (KMS)** is a service that almost all CSPs offer. A KMS makes key management easy, especially when using native cloud services. The KMS allows you to generate, rotate, and invalidate keys on demand. The KMS usually integrates with other cloud services, enabling you to create **Encryption Keys** for object storage, databases, and other services in a single tool. Most cloud native databases or object-storage solutions will automatically generate (or use) keys registered in the KMS, as shown:

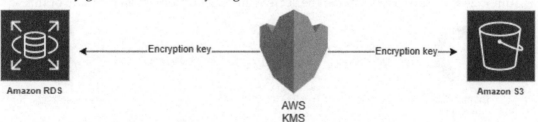

Figure 5.11: Example of AWS KMS integrating with object storage (Amazon S3) and a database (Amazon RDS)

Because of this integration, enabling encryption is often just a click of a button. As mentioned above, some KMS solutions allow BYOK. However, keep in mind that BYOK limits the capabilities of the KMS.

Secrets management

Another critical factor is the management of secrets. Secrets are any value that is restricted to a limited amount of identities or services.

For example, a secret can be an API token for the Google Maps API. If the API token is readable by unauthorized identities or services, they can call the Google Maps API. Calls to the API would result in costs, meaning others can cause costs to your organization without your knowledge or consent.

Unfortunately, many organizations disclose secrets in client-side web application code. They might call the Google Maps API from the client side, inadvertently exposing the API token to any user of their website (we will zoom in on this in *Chapter 11, Secure Development, Awareness , and Training*). However, there are many other ways to disclose secrets.

For example, some organizations include secrets in their source code. This means anybody with access to the code could abuse secrets. If you store your database configuration in source code, anybody who gains access to the code can now attempt to access your database. Throughout the past decade, many examples have been of companies being breached by disclosing source code containing secrets.

However, the cloud adds some other challenges as well. We talked about IaC earlier in the book. IaC requires us to define infrastructure as the code we want to deploy. However, this infrastructure (or the applications running on it) likely needs access to other resources. What you do not want to do, is include your secrets in your IaC. Once again, exposure to your code could lead to breaches of other resources.

Instead, you want to load your secrets during (or after) deployment. Most CSPs have created solutions for this called **secrets management**. Secrets management allows you to store secrets accessible by specific identities and services only. Because of this, you do not need to put your secrets in your code. Instead, you reference values in the secrets management tool. The secrets management tool will then ensure your service or identity is authorized and provide access to the secret value. Let us look at an example of this:

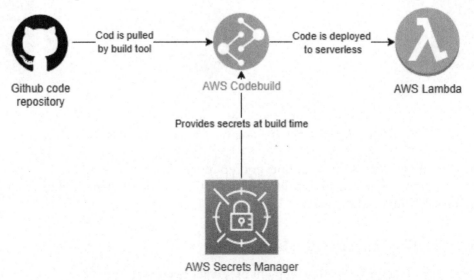

Figure 5.12: Serverless code deployment using AWS Secrets Manager

EXAM TIP: The CCSP exam is vendor agnostic. You do not need to know the names of tools provided by common CSPs. This book uses them as examples.

Another exciting benefit is that you can automatically rotate secrets. So, if you have configured service A to use secret A as its access token, updating secret A will also update the value service B uses to access service A. That way, you can easily rotate tokens without breaking your applications. In short, you do not need to manually update secrets throughout your applications. Instead, you can give new applications access to existing secrets.

EXAM TIP: The CCSP exam considers hard-coded secrets a deadly sin.

Please keep in mind that many non-CSP vendors offer secret management solutions. These solutions are useable in addition to or instead of cloud-native tools. Remember if your organization already uses secrets management outside of the cloud. Also, do not forget that secrets management is a SaaS service you can use for your on-premises environment.

EXAM TIP: Secrets management is the only easily and securely manage secrets in the cloud

The last benefit of secrets management is that developers do not need to know production secrets. If the team that manages the secrets does not manage the code, you can create a **separation of duties (SoD)**. SoD can limit the number of people accessing production databases, services, and storage solutions, which lowers insider threats.

Certificate Management System

Managing certificates is just as essential as managing secrets. Certificates are used to provide trust in identities. For example, certificates can be used to authenticate machines to each other or for users to gain confidence in the identity of a website. Many applications nowadays are web applications that rely on SSL or TLS for encryption during transit. Certificates play an essential role in the process.

Most CSPs offer a **certificate management system (CMS)**. Such a system allows you to create new certificates on the fly. These certificates can be for devices, services, and identities. For example, your organization might want to issue a certificate to every mobile device. Similarly, it might need to issue certificates for web applications. A CMS allows you to issue and revoke these certificates quickly and easily. In most cases, the CSP can automatically verify your domain ownership by creating DNS records for your domain name. Alternatively, if you host your DNS outside the cloud, you might be required to create DNS records for validation.

Most organizations will be best off using a cloud-native CMS. It makes it very easy to create and manage certificates. However, some organizations already issue certificates within their on-premises environment. It is almost always possible to import those certificates within the cloud environment.

EXAM TIP: a CMS allows you to create certificates, revoke them, and assign them services.

If you are using your certificates, you must revoke them where you generated or bought them. However, the CMS cannot automatically revoke or renew these certificates. Also, remember that certificates stored in the cloud could be accessible during a coordinated attack from within the CSP. After breach of your certificates, the attackers could abuse the trust in the certificate.

EXAM TIP: Using CMS has security risks, but the benefits are significant, especially for companies with many certificates or little IT capacity.

Avoid using wildcard certificates. If these types of certificates are exposed, attackers can impersonate more services easily. While using specific certificates only allows the impersonation of a single service.

EXAM TIP: The CCSP exam considers wildcard certificates to be insecure.

In the last section of this chapter, we will review how CMS, KMS, Secrets management, and storage solutions can come together in a storage architecture. However, first, we will look at data masking, obfuscation, anonymization, tokenization, and data loss prevention.

Data obfuscation, tokenization, masking, and anonymization

We have looked at some technologies that allow us to store data, secrets, certificates, and keys securely. However, it is more than just a matter of storing the data securely. It is also about what is in it.

When we store data containing PII, it will likely have a higher classification than data containing aggregated metrics or non-identifiable information. Let us see what data is more critical to protect, refer to the following table:

First Name	Hair color
Alice	Blonde
Margo	Black
Elliot	Black
Penny	Black

Table 5.7: Sample dataset with plaintext data

The following table shows examples of tokenized data:

First Name	Hair color
Aaaa	Blonde
Bbbb	Black
Cccc	Black
Dddd	Black

Table 5.8: Sample dataset with tokenized data

The following table shows examples of masked data:

First Name	Hair color
Firstname	Blonde
Firstname	Black
Firstname	Black
Firstname	Black

Table 5.9: Sample dataset with masked data

The following table shows examples of encrypted data:

Name	Hair color
a7dcef9aef26202fce82a7c7d6672afb3a149db207d90a07e437d5abc7fc99ed	Blonde
8e911a00cc3fb61771b4b246307e0e3c67b46c2d8a9ee40801811acb521db893	Black
a43cf62b60d346cce465dce704eb7aef23bf896eb8e5f21592ee3cd64f823a05	Black
61ba80ffbabe0ce4bbd7b16d19bfbc454ece346e88ee6a9c8e99a6ff704fd219	Black

Table 5.10: Sample dataset with obfuscated data by encryption

The four tables above show a dataset for determining which hair color is most prevalent among customers.

The **first table** includes the actual first name of the customer, while the other three contain values to anonymize the data. Because the data contains customers' names, the security requirements for this data are likely higher than the other tables.

The **second table** has replaced all first names with a token. The tokens are unique but completely hide the name. It is important to note that the value format is similar to a first name. This process is called **tokenization**. The formatting is essential to ensure that any system that uses the data does not malfunction due to the change in format. If you have a system that has strict limits on the size of a field, tokenization can be a good approach. The uniqueness of the token also allows you to combine other data sets, as the token can be linked to other tables containing the same token.

The following table contains masked data. The records are untraceable to a single person. The big difference between masking and tokenization is that masking does not require unique values. With masking, you should replace the values with something this is formatted similarly to the initial value (for the same reason as tokenization). It makes masking less useful for situations that require cross-dataset analysis.

The last table has replaced the first names with encrypted values of the names. The first name is no longer readable without decryption. However, the format of the name has changed significantly. The value is now much longer. Depending on the processing systems, this could cause further issues. We call this **data obfuscation**.

The point of the sample tables above is simple. Depending on what you do with data, you might be able to use anonymization to reduce the data classification. **Anonymization** is achievable through tokenization, obfuscation, or masking.

Tokenization is the best option if you have constraints on the data format and need to perform analysis across multiple datasets. As the unique value of a token, it allows you to link datasets.

Masking is suitable if you require a strict format, but the analysis does not require linking datasets.

At the same time, obfuscation is great for datasets that might seek to restrict access to specific values. After all, decrypting obfuscated data (with encryption) can be made readable. This means you can limit who has access to the source data by restricting access to keys.

No matter the approach, anonymization is an essential tool for storing data. It can be used to create test data sets based on production data without traceable production data. Instead of creating mock datasets, you can take and anonymize production datasets. It results in data sets that are safe to use in test environments. It is wise to examine if anonymization is useable within your data sets.

In many cases, you might consider anonymization and archival of data instead of deletion. That way, you can still analyze archived data (when needed).

EXAM TIP: Data anonymization can save your company money and time by removing or limiting the need for security controls from a certain dataset.

EXAM TIP: Never use production data in non-production environments without anonymization.

Data loss prevention

In the previous section, you have learned that anonymizing data can help you reduce the security efforts needed to secure data according to its confidentiality. However, when we handle highly confidential data, we can take additional measures to prevent (or detect) its leakage or loss. One of the technologies that help us do this is **data loss prevention** or sometimes **data leakage prevention (DLP)**.

DLP technologies attempt to detect the disclosure of data through unauthorized channels. For example, you could use a DLP solution to see employees e-mailing social security numbers or bank accounts to e-mail addresses outside the organization. Once a DLP tool detects such communications, it can block them, alert the user, or alert the security team (or all of these).

DLP solutions work in a variety of ways. Some DLP solutions check network traffic going out of a corporate network or cloud (network-based DLP). Others check communication going out of a host (host-based DLP). Another common form is DLP, which focuses only on e-mail clients.

Most DLP tools scan files, documents, messages, and network traffic for specific patterns. As mentioned previously, a DLP tool might be configured to detect the occurrence of social security numbers in e-mails. Unfortunately, DLP tools do not know if a social security number is sent. Instead, they use pattern matching (or regular expressions) that define what to look for. Regardless of the type of DLP technology, it will require you to define rules on data-sharing. Let us see how this works, refer to the following image:

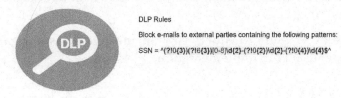

Figure 5.13: Sample detection using e-mail DLP

As you can see in the sample detection above, the DLP tool checks all e-mails for the occurrence of a social security number using a regular expression. It is blocked if the e-mail contains a social security number and is sent to an external e-mail address. However, the example above also illustrates the main challenge of DLP tooling. The e-mail on the left contains a mistyped phone number (it misses a digit). The DLP tool automatically flags the value as a social security number because it matches the regex. Because the e-mail was sent internally, it is not blocked.

Nevertheless, false positives can become a massive obstacle when you implement DLP tooling. For example, use DLP tooling to detect the disclosure of customer names or addresses. It might prove challenging to generate a rule that does not block legitimate data-sharing. Similarly, you will encounter false negatives as well. Because what happens if someone writes the social security number without dashes? The regex would no longer match, even though a valid SSN was sent.

The point here is that DLP can be extremely useful. However, its rule set must be developed with extreme care. If the rules are too general, you will block traffic that should be allowed. In contrast, a too-specific ruleset will miss data loss. Testing your DLP rulesets using notifications only to start is good practice. That way, your security team can evaluate where the ruleset identifies false positives and negatives and tinker with the ruleset until both are within acceptable bounds.

Network DLP is likely to miss data loss in encrypted communications. While host-based DLP is much more likely to capture data loss, it is almost always more expensive and time-consuming to configure. Email-only DLP will miss any communications that do not occur through e-mail, creating a blind spot for other communications like file-sharing platforms and messaging tools. So, when your organization chooses to implement DLP tools, consider where you apply them and experiment with building a ruleset that suits your organization's needs.

EXAM TIP: The CCSP exam considers DLP an effective measure against data loss. In reality, it all depends on the implementation.

Tiering, CDNs, replication, and backups

Throughout this chapter, we have focused on the confidentiality and integrity of data. However, security has another pillar, availability. As you know, cloud computing allows high availability of all its services, including storage. While it is essential to ensure our data is correct and cannot be accessed by unauthorized individuals, we must ensure it is available to those needing access. Storage tiering, replication, and backups are the main mechanisms to achieve this.

The first aspect, storage tiering, means that you can choose the level and speed of data availability in the cloud. In block and file storage solutions, you can pick the speed of your storage device. At the same time, object-storage solutions allow you to choose which SLAs must be met for your data. Most CSPs attempt to meet these demands by creating storage tiers.

You can generally distinguish three different tiers: hot storage, warm storage, and cold storage. Hot storage is the fastest storage you will get. Data stored in hot storage is readily available and is usually extremely fast. Warm storage is still fast but will not be top-of-the-line. In contrast, cold storage is usually not readily available. Limited availability means retrieving your data might take minutes, hours, or days.

As you can imagine, hot storage is the most expensive, while cold storage is the cheapest solution. Under these storing tiers, you will find different storage methods. For example, hot storage likely uses PCIe flash memory or fast SSDs, while cold storage might use backup tapes. After all, in the cloud, you pay for what you use.

When your organization operates in the cloud, picking the suitable storage tiers for your data is essential. Mission-critical data must reside on hot data storage. At the same time, data archival for seven years can take place in cold storage due to legal requirements. In most cases, you can set rules to move data from one tier to another automatically. For example, if your organization archives orders after six months, you can automate the move of records from hot to cold storage. Automatic re-tiering results in less available data but (massive) cost reductions.

EXAM TIP: Security is a game of trade-offs. Availability and costs must be balanced.

Another factor to consider is file-caching. Sometimes, files are requested very frequently. Most CSPs offer solutions that allow you to cache these files using a **Content Delivery Network (CDN)**. A CDN network has geographically dispersed storage locations that will enable quicker access. For example, suppose your company hosts corporate data in the European region, but American employees need to access files frequently. In that case, a CDN can cache the files in an American data center closer to the end user. That way, network performance plays a minor role in data availability, as shown:

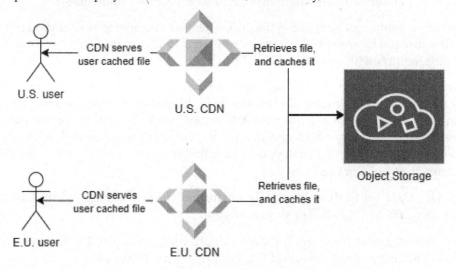

Figure 5.14: Caching files using a CDN improves availability

As shown above, the CDN caches the file retrieved from the **Object Storage**. It does not have to be retrieved whenever a CDN user requests the file. While caching greatly improves availability, you must ensure that your caches are invalidated when needed. If you cache files that change very frequently, users will receive an outdated version of the file. Therefore, caching works best for static files or files that rarely change.

EXAM TIP: A CDN is great for increasing the availability of static files or files that undergo infrequent changes.

Next to storage tiering and CDNs, we can use replication and backups to improve availability. By replicating data across at least two (but preferably three) Availability Zones (AVs), we can significantly reduce the chance data is lost in disasters or unavailable during (local) service outages. Earlier in this book, we covered how replication across regions and availability zones can prevent outages or disasters from making data unavailable. Sometimes, it might even be worth-wile to replicate data across regions or even CSPs. Every replication of your data increases your total storage demand and, thus, your costs. Once again, your organization must determine how important the data is and which costs are acceptable to protect the data.

EXAM TIP: The CCSP exam considers replication across three AVs the most secure option, while replication over two is more cost-effective.

Replication achieves redundancy of data and services. This means replication takes place to the same tier. Hot data replication must be to another hot data storage solution. Otherwise, replicating data will not improve the availability you want.

For example, suppose you have a database that you replicate from a high-speed database server to a small and slow database in another AV. In that case, the slow database cannot provide the same service if the high-speed database becomes unavailable.

Backups serve a different purpose. A backup is meant to be able to restore data if it were to be lost. Because data loss should not frequently occur, backup data does not have the exact availability requirements as replicated data.

Backup restore procedures take time, and your organization will manage as long as the data is available and restorable within the RTO. However, if replicated data as part of a redundant service is not readily available, it will lead to another service outage. For example, if you have to wait 15 minutes for backup data to be available, the impact is probably not very large. In general, you can say that warm or cold storage is more suitable for backups than hot storage.

EXAM TIP: Data replication is usually performed in hot storage, while backups are storable in warm or cold storage to save costs.

We will examine backup strategies more in-depth during *Chapter 10, Business Continuity and Disaster Recovery in the Cloud*, and *Chapter 17, Security Processes*.

Sample architecture

Now that we have the puzzle pieces needed to create a secure data storage architecture, let us look at the scenario:

An international online candy store allows customers to purchase candy through their website. The candy store must retain customers' orders for seven years to comply with local laws and regulations. The store thinks the protection of customer data is essential and wants to implement security measures to keep customer data from leaking after a breach. At the same time, the store requires that customers can securely place their candy orders without exposing their data. Since the candy store has high daily sales volumes, it does not accept more than 5 minutes of continuous downtime. Lastly, the company wants to be able to analyze candy orders over the last ten years.

If you read the scenario above, you can deduce several essential factors. The store values the confidentiality of customer data, and the store's availability is vital. It is required to retain records, and the company operates internationally.

Let us mirror these items against the technologies we discussed. At first sight, we would need to encrypt customers' data at rest and in transit to ensure confidentiality. Customer data and order data are usually structured data. Thus, the company would need a database. It mentions that data retention for seven years is required. So, we should archive orders and move them to cold storage to limit archival costs. Because the company operates internationally and requires high availability, we could use a CDN to cache static website files to speed up the website and ensure up-time across regions. Because downtime over five continuous minutes is unacceptable, we should replicate (and sync) the data across multiple availability zones to ensure service outages or disasters do not affect the availability.

The organization wants to analyze data from the last ten years. The company must store data for the previous seven years, so we can use tokenization to anonymize more than seven years old data. Doing so can save the company money while reducing maintenance efforts.

Let us look at what a storage solution that meets these requirements could look like in AWS:

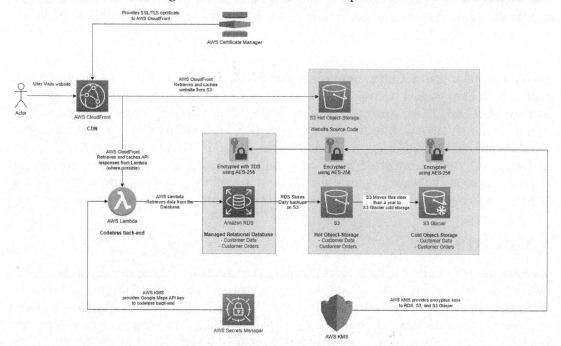

***Figure 5.15**: Sample of a simplified storage architecture in AWS*

In the architecture above, a user connects to the CDN, which offers an encrypted connection using an SSL/TLS certificate retrieved from the certificate management system, providing encryption in transit.

The CDN caches front-end and back-end responses for the website, ensuring high availability. The front end consists of static resources stored in an encrypted hot object-storage solution to provide fast availability.

The customer data and orders are stored in a relational database that uses TDE for encryption. The database creates daily backups stored in encrypted hot object storage for quick backup restoration. Once the backups are older than a year, they automatically move to cold storage. The object-storage solutions and the database rely on the key management system to encrypt and decrypt data. The back-end code uses the secrets manager to retrieve an API key for Google Maps to determine shipping times.

You do not see replication across AVs or the data tokenization in this diagram. They are left out to not overcomplicate the diagram. Nevertheless, you have probably noticed that this small architectural drawing is quite complex. In reality, the diagram would include many more components. However, it is essential to realize how the different storage technologies interact. Without a KMS, you cannot use native encryption for your database or buckets. Without a secrets manager, you cannot securely deploy your back-end code. At the same time, the certificate manager allows you to create a reachable CDN with the proper certificate (and domain name).

The essence of the diagram above is that you need all the technologies covered in this chapter to secure your data effectively. It would be best to have the basic building blocks, such as encryption before you even consider implementing high-level solutions such as DLP.

Before you take your CCSP exam, you should look at some of the systems you work with. Think about which technologies covered in this chapter are being used and what technologies could make your systems even better. While the CCSP exam does not require you to design an architecture useable at a specific CSP, you must understand what role the different components play in the cloud. It is also important to note that the example above is not how you must design your architecture. Architectures and considerations differ significantly between organizations and even systems. If your organization migrates to the cloud, check the CSP's best practices, templates, and architecture frameworks.

Conclusion

We have discussed many technologies that allow us to create a secure storage architecture. We can use encryption to store data securely at rest and in transit. Hashing will enable us to store passwords and verify file integrity. While a KMS, CMS, and secrets manager enables us to handle secrets (within the cloud) securely. Anonymizing data can help your organization limit the security effort needed to secure data effectively while allowing you to create valuable test data. DLP is an essential tool to prevent the compromise of data confidentiality, but it requires rigorous testing and configuration to be effective. Measures like backups, data replication, and the usage of CDNs are essential to ensure data is available when we need it. While backups are suited for cold storage, replicated data and caches, require hot storage to meet availability demands.

Data security requires a plethora of different technologies, policies, and processes. No single technology will keep your data secure alone, no matter what companies promise.

In the next chapter, we will learn about the cloud Infrastructure.

Learning goals

This chapter addresses the following CCSP exam outline learning goals:

Domain 2: Cloud data security

      2.2 Design and implement cloud data storage architectures

      2.3 Design and apply data security technologies and strategies

Join our book's Discord space

Join the book's Discord Workspace for Latest updates, Offers, Tech happenings around the world, New Release and Sessions with the Authors:

https://discord.bpbonline.com

CHAPTER 6

Cloud Infrastructure and Components

Introduction

Cloud infrastructure relies on similar components as on-premises computing. However, the management of cloud infrastructure differs significantly from the management of on-premises infrastructure. This chapter will explore what cloud infrastructure consists of, how we can manage it, and what standard components CSPs offer. Specifically, we will work on understanding the physical environment of the cloud. However, we will also reveal non-physical aspects such as networking and communications, compute resources, virtualization, and of course data storage and management of the environment.

Structure

This chapter covers the following topics:

- Physical environment
- Network and communications
- Compute
- Virtualization
- Storage
- Management plane

Objectives

This chapter teaches you how to set up and manage cloud infrastructure. You will learn the steps to secure the infrastructure and its management plan. As well as how to use common components CSPs offer to build a secure and functional environment. Throughout this chapter, you will build a strong understanding of what a cloud infrastructure comprises.

Physical environment

In cloud computing, the physical environment is usually of minor importance to the cloud consumer. Nevertheless, the CSP or (in the case of a hybrid cloud) the data center operator is still responsible for physical security. Even though your organization might not be responsible for adequately securing the physical environment, you are still accountable. As discussed earlier in this book, you must ensure that the correct checks and balances are in place to verify that your CSP implements the proper controls. In *Chapter 7, Data center security*, we will zoom in on this subject from the perspective of the CSP and data center operator. For now, we will focus on what you control in the cloud.

Network and communications

The first subject we will cover is networking and communications within the cloud. Through the book, we have discussed many facets associated with networking already. We explored the concept of regions, allowing us to build environments close to the users they serve or ensure compliance with local regulations and laws. At the same time, availability zones allow replication of services across different data centers to prevent local outages and disasters from interrupting services.

However, as you know, CSPs offer various networking technologies in the cloud. We briefly covered virtual networks, NICs, load balancers, direct connections, and VPNs. This chapter will dive into these components' functionality and security requirements.

Virtual networks/ virtual private clouds

Let us start with VNets and VPCs (the terms are used interchangeably). As we covered before, VNets are virtualized networks in the cloud. These networks logically isolate your network from other cloud consumers. So, your traffic might run on the same physical networking equipment but will not be visible to other users. VPCs are always bound to a specific subnet range. Meaning the VPC has a certain subset of IP addresses.

In essence, every cloud environment requires at least a single VNets . The VNet is the network in which all of the services will run. Whether these are SaaS or IaaS services does not matter. Almost all SaaS and PaaS services can directly run inside your VNet OR attach to the VNet.

In any case, a VNet is an essential building block to your environment. It is where you will attach your services and make them available to others. By default, VNet does not have internet access. Because the VNet is isolated from other networks, it cannot resolve locations outside the network. Your organization cannot connect to your VNet immediately, nor can it connect to, for example, the Internet.

CSPs generally offer two solutions for this. You can implement an **internet gateway (IGW)** or a **Network Address Translation Gateway (NGW)**. Keep in mind that CSPs might use varying names for these as shown:

Vendor/ Technology	Microsoft Azure	Google Cloud Platform	Amazon Web Services
Internet access from the cloud only	Internet access allowed by default	cloud NAT gateway	NAT gateway
Internet access to and from the cloud	Attaching public IPs	Attaching public IPs	Internet gateway

Table 6.1: *Differences in network implementation amongst CSPs*

An internet gateway allows resources inside your VNet to connect to the Internet. However, it also allows external systems to connect to resources in your VNet. If you are familiar with networking in an on-premises environment, this likely sounds familiar. To do so, you must add routes to the routing table. Routes define how specific traffic propagates throughout the network. Adding a route to direct non-internal traffic to the IGW allows your services inside the VNet to reach the Internet. Unlike an IGW, an NAT GW only allows your VNet services to connect to other networks. So, your services might be able to talk to the Internet (or other VNet) but not vice versa.

EXAM TIP: It is crucial to understand the differences between an IGW and NGW.

As you might understand, IGWs and NGWs are essential to ensure the correct connectivity for the service in your VNet. If you want to manage your services directly, for example, you want to SSH into a virtual machine in a VNet, you will need an IGW. However, if you just want the virtual machine to pull daily updates, an NAT GW is sufficient. Another critical difference is that IGWs are generally useable by all VNets, while NGWs are specific to a single VNet.

EXAM TIP: The CCSP exam is vendor agnostic. Nevertheless, you must understand the general concepts behind the technology. Do not waste your time studying CSP-specific implementations and differences.

Please refer to the following table:

Gateway Type	IGW	NGW
Allows internet access	Yes	Yes
Allows external access	Yes	No
Network specific	No	Yes

Table 6.2: *Gateway types*

Let us see what this looks like in the figure as follows:

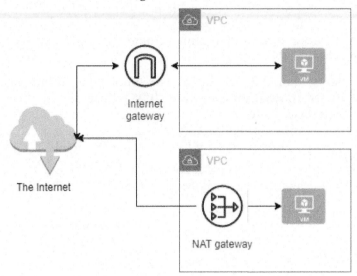

Figure 6.1: Connections allows through IGW versus NGW

Using an IGW requires the services in your VNet to have a public IP address. After all, you must have an address to reach the service. Typically, **VPC** resources are automatically assigned a public IP address. The given address is dynamic, meaning it will change over time. Whenever the service shuts down or hibernates, it releases the IP address. The assignment of a dynamic IP address can cause headaches. If you manage a machine in your VNet, you might not be able to reach at on the same IP even during the same day, as shown :

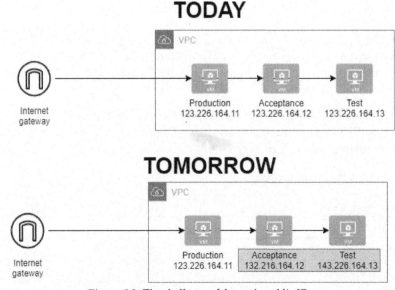

Figure 6.2: The challenge of dynamic public IPs

Let us examine the scenario above. Your organization runs a **Production**, **Acceptance**, and **Test** environment (for ease of explanation in the same VPC). However, your organization shuts down the **Acceptance** and **Test** environments at night to cut costs. After all, the developers do not work at these times. The next day, when all the developers return to work, they cannot reach the **Acceptance** or **Test** environment. The DNS records for **test. example.com** and acceptance.example.com now point to completing different applications owned by another company. While connecting with SSH to the IPs causes an incorrect credentials error.

In the example above, the machines are accessible using their dynamic IPs. As soon as the machines shut down, they released their IPs. In the meantime, someone else started new machines that picked up your old IP. If you had set DNS records to these dynamic IPs, they are not pointing to someone else's machine. Similarly, you cannot reach your machines until you look up the new IP address. Not only has the situation created a lot of annoyance with your development team, but it also creates a security risk. What if you were hosting an API and sending credentials to the dynamic IP belonging to someone else? You might have inadvertently compromised service or user credentials. Luckily, CSPs have devised smart ways to solve this problem, which we will examine below.

EXAM TIP: You must understand the danger of using dynamic public IP addresses.

Elastic IPs/ static public IPs

One of the solutions is called an **Elastic IP** or **static public IP**. These IP addresses are static, meaning they do not change. As a cloud consumer, you can rent these addresses and assign them to your hosts. By doing so, you can ensure your systems are always reachable over the same IP. Unfortunately, elastic IPs have a downside. Many CSPs will charge you if you reserve an EIP but do not use it.

For example, your organization has big spikes in load. Therefore, your organization scales machines up and down throughout the day. If you want every machine to have a static IP, you must reserve an elastic IP for every machine you potentially spin up. However, when you stop a device, the elastic IP is returned to your elastic IP pool (and can technically be assigned to another). At that point, the EIP is considered not to be used, and the CSP will charge you a fee. While these fees are generally not high, you can imagine the costs might increase if you are using thousands of instances. It might even inadvertently cause extra charges if you shut down machines when unused.

The costs you incur are mainly to motivate organizations not to over provision their elastic IPs. The free is charged because the CSP has to reserve these IP addresses. If all their customers just dedicated 1000 elastic IPs, the CSP would not have enough addresses to serve all their customers.

The main takeaway here is simple. Elastic IPs are extremely useful, but carefully consider when to apply an elastic IP and calculate the impact of leaving these addresses unused.

Load balancing

Aside from elastic IPs, there is another solution to the dynamic IP problem. Load balancers can be extremely useful in this situation. Load balancers are servers that redirect (and spread) traffic between other hosts. Essentially, you would use a load balancer (with an elastic IP) connected to a VNets.

The load balancer uses a **Load Balancer Group** to direct traffic. The load balancer group is (usually) a collection of virtual machines or other services. The load balancer is aware of changes in the IP addresses and will route to the correct device, even if the IP changes. The load balancer can reference these instances directly without requiring a static IP.

Load balancers are essential when you pool resources and require scaling. Depending on the instance and availability, the load balancer will spread your traffic across these instances (in different zones). For example, run your web application on VMs in multiple VNets across several availability zones. You can add all the instances of your web application to a load-balancing group, as shown:

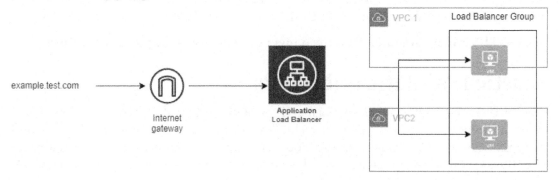

Figure 6.3: Example of an application load balancer

It is important to note that load balancing is often used for web applications but not necessarily for management and administrative tasks. Remember, load balancing is to achieve high availability. After all, load balancers distribute the load to prevent service unavailability. Nevertheless, how they work can negate the need for static IPs within your VNets.

When discussing load balancers, you must realize you will encounter them in two forms within the cloud: **Application Load Balancers** (**ALBs**) and **Network Load Balancers** (**NLBs**). ALBs route traffic at layer 7 of the OSI model (the application layer). Operating at this layer makes them aware of the content of the communication. For example, it can examine the contents of a web request and route traffic to a specific machine based on a session token or cookie. Because of their in-depth access to communication, ALBs can even add request headers or transform requests where needed. ALBs usually offer limited protocol support. Most ALBs support HTTPS and HTTP but might not support any other protocols. Therefore, ALBs are not at all suitable for many machine management tasks.

An NLB is only capable of routing traffic based on the limited information it has available. Unlike ALBs, NLBs route traffic at layer 4 of the OSI model (Transport layer). At layer 4, the load balancer has much less understanding of the contents and context of a request. However, NLBs do (generally) support more protocols than ALBs do.

In short, you could say that an ALB is an intelligent load balancer while an NLB is not. When possible, you should use an ALB over an NLB. Of course, there are some other differences in implementing NLBs versus ALBs. However, do not expect these on the exam, as they are often vendor specific.

> **EXAM TIP: ALBs are more advanced than NLBs because they can understand the context and content of the communication.**

Stepping stones

Dynamic IPs are impractical and can cause security issues. Load balancers are great for serving applications but not for managing servers. So, what solution should you use to manage your devices? A good solution is a stepping stone called a **jump server** or **jump box**. A stepping stone is a server that runs in your VPC with a static IP address. This means you can always reach this server on the same IP. This server connects to other machines within your VPC based on their private IP addresses. That way, it does not matter if they are assigned dynamic IPs because the jump box can connect to the machine using their (static) private IP address.

Stepping stones have a couple of benefits (when implemented correctly). Firstly, a stepping stone allows you to block traffic from public networks to your other machines. Blocking such traffic reduces the attack surface by simply exposing fewer machines. Secondly, you only have to pay for a single static public IP. There is no need to reserve static IPs for all your hosts because you can manage them through the jump box, while you can expose your applications through the load balancer. Let us take a look at how this could look:

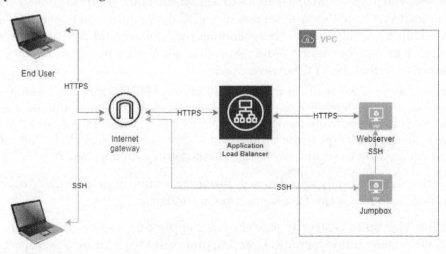

Figure 6.4: Combining a Jump box for management and ALB for the Webserver

As you can see above, the ALB can always route traffic to the **Webserver** because it is registered in the load balancer group. The jump box can always connect to the **Webserver** based on it is private IP address. Therefore, you only need a static public IP for the jump box and not for any VMs used for the **Webserver**.

Stepping stones have more benefits. Because only the jump box is used for management, you can limit the access to management protocols like **Remote Desktop Protocol (RDP)** or **SSH** to just the **Jumpbox**. That way, attackers cannot directly target server management protocols without prior access to the **Jumpbox**. Because administrators should only access the **Jumpbox**, we can lock down the **Jumpbox** much tighter than the **Webserver**. For example, you can use security groups to only allow access from a corporate IP or usual mutual certificate authentication to only allow access from specific client machines. Doing so can reduce the chance of an attacker gaining access to your **Jumpbox**.

Security groups/Access control lists

We discussed security groups and ACLs throughout this book. SGs default deny any traffic and are used to create *allow rules* only. The beauty of SGs is that they can be applied directly to a network interface. For example, an SG applies to a **load balancer** or a **virtual machine**. So, you can easily use security groups to allow access from a stepping stone to a VM you want to manage. By ensuring all your VMs only allow the traffic they need, you limit the chances of an attacker pivoting (moving from one machine to another) within your VPC. Limiting pivoting possibilities will ultimately make the hacker's job far more complex.

EXAM TIP: Try to limit allowed communications with a VPC to the bare minimum

ACLs are applied at the VPC level and do not offer the same granular control SGs offer. Nevertheless, you might want to use ACLs to restrict and allow traffic to your VPC broadly. For example, if you have five web servers in a VPC that require access over HTTPS from the Internet but do not allow any other incoming traffic, you could use rules to allow only HTTPS and deny all other traffic. Doing so would allow your machines to communicate with each other within the VPC however freely.

The better solution is to create an SG that only allows HTTPS traffic and assign it to the NICs associated with the five web servers. That way, you prevent traffic between these web servers. Now, if you were using a load balancer, you could opt only to allow HTTPS traffic from the load balancer to the VM instead of direct access through the Internet. Proxied access brings us to the next topic in this chapter, encryption in transit.

EXAM TIP: Security groups are more granular and offer higher security than ACLs. The trade-off is that SGs can take more time to configure

REAL-LIFE TIP: Build a security model before applying security groups. It is vital to limit SGs to a manageable amount. Creating groups by application or service type can be a good start.

Encryption in transit

We have talked extensively about encryption and encryption in transit. However, we must consider some important factors when creating cloud networks. For example, take a look at *Figure 6.5*. In this figure, the ALB connects to the web server over HTTPS. For this to work, the webserver must allow connections over HTTPS, which means it must contain a valid certificate that the ALB can accept.

Sometimes, your backend applications behind a load balancer might not offer encrypted communication channels, or your organization might find it too challenging to manage certificates on all the web servers. After all, certificates must be valid, and if you have a dynamically scaling environment, any new machine would need to obtain the certificate before participating in the load balancer group.

Whatever the reason, many organizations opt not to encrypt the connection between the ALB and the webserver. Instead, the ALB serves the certificate for your application to the end user. The traffic is then proxied from your ALB to the VM. Meaning any machine in the VPC could listen in on this traffic. If an attacker could obtain access to a single machine or service in your VPC, they would likely be able to listen in on ALL the traffic sent out to the servers in the VPC.

The process above is called **SSL/TLS offloading**. Nowadays, this way of working is widespread. Unfortunately, it is also a very insecure approach. An easy solution to the problem above is the following:

If your service does not support **HTTPS**, consider creating a web server on the virtual machine (or container). The web server can then expose your service over **HTTPS** to the load balancer and proxy the traffic to the internal service. That way, the unencrypted traffic is contained in the **Virtual Machine** or container itself, refer to the following figure:

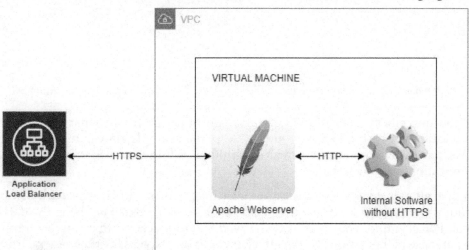

Figure 6.5: It is better to limit unencrypted traffic to a VM or container instead of a VNet

Suppose you cannot or do not want to disperse certificates to these web servers. In that case, using self-signed certificates (so not signed by an authority) is better than allowing unencrypted communications within your VNet.

EXAM TIP: SSL/TLS offloading is insecure because of traffic exposure within the VNet.

EXAM TIP: End-to-end encryption never exists with SSL/TLS offloading

Zero Trust

If you have been in the security industry for a while, you will have heard of *Zero Trust*. Like cloud, Zero Trust is one of the new buzzwords in IT. So, what is it all about?

Zero Trust is a relatively simple concept. In an environment built on the principle of Zero Trust, you assume that your network, machines, and identities are compromised. As a result, you do not trust any system, network, or identity to gain free reign in your environment. Instead, you limit access, communication paths, and privileges to the absolute minimum.

Throughout the previous sections, we have seen some of the items you want to implement in a Zero Trust environment. The most important one is micro-segmentation. In a micro-segmented environment, you block all communications between services and devices by default. Let us look at an example, refer to the following figure:

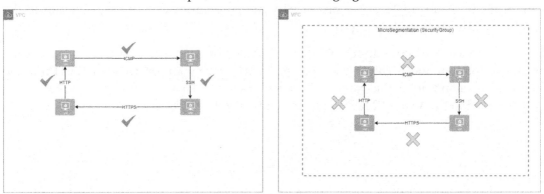

Figure 6.6: VPC without micro-segmentation left, VPC with micro-segmentation using an SG

When you implement a zero-trust network, you must figure out what services have to communicate with each other. As you can see in the example above, in the figure on the left VMs can freely communicate with each other. While in the figure on the right, all communications are blocked.

Rather than allowing every VM to communicate freely, you should use a security group that only allows the webservice backend to communicate to the database using the database's protocol. For example, you might have a web service backend that must communicate with a database in the same VPC. An attacker could only access the database by breaching it or the web service. At the same time, a breach of any other VM in the VPC will not allow them to reach the database.

EXAM TIP: Microsegmentation is an integral part of the zero trust puzzle.

EXAM TIP: Zero Trust demands a deny-by-default approach

Another vital part of Zero Trust that we covered is the need for encryption in transit. Of course, Zero Trust encompasses much more than this, but remember that these are some of the most important facets of networking. If you assume your network and systems are breached, you do not want to broadcast unencrypted data on that network.

EXAM TIP: Zero Trust is not a technology. It is a way of thinking and working that uses a variety of technical (and non-technical) controls.

VNet/VPC peering

Similar to on-premises networking, you might require that service and machines from one VPC can talk to others in another VPC. CSPs have designed something for this called **VNet** or **VPC** peering. By peering VNets, you allow hosts from these networks to speak with each other. Peerings can be set up automatically and require an NAT GW per VPC (to communicate outside of the VPC) and routes for the resolution of hosts in other VPCs. Almost all CSPs offer to peer in an easily configurable interface. Sometimes, you might even be able to peer networks across regions. Allowing you to create a global network where services can communicate directly without traversing the public Internet. An important limitation of VPC peering is that peering only works between networks hosted within the same cloud. You cannot peer an Azure VNet and an AWS VPC.

VPNs

Another approach to connecting to your cloud network is using a **virtual private network (VPN)**. As discussed earlier in this book, a VPN creates a tunnel over an underlay network. The tunnels isolate the traffic from the underlay network and ensure (using encryption) that the traffic is not readable to others on the underlay network.

Creating a VPN can be done in a couple of different ways. The first one is called **host-to-host**. With one of these tunnels, the VPN includes two machines only. These machines can then communicate with each other through the tunnel. Let us look at an example:

VPN Connection

Figure 6.7: Host-to-host VPN over the Internet.

A host-to-host VPN requires both hosts to run VPN software to establish the tunnel between the two devices. This type of VPN is helpful if you are trying to give access to a single host, but if you require your cloud network to be accessible by your on-premises network, you would need a site-to-site VPN, as shown:

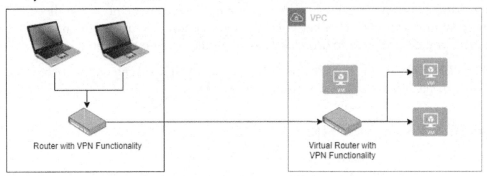

Figure 6.8: *Site-to-site VPN with a virtualized VPN appliance*

The example above shows a VPN that includes the whole on-premises network and the VPC. The router in the on-premises environment connects to a virtual version of the same router in the cloud. These two devices create a tunnel allowing traffic between VMs in the VPC and laptops in the on-premises network. In the sample above, your organization must manage a virtualized instance of a router or VPN gateway in the cloud. If the VM fails, the VPC is unreachable, or the router is misconfigured, your environment will not work.

Many CSPs understand that maintaining these virtual appliances brings a lot of extra work and license costs (and is not always reliable). So, these CSPs offer managed VPN solutions, allowing you to create a VPN between your on-premises and cloud network. Most offerings allow host-to-host or site-to-site and require configuring or installing a customer gateway in your on-premises network. The customer gateway, which can be an existing router or firewall but may be a virtual appliance, connects to the transit gateway in the cloud. Let us see what this could look like:

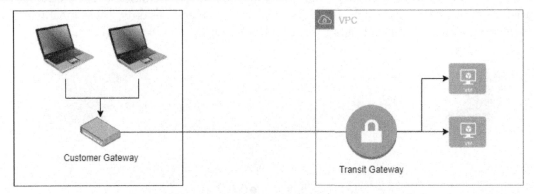

Figure 6.9: *Site-to-site VPN with a managed VPN service*

Remember that routes are needed in the VPC route table to allow devices to resolve each other. If you create a VPN using your own (virtual) appliances, you must ensure these routes are in place. Managed solutions may create them for you. Additionally, you must ensure that the VPC and the on-premises network addresses do not overlap. If they do, you will experience connectivity issues.

EXAM TIP: Customer-managed VPNs require more work from the customer, allow more customization, and may be cheaper.

EXAM TIP: Managed VPN services (generally) provide better availability and scalability but come at a cost.

When you choose between a customer-managed VPN solution or a managed VPN service, remember to vet either solution for its security properties. Different solutions allow different protocols, encryption algorithms, and key lengths. It is essential to pick a solution that offers sufficient availability, throughput, and security. You might even want to consider portability and interoperability with other CSPs. After all, you may also want to establish VPN connections between different CSPs in multi-cloud environments.

EXAM TIP: For the exam, VPN connections are often considered more secure than direct connections over the Internet. However, many Zero Trust advocates argue this point.

For the CCSP exam, you do not need in-depth technical knowledge of how VPNs work. However, you should know a couple of standard implementations. Two of the most common ones are **IPSec** and **TLS/SSL-based VPNs**. IPSec or TLS/SSL encrypts tunneling protocol (like **GRE** or **L2TP**) in these VPNs. It is essential to realize that a VPN always consists of a tunneling protocol and encryption.

Direct connections

While VPNs are a fantastic way to connect on-premises networks to the cloud or even multiple clouds, there are a few drawbacks. Firstly, the VPNs we discussed run over the Internet. Unfortunately, the Internet does not provide SLAs. An outage of the connection to the Internet or local overloads of the provider network will impact the availability of the VPN. Similarly, when traffic traverses the Internet, it travels through loads of different equipment. At every piece of equipment (or sometimes even the cable), parties (like governments or hackers) can intercept your traffic. While VPNs allow traffic encryption, you must pick strong encryption algorithms and long enough key lengths to prevent these parties from getting their hands on your data.

For some businesses, data is so sensitive that transmitting it over the Internet is unacceptable. As we covered earlier, a solution exists, namely a direct connection. You know a leased line if you are experienced in data center networking. A leased line is a logically or physically reserved cable transporting your data at a certain speed. Unlike the Internet, **Internet Service Providers (ISPs)** and **Data Center Operators (DCOs)** offer an SLA for these connections. Instead of using the Internet for a VPN, you could (in some cases) reserve a direct connection from your data center to the cloud.

The benefit of a direct connection is simple. Your data is not transported through the equipment of the parties you do not trust, but more importantly you will be provided with an SLA, meaning your CSP and ISP/DCO are responsible for providing you with the availability you pay for.

So, should you encrypt data if data is transported over a network you trust? The answer depends on your organization's risk appetite or willingness to take a risk. If your organization operates under the principle of Zero Trust, you should never trust any network. This means you should still encrypt traffic on direct connections. You could do so by creating a VPN on the direct connection or encrypting the data before sending it. However, security professionals around the world debate this topic. Some say encryption should never be needed on direct connections.

In any case, the CCSP exam does not consider tunnel encryption required for these connections. Nevertheless, it would be best to use protocols that offer encryption in transit where possible. For example, use HTTPS over a direct connection over HTTP.

EXAM TIP: The CCSP exam does not expect you to encrypt traffic on a direct connection

Web Application Firewall

Earlier in this chapter, we discussed security groups and ACLs more thoroughly. **Web Application Firewall (WAF)** is a crucial addition to these building blocks. As discussed in *Chapter 1, Understanding cloud computing concepts*, and the cloud reference architecture, WAFs are intelligent firewalls that are context-aware and can perform request-level filtering. For example, WAFs can detect attacks like cross-site scripting or SQLI. Once you have implemented SGs and ACLs to limit the incoming traffic to your network, you can enable a WAF to work with your ALB to scan incoming requests to your web application.

Because WAFs read the requests it receive, they also must be provided context about what requests are acceptable and which are not. That way, you do not only restrict access to the protocol level, but you can also block malicious requests to your server at the application level. Many CSPs offer default rule sets for WAFs, but a lot of tuning will be needed to really utilize their full potential. For example, let us look at the following WAF rules:

Rule 1	Rule 2
Allow request when:	Deny request when:
Method: GET	Method: POST
Content-Type: application/JSON	Content-Type: text/HTML
	Body contains <script>

Figure 6.3: Sample rules for a WAF

Rule 1 says to allow requests using the **GET** method, and the content is in JSON format. This rule will decline requests that are not marked as application/JSON. However, it does not verify if the request's body contains JSON. While this rule looks smart, attackers can easily evade it and send non-JSON content. Instead of using a rule like this, you might want to verify that the request body consists of valid JSON that follows a (semi-)structured format.

Rule 2 is more specific than Rule 1. It says to deny POST requests using text/**HTML** formatting and contain the HTML **<script>** tag. The purpose of this rule is likely to block XSS attacks. However, there are many more ways to inject JavaScript inside HTML code. Looking at this rule, even writing **<SCRIPT>** will already evade this rule.

The point is that you must carefully consider what rules you implement in a WAF. You can choose to block requests that occur in a known attack database, or you can create rules that only allow requests that exactly match the format your application expects. Similarly to normal firewalls, you will be the most secure if you deny all traffic by default, except for the requests you know to be valid.

EXAM TIP: WAFs can be highly effective but require much effort and testing.

EXAM TIP: WAFs often integrate with ALBs to protect all instances of your application at once

REAL-LIFE TIP: Less is more. Keep WAF rules manageable (in size and number) and clear to prevent false positives.

Denial of Service protection

This chapter has talked extensively about the different cloud networking aspects. Broad access is the main difference between cloud and on-premises computing. As we have seen, it poses new risks. Attackers can access more systems directly, and poor configuration can substantially increase the organization's attack surface. Until now, we have primarily discussed how this affects the confidentiality and integrity of these systems.

Unfortunately, the availability of your cloud environment is also under consent threat. After all, what happens if you have publically reachable server instances that are reachable to attackers? If you have been operating in the security realm for a while, you know that attackers are probing servers indiscriminately at a large scale. For example, on the webserver hosted in a home data center, you may receive thousands of probes and payloads with malicious content daily.

The same is true for any cloud environment with publicly exposed assets. Attackers are consistently probing any machines that are publicly reachable for attack venues and known vulnerabilities. Once identified, your device becomes subject to various attacks. Depending on your organization's profile, activistic attackers might attempt to bring your public-facing services down using DoS attacks.

Luckily, most CSPs offer standard protection against simple (volumetric) DoS attacks. Because the CSP provides you with SLAs on the availability of your services, they will protect you against these attacks. However, some attacks are not covered by the CSP. These more complex attacks, like **Reflective Denial of Service (RDoS)** or **Distributed Denial of Service (DDoS)** attacks (or a combination of them), can significantly disrupt the availability of your services.

During an RDoS attack, a computer impersonates a machine and sends requests to other devices. These devices respond to your machine instead of the attacker's and cause massive traffic that might render your machine unusable. You can compare an RDoS attack to the following:

Alice posts on social media that she is giving a party with free food and drinks at 92 hacker street. Thousands of people arrive at 92 hacker street and try to get on the property. The owner of 92 hacker street did not expect thousands of people to show up at their property. Because there are so many people, they cannot clear out the property, making it temporarily unusable.

The same happens during an RDoS attack. However, instead of saying there is a party at a certain address, Alice's computer sends out requests that require a response. Instead of sending them out from her IP address, she fakes Margo's IP address. Rather than responding to Alice, everybody sends their response to Margo, rendering her computer unusable.

A DDoS attack works differently; during such an attack, the attackers make requests to a target system from many other devices (often ten of thousands or more). The traffic these devices generate overloads the target machine rendering it incapable of handling legitimate requests.

Now, if you combine these attacks, you get a RDDoS attack. In that attack, many different systems impersonate the target machine and cause other devices to send their responses to the target machine.

EXAM TIP: The CCSP exam expects you to understand the danger of DoS, DDoS, RDoS, and RDDoS.

As mentioned previously, many CSPs offer protection against these attacks. The protection is often expensive and not enabled by default. Depending on your organization's threats, you might want to consider purchasing this service.

However, even if you do not have enough budget, there are actions you can take. For example, you can block common protocols like **Internet Control Message Protocol (ICMP)** often used for these attacks. You can also install software on hosts that detect these attacks and block traffic. Most web server software packages offer such plugins. Of course, usage of VPNs, direct connections, and a WAF can also greatly reduce the risks associated with these attacks.

EXAM TIP: Extensive DoS protection is expensive but sometimes necessary

API Management

The last standard networking tool we will discuss is called **API Management (APIM)**. Most (large) CSPs offer APIM solutions. APIM is a fantastic tool that functions as a combination of an ALB and WAF while allowing you to create serverless APIs at the same time.

APIM allows you to create a central point to manage your APIs. You can configure URLs pointing to different backend applications in the tool. For example, if a single domain hosts multiple APIs, you can quickly point the correct path to the associated API. While only having to configure a certificate and security requirements once. APIM allows you to add authentication to applications by requiring authentication for specific URLs.

At the same time, APIM is configurable to perform checks on the request body (as discussed in the WAF section) or even transform requests or responses to another format. For example, APIM can convert SOAP requests to REST and reverse them.

As mentioned previously, APIM can also point URLs directly to serverless code. You can quickly create new API endpoints that execute code without creating the code for the web interface.

It is important to note that while APIM has high availability as a SaaS solution, the underlying applications that APIM uses might not. APIM solutions often integrate with CDNs, allowing localized caching to improve availability. Let us examine what APIM could look like in a sample environment, refer to the following figure:

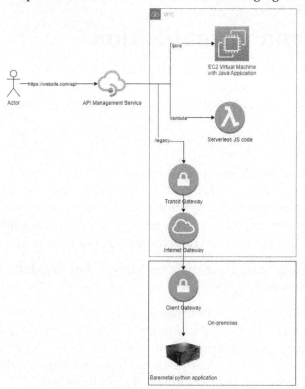

Figure 6.10: *Sample environment with APIM*

As you can see above, an external user might call APIM with a URL. APIM will proxy the traffic to the correct underlying service based on the specified path. URLs with /java will go to a VM in the AWS Cloud, while requests with /lambda will go to a serverless application in the cloud. However, URLs with /legacy are routed over a VPN to the on-premises network.

While the first two features are great, the last option is attractive. If your organization exposes many applications from its on-premises network, they likely incur a lot of attacks on its public servers. Now, you can use APIM to make your internal APIs available through the cloud. By doing so, you will benefit from the DoS protections of the CSP and any other protections you implement in APIM. For example, if you implement request filtering or a WAF, you can block most malicious traffic in the cloud. Thereby, APIM can allow you to reduce the direct attack surface to your on-premises network.

Similarly, you could use APIM to provide a REST API from the cloud that automatically converts REST requests to SOAP and then transmits the requests to on-premises backend services that only use SOAP. That way, you can quickly modernize your web service without simultaneously rebuilding all services from SOAP to REST.

You might have guessed, but the author of this book is a massive fan of APIM solutions. You should know how APIM can improve security by reducing the attack surface on web services (both on-premises and in the cloud).

Compute and virtualization

In the first part of this chapter, we talked about the common networking components you will need to build a (secure) cloud environment. Of course, CSPs offer many services aside from networking. Let us start by looking at some of the computing options CSPs offer:

Serverless

You may have heard of serverless computing before. Contrary to what the term suggests, there are absolutely servers in play in this form of computing. However, it is called **serverless** because the customer does not manage the service. The CSP offers you an environment where you can run your code without having to do any configuration on the underlying servers. In essence, serverless computing is a PaaS offering.

EXAM TIP: Serverless computing involves servers, but the cloud consumer does not manage them. Serverless is PaaS.

Serverless is an excellent tool that allows developers to quickly create applications without worrying about building and maintaining the underlying infrastructure. It is important to realize that moving your application to serverless only works if it is written in a supported language. Most serverless platforms offer various useable languages to run code (JavaScript, Python, and Java are almost always provided).

EXAM TIP: Serverless does not work for every programming language

So, how do we work with a serverless platform? Well, the platform often offers an online **Integrated Development Environment (IDE)**. The IDE allows you to type code directly into the service and run it immediately, as shown:

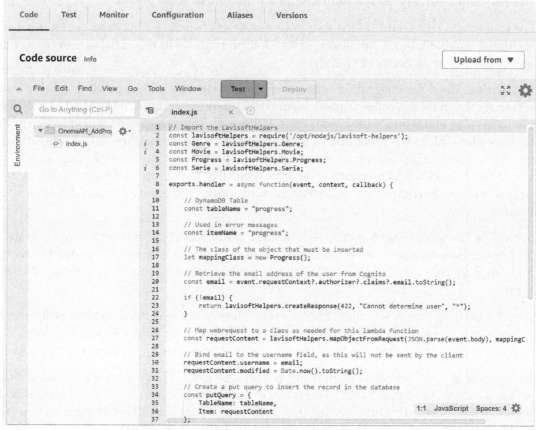

Figure 6.11: *Serverless JavaScript application in AWS Lambda*

However, many organizations elect to use existing development and deployment tooling. For example, you can write code for a serverless platform on your laptop, sync it to **GitHub** (or another version control software), and then deploy it to the serverless platform using a (cloud) deployment tool. The benefit of using normal development processes is that you can include (security) testing and scanning like usual. Many serverless platforms allow you to virtualize the platform locally to test your code before uploading it to the cloud. So, the decision on the development strategy is highly dependent on your organization's requirements and existing processes.

Another remarkable feature of serverless computing is that it can often directly integrate with other cloud services. For example, your serverless platform can use roles and identities defined in the cloud IAM tool to access other services. Roles allow you to define which service is allowed to perform what actions where. Using roles is a crucial way to establish an environment with the principle of least privilege in mind (only providing access to the necessary resources).

EXAM TIP: Serverless integrates with many other cloud native services—increasing security and allowing setups following the principle of least privilege.

For example, a role could define that your serverless function can access a cloud-based relational database. But it can also restrict what you can do in this database. Perhaps the serverless code only needs to read data.

In any case, the tight integration with other cloud tools can make accessing other cloud services extremely easy (and more secure) for your serverless code. Most serverless platforms also allow integration with their APIM tool. This integration will enable you to tie a specific URL to the execution of your serverless code (sometimes called a function). Instead of building an extensive software package that creates an API with endpoints, you can create an APIM instance and code for every URL in serverless functions. By doing so, you limit code complexity and size while increasing the agility of your development teams.

Serverless has some other benefits. As with any cloud service, you pay for what you use. You do not have to pay for an application that may or may not be used. You pay for every invocation of your code. The benefit is that if you do not run code often, you do not pay for it.

Another exciting aspect is scalability. Since serverless is a PaaS service, the CSP will ensure your functions are available following the SLA. Depending on your CSP and the provided SLA, serverless computing can save money and improve your application's availability.

It may sound like serverless computing is the holy grail. However, keep in mind that serverless does not support every language. In some cases, it also limits the duration and memory consumed. If your organization is looking to go serverless, it may be wise to build a new application first before you migrate existing services to serverless. That way, you can gain insight into serverless opportunities and limitations.

EXAM TIP: Serverless computing is not suitable for all situations

REAL-LIFE TIP: Serverless computing requires a change in your development teams' mindset. Try to build a new application serverless before migrating existing applications.

Containers

As discussed, not everything is suited for serverless computing. One of the main drawbacks is that code movement to another CSP is not easy. While your code stays the same, its deployment is different between CSPs.

Suppose you have been working in IT for a while. In that case, you have likely encountered container technology, which is a great option to accommodate more specific needs (such as languages) while ensuring high portability.

A container is, in essence, a stripped-down virtual machine. Instead of including all the code and packages needed to run an operating system (like a GUI, for example), a good container only contains those required to run the software you need. The benefit of a container is that it uses fewer resources than a VM (due to a smaller amount of services and packages). However, they can also be more secure than VMs simply because fewer packages means less attack surface and thus likely fewer vulnerabilities.

EXAM TIP: In the CCSP exam, containers are considered to be more secure than VMs

Because virtualized containers can run on any host system that supports that specific container technology, one of the most well-known container platforms is **Docker**. If you install Docker on any machine, you can run Docker containers on it. Regardless of the operating system and packages of the host. The beauty of this is that it is ultra-portable. A developer can work on a MacBook, a Linux machine, or a Windows host and get the same result from the same code. Because of this portability, you can quickly move containers from one CSP to another without requiring anything but setting up hosts to run the containers.

EXAM TIP: Containers are extremely portable and are easily used when moved to CSPs and on-premises

However, managing a container platform can be a lot of work. Most CSPs acknowledge this and offer managed container platforms. These platforms allow you to upload your container, specify the availability, and the platform will automatically create your containers for you. These services allow you to transfer management of the container platform, but they also allow you to build a highly available environment quickly. After all, you can specify the availability of your software, and the container platform will automatically create new containers if the load increases or stop them if the load decreases. Of course, these offerings come at a (hefty) price.

Platforms like this exist outside of the cloud as well. Kubernetes is a well-known example of such a **container orchestration platform**. Instead of using a managed service, you could also run such a platform on a virtual machine (or a container) and manage your containers that way. However, remember that cloud native tooling offers more extensive integration options.

EXAM TIP: Effective container orchestration is essential in the cloud

Even though containers are considered more secure, they still require security practices. It is necessary to scan containers for vulnerabilities and misconfigurations. We will discuss more about this in *Chapter 11, Secure Development (SSDLC), awareness, and training.*

REAL-LIFE TIP: Containers are very suitable for micro-service workloads

Virtual machines

Not every organization uses containers. Some organizations might have other virtualization environments within their on-premises data centers. Organizations sometimes want to lift and shift these machines to the cloud. One option could be to run your current Hypervisor in a virtual machine in the cloud. That way, you could quickly move virtual machines from your on-premises network to the cloud. Many hypervisor companies (like VMWare) even allow you to shift workloads between the cloud and on-premises environments that way.

Alternatively, you could rebuild your virtual machines within the virtual machine services provided by the cloud service provider. All major CSPs offer the ability to create new VMs quickly. Frequently, they provide standard images that you can use directly. However, you can also buy/download VM images from the CSP store. Other organizations might maintain and sell such images. The images can be pre-hardened, scanned for vulnerabilities, and fully pre-configured. By using existing images, your organization can reduce its maintenance efforts. Using managed images that third parties update can be a way to minimize management efforts, but your organization must still verify (or Trust) that the third party did the right thing

Similar to containers, you should always scan and monitor virtual machines. Most CSPs offer cloud-native tools that allow you to scan your virtual machines for misconfigurations and vulnerabilities automatically. Other tools are also available to automatically gather logs from your VMs in central cloud logging tools.

Underlying infrastructure

Whether using VMs, containers, or serverless, CSPs are responsible for managing the physical machines on which your applications are virtualized. In most cases, CSPs are also responsible for managing the hypervisor used to run your virtual environments. While you can pick the availability requirements (for serverless and containers) and hardware requirements for VMs, you do not need to worry about hardware failures.

Scaling

A significant part of any cloud environment is scaling. As we discussed, serverless computing can scale entirely automatically. Similarly, container management platforms can also scale your container environment on demand. Luckily, the same applies to VMs. By creating scaling groups, you can automatically **horizontally scale** (so increase the number of VMs) or **vertically scale** (increase hardware for your VM). By using load balancing groups and scaling groups in conjunction, you can ensure your compute availability is always sufficient. At the same time, you can reduce costs by scaling down VMs, containers, and serverless computing when you are not using it.

EXAM TIP: For the CCSP exam, you must understand horizontal versus vertical scaling.

While scaling and virtualization go hand in hand. There are also risks to virtualization and unlimited scaling. The main problem that can occur is called (virtual machine) sprawling. Sprawling occurs when an organization overprovisions virtual resources to the point where they become too numerous to manage. For example, if an organization created thousands of VMs that each contain a micro-service, it can become highly challenging to manage. It is essential to devise a good strategy to deal with the management of virtual resources.

One of the main things your organization must organize is lifecycle management. When and how do we create resources, and when do we use them? In an on-premises environment, you already paid for the hardware, so many think they should make as many VMs as the hardware will support. However, in the cloud, you pay per machine. So, your considerations for isolating workloads on different VMs may have to differ. Additionally, you might want to consider running specific one-time workloads in a VM and removing the machine afterward.

In any case, your organization must devise a strategy on when to create, modify, and delete resources. If you do not, VM sprawling is likely to occur. Once it happens, your organization is much more likely to (inadvertently) create or uphold security vulnerabilities.

Hypervisor attacks

Another item you must be aware of when you virtualize compute workloads (for example, containers or VMs) is hypervisor attacks. During these, attackers seek to break out of the virtual environment and gain access to the hypervisor that runs the virtual compute resource. By doing so, they could gain control over all virtualized resources. Such access could shut down machines, steal data, and inject malicious workloads. When you use virtualization services the CSP provides, they are responsible for preventing these attacks. However, if you bring your hypervisor to the cloud, you must take measures to avoid this.

EXAM TIP: Depending on your setup, you might have to prevent hypervisor attacks

Other compute technologies

Many CSPs offer additional computing solutions. For example, CSPs might offer **Machine Learning (ML)** of **Artificial Intelligence (AI)** as a cloud service. Similarly, CSPs have offerings to automatically process large amounts of data from databases (or data lakes). Unfortunately, most of these offerings vary greatly between CSPs, which makes it challenging to outline their functionality. If you are interested in these applications, you should investigate the options different CSPs have to offer.

Storage

In addition to computing and networking, all CSPs offer storage solutions. Throughout the book, we discussed how data types affect storage needs. Following, we will briefly revisit some of these items.

File storage, object storage, and block storage

In *chapters 4* and *5* (*Discover, Classify and Manage Cloud Data* and *Cloud Storage Architectures and Their Security Technologies*), we have talked extensively about data and storage solutions. Structured data is best stored in relational databases, while semi-structured data is suitable for non-relational databases. Unstructured data is best stored on object or block storage solutions.

However, as we saw previously, we also deal with different types of computing. For example, how can you store data for a virtual machine? Well, VMs allow you to attach block storage solutions. These solutions allow you to pick between SSDs or HDDs and often allow you to pick speed and size requirements. In essence, block storage functions as a virtual hard drive for your virtual machine.

File storage can be used to share files between different virtual machines and containers. Think of file storage solutions as a network drive. You do not have the freedom to decide between HDD or SSD storage, but you can qualify for speed and availability requirements. These file storage solutions can be mounted to various machines, allowing you to efficiently share data between various virtual compute resources.

As discussed earlier, assigning roles can easily allow your container or serverless platform to access a specific database. However, when you run workloads (or applications) on your virtualized compute, they are likely best suited using file storage or databases. After all, if you run a Python application on a serverless platform, you might need to store order data in a database. Alternatively, you might need to pull video files from an object or file storage solution to display to your users.

Data lakes

One of the solutions we have not yet discussed is data lakes. Data lakes are used for data analytics and big data. A data lake is nothing more than a collection of various data sources (databases, object storage, file storage) that are used in conjunction to perform analysis. While analysis of massive amounts of data can be instrumental, remember that it also makes data lakes an attractive attack target.

Management Plane

An essential part of cloud infrastructure is the management thereof. The cloud allows us to scale environments on demand from anywhere. However, doing so requires specific tools and even poses risks. In this section, we will discuss managing the cloud infrastructure.

Cloud console

One of the most common ways to manage your cloud environment is through the cloud console. This console is a web-based **Graphical User Interface (GUI)**. It is accessible online from any location (unless otherwise configured). The console allows you to create, alter or remove new resources easily. For example, creating a VNet or starting a container can be done with a few clicks. While the cloud console is easy to use, it requires manual interactions from an engineer or administrator. Especially in large cloud environments, you are unlikely to perform every management task in the cloud console, refer to the following figure:

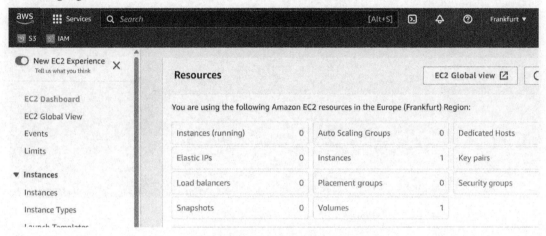

Figure 6.12: Sample of the AWS Cloud console

Command Line Interface

CSPs often allow access through a **Command Line Interface (CLI)**. A CLI can be installed on a host system, allowing access to the cloud environment through a text-based interface. The CLI executes commands manually or programmatically. For example, you can use commands to create a new VNets or create ten new VMs in a scaling group. Because the CLI allows programmatic interaction, it can be more scaleable than the cloud console.

For example, you could use the CLI to deploy multiple VMs simultaneously or to migrate numerous machines from one VM to another. The CLI allows you to use code templates to deploy your infrastructure.

A sample of a cloud CLI is shown, refer to the following screenshot:

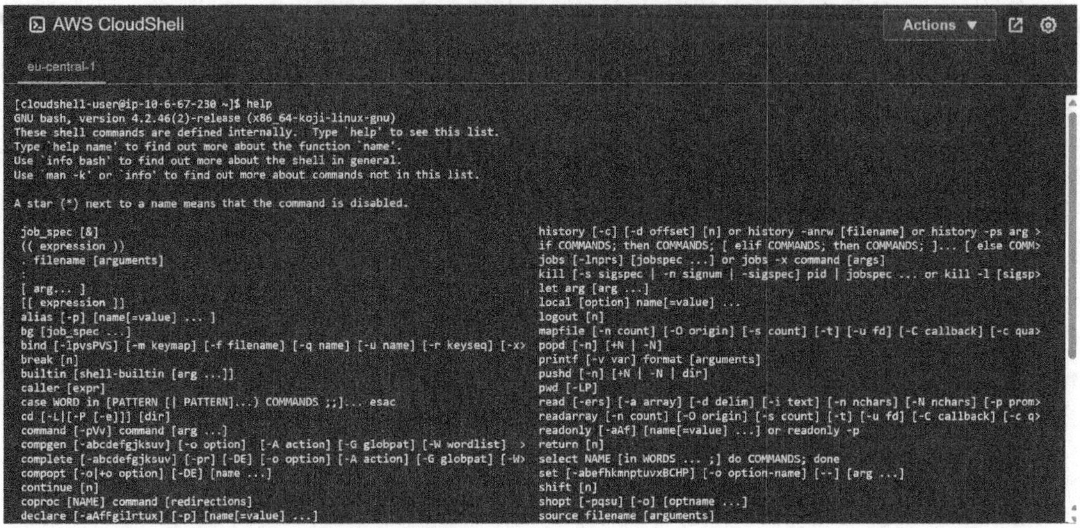

Figure 6.13: Sample of the AWS Cloud CLI

APIs

Aside from management through the console and the CLI, management can also occur through APIs. Depending on your service, the CSP might have full or limited management functionality through an API. The API allows programmatic access, similar to the CLI, but can be used without needing a CLI application.

For example, a web application in the on-premises environment can directly communicate over the Internet with an API to create a new VM. An exciting opportunity this presents is that you can fully automate everyday tasks and put them in your web interface. Instead of having system administrators install a CLI on their endpoints, you can use one central application for all your administrators to use. While still being able to make changes quickly at a large scale.

Infrastucture as Code

Previously in this book, we discussed how IaC is necessary to deploy cloud environments at scale. IaC allows CSPs to manage their vast environments quickly while adhering to demanding customer SLAs. However, IaC also plays an important role in managing your own cloud. As we discussed earlier in this section, updating your environment through the cloud console is tedious and time-consuming at scale. Rather than clicking manually through an interface, you can use the CLI or an API to deploy IaC.

However, what does IaC look like? While it sounds complicated, IaC is nothing more than configuration files often written in YAML or JSON. These files are interpreted by the CLI, API, or cloud service and form templates for managing existing or creating new environments.

The main benefits are that you can easily deploy many of the same templates at once. However, it also allows you to deploy these systems in a repeatable manner without manual intervention. Properly used IaC will reduce deployment errors and improve scalability.

Security

The management plane of the cloud is a prime target for attackers. From the management plane, you can significantly damage a cloud environment, create malicious machines, and steal data. It is essential to lock down access to the management side of the cloud as much as you can.

Generally, it would be best if you considered the following;

- Change default credentials
- Require two-factor authentication for access
- Create personal accounts
- Log access and usage
- Do not use the root user for everyday tasks
- Use minimalized access privileges
- Give every API or CLI user separate security tokens (with minimal access).

If you consider the items above, your cloud environment is less likely to be used against you. We will dive into securing the management plane and the logging you should implement later in this book.

Conclusion

This chapter introduced you to some of the fundamental cloud infrastructures most CSPs offer. Many CSPs provide different and more extensive services. Nevertheless, every cloud environment is built on these building blocks.

You have learned that VPCs form the core of cloud networks and allow communication with the Internet, other clouds, and even on-premises networks. Various security controls like ACLs, SGs, and WAFs are necessary to ensure you can access your environments securely.

Load balancing and virtualization are key components to allow your cloud environment to scale. Regardless of whether you use serverless computing, containers, or virtual machines, you must ensure that compute resources are adequately secured.

VPNs and direct connections are essential components in connecting your cloud network to the on-premises network securely and reliably. At the same time, APIM will allow you to quickly create new APIs or transform existing APIs to current-day standards.

We also covered the management of cloud environments. CLIs, APIs, and cloud consoles are the main ways to manage the cloud. While CLIs and APIs scale well and allow for Infrastructure as code, cloud consoles are not as scalable.

This chapter has given you the basic understanding of cloud infrastructure needed to delve into security control applications, risk management, security architecture, and secure development in the cloud. In *Chapter 7, Datacenter Security*, we will look at the physical security of the components discussed here.

Learning goals

This chapter addresses the following CCSP exam outline learning goals:

Domain 3: Cloud platform and infrastructure security

      3.1 Comprehend cloud infrastructure and platform components

Join our book's Discord space

Join the book's Discord Workspace for Latest updates, Offers, Tech happenings around the world, New Release and Sessions with the Authors:

https://discord.bpbonline.com

CHAPTER 7
Datacenter Security

Introduction

This chapter explores the facets of physical data center design. Cloud consumers leverage the CSP's **data centers (DCs)**. If you work for a CSP, it is essential to understand the details of data center design. As a cloud consumer, you must select a CSP that meets your demands. Therefore, it is necessary to understand the physical, environmental, logical, and resiliency aspects associated with DCs.

Structure

This chapter covers the following topics:

- Physical design
- Environmental design
- Resilient design
- Logical design

Objectives

This chapter will examine the options for DC acquisition and how to correct physical design to ensure your DCS are secure and functional. Environmental design allows you to ensure your equipment can function to the best of its ability in any circumstance. The chapter will also explore making a DC design resilient against man-made and natural threats. Lastly, you will learn how logical design allows a **data center operator (DCO)** to serve multiple customers at the same time.

Physical design

Datacenters are a widely discussed subject. Some groups fight against creating new DCs while advocates point out their necessity. Regardless of your stance on DCs, built data centers must be safe and secure. This section will examine common areas of interest in DC design. For example, should you build your own data center, or is it better to leverage existing DCs? We will also look at the location of a DC and the effects of security, safety, and regulatory requirements on the design.

Buy, lease, or build

Firstly, many organizations need data centers. However, DCs are generally expensive to build. Local governments might have regulations or restrictions that make the creation of new data centers difficult or even impossible. So, how should your organization go about acquiring DC capacity?

The most important question to ask is what you are trying to achieve. If you are hosting one or two servers, leasing rack space is likely your best bet, but if you provide services to other customers and need to store data for hundreds of customers, you might want to consider buying or building a data center.

In the end, it mainly depends on costs. Buying and building a DC requires significant upfront capital. As mentioned previously, data centers are costly. Most organizations do not have the budget to build or buy one. Whenever you create a data center, you face a long-term project. Constructing a data center takes time. Sometimes, it might take years to get approval to start building.

So, as a general rule of thumb, building is likely not the right option unless you provide data center/cloud services to others. How about buying an existing DC? Unfortunately, data centers are a rare commodity. While purchasing a DC saves time, you might be unable to find any DCs for sale. If you do, you can guarantee the costs of such a purchase would be significant.

What does this mean for small-sized companies? Well, most organizations will be limited to leasing rack space. The benefit of leasing is that, similarly to cloud computing, you are not responsible for anything outside your rack space. The DCO will provide the physical building, power, cooling, access control, and so on. By taking these responsibilities, your organization does not have to hire hundreds of operators and technicians to maintain and run the data center. Another significant benefit of leasing rack space is having minimal upfront costs. You will pay the DCO for the racks that you use. Sometimes, you might still have to purchase or rent connections, such as dark fiber or redundant ISP hookups. However, your upfront costs are limited mainly to the equipment you want to use.

It may sound like leasing is a perfect solution. It requires less personnel, small upfront costs, and transfers many responsibilities to the DCO. However, remember that, similarly to cloud computing, you must relinquish control. Your organization must rely on the DCO to logically and physically separate your networks and equipment from other customers. Additionally, you will have to trust their access control, security, and safety protocols. So, if you want to maintain your data center space, ensure you vet the vendor, establish SLAs, and verify compliance with applicable laws and regulations. For example, your organization may have to comply with standards like the FIPS 140-2/3, the ISO 27001:2022, or PCI-DSS. Each standard and regulation has specific requirements you must incorporate in your DC. Let us look at some of the expected benefits and drawbacks of the various options:

Choice	Benefits	Drawbacks
Buy	Short timeline, full control, audibility	High upfront costs, limited availability, extensive personnel needs
Build	Build to specification, more control, audibility	High upfront costs, long timeline, extensive personnel needs
Lease	Low, upfront costs, limited need for personnel transference of responsibilities, short timeline	Limited control, compliance, and audit challenges

Table 7.1: Common benefits and drawbacks of DC acquisition models

Location

Once your organization has determined if it is buying, building, or leasing a DC. The next question is its location. DCs have some particular demands (that we will explore later in this chapter). They require the availability of fast internet connectivity, reliable power, and water supply. Without these factors, your DC will not be able to operate reliably.

However, there are many other facets to consider—for example, the distance of the DC to your customers. The closer your DC is to the users, the faster it can provide service, but closer is not always better. The location of a DC can bring along risks as well. Building a DC in a flood plain or high-risk tornado zone is probably not the best idea. In any case, these types of factors are called environmental or natural threats. It would be best to consider these factors when you purchase, lease, or build a data center. The effects of a natural disaster can be significant. Equipment and data can be destroyed, services disrupted and lives lost.

EXAM TIP: Evaluate DC locations for availability and reliability of utilities, but more importantly, for environmental and man-made threats.

Aside from environmental threats, your location might also result in man-made threats. Building a DC in a highly disputed area can result in protests, theft, and even vandalism. As mentioned previously, many people and activist groups are reluctant towards DCs.

We briefly talked about the distance between a DC and its users. However, there is another factor we should consider. What happens if the DC is destroyed by a flood or the internet connection for a large area is disrupted? A single data center is insufficient if your organization wants a resilient environment.

Like availability zones in the cloud, you will want multiple DC locations. Geographic dispersion of these locations is essential so that a major service outage or disaster does not affect both areas. Unfortunately, the distribution of DCs also poses other challenges. For example, if you buy or build a DC, you require personnel to run these DCs. If one of your DCs is in Seattle and the other in New York, you will need staff for both DCs. However, you might not if your DCs are within a 50 mile radius. It is essential to weigh the drawbacks of dispersing your DCs over a large area versus the reliability benefits.

EXAM TIP: Every data center faces specific threats. A DC near a fault line requires a different design than one in a flood plane. The physical design requirements depend on this.

Security and safety

Throughout this chapter, we have been discussing safety and security. These terms are often used interchangeably. However, they have very different meanings.

Safety refers to the physical safety of humans and animals. At the same time, security refers to preventing financial or physical damage to objects. Safety and security do not always go hand-in-hand.

EXAM TIP: In the CCSP exam, safety always trumps security

For example, in the case of a fire, you could use gas to bind or extract oxygen from the air. By doing so, you can quickly extinguish a fire. However, every human in the room will suffocate due to a lack of oxygen. So, in the CCSP exam, using this gas to save your equipment is not an acceptable solution. After all, it puts security over safety.

It is essential to understand two terms that come forth from this concept. Fail securely and fail safely.

For example, if a fire breaks out, your DC emergency doors should unlock to allow employees to escape. However, opening these doors creates a situation where attackers could enter your building and tamper with or steal equipment. In this example, the designers choose a *fail safely* method of approach.

For example, let us say you use a badging system to provide access to your DC. Due to a system error, the badging system does not work. If you follow the concept of failing securely, all doors should remain locked until the system restores. However, while this approach keeps unauthorized people from entering, it might also prevent people from leaving the building. In case of disasters, this could cause significant safety issues.

When you design security controls, try to achieve secure and safe failure simultaneously. If this is not possible, you should always choose to fail safely over fail securely. Of course, you might encounter situations where safety is guaranteed by secure failure.

For example, if someone attempts to tamper with an HSM, it might erase all the keys in the appliance. The HSM does not directly affect safety but ensures the keys are secure by failing securely.

Now that we understand the difference between failing securely and failing safely. Let us take a look at safety and security considerations for DCs.

Firstly, DCs have to incorporate measures to protect employees in the case of disasters and emergencies. Some standard requirements are:

- (fire) escape doors

- smoke and fire detectors/ alarms

- human-safe fire control measures

- flame retardant materials

Aside from fire control measures, you should also implement worker safety within the DC. Hearing protection, protective eyewear, construction shoes, server lifts, and so on, are essential tools to ensure worker safety.

Aside from safety, a physical data center design has to incorporate physical security measures. When we talk about security controls, we commonly organize them into two systems. The first system consists of the following:

- Deterrent

- Preventive

- Detective

- Corrective

As you can see above, the first model separates control by the function. The second model splits controls by control type:

- Administrative

- Physical

- Technical

EXAM TIP: In the CCSP exam, you will encounter both models (sometimes in conjunction

During the physical design of a data center, you must incorporate controls from each domain to secure the premises. For example, a physical, deterring control could be a fence around the premises. If you make the fence high enough, it will deter trespassers (making it preventive). Because the fence is a physical measure, it would be considered a physical control.

An example of a detective control can be a camera system. Such a system can be used to detect intruders or perform analysis after an incident. At the same time, a camera system could also function as a deterrent. It is important to remember that not all controls are a single category.

Now, let us look at some of the physical data center's threats and the controls we must incorporate. Common threats are:

- Intrusion

- Vandalism

- Theft

- Corporate Espionage

A key component to thwarting these threats is access to the data center. We should take different measures to achieve the same goal (prevent unauthorized access). Just as with technology, we should approach DC security from a defense-in-depth approach.

For example, we could use a combination of the following controls:

- 6-foot fence (deter)

- Security guards (detect, deter, and correct)

- Guard dogs (detect and deter)

- Outside cameras (detect)

- Bollards to prevent cars from being able to reach the DC (prevent)

- Lighting around the premises (deter)

- Doors with a badge and biometric access (prevent)

- Employee badging (detection)

- Visitor badging (detect)

- Camera's in the DC (detect)

- Badge access within the DC (prevent, detect)

As you can see in the example above, we could use a combination of many controls to achieve the control functions. When you design a DC, using multiple controls for every function is essential. After all, what happens if the guard dogs have to go to the veterinarian? If they are your only detective/deterring control, this would be a problem.

Remember that the list above is not exhaustive. Many different controls exist. However, for the CCSP exam, you should know the following controls by heart:

Window placement is vital to prevent unauthorized access. When constructing a DC, you should not place windows that allow entry into the DC from the ground.

Lighting is used to deter intruders. Keep in mind that lighting should be placed strategically around the building. When placing lighting, ensure you do not blind security guards or other personnel, not that you place the lights directly over them.

Turnstiles are a physical preventive control. A turnstile requires you to swipe a badge, after which it will let one person through. You have likely encountered this system at train stations or other similar places. The benefit of a turnstile is that it is much more challenging to piggyback. During a piggybacking attack, the attacker follows an authorized person into a building. They rely on the target to open the door using their badge (or biometrics). After which, they slip through the door.

Man Traps are also physical preventive controls. Similar to a turnstile, they seek to prevent piggybacking attacks. However, a man trap is more elaborate. The system consists of two doors with an open area in the middle. A person enters through the first set of doors, after which they close immediately. At this point, the person authenticates by badge or biometrics, and the send door opens. The person can enter the area, and the second door closes behind them. This method prevents people from following you, especially if the middle room implements a security camera or other detective/preventive controls. You have likely seen man traps at airports (or government buildings).

Biometric locks use the physical characteristics of a person to prove their identity. For example, a fingerprint, iris, palm, or retina scan. Because biometrics belong to a person physically, it is more difficult to gain unauthorized access. After all, you must force someone to provide their palmprint or fingerprint. However, badge locks are openable by simply stealing or finding someone's badge. An essential factor to consider with biometrics is the sensitivity of the system in use. If a system has many false rejections, it prevents employees from accessing a room they are authorized to access. False acceptances allow someone who should not have access to gain access.

EXAM TIP: Biometrics are more secure than badges but have privacy concerns.

As a general rule of thumb, you want a system with more false negatives in a high-security environment and one with more false positives in a low-security environment. After all, false negatives hinder the end user's experience, while false positives compromise security.

Every system is measurable for its sensitivity. The amount of false rejections calculates the **false rejection rate (FRR)**. At the same time, the number of false acceptances represents the **false acceptance rate (FAR)**. The FRR and FAR are often shown in a diagram. The point where they meet is called the **crossover error rate** (**CER**). The CER is the measure of the sensitivity/security of a system. A low CER means a high amount of false acceptance, while a high CER means the opposite, as shown in the following figure:

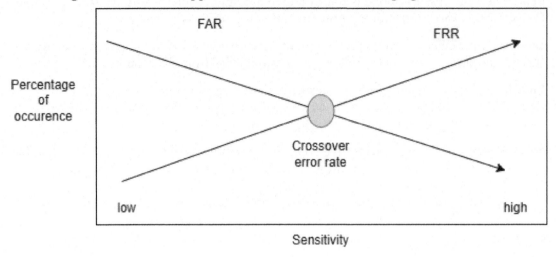

Figure 7.1: *The relations of FAR, FRR, and the CER*

It is essential to understand that the CER of a product is a static value. You cannot configure the FAR, FRR, or CER. It is a property. If the CER is insufficient for your purpose, you must choose a different system.

EXAM TIP: FAR, FRR, and CER are static properties belonging to a product. You cannot change them.

As mentioned earlier, biometrics are more secure but present some privacy concerns. Some areas might not allow organizations to store biometrics data, and sometimes, employees might not be willing to do so regardless of regulation. Retina scans are known to reveal medical data about their owners, making the scans a widely debated method. Palm scans are generally considered the least secure biometric. In any case, securing biometrics data correctly and applying it where necessary is crucial. It is also important to note that biometrics are often used with badges to create physical **Multi-factor authentication** (**MFA**).

Let us look at an example of MFA within a DC environment. Imagine a technician that needs to gain access to a specific area of the DC. The area contains sensitive governmental servers. Such an environment could be protected more extensively by requiring MFA. An application of MFA could be a keypad lock that also requires the technician's finger print (something you are and something you know). Similarly, for extremely highly sensitive data, you may need a retina scan, a badge, and a keypad lock. That way, you combine (something you are, something you have, and something you know.

EXAM TIP: MFA is an essential tool in physical access control.

Intrusion detection

Another exciting technology to implement for security purposes is intrusion detection. If you like home automation, you have likely worked with this technology. For example, you can implement door, window, and **infrared (IR)** sensors to detect movement or entry within a DC. If your DC has no on-site technicians at night, these sensors can be a detective control. If a door is opened within the DC, while no one should be there, you are likely in a breach situation.

Let us look at the different IDS technologies that can be implemented in a DC. Firstly, there are photoelectric sensors. These sensors measure the light coming from a specific light source. A typical application of these is the famous laser beams burglars try to avoid when robbing a bank. Disrupting the laser beam triggers the photoelectric sensor, indicating intrusion.

Another type of sensor is an ultrasonic sensor. These sensors use ultrasonic pulses to detect the proximity of an object. By doing so, the sensor can detect anything that walks by it closely.

A third type of sensor is called a **microwave sensor**. The sensors use high-frequency radio waves to detect motion by measuring the time it takes for its signal to return. If something moves through its waves, it will reflect the waves, and the sensor can detect the movement.

The fourth type of sensor is called **passive infrared**. These sensors measure infrared light sent out by objects in a room. When a person walks through the sensor's detection range, the sensor can measure the person's presence by its IR signature.

The last type of sensor is called a **pressure sensor**. These sensors work much like the traps in the Indiana Jones movies. Once a person walks on a pressure-plated tile, it detects that person's presence.

As you can imagine, all of these sensors have strengths and weaknesses. Mixing and matching different types of sensors is essential to prevent attackers from circumventing detection. Keep in mind that more IDS sensor technologies may exit and be applied.

Construction materials

When you build a DC, you must ensure the materials used suit the environment. Materials should be flame-resistant and retardant while preventing leakage from **Electro-Magnetic (EM)** signals. Ceilings and HVAC must not be useable to bypass access control systems.

Regulatory requirements

Aside from some reviewed controls, your organization must consistently monitor applicable building codes and legal and regulatory requirements. For example, your local government might require that you implement specific security or safety measures (like fire escapes). Conversely, regulations might prevent your organization from storing employee biometric data. In those cases, you may not be allowed to implement biometrics for access control measures. In any case, the measures you implement must always comply with the building code and local laws and regulations.

EXAM TIP: The CCSP exam expects you to understand fundamental physical security controls in a DC.

Environmental design

We already covered how the location of a DC affects its safety, security, and reliability. However, the environment within the DC is detrimental to the computing applications inside. This section will examine some standard controls that require implementation to ensure the DC will keep functioning.

Electric

First off, DCs consume a tremendous amount of power. Depending on the number of servers, switches, and the chosen hardware, its power draw will be more or less significant. Nevertheless, one thing is for sure, DCs need consistent and reliable power.

Disruption of the power supply to a DC renders the equipment unavailable. To prevent this from happening, DCOs and CSPs take various measures. Most commonly, DCs connect to a reliable power grid, potentially provided by two energy companies. Additionally, a DC must have (fuel-based) generators. These generators are connected to the DC power grid and are activated automatically when the power supply is interrupted. They are providing the equipment with emergency power during the outage.

However, a power outage can occur almost instantaneously. Generators have to be started and will take time (usually minutes) to become operational. Minutes without power would still cause all systems to go offline. Most DCs are also fitted with large batteries to prevent this from happening. These batteries are commonly called **uninterruptible power supply (UPS)**. The DC might employ a UPS that powers all of the DC (which usually consists of multiple units), or every rack might have a smaller UPS.

As the name suggests, the UPS will not lose power if the connected power grid fails. Maintaining power is possible because the UPS delivers its power through a battery instead of directly. The battery acts as a proxy for the power grid, so if the power goes down, it keeps unloading until it is empty. However, the power delivery was not interrupted because the power was already coming from the battery (it was just being charged consistently).

The combination of redundant power grids, generators, and UPS can prevent your DC from becoming unusable after a power outage. Following you can see a schematic of how this works:

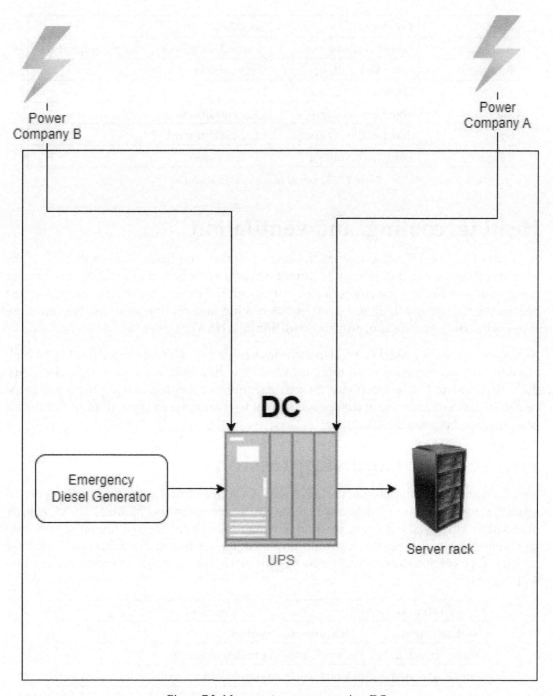

Figure 7.2*: Measures to ensure power in a DC*

Aside from the total loss of power, which we call a **blackout**, we have other power issues we should consider. Let us take a look at common electrical problems and their:

Name	Problem	Solution
Blackout	Long loss of power	Redundant power hookups, generators
Brownout	Long low voltage	Clean power
Fault	Short loss of power	UPS
Sag	Short low voltage	Line conditioning
Spike	Short high voltage	Line conditioning
Surge	Long high voltage	Clean power

Table 7.2: Electrical issues and their solutions

Heating, cooling, and ventilation

Aside from power, DCs also require the correct climate conditions within the DC. If the temperature is too hot, the equipment cannot perform to the best of its capabilities. Damage to equipment is likely if the environment is too cold. Either way, working conditions must be safe for technicians. DCs use a variety of heating and cooling systems. We call these systems **heating, ventilation, and air conditioning (HVAC)** systems.

As you may have noticed, HVAC also includes ventilation. The reason for this is that high humidity causes corrosion of equipment. While low humidity can cause static electricity. Both corrosion and static electricity can cause significant damage to equipment and must be avoided. Combining these factors is essential to ensure the relative humidity of the air is acceptable (between 40 – 60%).

Fire detection and suppression

We talked about fire suppression earlier as well. Of course, fire is not a good environmental condition for a DC. As we discussed, some fire suppression mechanisms favor security over safety. However, not every method is suitable for every type of fire either. As with any other security measure, you should implement a defense-in-depth approach and use multiple types of detectors to avoid false negatives. Let us take a look at common detection systems first:

Detection	Method
Heat activated	Measures temperature
Flame activated	Uses IR imaging to detect flames
Smoke activated	Detect using a photoelectric device

Table 7.3: Fire detection systems

As you can see above, three main ways to detect a fire exist. Every type of fire also requires different methods to suppress them. Every fire needs temperature, a combustible, and oxygen. Other suppression methods always target one of these facets. Let us look at some of the standard methods :

Measure	Effective for	Drawbacks
Fire extinguisher – Class A	Common combustibles	Not suitable for every fire, damages electrical equipment
Fire extinguisher – Class B	Flammable liquids	Not suitable for every fire, damages electrical equipment
Fire extinguisher – Class C	Electrical appliances	Not suitable for every fire
Fire extinguisher – Class D	Combustible metals	Not suitable for every fire, damages electrical equipment
Fire extinguisher – Class E	Flammable gasses	Not suitable for every fire, damages electrical equipment
Argon gas	Any fire	Unsafe for humans
CO2 gas	Any fire	Unsafe for humans
Sprinklers	Any fire	Damages electrical equipment

Table 7.4: Common fire suppression mechanisms

As you can see above, many ways to suppress a fire exist. Different fire extinguishers are useable to fight varying types of fires. Gasses are useable against virtually every fire, similar to sprinklers. However, using gas to extinguish a fire in an area with humans is extremely dangerous and almost always fatal. It is essential to pick different fire-suppressing measures and implement them within the DC with care. For example, implementing sprinklers may be effective, but they will destroy your equipment. While implementing gas means you cannot activate it until the evacuation of the area. If you only implement extinguishers, you cannot fight a large fire or a fire in multiple areas.

EXAM TIP: Gas is commonly used in DCs because it spares equipment. Gas is not deployable until complete employee evacuation. If you implement gas fire suppression, safeguards must be in place to prevent early deployment.

For the CCSP exam, you must understand some of the different sprinkler systems. Let us examine them below:

Wet pipe systems are always full of water. The benefit is that they can quickly disperse water when the system is triggered. Heat sensors on the sprinklers often activate these systems automatically, so they activate separately. However, a significant drawback is that leakage of the pipe system can cause damage to the equipment located under the pipes.

Dry pipe/Deluge systems do not contain water in the pipes by default. Instead, the system fills with water after triggering a sensor. Because the lines are empty, it takes longer for the system to deploy water. However, leakage in the pipe system will not damage equipment before a fire.

Preaction systems combine a dry pipe and a wet pipe system. The lines are empty like a dry pipe system in a preaction system. When the sensor is triggered, the system fills itself with water. However, not every sprinkler activates automatically. Instead, every sprinkler has a link. If the temperature at that sprinkler is high enough, the link will melt, and the water will deploy. The significant benefit is that sprinklers only activate in areas without fire.

EXAM TIP: Sprinklers are a common topic in the CCSP exam.

Cabling

Another aspect of environmental design is cabling. Installation of cables must be safe and secure. Most DCs use raised floors to run cables through. That way, cables are not on the floor and in the way of technicians but are still easily reachable while preventing cable damage.

Multi-vendor pathway connectivity

Another item a DC must take into account is the connectivity to the internet. After all, clouds should have broad access by definition. Since an enormous amount of data will go in and out of the DC, the CSP or DCO must ensure connectivity to a reliable and sufficiently fast connection. Not only that, but they should also ensure they have backup connections. After all, you do not want a DC to go offline because of a single ISP service interruption. Another aspect that plays a role here is direct connections. As discussed earlier in this book, many CSPs allow you to connect directly with their DC. It is wise to facilitate as many customers as possible to have incoming connections for as many ISPs as possible. That way, customers can create a leased line between their location and your DC, regardless of their provider.

Resilient design

You may have noticed that designing for resiliency is an essential topic in this chapter. Redundant power supplies, internet connections, and HVAC systems are crucial to prevent DCs from becoming unavailable. Throughout the DC design process, it is essential to examine, at every step, what effects the failure of your design would have. What happens if a lock breaks down? Can someone enter the building, or are other security measures in place? What happens if a storm destroys a powerline? Does the whole data center lose power?

By asking yourself these questions, you can evaluate your steps to ensure resilience in every domain. A DC must be resilient against natural or man-made threats, whether affecting the systems within the data center or the physical building itself. Resiliency even extends beyond single DCs. Rather than ensuring one extremely resilient DC, you must still consider that the DC can be rendered unusable. By implementing multiple DCs and replicating customer data, you can create resilience at a service level instead of a physical level.

For CSPs, this service-based resilience is the ultimate end goal. After all, a SaaS may only be allowed to have hours of downtime in a year. To offer this, the CSP must fit their DCs with redundant servers, switches, access control systems, and so on and ensure data and service replication across DCs. Following, you will find an example of how resilience can work throughout the DC:

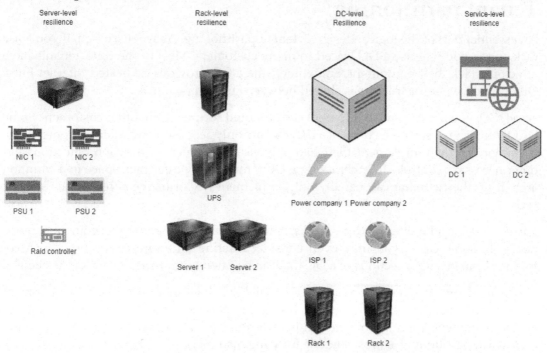

Figure 7.3: Resilience is vital at every level of the DC

EXAM TIP: Resilient design has many levels. Systems and end-user services must be resilient, systems must be resilient, and DCs must be resilient.

Nevertheless, resilience works through to the lowest levels of the DC. Servers should have multiple CPUs, NICs, and power supplies to ensure the failure of these small components does not render the machine unusable. Similarly, hard disks may have to be configurable to use a **random array of independent disks (RAID)**. Using RAID (in some modes) can prevent hard drive failure from resulting in data loss.

Regardless of the nature of your DC component, from power and connectivity to access control, you must design your systems to account for failures.

EXAM TIP: Resilience and defense-in-depth go hand-in-hand.

Logical design

The last topic of this chapter is logical design. We have already covered some of DC design's physical, environmental, and resiliency aspects. However, once you have built, leased, or bought your DC, logical design is essential to ensure the systems within are only useable by authorized parties.

Tenant partitioning

An essential part of the logical design is tenant partitioning. As we discussed, if you lease rack space, you will use a DC leased to many customers. Most of the time, tenants have a rack to stack their equipment. Sometimes, the DCO provides dedicated internet lines. Other times, the infrastructure is shared between customers.

As a DCO, you must ensure equipment can be stored securely from other customers. Some DCOs offer cages, secure sections of a DC, that are only accessible to certain customers. The customer can then implement their badging systems, cameras, intrusion detection, and other necessary controls. In other cases, a DCO might only offer rack space in a common area. If so, the customer can usually only implement key or badge access to the specific rack.

You should consider offering cages, racks, or a combination depending on your customers' needs. In some cases, you may even consider offering an entire co-location. Such co-locations can be larger sections of a DC that can be fitted with security controls as needed.

However, if you are operating as a CSP, you will likely have a limited ability to implement physical measures to partition tenants. Instead, hypervisors and virtual networking can isolate customers. Your organization must determine what types of clients you will serve and which partitioning is most suitable for your customers.

Access control and identities

This chapter has discussed badge access, biometrics locks, and other access control technologies. However, we have not covered one essential item on how identities and access control tie together. Many DCs offer the ability for customers to administrate their access. Sometimes, a DC administrates authorized users for all their customers through a local database. Customers might also want to manage their access to the DC, co-location, or rack. Customers can then provision and de-provision access through badges or biometrics. Some CSPs even integrate their access control systems with their identity provider. By doing so, an employee with a badge that was laid off can automatically no longer access the DC.

While integrating an identity provider in the access control lifecycle is beneficial, it can also have a downside. For example, if the identity provider is unreachable, no one will be able to gain access to the DC. It is important to ensure a balance between secure failure and access. For example, you might want to register an emergency badge that is locked in a safe to maintain access to the DC in case of that event.

EXAM TIP: Federation is also applicable to physical access controls

Another aspect to take into account here is logging and visitors. First, you should ensure that every access action with the DC gets logged. You must register who enters and leaves the DC and who enters and leaves what area. By doing so, you can detect malicious activity and register the presence of humans in certain areas. If you deploy gas fire suppression, such logs can help you prevent the activation of a gas system while employees are in the area.

Video recordings can also form an essential part of access control monitoring within the DC. By monitoring access at every entry and exit of a DC, you can detect unauthorized entry and ensure full employee evacuation.

Lastly, it is essential to note that visitors should always be accompanied when entering and working in a DC. Visitors should also receive and wear a physical badge.

EXAM TIP: The CCSP exam requires logging of access and physical escorting of the visitor.

Conclusion

DC design is a complicated process. Whether you build, buy, or lease a DC requires consideration. Natural and man-made threats dictate how risky specific locations are for your DC. At the same time, some places may provide significant upsides for DCs. Sometimes, legal and regulatory requirements will strongly influence your DC design.

Some of the essential items to consider in DCs are security and safety. By creating a layer of security measures, you can ensure that the failure of a single control does not compromise security. While security is essential, it should not compromise safety. By balancing secure and safe failure, your DC will be more resilient.

Aside from security and safety, many environmental factors are important. Is the DC climate optimal for humans and equipment? Does the DC have enough power? Implementation of HVAC, resilient power, and internet connections are essential parts of good DC design. The resiliency of a DC takes place at many levels, from individual cables to servers to entire co-locations. Everything in the chain must be resilient to an excellent end product, but even when your DC is completed, you are not done. It is essential to offer tenant separation options suitable to your customer base. Access control and visitor management are also essential factors to consider. All in all, DC design is complicated. Many small organizations are not equipped to do it. As a CCSP, you can lead your organization toward the right decisions.

In the next chapter, we will learn about risk management practices in a cloud environment.

Learning goals

This chapter addresses the following CCSP exam outline learning goals:

Domain 3: Cloud platform and infrastructure security

   3.2 Design a secure data center

Join our book's Discord space

Join the book's Discord Workspace for Latest updates, Offers, Tech happenings around the world, New Release and Sessions with the Authors:

https://discord.bpbonline.com

CHAPTER 8
Risk Management in the Cloud

Introduction

Security is about balance. Systems are highly securable, but the costs may be substantial, and the system's availability will likely suffer. Managing organizational risks is essential to determine what measures should or should not be taken. In chapter eight, we will examine risk management in general. Throughout the chapter, we will also zoom in on various challenges of risk management in the cloud.

Structure

This chapter covers the following topics:

- Risks
- Risk assessments and the risk environment
- Risk mitigation strategies and treatment
- Risk frameworks
- Metrics for risk management
- Assess vendor/provider risk management programs (controls, methodologies, policies, risk profile, risk appetite)

- Cloud vulnerabilities, threats, and attacks

- Difference between data owner/controller versus data custodian/processor

- Breach notifications, SOX, GDPR

Objectives

This chapter will teach you how risk assessment allows your organization to treat risk proportionally. You will learn how various risk frameworks and treatment strategies can help your organization remain in control. This chapter will also teach you about the specifics of risk management in the cloud. We will look at managing risks in your vendor landscape while also diving into the necessity of metrics to evaluate the effectiveness of risk management. Throughout the chapter, we will discuss how the different roles of data handling significantly affect risk management in the cloud, specifically when breach notification laws, **Sarbanes-Oxley** (**SOX**), and GDPR are involved. At the end of the chapter, you will understand what elements a risk management program must contain for an organization with a cloud presence.

Risks

Before we dive into risk management, let us examine what risks are. Risk consists of two factors; Likelihood and impact. The likelihood is a measure of the chance that something will occur. Many variables influence the probability of a risk.

EXAM TIP: Risk = likelihood x impact

For example, if you have an IT environment with many vulnerabilities, you may have a higher likelihood of getting hacked. Similarly, if your company stores highly confidential or valuable data, your organization is likely targeted by more threat actors, thus increasing the likelihood of getting hacked.

In the example above, we talk about hacking. However, risks can pertain to many factors. In the last chapter, data center security, we discussed natural disasters. When you determine the risk for earthquakes, you will have a higher likelihood in one area versus another. It is essential to realize that likelihood influences risks of every kind.

The other factor, impact, means the damage sustained when a risk occurs. This damage is not merely physical or even monetary. Let us examine a hacked organization. If the organization stores **Social Security Numbers** (**SSNs**), a hack exposing this information will likely damage the organization's reputation. Aside from the damage to the reputation, disruption of business activities causes a loss of revenue. You must ensure you consider all factors to risk impact.

EXAM TIP: Impact is more than monetary damage and must include damage to reputation, customer trust, and other factors.

Now that we understand that risks consist of impact and likelihood, we must discuss how risks are classifiable. You may have realized that likelihood x impact does not produce a simple value. Nevertheless, we must be able to compare risks against the risk appetite of the organization but also against each other.

In general, you can use two ways to classify risks. Qualitative risk classification relies on descriptive names. These terms describe how damaging the occurrence would be to an organization. For example, qualitative risks may have a catastrophic, severe, considerable, or minor impact.

For example, an organization may deem an impact that bankrupts the organization as critical, while an effect of low could damage less than 10,000 USD.

Many organizations tie risk classification to data classification. If a risk compromises highly confidential data, it may automatically be deemed a high risk. However, similarly to data classification, there is no one answer to the qualitative impact classification; it wholly depends on your organization. When you use qualitative risk classification, your organization will have to define thresholds for every level.

When you use qualitative classification, your impact is often depicted similarly. For example, the likelihood may be highly unlikely, unlikely, likely, or highly likely. Determining the bounds for these levels is up to your organization.

If your organization uses qualitative risk classification, you will need a risk classification matrix to determine the risk classification based on the combination of impact and likelihood. Following, you can see an example of a matrix:

Likelihood/Impact	Minor	Considerable	Severe	Catastrophic
Highly unlikely	Low risk	Low risk	Low risk	Medium risk
Unlikely	Low risk	Low risk	Medium risk	High risk
Likely	Low risk	Medium risk	High risk	Critical risk
Highly likely	Medium risk	High risk	Critical risk	Critical risk

Table 8.1: Sample risk classification matrix

A risk classification is an essential element in managing risks within an organization. As you can see above, a risk classification matrix combines the impact and likelihood to create a risk classification (sometimes called **risk score**). The type depicts how important a risk is to an organization and forms the main driver for risk treatment decisions.

Aside from qualitative risk classification, we can also use quantitative risk classification. In quantitative risk classification, we use numerical measurements to depict risk. For example, the impact is measurable in US Dollars. At the same time, the likelihood is measurable in expected occurrences per year. By measuring impact, you can measure risk more granularly. After all, in qualitative risk management, you may have five risks with different likelihoods and impacts that still have the same end classification (as seen in *Table 8.1*).

Let us look at an example. A company has a DC that costs 5 million dollars to build, and the data center is built in an area where two earthquakes occur yearly. The company has taken measures to prevent earthquake damage. However, an earthquake is expected to destroy 10% of the DC.

If we applied quantitative risk management to this example, we could use the following formulas:

Single Loss Expectancy (SLE) = Exposure factor (EF) * Asset Value (AV)

Annualized Loss Expectancy (ALE) = Annual Rate of Occurrence (ARO) * Single Loss Expectancy (SLE)

In the example above, the asset value is the DC. The DC is valued at 5,000,000. The exposure factor is the asset percentage destroyed if the earthquake happens (10%). Based on these numbers:

SLE = 0,1 (EF) * 5,000,000 (AV) = 500,000

An SLE of 500,000 means that every time the risk takes place, it costs the organization 500,000 dollars. Now, we can also calculate the ALE. As stated in the example, an earthquake occurs twice every year. Meaning the ARO is equal to 2. Let us look at what this means:

ALE = 2 (ARO) * 500,000 (SLE) = 1,000,000

An ALE of 1,000,000 means the company should expect to suffer 1,000,000 dollars in damages from this risk yearly. The organization should consider building the data center in another area, considering the ALE.

EXAM TIP: During the CCSP exam, you must be able to calculate the SLE and ALE of a given risk.

EXAM TIP: You should consider writing down the formulas on your exam note paper to help you calculate values during the exam.

So, why would you use qualitative risk classification if you can get more granular, easy-to-understand values by quantitative analysis? The answer is simple: sometimes, determining the dollar amount associated with an impact is too time-consuming or difficult. Similarly, it may be too difficult to decide on a reliable ARO. If you cannot determine these values with good precision, it undermines the value of quantitative risk analysis.

TIP: Qualitative risk classification is easier to communicate and prioritize but may only sometimes be practical.

Risk assessments

Risks are about impact and likelihood. They are expressible through quantitative and qualitative classifications. However, how do we determine what risks an organization faces and what the impact and likelihood are? We call the process of doing this risk assessment.

During a risk assessment, the assessor identifies an organization's risks. An assessment can have a broad or narrow scope. For example, a risk assessment can be conducted on the entirety of an organization. However, it can also be performed on a single application within the organization's landscape. Broad-scope risk assessments are likely to incorporate a different amount of effort on the level of an application than a precise assessment. That makes it essential to conduct risk assessments at various organizational scopes.

For example, your organization may want to identify risks at a macro level. An example of this could be a specific functional area's economic or political climate. However, risk assessments could also focus solely on the acquisition of a new subsidiary or the creation of a new product.

The point you must understand is that risk assessments are not created equal. A company-wide risk assessment is unlikely to identify risks that stem from vulnerabilities in a specific software package. A web application risk assessment will not identify that the DC it runs in is at risk of earthquakes.

As with everything in security, you need a layered approach to risk assessments. An organization must gain an understanding of risks throughout the organization. From macro-level risks to specific application risks, they require assessment. When discussing risks that affect the organization, we refer to them as **strategic risks**. At the same time, risks that target business processes and information systems are called **tactical risks**.

The reason for this is simple, companies have a **risk appetite**. Risk appetite represents the risk a company is willing to take to succeed. After all, risk-taking is necessary to achieve some results. In contrast, risk-taking in other areas could harm the organization's health. For the company leadership to be able to make risk-based decisions, they must understand the risks they are facing.

For example, if a new business was to bring in 2,000,000 in yearly revenue, but the ALE of the associated risks is 2,500,000, leadership may decide to wait to start the new business. Similarly, if a new product creates 6,000,000 in profit, and the associated risks have an ALE of 250,000, the product may be worth it. As security and risk management professionals, we must provide leadership with the data they need to make these decisions.

Now, risk assessments are a complicated process. Luckily, many organizations and institutions have already defined ways to conduct them. Commonly referenced documents on this topic are the **Risk Management Framework (RMF)**, and the *SP 800-30 Rev. 1, Guide for Conducting Risk Assessments*[1], created by the NIST. In SP 800-30, NIST outlines ways risk

---

[1] *SP 800-30 Rev. 1, Guide for Conducting Risk Assessments | CSRC (nist.gov)*

assessments can be conducted and how they should be used throughout the organization. At the same time, the RMF outlines a framework with steps for risk management. We will examine both in more depth later in this chapter.

According to the NIST, there are four essential steps to conducting risk assessments. The first step is to prepare for the assessment. During preparation, you must understand the scope of the assessment and the risk environment of the organization. It is essential to understand why you will conduct the risk assessment. Is it needed to launch a new product, is your organization looking to certify against a standard like 27001, or is it simply to reduce risks at the tactical level? Once you understand the purpose, it is essential to scope the assessment. As we discussed, assessments can take place from a strategic to a tactical level. By defining the scope, you can ensure you cover only a little of the organization. The preparation phase is also a great time to identify what information you will use during your assessment and if there are any roadblocks or constraints you must consider. For example, you may not be able to access all facets of a system, or a critical stakeholder may be on vacation during your assessment. The last vital part of the preparation phase is determining the risk model and classification strategy. Decide if you will classify risks quantitatively or qualitatively and study the organization's risk classification matrix.

The second step of the process is conducting the assessment. You must identify threats, sources, and events as part of the assessment. Threat sources can be threat actors such as criminal organizations and environmental threats. Threat events are situations that cause risk, for example, earthquakes or hacks. It is far more likely to be attacked by criminal organizations than it is to be attacked by state actors. By thoroughly preparing during phase one, you can ensure you best understand the context of your organization. You will experience that this greatly simplifies the process of identifying threats. Remember the candy store from several chapters back?

You are trying to determine how feasible a threat source can cause a threat event. Once you understand the threats your organization faces, you must identify if any vulnerabilities or predisposing conditions exist. For example, if your environment contains many software vulnerabilities, it is more likely that a hacking group will be able to breach your environment. Similarly, if your DC is built near a fault line, you are predisposed to fall victim to earthquakes.

Vulnerabilities and predisposing conditions are vital in determining the likelihood of occurrence. Remember that risk is likelihood multiplied by impact. When determining the likelihood, you must consider the capacities of the threat source, vulnerabilities, and predisposing conditions. For example, a state actor is generally more capable than a script kiddie. So, suppose your organization is likely to be targeted by state actors. In that case, the likelihood of a complicated hack occurring is more likely than for an organization only targeted by script kiddies looking for low-hanging fruit.

Once you understand the likelihood, you should examine the impact of a risk occurring. Generally, it would be best to quantify the risk when possible. Leadership can more easily understand quantitative versus qualitative risks; however, if you cannot, try to depict the impact of risk as simply and straightforwardly as possible.

Now that we have gained an understanding of the likelihood and impact, we can determine the risk. It is essential to formulate risks in a clear and precise manner. Remember, you should pick the method of risk classification before you start the assessment.

Now, the third step in the process is arguably the most crucial. Step three is communicating the results of the assessment. Risks have to be communicated within and throughout the organization. With proper and clear communication, risks are likely understood, which may lead to a lack of or excessive action.

For example, if you conduct a risk assessment on the scope of an application, you may decide to use a risk classification matrix at the application level. Such an assessment may produce many critical risks at the application level. If you communicate to your leadership that you have five critical risks, this can cause panic. Leadership may decide to shut down the application straight away. This is because leadership is likely to look at risk classification at the strategic level (that is where they operate). When you communicate your report, it is essential that you clearly describe the context of the assessment and the impacts on the organization. Remembering that you should prioritize risks within your report is also important. Present risk information in a manner that allows leadership to determine which risks require their attention the most quickly.

Risk assessment is hardly concluded after the results are communicated. The fourth step of the process is maintaining assessments. Once risks are identified, they must be monitored. The reason behind this is that the context of risks changes. Other controls may mitigate some risks, applications may be retired, or the impact of risks may increase once new data is added to a database. By continuously re-assessing risks, your organization can stay on top of the latest status of risks. After all, risks change in importance, and an organization must focus on suitable risks. Risk monitoring is also essential to establish whether risk treatment is effective.

Following you can see a table summarizing the steps of the risk assessment process:

Step	Actions
1	Prepare for Assessment
2	Conduct Assessment
3	Communicate results
4	Maintain assessment

Table 8.2: Steps of the risk assessment process

EXAM TIP: The NIST SPs are essential in the CCSP exam. You should review them before taking the exam.

Risk treatment and mitigation strategies

Now that we understand the four steps of risk assessments and the roles of communication and context in them. Let us look at what can be done with the results of risk assessments.

There are four different ways to deal with risk. Firstly, an organization can choose to mitigate risks. Risk mitigation means that the organization will implement one or more controls that reduce the risk to an acceptable level (based on the organization's risk appetite). It is essential to realize that risk mitigation rarely entirely removes the risk. Instead, it reduces its impact of severity. The risk that remains is called **residual risk**. An organization should always accept residual risks after mitigation.

For example, adding MFA to admin accounts reduces the likelihood of an attack using administrator credentials. However, adding MFA increases the impact of such an attack. However, because the likelihood of success is significantly reduced, a critical risk may be reduced to low risk. The low risk may be accepted following the organization's appetite, as allowing administrators to log in also benefits the organization.

EXAM TIP: Risk meditation rarely entirely removes a risk.

The second approach an organization can take to risk is called **transference**. When a risk is transferred, another organization's responsibility is essentially made. Risk transference is extremely common in cloud computing.

For example, using a SaaS product can transfer the risk of DDoS attacks to the CSP. After all, the CSP promises your organization availability according to an SLA. DDoS attacks are now a risk for the CSP instead of the cloud consumer.

The following approach is risk avoidance. When an organization chooses risk avoidance, it takes away the source of the risk. For example, if you have a DC that is at risk of earthquakes, selling the DC would be risk avoidance. Because the DC no longer belongs to the organization, it is no longer a risk. Risk avoidance is generally not an ideal solution. After all, most of the time, risk sources exist for a reason; they may bring in profit or be essential to an organization. However, risk avoidance can be an important consideration for new products or even old products that might be retired in the (near) future.

The last risk treatment method is **risk acceptance**. We discussed risk acceptance earlier as part of risk mitigation. In essence, risk acceptance means that the organization is aware of the risk but feels the risk is within the organization's risk appetite. A reason for risk acceptance can be that the source of the risks may produce much more value than the risk that threatens the organization. Alternatively, risk acceptance can also be a good option if the risk mitigation costs exceed the risk classification.

For example, if a risk produces an ALO of $ 100,000$ but the costs to mitigate the risk are $ 200,000$ per year, the organization may be better off taking their chances.

Regardless of your organization's risk treatment strategy, the risks require management. First, all organizational risks should be captured within a risk registry. Such a registry can be an overarching registry for the entire organization but may also be scoped at an application, process, or departmental level. Once a risk registry is created, it is vital that the risks within the register are monitored, re-evaluated, and re-assessed regularly. Reports/briefings/dashboards should be made to leadership regularly on the registry. By doing so, leadership is enabled to quickly act on changes in risk classification and anticipate investments and staffing needs to address risks.

Risk frameworks

As we discussed earlier, your organization does not have to reinvent the wheel on risk management. We have already discussed the role of risk assessments as part of risk management. However, simply assessing risks will not help your organization. It is vital that an organization manages new and existing risks and takes the proper steps throughout its lifecycle to ensure all risks are actively managed and do not exceed the organization's risk appetite.

Fortunately, many organizations have built frameworks to help organizations set up a risk management program. Let us look at some of the commonly used frameworks within our industry below:

Firstly, NIST has designed the **Risk Management Framework (RMF)**. The RMF was explicitly created for governments and government subtractors in the US. However, it has proven to be an essential asset to many other (international) organizations. The RMF outlines seven steps for managing risks throughout their lifecycle, as shown:

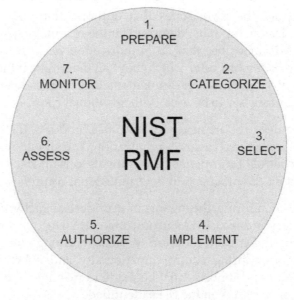

Figure 8.1: *Seven steps of the NIST RMF*

As you can see above, the RMF contains seven steps. The first step, preparation, helps an organization determine the key risk management roles. It also seeks to determine an organizational risk strategy and a risk appetite. Another important outcome of this step is an organization-wide risk assessment, common controls, and a strategy for continuously monitoring risks.

The categorization step is used to determine what risks the organization faces. During this step, risk assessments are conducted at various organizational levels. These assessments allow for system characteristic documentation, security categorization of applications and information, and formal approval from the leadership.

After the organization understands its risks, the selection step seeks to select and **tailor control baselines**. Control baselines are standard controls that should be applied to every piece of data or system at a particular classification. While tailoring means optimizing controls for your specific organization. Other outcomes of this step are assigning specific controls to systems to reduce risks and developing security and privacy plans that establish the processes and approval surrounding control selection.

During the fourth step the controls described in the privacy and security control plans from the select step are implemented. After implementation, the plans are updated to reflect which controls have been successfully implemented.

The fifth step, asses, seeks to establish if the controls implemented during the implementation phase function correctly. During the assessment step, an organization should appoint assessors, create, and approve assessment plans, conduct the control assessments, and report/document the results. Based on these results, an action plan must be established on how ineffective or non-functional controls will be corrected.

After assessing controls, the RMF states that authorization must take place. During authorization, senior leadership must determine if the residual risks are acceptable to the organization. The RMF prescribes that an authorization package is used to present all information to senior leadership, after which they can determine if the risk has sufficiently been reduced or if new controls must be implemented. Senior leadership can only approve or allow systems and processes to be used with additional controls.

Keep in mind that frameworks are never ready-to-use products. Instead, they provide the tools to set up processes tailored to your organization. You should not expect frameworks to prescribe which controls to implement to mitigate certain risks. Instead, it will help your organization set up the processes to determine what controls you should use.

During the last phase, monitoring, the organization undertakes activities to keep situational awareness about privacy and security. As an outcome of this step, systems and environments must be monitored by the created monitoring plans, and ongoing assessments must be conducted to evaluate enduring control functionality and effectiveness. Additionally, analysis of the activities and reports must be made to management to allow them to re-authorize or de-authorize based on the risks identified.

EXAM TIP: You must have a high-level understanding of the RMF steps to pass the CCSP exam.

Other important risk management frameworks are the COBIT **Enterprise Risk Management (ERM)** framework, the ISO 31000 ERM framework, and the COSO ERM Integrated framework, let us contrast these frameworks:

Framework	Industry	Scope
NIST RMF	(US) Government	Internal and external
ISO 31000	Broadly applicable	Internal and external
COSO ERM	Broadly Applicable	Internal
COBIT ERM	Focused on IT	Internal and external

Table 8.3: Contrast between risk management frameworks

Remember, when your organization is setting up an (enterprise) risk management program, it is best to evaluate the benefits and drawbacks of these frameworks.

Metrics for risk management

As you may have noticed, the NIST RMF focuses heavily on reporting to leadership and getting approval for risk management activities. The difficulty of risk management is that risks throughout an organization can have vastly different natures. You may experience economic risks, natural risks, cyber risks, and so on. Only some leaders may have a thorough understanding of all these facets. Nevertheless, senior leaders must make decisions on how risks are handled.

As a cybersecurity professional, you must help your leadership understand individual risks and risks at a broader scale. Leaders must easily understand if a specific application is risky without delving into technical details and jargon (in which they may not be well-versed).

An essential tool to do this is metrics. Metrics allow you to quickly provide management (and team members) with valuable decision-making material. Trends are especially a powerful tool in risk management. For example, a sharp increase in risks will show management that their (new) activities are risky, while increases in ineffective controls indicate that risk mitigation is not being done correctly.

Generally, metrics should be descriptive and expressed in numbers where possible. Let us look at an example of this:

Secure applications   Applications without open risks

       4000   40% (4000/10000)

Considering the above risks, which metric do you think management will understand better? The first metric is described as *secure applications*. However, what does secure mean? The second metric is described as *Applications without open risks*. That metric much better describes what it depicts.

A similar effect can be seen in the expression of the metric. The first metric displays an absolute number of 4000. Managers may feel the organization is doing excellent when they see this number. After all, 4000 secure applications sound like a good achievement. However, when you provide context as part of the metric, as seen in metric two, the manager will realize that 6000 applications are not without risks. It is evident that the framing of these metrics significantly impacts how they are perceived, even though they represent the same numbers.

When your organization builds its risk management processes, sit down with senior leaders and determine which metrics are valuable to them. Managers may only be interested in trends rather than absolute numbers or percentages. When possible, try to define the metrics as the program's **Key Performance Indicators (KPIs)**. For example, a KPI may show the percentage of applications undergoing assessments per month.

Aside from KPIs, you will want to define **Key Risk Indicators (KRIs)**. KRIs are similar to KPIs in the sense that they are essential metrics. However, KPIs focus on the performance of processes, teams, and businesses. KRIs instead focus on the amount of risk associated with something.

EXAM TIP: You should use KRIs and KPIs to evaluate your risk management program.

A great KRI can be the percentage of accepted risks. If management sees a month-over-month rise in this KRI, they know the organization is broadening its risk appetite. Management can then evaluate if broadening the risk appetite aligns with their plans. Let us take a look at common KRI's in the cloud:

Key Risk Indicator
Percentage of cloud policy compliant devices
Number of global administrators
Cloud applications without owners
Number of external collaborators
Time to respond to incidents
Number of unauthorized access attempts

Table 8.4: Samples of key risk indicators in the cloud

The sample KRIs above provide valuable information to an organization operating in the cloud. For example, many global administrators indicate that the organization may not operate with the principle of least privilege. Which makes the organization susceptible to a variety of attacks. Similarly, a long time to respond to incidents may indicate that your organization may be unable to promptly limit the damage of an on-going attack.

REAL-LIFE TIP: When you create a metric, it should serve a specific goal. For example, a metric drives decision-making on a specific subject.

Vendor risk management

Earlier in this chapter, we discussed risk transference as a common risk treatment method in the cloud. Dealing with vendors or suppliers complicates risk management significantly. Your organization is responsible for managing risks associated with your vendors and suppliers. Whether these risks pertain to how a vendor operates their organization or the products you use does not matter. Whenever you select vendors, you must evaluate the vendor's security controls to see if they reduce risks to an acceptable level.

As part of this verification, you can ask your vendors to share risk management metrics and policies with your organization. You must work with vendors that look at risk in a similar manner as your organization. For example, if your organization has a very small risk appetite, it would be unwise to work with an organization with a very large risk appetite. After all, an organization with a large risk appetite is likely to take risks that are unacceptable to an organization with a small risk appetite.

The more vendors and suppliers you work with, the more complicated it becomes to watch all these parties. Nevertheless, you must do so. By setting up a third-party or vendor risk management program, your organization can do so in an organized fashion.

Such programs should seek to evaluate vendors and suppliers on a set schedule (at least yearly). When your organization changes its risk appetite, it is essential to re-evaluate if your vendors and suppliers are still a good fit.

Especially in the cloud, it can become challenging to gain insight into vendor risks. After all, you will use many different products with varying risk levels. The on-demand nature of cloud computing also invites to start using new products quickly. However, your organization should ensure that they review the risks associated with new services within your existing cloud environment before use. You must avoid the ease of on-demand becoming a risk to your organization.

Like enterprise risk management, you should evaluate your CSPs for varying risks. Ask yourself how secure their services are and their reputation, but also wonder about a CSP's financial stability and political context.

For example, if you are an American organization, you may want to avoid using a Russian or Chinese CSP due to political tensions between the US and these countries. It is essential to remember that risks surrounding vendors are complex and require diligent evaluation like risks within your organization.

Cloud vulnerabilities, threats, and attacks

While cloud computing has some advantageous features, it poses specific threats and creates new vulnerabilities. Broad access means that the attack surface of a cloud environment can quickly become more significant than in traditional environments. At the same time, on-demand provisioning allows the creation, modification, and deletion of new services in ways previously unimaginable. While this is great, it also poses risks for new attacks through which adversaries can create dangerous systems or infrastructure within your cloud in minutes.

Another facet to consider is that cloud infrastructure is maintained by a CSP and shared with other parties. Contrary to on-premises computing, you transfer many risks to the CSP whenever you use a cloud computing platform. Some organizations, very risk-averse ones, might not find this acceptable. After all, you must trust the CSP to handle your data and services properly.

For example, if a CSP does not have proper methods of disposing of storage devices, your organization's data may end up on the street.

While CSPs have very tight security, you should thoroughly evaluate all CSPs you work with. Many CSPs that offer SaaS build their platforms on top of cloud platforms. You may have to evaluate your direct partner and the vendors they use for their product.

The critical thing to understand is that cloud computing creates new risks by its very design. These risks must be evaluated and managed by your organization. Blindly trusting a CSP will put your organization in a precarious situation.

Roles in data handling

We just discussed that CSPs and other customers share infrastructure with your organization. However, when you use cloud services, you also share data. Sharing data means sharing responsibility. Understanding the different roles (and responsibilities) that come into play when sharing data is essential. Many laws and regulations may have requirements based on your and your partner's roles.

In general, we distinguish three different roles when it comes to data. The **data subject** is the person or entity whom the data is about. At the same time, the **data controller** (sometimes called the **data owner**) is the entity that determines why and how the subject's data will be used. A **data processor** (sometimes called **data custodian**) is the entity that stores, collects, transmits, and processes the data.

Your organization is the data controller when you solely use cloud computing in your environment. At the same time, the CSP is likely the data processor. In contrast, your customers (and employees) are data subjects. However, you may be a data processor and controller in a hybrid cloud environment. In multi-clouds, you will likely have multiple data controllers and processors. However, in traditional on-premises computing, you are almost always the controller and the processor.

As you can imagine, it can become complex to determine who holds responsibility for what in complex environments. Generally, we can state that the data controller is liable for ensuring data handling occurs in a compliant manner. Nevertheless, the data processor is responsible for ensuring that the processing takes place compliant. Whenever you decide to use cloud services, it is essential to define with your CSP who the controller and processor of what data is. More importantly, you must ensure that the CSP complies with all laws and regulations for your control data. After all, if you contract a CSP that is not compliant with laws and regulations that apply to your organization, you can incur hefty fines and reputational damage if something goes awry.

EXAM TIP: Data controllers are liable for compliant processing, while processors are responsible.

Common laws and regulations

So, what are some of these laws and regulations that you must consider when managing risks? Unfortunately, it entirely depends on the areas you operate in. Daily, new laws and regulations are formed around data protection and security. Whenever your organization investigates legal and regulatory requirements, it is highly advisable to consult specialized attorneys.

Most cloud service providers offer functionality within their cloud environment to ensure compliance. For example, in Azure you can configure initiatives. These initiatives contain policies that ensure your resources are audited against control requirements. An example of an initiative could be the ISO 27001 standard. By enabling such an initiative, all your resources can be audited for compliance, and new resources can be forced to comply with the policies that are part of the initiative. Most CSPs, offer such functionality to comply with common laws, regulations, and standards like GDPR, ISO 27001, NIST, and PCI-DSS.

However, for the sake of the CCSP exam, you must be familiar with a few laws and regulations that we will review as follows:

Breach notification laws

Many countries (and all US states) currently have breach notification laws. Such laws require the data controller and the data processor to disclose any breach of (customer) data. While processing or controlling data, you must have processes to ensure you comply with these laws. Many breach notification laws impose hefty fines on organizations that are found to have hidden data breaches. Sometimes, your CSP may be required to disclose a breach to your customers without your organization's interference. In those situations, it is important to have pre-established communication plans that allow you to notify customers quickly of a breach at a vendor. By doing so, your organization may be able to (somewhat) limit reputational damage from the breach.

Whenever you work with a CSP, you must establish processes with the CSP regarding how data breach notification will take place. These processes must also document and outline which laws apply to either party. Due to the quickly changing nature of data protection and privacy law, monitoring these developments in depth is highly advisable.

GDPR

The **General Data Protection Regulation (GDPR)** is the most well-known data protection regulation. The GDPR applies to residents of EU members, even outside the US. Your organization must evaluate if GDPR applies to (some) of your data. If it is, you must ensure your organization and your CSP comply with all GDPR provisions to avoid severe fines.

One interesting provision of the GDPR is *the right to be forgotten*, meaning that data subjects can request that the data owner remove all their data. Another provision is the Right *to be informed*. This right means that you must inform data subjects that you are collecting data about them. One of the main ways you see this provision play out is mandatory cookie banners before collecting data as cookies. Other provisions in GDPR restrict how data is processed, ensure data subjects can have their data rectified, and allow subjects to request all data stored about them.

An overview of the rights is shown:

The right to be informed
The right of access
The right to rectification
The right to object to processing
Rights in relation to automated decision-making
Right to be forgotten.
Right to data portability
Right to restrict processing.

Table 8.5: The eight rights imposed by the GDPR

As you can imagine, these GDPR rights profoundly impact the controls that must be implemented to be compliant. Data labeling, categorization, and retrieval/disposal processes must be in place to comply. As a CCSP, you should have a basic understanding of these provisions. However, consult a specialized attorney or data protection specialist whenever you deal with legal matters.

California Consumer Privacy Act

In 2018, California created the **California Consumer Privacy Act (CCPA)**. That act was the first US-based privacy act similar to the GDPR. While CCPA only applies to for-profit California businesses, it has laid an essential foundation for other states to build off. Currently, California, Virginia, Connecticut, Colorado, and Utah have comprehensive data privacy laws. However, many more states are expected to follow in their footsteps. Whenever you choose to do business or store your data in one of these states, you must ensure compliance with their laws.

Sarbanes-Oxley

SOX or **Sarbanes-Oxley** is a law passed in 2002 in the US. The law seeks to protect investors against accounting fraud. The law imposes requirements for financial auditing and reporting on US public corporations. Whenever you work with a CSP, it is crucial to establish if they are required to comply with SOX and if they are currently.

Other laws and the exam

Many countries have different laws surrounding data privacy and protection. Australia, China, India, Chile, and Canada are among the countries with their laws. However, it is essential to remember that the CCSP exam is US and EU-centric. During the exam, you are less likely to encounter questions about laws outside of the US and EU. Nevertheless, your organization may have to comply with some of these laws.

Conclusion

Throughout the chapter, you have learned that risk consists of a likelihood of occurrence and an impact on occurrence. Qualitative and quantitative classifications allow us to describe risks in an understandable way to management. Management teams must define risk appetite, a measure of acceptable risk to an organization. By conducting risk assessments, your organization can identify risks within and outside the organization. Because every organization is different, threat actors may vary significantly between organizations. This means your organization must properly evaluate its risk context.

Once risks are revealed through assessments, it is essential to continue managing them. Frameworks like the NIST RMF allow your organization to build a risk management program that continuously evaluates and monitors risks. Risk management allows your organization to take adequate risk treatment options. These options range from mitigation, transference, and acceptance to risk avoidance.

A vital part of effective risk management is communicating risk management results as metrics. Organizational leaders may not understand highly technical results but can interpret and make decisions based on clear and well-defined KPIs and KRIs.

While cloud computing brings us many opportunities, vendors' and suppliers' heavy involvement complicates risk management. Broad access and on-demand self-service create less prevalent risks in traditional on-premises environments. Therefore, it is essential to thoroughly evaluate if a vendor fits the organization's risk appetite.

Once you determine this, your organization and the CSP must establish data control and processing responsibilities. By defining roles and responsibilities, your organization and the CSP can ensure compliance with laws and regulations like GDPR, CCPA, breach notifications laws, and SOX.

The next chapter will examine security controls within a cloud environment. You will learn about different types of controls like IAM, system protection, and auditing.

Learning goals

This chapter addresses the following CCSP exam outline learning goals:

Domain 3: Cloud platform and infrastructure security

   3.3 Analyze risks associated with cloud infrastructure and platforms

Domain 6: Legal, risk, and compliance

   6.4 Understand the implications of cloud to enterprise risk management

Join our book's Discord space

Join the book's Discord Workspace for Latest updates, Offers, Tech happenings around the world, New Release and Sessions with the Authors:

https://discord.bpbonline.com

CHAPTER 9

Cloud Security Controls

Introduction

Throughout the book, we have looked at various security controls already. The controls ranged from security controls in DCs to encryption throughout your environment. In chapter nine, we will focus on system protection, IAM, and auditing in the cloud. You will learn that identity and access management are not only essential controls but also allow your organization to provide correct and necessary access efficiently. Also, you will be taken into the cloud auditing world and the specific challenges we face when collecting and correlating logs. Lastly, the chapter will help you understand physical and environmental controls as well as technical controls for systems, storage, and communications.

Structure

This chapter covers the following topics:

- Physical and environmental protection
- System, storage, and communication protection
- Identification, authentication, and authorization in cloud environments
- Audit mechanisms (log collection, correlation, and packet capture)

Objectives

This chapter will teach you about security controls specific to cloud environments. Throughout the chapter, you will gain an understanding of physical and environmental protections for the security of systems, storage, and communications. This chapter will explain how IAM works in cloud environments and what considerations are important. Lastly, the chapter explains how logging works in the cloud and how to analyze logs for security purposes.

Physical and environmental protection

Throughout the data center security chapter, we have looked at physical and environmental protections that should be in place. We covered various controls—biometric and regular locks, cameras, turnstiles, mantraps, bollards, fences, guards, and so on. To avoid repetition, you can reference *Chapter 7, Datacenter Security*, for more information about physical and environmental controls.

However, it is vital that you are aware of some physical controls that apply to offices. Many rules for physical access similarly apply to offices in DCs. However, offices and remote workers have some other requirements.

For example, laptops may need to be fitted with cable locks or privacy screens. Cable locks can prevent thieves from stealing the physical device, while privacy screens can reduce the risk of shoulder-surfing (looking over one's shoulder to see what is on their screen).

System, storage, and communication protection

If you started this book from the beginning, you know we have already examined various system, storage, and communication protection measures. The primary controls we have discussed are centered around encryption. However, more than merely data encryption is required in transit and at rest.

Cloud environments rely (mostly) on shared infrastructure. As we discussed, this opens your systems, storage, and communication to interference from other parties. These parties can be external attackers, CSP employees, and other CSP customers. While encryption ensures that these parties cannot simply read data from our disks or communication channels, we still need protection if systems are breached.

For example, if an external attacker can compromise a server in our cloud environment, they might be able to access data as an authenticated user on the server. In turn, the attacker can exfiltrate and encrypt the data from our cloud environment (ransomware attack). While encryption in transit at rest and in transit is excellent, it will likely not fully protect us from such an attack.

Similarly, implementing a WAF might protect us from malicious requests targeting an API, but what can we do if an attacker has gained access to a compromised SSH key that provides access to a jump box?

Well, there are many controls that we should implement on our systems to both detect and prevent such attacks from occurring. The challenge of the cloud is that a system may be comprised of solutions at different service levels. IaaS systems will generally require more controls on the cloud consumer side than SaaS tools. In any case, let us look at some of these controls at the system level.

Host-based intrusion detection and prevention

One useful security control to apply is host-based (HIDS/HIPS). In previous chapters, we discussed **network-based IDS/IPS (NIDS/NIPS)**. While NIDS/NIPS can detect and prevent intrusion at the network level and is thus less work to implement, it has some significant drawbacks. Our security controls cause the most crucial drawback. Traffic that is sent over a network should be encrypted. Unfortunately, this means that traffic intercepted by a NIDS/NIPS is also encrypted. Encryption significantly limits how a NIDS/NIPS can analyze the traffic.

It is possible to decrypt the data for analysis through NIDS/NIPS. However, because of the compute-heavy encryption and decryption, this can cause some serious performance issues. Aside from the fact that decryption and encryption at the NIDS/NIPS mean that keys must be shared across the network. Especially when many workers are remote (especially for cloud-based environments), you may need a corporate network to install any network security measures on. If you are building a zero-trust architecture, you should aim to secure your endpoints similarly, regardless of the underlying network. Hence, it is highly advisable to implement HIDS/HIPS instead of NIDS/NIPS, as the network-based tools only work when connected to that network.

Fortunately, HIDS/HIPS provides a solution. HIDS/HIPS is installed on a host machine. The machine could be a server, networking device, phone, or other endpoint. The HIDS/HIPS detects intrusions solely on the machine itself. However, because the detection takes place on the host, the contents of all traffic can be read. The drawback to HIDS/HIPS is that it requires managing the tool on all endpoint systems. Depending on the system, you might need different configurations, signatures, and so on. Aside from this, HIDS/HIPS can be a costly control to implement. Any form of intrusion detection requires extensive tuning and optimization to limit false positives and improve detections.

EXAM TIP: HIDS/HIPS is more effective than NIDS/NIPS but also requires more resources (time, money, and work)

Data loss prevention and proxying

Another interesting tool is data loss prevention tooling. DLP attempts to identify and prevent the exfiltration of specific data from a machine. An essential pre-requisite for this is defining the data the DLP tool must look for. Like an IDS, DLP tools can be installed at the network or the host level. Sometimes, DLP can even apply to a single service (like e-mail). However, remember that, like IDS/IPS, a DLP tool cannot make sense of encrypted data. Using host-based tools is usually your best solution.

As discussed earlier in this book, DLP searches for patterns in data using regex. For example, it can search e-mails or files for the occurrence of payment data or SSNs. Using regex means that DLP is not perfect. It might block data that should be allowed to share or miss formatted data so that DLP does not detect it.

For example, if your DLP looks for social security numbers in a format of 3 digits, a dash, two digits, a dash, and four digits, someone can share SSNs without detection by leaving out the dashes. Similarly, someone could use a **Caesar cipher** or stenography (hiding a message in an image) to deceive DLP tooling.

So, if DLP is so easily deceived, is it still worth it? The answer is that it depends. It could be very effective if your organization understands the data that traverses the organization and data-sharing channels are clear and monitored. However, it would be best if you never relied on DLP alone.

A more traditional approach to DLP could also be using forwarding proxies. These proxies are (virtual) network appliances that receive and re-route (external) network traffic. For example, a forward proxy can be installed so that all traffic to the internet goes through the proxy first. Once the traffic comes to the proxy, it can be blocked, flagged, or allowed.

Proxies are an effective way to limit traffic to specific IP address ranges or applications. For example, you could limit traffic to **docs.google.com** through a simple rule. However, proxies rely on regex testing and lists of abusive or poor reputation domains like other DLP tools. Attackers could easily register a new domain and use this domain as a reverse proxy for their malicious application. It is very unlikely that a forward proxy could detect this.

In any case, a proxy can be used as a DLP tool. Many host-based DLP tools have some forwarding proxy component. Remember, proxies are more effective when installed on a host, especially if the host is supposed to work on non-managed networks.

REAL-LIFE TIP: Network-based proxies are becoming ineffective when switching to remote work (without VPNs)

Host-based firewall

We have already examined various types of firewalls. Stateful firewalls can inspect packets and who sends and receives them. While stateless firewalls only inspect where boxes are going. Application firewalls or **nextgen firewalls** (**NGFWs**) can even understand what is sent inside the package.

These firewalls allow us to limit traffic to or from specific networks. However, they can also be installed on a host. While you might not know this, almost every computer you use daily has a host-based firewall. In the cloud, you can use security groups to quickly group different hosts and create firewall rules. However, in some cases, you may want to install a host-based firewall inside a container or virtual machine.

EXAM TIP: You must understand the difference between stateful, stateless, and NGFWs

Anti-virus

If you rely on the container or virtual machines, install anti-virus software for these systems. Anti-virus software searches a system for files (or behavior) that matches signatures. These signatures are hashes of known malicious files. The benefit of anti-virus software is that they are very good at detecting known viruses based on their signatures.

Unfortunately, many viruses can encrypt themselves to hide from anti-virus software. Nevertheless, anti-virus is an essential control to prevent breaches through known **viruses**. Depending on the system, your organization should consider subscribing to a service that provides daily updates to known signatures. That way, your anti-virus tooling will detect newer viruses as soon as signatures are available (the same applies to DLP, firewalls, and IDS/IPS).

Vulnerability scanning and secure configuration

Aside from scanning systems for viruses, we must also scan them for vulnerable software and configuration. While viruses are malicious software by nature, vulnerabilities are legitimate software that attackers can exploit to compromise your system all the same. Using vulnerability scanning, you can identify if your system uses previously found vulnerable software. Vulnerability scanners rely on vulnerability databases such as **Common Vulnerability and Exposures (CVE)** and can locate susceptible software versions. Remember that vulnerability scanners will not detect new and unknown vulnerabilities. These vulnerabilities are called **zero-day vulnerabilities**.

When you deploy systems in the cloud, you should check every part of your system for vulnerabilities. When you use VMs, you should scan the entire OS; if you use containers, you should check the container image; even if you use serverless systems, you must check the code for vulnerabilities.

Baselining and secure configuration

Aside from detecting vulnerable versions, we must also identify insecurely configured systems. For example, you may be using a secure version of an SSH server. Still, it might be vulnerable to many attacks if you do not apply the correct security configuration.

The primary control we must implement to prevent this is security control baselines. A baseline is a set of mandatory security configurations that should be applied across systems or groups of systems. These baselines ensure your software packages are configured to limit known vulnerabilities and attack surfaces.

As with many things in security, you should not start by developing your baselines. Instead, rely on trustworthy and tried baselines such as NIST **Security Technical Implementation Guides (STIGs)** and **Center for Internet Security (CIS)** benchmarks. STIGs are required for US government agencies and contractors, while CIS benchmarks are oriented toward a broader audience.

EXAM TIP: STIGs are required for the US government and contractors

STIGs and CIS benchmarks are a great place to start. However, security requires customization for your organization. By cherry-picking and tailoring, you can ensure you implement your organization's desired configurations. Cherry-picking means you only select the deemed helpful controls for your organization. Tailoring means that you adjust them as needed.

In any case, you should rely on baselining to secure your systems at every service level. For example, you should configure a SaaS service like **S3 (Simple Storage Solution)** following the well-architected framework and design inspector recommendation. Similarly, you should configure an Azure VM or container by the baseline most applicable to your organization.

An essential part of good baselining is testing them. You must ensure that the security configuration is in place when a system or service is created. However, you should monitor if it remains in place over time. That way, you can apply new baseline requirements as new insecure configurations are discovered while ensuring that work on your systems did not accidentally compromise your configuration. Please remember that any changes to baselines should be made through a (secure) change management process to ensure proper security.

EXAM TIP: Effective baselining requires tailoring and cherry-picking.

EXAM TIP: Baselines must be monitored and tested over time

Principle of least privilege

The principle of least privilege is one aspect of baselining that requires extra attention. We have covered this concept frequently in this book already. In baselining, the least privilege should be applied to how you run your systems. You must ensure that services within your systems, and your systems in general, function with the absolute minimum of privileges required.

For example, running a webserver like **Nginx** or **Apache** as a www user is better than the root user. That way, if an attacker can compromise the web server, they do not automatically gain root privileges on the underlying system. In the cloud, you should also review if your services have minimal communication privileges with other services. If you create a serverless code that must communicate with a database, ensure it can only read the tables it needs. However, if you run a full-fledged VM, you must also ensure it is properly isolated from other VMs in your vNet.

Whenever you compile baseline requirements, consider the privileges used within your systems.

Infrastructure as code and immutable systems

Using immutable systems is one way to ensure that secure baselines are in place. Immutable systems cannot be changed over time. Meaning their configuration and software remain consistent throughout the lifecycle. If a machine crashes or software must be updated, a new system is created, and the old one is shut down instead of changing the existing system. Using this approach, your organization can ensure that changes to a system are only made through authorized processes. Prohibiting ad-hoc changes within an existing system can significantly reduce the risk of accidental configuration drift (straying from your baseline).

One of the main ways to achieve immutable systems is by using IaC. IaC allows us to deploy entire systems as configuration quickly. These quick deployments will enable us to create a new system when an update is needed rather than making manual changes. However, remember that immutable systems also require locking the system down to prevent changes. An essential way to do this is not to allow direct administrative access to a system. In some cases, you can also use operating systems that do not allow changes to be made after deployment. That way, even if someone gains access to the system, you can prevent changes.

Once again, immutable systems do not prevent vulnerable systems. However, they can significantly reduce configuration drift. By doing so, your organization will control your systems and the software on them, which allows you to prevent common vulnerabilities of misconfigurations.

Mobile device management

Depending on your organization's work model, your employees may or may not work in an office. Regardless of their work origins, you may want to configure mobile devices with MDM tooling. MDM tooling implements some of the security controls above, like baselining, DLP, HIDS/HIPS, and anti-virus. However, MDM can also be used to gain remote-wipe and locator functionality. These functionalities allow your organization to disable stolen or lost devices without requiring physical access.

While MDM is not specific to cloud computing, many organizations that use cloud computing also allow remote work. Whenever employees take devices to and from the office, it is essential to implement MDM to prevent damage if a device is stolen or lost. Even when employees work at the office exclusively, using (limited) MDM functionalities is advisable.

Identity and access management

IAM controls are some of the most important controls you can implement in the cloud. Since cloud environments offer broad access and on-demand self-service, it is more vital than ever to provide (and deny) access properly. Malicious users can easily destroy entire cloud environments, rack up high costs, or even abuse your environment for nefarious purposes.

Earlier in this book, we already discussed decentralized versus decentralized identity management. You may remember that centralized identities are easier to manage. Centralizing identities can more easily prevent duplication and ensure data integrity.

In cloud environments, you can integrate with existing identity providers on-premises. Alternatively, you can use a fully managed cloud-based directory or a directory from another cloud provider. Whenever your organization evaluates its options, you must ensure that your chosen identity provider properly integrates with all your platforms. The main thing you want to avoid is using a directory for most of your applications but requiring separate identities for a variety of systems. Otherwise, you will end up with centralized and decentralized identities, negating the benefits of centralized identity management.

How you manage identities is essential. However, there are also security controls you must implement inside your identity tool/directory. You should ensure that identities are assigned to a single person. By doing so, you establish non-repudiation. Non-repudiation will be essential if an (inside) actor uses an account for malicious purposes. After all, if an account is shared between many employees, log files will not likely point you to the perpetrator.

Aside from assigning the correct privileges, you must also closely monitor the lifecycle of identities. Employees are likely to enter, leave, or change jobs. At any of these points, actions must be taken to grant, alter, or revoke privileges or add or remove identities. If your organization does not properly manage the identity lifecycle, your organization will be at risk of attackers exploiting credentials from former employees. Additionally, employees may accumulate too many privileges, allowing them to perform tasks that can endanger the organization and its data.

Thirdly, when we manage identities, we should assign privileges using the principle of least privilege. Any user account should only have minimal rights to perform a job. In general, there are a couple of different models to achieve this:

Role-based access control

One of the most common ways to assign privileges is through **Role-based access control (RBAC)**. RBAC defines privileges based on the role a user has. For example, the admin role may create, update, and delete data. At the same time, the role of a recruiter may only be allowed to create and update data. Often, these roles are matched to employees' job roles. However, roles can also be more generalist. Sometimes, employees may need to be assigned multiple roles.

For example, an employee in a DevOps team may need the role of software developer and system administrator. Remember to limit access to the absolute minimum regardless of how you define roles.

REAL-LIFE TIP: Refrain from using the root account for a cloud environment for management. The root account should be a last resort to access the environment.

Attribute-based access control

Attribute-based access control works differently than RBAC. Instead of determining privileges based on someone's role, they are determined on known attributes. For example, an attribute may be the office location you are assigned to. That office location could then be used to ensure your badge only has access to that location. Similarly, an attribute could be your level in an organization, the country you work from, or your department.

As you can imagine, ABAC has more granularity than RBAC. For example, if you have software engineers in different countries, they would likely all have the role of a software engineer. However, when using ABAC, you can further restrict the privileges based on the country the developer is in.

It is essential to realize that multiple access control paradigms simultaneously can confuse. Similarly, using extremely complicated rule sets for access may make managing privileges easier and lead to conflicts. For example, suppose you use RBAC to give your developers access to all test systems, but an ABAC control is in place to only allow access during the day. In that case, developers may need clarification as to why they do not have access at night.

Regardless of your chosen approach, ensure it fits your organization's needs. Also, be aware that your organization can evolve from one model to the next. Many organizations start with basic RBAC and build out to an ABAC system as demands evolve.

EXAM TIP: Most CSPs provide RBAC and ABAC

Discretionary access control

DAC is an access control principle that allows someone who has access to provide access to others at the level. For example, if you can read data yourself, you can provide others access to that data as well. DAC is commonly used within filesystems. While you will encounter DAC within your cloud environment (if you use filesystems), it is rarely used for access to the cloud environment.

Mandatory access control

Another less common access control paradigm is MAC. MAC is used frequently within government agencies. MAC relies on clearance levels. For example, if your data is classified as highly confidential, access should only be provided to those cleared at that level. MAC is rigid and rarely applied within cloud environments.

Access controls

Now that you understand that there are different ways to assign privileges (and they should be assigned sparsely), we must look at other access controls you must implement in the cloud.

Two-factor authentication/ multi-factor authentication

One of the most important (and effective) access controls in the cloud is the usage of **two-factor authentication (TFA)** or even **multi-factor authentication (MFA)**. Throughout this book, we have covered this concept several times already. However, it is essential to reiterate the importance. As you know, cloud environments offer broad access. In many cases, anybody with an internet connection and correct credentials can access your organization's cloud environment. If malicious actors can access your cloud environment, they could cause significant harm to business continuity and substantial financial damages.

By enforcing TFA/MFA, you can ensure that disclosure of credentials such as private keys, username/password, or service tokens cannot directly result in access to the cloud environment. Instead, the attacker would require access to the additional factor as well. Because the attackers usually do not have the exposed credential holder's phone, token, or e-mail, the chances of successful attacks diminish significantly.

REAL-LIFE TIP: ALWAYS implement MFA for identities that access management functionalities of your cloud environment.

Separation of duties

One of our concerns is collusion. Within a cloud environment, malicious actors could abuse their access to perform nefarious actions. For example, if a developer has access to write code and deploy it to production (without safeguards), a developer could knowingly (or unknowingly) disrupt an application or even launch malicious code. One of the most important controls to implement to prevent this is the separation of duties. SoD is tightly related to the principle of least privilege. It seeks to ensure that a single person cannot perform critical tasks.

In the example above, you should ensure that your developer has the privilege to write code and submit it for review and release. However, another entity should be required to review the code and clear it for release. By doing so, you can ensure that a single actor cannot disrupt critical systems alone.

Two-person control

Aside from SoD, you may also want to implement two-person control. You may have seen this principle in war movies before. Think of a nuclear installation requiring two officers to turn their launch keys simultaneously to fire a missile. You can implement similar controls in your cloud environment. For example, when you create many new instances, requiring two parties to consent to the launch can be helpful. Similar to SoD, this prevents a single actor from being able to take damaging actions within your cloud environment. However, SoD can be performed by two actors with the same role. For example, two-person control may require two developers to review a software release before launch. At the same time, SoD would require a software engineer and perhaps a system administrator to perform separate tasks rather than the same task.

Passphrases and passwords

Aside from implementing MFA, it is wise to implement policies and controls that enforce strong passphrases (or passwords). Earlier in this book, we discussed how quantum computing poses a threat to breaking current-day encryption algorithms. However, a similar threat looms for passphrases and passwords. Many tools exist to enumerate passwords based on password lists that can even be targeted at a single person or company.

The main tools to fight these enumeration attacks are MFA and strong passphrases and passwords. Contrary to what many believe, length is the essential factor to strength for passphrases and passwords. By requiring long passwords or passphrases, the time required to enumerate passwords increases exponentially (with every required letter).

Requiring special characters and numbers increases password strength. However, a 10-character letters-only password is more secure than an 8-character password with special characters and numbers.

At the time of writing, it is highly advisable to require passwords/passphrases that are 14 characters or longer. Please note that passphrases and passwords are used interchangeably. The difference between a password and a passphrase is simply that a passphrase consists of a phrase that is easy to remember but hard to enumerate. Passwords, historically, discouraged the usage of known words (due to enumeration). It is important to note that the NIST has advised the usage of passphrases over passwords to improve the user experience while allowing for higher length requirements.

Lockouts

Another critical factor in preventing enumeration is lockouts. Account lockouts are a mechanism that blocks the account for a pre-determined amount of time after a pre-set amount of authentication failures occurs. Account lockouts impact users, as the legitimate user will also be locked out. However, they are incredibly successful in stopping enumeration attacks significantly when lockout durations increase after successive account lockouts.

Rotation and invalidation

We cannot always prevent credentials from leaking. Because of this, it may be helpful to implement controls that enforce credential rotation and invalidation. Automatic rotation is a mechanism that changes credentials automatically after a pre-defined period. If you use the native credential or secret management tooling, you likely will have this capability at your disposal. The powerful part is that these tools rotate your credentials throughout your pipeline.

For example, they can rotate the token used to access a database but, at the same time, update the token used by the service that calls the databases. That way, your organization only experiences downtime or extra work due to credential rotation. However, it does benefit from the reduced risk of abuse of exposed credentials.

It is important to note that at the time of writing, the NIST no longer recommends forced rotation of passwords. Over time, it has been shown that frequent password rotation leads to password reuse, or a slight variation of passwords, and diminishes password security.

However, tokens, keys, and certificates used to gain access to your cloud environment (or within the cloud) must still be rotated regularly, and old credentials must be invalidated after rotation.

Session lifespan

A common way in which attackers gain access to cloud environments is by abusing existing sessions. In some cases, attackers may be able to steal session information (session hijacking). While session hijacking is usually fairly complicated, it may be as simple as gaining access to an unlocked computer and using a user's already authenticated session.

Regardless of the attacker's approach, you can limit the risk of session hijacking by ensuring sessions are not excessively long. For example, if your employees work only 8 hours daily, you may want to invalidate sessions after 8 hours. After all, your employees are unlikely to work more than those 8 hours, negating the need for longer sessions. By reducing the session length from (for example) 1 month to 8 hours, you can significantly reduce the effectiveness and consequences of session hijacking attacks. After all, attackers have less time to steal existing sessions, and if they succeed, they have less time to abuse them.

In general, you should limit your session lifespan to a minimum. However, remember that your users will likely become annoyed if they have to re-authenticate frequently. Try to find a balance between user frustration and security.

Out-of-band management and emergency credentials

One control that needs to be addressed is out-of-band access or emergency credentials. Both of these measures are important when your well-designed system has failed. For example, how do you access your cloud environment if your identity provider is unreachable, but all your identities are stored there?

In those situations, you may want to have emergency credentials at hand. Such credentials are often tied to an admin-level account not associated with any user. The credentials should be tied to an identity registered in the cloud-native identity tool (not in your directory). Instead of using this account for daily activities, it sits dormant. The credentials should be stored in a safe and can be accessed in the case of a disaster in which you cannot gain access to the cloud environment. Your organization may elect to make the root user of the cloud the emergency credentials.

In another situation, your organization may lose access to your cloud environment. For example, because the internet connection fails. If your organization is at risk of such events, you may want to consider out-of-band management for your cloud environment. OOB is common in on-premises computing. OOB networks can provide administrator access to the physical device (or even virtual management interface) in case remote management is no longer possible.

However, you are unlikely to have direct access to a physical device in a cloud environment. This means OOB management is more complicated. However, if your main way to communicate with the cloud is the internet, consider establishing a direct connection to the CSP. You can still reach your cloud environment through such a direct connection, even if your internet connection is disrupted.

Most of the time, it is more practical to implement backup solutions for your connection to the internet, such as **software defined wide area networking (SDWAN)** or even mobile hotspot solutions. Nevertheless, in some use cases, you may need alternative methods to connect to the internet (and thus the cloud), making OOB management over a direct connection the only alternative.

REAL-LIFE TIP: OOB through direct connections is costly. Unless you require such a connection for functionality, consider backups for your internet connection.

Mutual certificate authentication

The last control we must discuss in the authentication realm is mutual certificate authentication. Throughout the book, you have encountered this term. **Mutual certificate authentication (MCA)** is a way for a device to prove its identity to service and vice-versa. You can add another layer of security by implementing MCA as a requirement to access your cloud environment. MCA allows you to verify if a device contains a known, signed, and valid certificate. The certificate can be used to assume the connecting device's identity reasonably. That way, you can ensure that an authenticated user can only connect from a company-managed device.

Unfortunately, many organizations overlook this control. They require strong passphrases and even MFA. However, these controls still allow an authorized user to access the cloud environment from a non-managed device. This could allow the user to exfiltrate data from the cloud to the unmanaged device. Because the organization does not manage the device, there will be no controls to stop data from leaking after it has reached the unmanaged device. Such data leakage can have disastrous consequences for your organization.

REAL-LIFE TIP: MCA is vital to ensure that only managed devices access your Cloud environment.

Audit mechanisms

We have discussed various system and IAM-based controls that should be implemented in a cloud environment. However, more than merely implementing controls and hoping they work is required. We must audit control effectiveness to ensure our controls do what they are designed to do. However, we must also monitor for new or existing problems that still need to be addressed. In the next section, we will explore some controls that must be implemented to audit the cloud environment, its usage, and its users.

Logging

Logging is the most fundamental control we must implement to ensure we can evaluate control effectiveness and anticipate new threats and attacks. The practice of logging means that we record actions and their actors within the environment. Logging should occur in many places (especially within the cloud). Monitoring should be in place for access to your environment, for actions performed on the management side, for actions within your systems, for traffic on your network, for the usage of your applications, and so on.

Generally, the more places you gather log data, the more complete picture of your environment you can form. However, when you gather this data, it is essential to pay attention to the following:

Firstly, you must ensure that logs cannot be tampered with. If you create logs on an employee's computer, you do not want them to alter these logs. After all, you may need these logs to show why an employee's computer was compromised. If the attacker can expunge the logs, you may be unable to identify what happened. To achieve this, we must do two things. Logs must be immutable (ergo, they must not be editable or removable), and logs should be stored centrally. By logging into an external system, you can ensure that the logs cannot be lost if the device is destroyed or access to it is lost.

Secondly, you should ensure that logs are, as much as possible, written in a standard format. As we discussed, logs can originate from many different systems built by different vendors. Frequently, these logs follow a different format. Having log files in various formats makes them more challenging to interpret. Tools exist to transform log formats from vendors to standard log formats such as **Syslog**. The tools that can perform the actions are often called **log aggregators**, as they may also transport logs from individual devices to a central logging system.

Another thing you must consider is what data you log. Most of the time, you should log who did what and when—unfortunately, the what may contain data that should not be stored in log files such as PII. You must attempt to remove or anonymize such data from log files. Doing so will make it easier to comply with local laws and regulations while reducing the amount of security controls needed to protect log data.

In cloud environments, you will often find many native logging platforms. CSPs will offer logging throughout their different service-level offerings. For example, you can install a logging agent on virtual machines that log to a central log repository in the cloud. However, you are also likely to be able to collect logs from databases, authentication platforms, and (administrative) APIs. The extensive logging options in the cloud allow organizations to gather staggering amounts of data quickly without much effort.

Monitoring

Logging itself is crucial, however, more than logging alone is needed. Monitoring is where logging becomes meaningful. We can identify attacks and measure control effectiveness by inspecting log files and searching for (malicious/odd) behavior and known patterns. Most cloud platforms offer extensive platforms to perform monitoring. They offer automated alerting tools that notify (alerting) your organization of default or custom detections. In most cases, CSPs have even built their monitoring systems so that you can automatically tie actions to specific detections.

For example, if you detect a high amount of CPU usage of a VM, monitoring could allow you to adjust the CPU capacity or launch new VMs automatically.

As you may have noticed from the example above, monitoring should occur on far more than just security. Your organization must ensure monitoring is in place to support business continuity. You may want to measure the usage of systems to prevent poor customer experience or to reduce costs. At the same time, monitoring can provide you with valuable information about your application's marketability or your website's exposure.

Frankly, the options for monitoring are nearly limitless. Unfortunately, this also creates a downside. Gathering too many (unimportant) logs can limit the organization's ability to focus on the data that matters. You must consider if you need all the data you log, and if not, that you stop unimportant data.

Security incident and event monitoring

While logging and monitoring are much broader than security, it has become more and more relevant in security. Many CSPs have acknowledged this and offered **security incident and event monitoring (SIEM)** capabilities. A SIEM aims to identify security events and determine if they are negative. A SIEM's power lies in its ability to correlate log data from different sources and perform a large-scale analysis. Security events are related to security actions, such as (failed) logins, virus scans, and so on. At the same time, security incidents are security events with an adverse effect, for example, a login with stolen credentials.

For example, SIEM might look at network access logs, authentication logs from a device, and logs from the mail server to determine whether someone has accessed an employee computer from China to exfiltrate data using an e-mail.

SIEM is not an all-knowing being, like IDS/IPS systems, SIEMs are trained to recognize signatures and analyze behavior. However, to analyze behavior, the system must be trained to understand the baseline behavior in your organization.

For example, an SIEM might mark a login as suspicious if it occurs after normal working hours. However, it must first be fed enough log data to understand the normal working hours.

Similar to **machine learning (ML)** or **artificial intelligence (AI)** applications, SIEMs have to be trained (or pre-configured) on behavior and rule sets (many CSPs use ML and AI in their offerings).

It is essential to consider a couple of things before implementing a SIEM within your organization. Firstly, you should consider if you have the knowledge and capacity to build, train, and maintain the system. Analyzing security events and incidents is complicated. These tasks should be delegated to everyone. If your organization decides to implement a SIEM, you must ensure you have well-trained and capable personnel.

Secondly, you should consider how you implement SIEM. Many vendors offer SIEM solutions. Some can be implemented within the cloud; others work on-premises only, and some can simultaneously analyze log data from many different cloud platforms. There is a cost aspect to this. Most SIEMs are costly, but some are free. Sometimes, your CSP might offer a SIEM integrated into your cloud environment (for example, **Microsoft Sentinel**). SIEMs provided by CSPs can utilize data from many customers to train and may have superior detection capabilities and integration with your environment. Conversely, a CSP-provided SIEM might only be able to analyze that specific cloud environment.

Security operations center

We just covered that you need the right personnel to manage a SIEM. Many organizations elect to build or hire a **security operations center (SOC)** (as a Service). A SOC is a team that is trained in analyzing security events and incident data and, often, can perform incident response and forensics. Due to the nature of their job, a SOC is usually a 24/7 team that operates continuously. Depending on your organization's size, their operation might be done using shifts or on-call rosters.

Once again, a SOC requires specialized personnel. Many small organizations do not have the knowledge and skills to create their own SOC. However, some large organizations may want to avoid creating their own SOC. Luckily, many providers offer **SOC as a service (SOCaas)**, sometimes called **Security as a Service**. These companies have specialized personnel that analyze your log data either in your own SIEM or pull your log data into their SIEM. They will then analyze security events and incidents, alert your organization, or even take steps to thwart an attack.

SOC as a Service is always costly. However, there may be other viable solutions for some organizations. In general, using SOCaaS has some profound benefits. After all, a service provider specialized in SOC deals with many different customers and experiences a variety of attacks. That knowledge and training can help them more effectively identify and stop threats to your organization. An organization with an internal SOC may have far less exposure to events and incidents, which can lead to reduced effectiveness.

EXAM TIP: The CCSP exam does not consider SOCaaS more effective than an internal SOC.

Regardless of your organization's model for a SOC, it would be best to be wary of alert fatigue. The concept of alert fatigue means that your organization receives many alerts based on broad detections (or poor training of the SIEM). Many of the alerts in these cases are false positives. Due to that, team members may become overwhelmed and miss legitimate incidents. Alternatively, legitimate security incidents may be ignored as analysts incorrectly identify them as false positives. If your organization wants a successful SOC, you must ensure proper training of your personnel and SIEM and minimize the altering of false positives.

Security orchestration, automation, and response

Once you establish or contract a capable SOC, you can explore the SOAR domain. As the name suggests, SOAR seeks to automate security tasks and responsibilities, which means that SOAR can perform tasks independently. By doing so, you can ensure that response to security incidents is significantly faster and more scalable.

For example, SOAR can be used to automatically isolate endpoints that are identified to have been infected with ransomware. Instead of requiring a SOC analyst to perform actions to isolate the device manually, SOAR can do this instantly and automatically. Doing so can reduce the chances the ransomware has to spread.

SOAR is extremely broad and can be applied in many ways. Some SOCs may use serverless code to perform actions. Others may trigger shell scripts on servers or even use cloud-native APIs. Many platforms even offer standardized SOAR capabilities by default. While

SOAR is complicated, it can significantly reduce the workload of SOCs while drastically improving its capability to respond to incidents.

Job rotation and mandatory vacations

While not technical controls, job rotation, and mandatory vacations can play a valuable role in your organization. Mandatory vacations can force employees with significant privileges or sensitive job functions to take vacation time. During this vacation time, they can be replaced by another employee. The replacing employee can then vet the work performed by the employee on vacation. Through this mechanism, your organization can monitor for fraud and prevent collusion.

Similarly, job rotations can be used to ensure a position is not held too long by a single person. After all, extended access to a position could also allow fraud to occur. By rotating a job, you can ensure that the work is vetted by a different employee after the rotation.

Conclusion

Throughout this chapter, we reviewed many controls that should be implemented in a secure cloud environment. From system-based controls, such as baselining, anti-virus, and HIDS/HIPS, to access control measures, such as an MFA and account lockout, every control plays a vital role in establishing a layered defense. However, more than implementing controls alone is required. We must log and monitor to anticipate new threats, identify incidents, and measure control effectiveness. SIEMs, SOCs, and SOAR can play an essential role in quickly analyzing security events across the organization and acting on them promptly. Strengthen by administrative controls such as job rotation and mandatory vacations, your organization will have a defense-in-depth approach to cloud security.

In the next chapter, you will learn about the vital practices of business continuity and disaster recovery. You will gain insight into how they are used and what challenges and opportunities the cloud presents to them.

Learning goals

This chapter addresses the following CCSP exam outline learning goals:

Domain 3: Cloud platform and infrastructure security

       3.4 Planning and implementation of security controls

CHAPTER 10

Business Continuity and Disaster Recovery

Introduction

For an organization to be effective, it must be able to run its critical processes. An organization's capability to do so is called **business continuity** (**BC**). The BC of an organization can be threatened in many ways: natural disasters, cyberattacks, broken equipment, and so on. By creating a strategy for dealing with business continuity disruption and **disaster recovery** (**DR**), your organization can more quickly re-establish BC and limit the damages of a disruptive event. This chapter will review the essential components of these strategies and how business requirements fuel them. We will also look at the process of creating, implementing, and testing BC and DR plans. These plans will allow your organization to translate strategy into clear, effective actions.

Structure

This chapter covers the following topics:

- Business continuity and disaster recovery strategy

- Business requirements (RTO, RPO, and recovery service levels)

- Testing of BC/DR plans

Objectives

This chapter will teach you the essential elements of BC and DR strategy. This chapter will help you understand how RTO, RPO, and recovery service levels are primary inputs for these strategies. Throughout the chapter, you will build an understanding of common approaches and controls required for BC/DR. Lastly, the chapter will teach you how you can effectively create BC/DR plans, implement and test them.

Business continuity and disaster recovery strategy

Every organization has unique requirements when it comes to BC and DR. Some organizations may perform critical tasks that could lead to a significant impact on safety. Other organizations may experience financial impact from impacted business continuity. Like data classification policies and strategies, your organization must develop a plan for dealing with business continuity disruptions. One possible way for BC to be disrupted is through disasters. Disasters can range from natural disasters like earthquakes to cyberattacks. Because disasters usually impact business continuity, developing a strategy for dealing with disasters is essential.

The challenge of the BC/DR strategy is that the scope is vast. If you sit down and think, you can come up with many scenarios that disrupt your business continuity. Some events can be as simple as key figures in your organization being out on sick leave. Whenever your organization starts working on BC/DR strategy, it is essential to establish some key factors first.

First, your organization should develop a policy considering any regulatory and legal requirements about BC/DR. For example, your organization may be required to maintain a BC/DR plan and test it annually. Your organization needs to gain insight into those requirements and establish a policy to ensure your organization can become compliant.

Secondly, your organization must conduct a **business impact analysis (BIA)**. As we covered previously in this book, a BIA will help your organization identify critical business processes and assets. A BIA will also reveal the impact of these processes' disruption or the assets' unavailability.

Once your organization understands what processes and assets are critical to the organization and what impact they cause, you must examine your organization's business requirements. Earlier in this book, we already talked about **recovery time objective (RTO)**, **recovery point objective (RPO)**, and **maximum tolerable downtime (MTD)**. Your organization will have to consider these values when building a strategy for BC/DR. The RTO, RPO, and MTD will also determine how many resources you will dedicate to BC/DR and which processes and assets need the highest priority in case of a disruption or disaster.

Based on your business requirements, you can start compiling a set of preventive controls. These controls will help your organization prevent disruptions from impacting the organization. Preventing impact does not always mean that you can avoid the event or disaster from occurring. However, you can take measures to reduce or negate the effect. One typical example of this is redundancy. By creating your cloud environment across different data centers (and replicating data), you can ensure that the destruction of a single data center only partially disrupts your organization. Similarly, you can make data backups and store them in multiple locations to prevent total loss. As with any control, it is essential that you not only identify and implement them. You must also test and evaluate them. Controls may become ineffective, insufficient, or redundant over time. By testing regularly, you can reduce costs while ensuring effectiveness.

Once you have implemented preventive controls, it is essential to establish various contingency strategies. It would be best if you created plans for different situations that can cause BC to be disrupted (including disasters). For every scenario, you must identify roles and responsibilities, steps toward recovery, and a strategy for testing the plan. By anticipating these scenarios before the occurrence, you can ensure your organization is prepared and stays calm during a BC disruption.

After creating different plans for various scenarios, it is essential to test your plans. For example, if you replicate a cloud environment across regions, can you effectively switch from one region to another? Aside from the feasibility of the plan itself, you must also train your personnel to understand the plans and be able to execute them. An essential part of this is conducting BC/DR exercises that allow your organization to practice the execution of the plan.

After you have trained personnel and executed exercises to test the plans, you must review the plans. Review sessions with various stakeholders and participants will allow you to improve your plans, evaluate effectiveness, and ensure plans are updated accordingly.

Whenever your organization devices a BC/DR strategy, you will want to have the following end products:

- General policy describing the organization's approach for BC/DR, including any legal and regulatory requirements. The policy should include provisions for creating, evaluating, and testing plans. It is helpful to reference the RTO, RPO, and MTD established by the organization.

- Specific BC/DR plans outline various scenarios that could disrupt BC. The plans must include roles and responsibilities and a step-by-step procedure to follow during a disruptive event or disaster.

- Test plans and training exercises for BC/DR plans. As we discussed, you must test and evaluate your plans to ensure they are effective.

NIST 800-34: Information system contingency planning process

Defining a BC/DR strategy is a challenging task. Your organization will have to consider many different scenarios and controls. Luckily, the NIST has released the contingency planning guide for Federal Information Systems (NIST SP 800-34)[1]. The SP 800-34 provides a seven-step process for contingency planning. The seven steps outlined below provide clear guidance on how your organization can work on creating a BC/DR strategy. However, remember that your strategy will be unique to your organization. SP 800-34 is not a useable plan or policy but rather a guide for your organization to create your own. Let us take a look at the seven steps of contingency planning:

Develop contingency planning policy
Conduct business impact analysis
Identify preventive controls
Create contingency strategies
Develop contingency plan
Plan testing, training, and exercises
Plan maintenance

Table 10.1: Seven steps of contingency planning in NIST SP 800-34

EXAM TIP: On the CCSP exam, the first thing an organization should do, is conduct a BIA.

Business requirements

Now that you understand the high-level process of determining BC/DR strategy, we must zoom in on business requirements. Business requirements are essential to an effective BC/DR strategy, as discussed. After all, the core business of an organization is its value. IT and security fulfill a supporting role in ensuring these requirements can be met. Contrary to what some believe, IT and security should not provide the requirements or capabilities for BC/DR. Instead, business stakeholders must investigate and understand what their needs are.

For example, if a business has an MTD of 2 hours, IT and security should provide solutions to ensure this MTD is not reached. Often, you see organizations where IT and security require a pre-defined set of controls. However, if your RPO is one month, it is non-sensical to perform back-ups every hour. After all, the business does not require an RPO of one hour. Your organization will likely waste valuable resources by uniformly forcing IT and security standards within a BC/DR context.

---

[1] *https://csrc.nist.gov/publications/detail/sp/800-34/rev-1/final*

As an IT or security professional, you should focus on helping the business understand the impact of outages and explain the effort and costs associated with (preventive) controls. For example, many business stakeholders say they require 99.999% up-time. That uptime percentage means only 5 minutes and 13 seconds of downtime is tolerable in a year. The costs of maintaining a 99.999% environment can be significant. As an IT or security professional, you should work with your business stakeholders to determine if the requirements are accurate and the costs are justified. Many business stakeholders need to fully realize that having 99.999% uptime may cost additional hundreds of thousands of dollars, while a 99.9% availability may also be justifiable based on the MTD.

RTO, RPO, and recovery service levels

As outlined above, your organization must accurately determine the RTO, RPO, and MTD. Underestimating an MTD can lead to highly inflated costs while overestimating an MTD can lead to the organization ceasing to exist. It is vital that your organization uses these values honestly to support its recovery service levels. Service with an MTD of 2 weeks does not require 99.999% availability, probably not even 99.9%.

Controls

Let us dive into what business requirements can mean for controls. Many disasters or disruptive events are centered around data or systems becoming (temporarily) unavailable. Therefore, some of the most common controls in BC/DR are based on the redundancy of systems and data.

Backups

One beneficial control is backups. Backups can be applied in multiple contexts. For example, you may want to use backup generators to ensure a power failure does not cause a disruption. However, backups can also pertain to specific data sets that must be secured from destruction.

While backups do not prevent disasters or disruptive events, they greatly aid recovery. For example, if an organization has backups of endpoints, data could more easily be restored after a successful ransomware attack on these endpoints. Similarly, storing backups outside of the data center (or in the cloud in another AZ or region) can ensure that the physical destruction of a data center does not destroy the data.

For the CCSP exam, you must be familiar with some common backup strategies applied to data backups. Firstly, you can use full backups. These backups store all the data in a specific scope. Full backups require the same amount of storage as the data (when not compressed); they are easy to restore but are relatively slow.

You can also use incremental backups. An incremental backup only includes files that have changed since the last backup. Incremental backups require much less space and are significantly faster than full backups but are more challenging to restore. After all, you would have to restore the last full backup and every incremental backup after this to restore the data to its latest state.

The last type of backup is called differential backup. A differential backup includes only the changes made to data since the last full backup. The benefit is that differential backup can be quickly restored as you only need to apply the last differential backup after restoring the last full backup. However, if files change frequently, differential backups may become very large.

EXAM TIP: Differential backups are faster than incremental and full backups

In practice, you will see that backup strategies are often used in conjunction. An organization may make a full monthly backup, differential backup every week, and incremental backups daily. It is essential that you devise a backup approach based on your RPO. After all, you do not want to waste money and time on creating unnecessary backups or put the organization in danger by making too few backups.

Regardless of your backup strategy, your organization must test the process of restoring backups. Many organizations have made the mistake of creating backups and realizing during disaster recovery that they could not restore backups. Similarly, you should conduct anti-malware, encryption, and integrity scanning (using hashes) to ensure secure backups.

EXAM TIP: You should encrypt backups

Redundancy/ fail-over

Backups are a great way to limit damage after a disruptive event. However, we also have some controls that can prevent an event from causing a disruption. Broadly put, these controls rely on creating redundancies at various levels. Redundancy means a process, system, or data is available in multiple ways to ensure continuity.

For example, you may achieve redundancy at a system level by creating two virtual machines to run the same application. If one VM fails, the other one can take over. Of course, redundancy comes with some challenges. You may have to replicate data or services between systems, databases, availability zones, or regions. By creating redundancies, you can ensure continuous availability for a single application or even your whole environment. When talking about redundancy, we generally use the following terms:

Hot site

A hot site is a live environment fully redundant and ready to activate once an outage occurs. A hot site may be a physical data center that is racked and stacked with equipment and is regularly updated with the most recent data from the live environment. Hot sites are expensive but can allow immediate fail-over to negate downtime completely. In the cloud, a hot site may be a duplicated environment in another availability zone or even region.

Warm site

Contrary to a hot site, a warm site may be pre-wired and may have some limited equipment to perform fail-over. However, a warm site is still being prepared for immediate fail-over. Instead, additional work, such as copying data, installing additional hardware, and performing configuration, may be needed. In the Cloud, a warm site may be a pre-configured vNet, and pre-configured systems and services that can be spun up (automatically) when needed. The benefit of this approach is that you do not have costs for running your warm site when your primary environment is still operational. However, warm sites can take days to a couple of weeks to activate, especially in on-premises environments. In the Cloud, creating a warm site with minimal costs is easy.

Cold site

A cold site is the least expensive redundancy measure. A cold site is usually an area where a fail-over environment can be set up. An on-premises cold site may need to have hardware installed. Instead, it may be a pre-wired empty rack or data center where your systems are not operational. A cold site approach is cheap but takes significant time to get operational. In the cloud, a cold site could be an open cloud environment in another AZ or region or at another CSP. Cold sites are primarily an option for on-premises data centers, as the costs may be so significant that an organization cannot buy double the hardware to ensure redundancy. However, if your organization operates in the cloud, using a friendly site offers quicker fail-over with little to no added costs.

Mutual agreements

If your organization uses on-premises computing but does not have the money to create a cold, warm, or hot site, you could consider a mutual agreement with another organization. Such an agreement can be struck with an organization with similar (security) requirements. Instead of each creating your own hot, warm, or cold site, you create a shared environment. The environment can then be used by the party that requires it. Of course, sharing infrastructure or physical locations creates significant risks and will only work if the organizations can share the functionality of the backup site. With the advent of cloud computing, mutual agreements will likely become less valuable.

On-premises and cloud

If your organization uses on-premises computing, you might not need to create a physical hot, warm, or cold site. Instead, you may be able to develop a fail-over environment in the cloud. In many cases, your operational costs to do this may be lower as you would not be required to purchase hardware. However, remember that you are still likely to have to pay for licenses for any appliance you want to virtualize.

Succession planning

A commonly overlooked control in BC/DR is succession planning. For example, what do you do if your CEO is unreachable, dies, or is incapacitated during a disaster? Your organization will likely need more time to consider appointing an interim CEO if the disaster also affects its business continuity. Your organization should make a succession plan for critical figures to avoid such situations. Creating such a plan lets you inform parties ahead of time that they must step in in case a key figure can no longer fulfill their duties. While some may consider this practice morbid, it is precisely for this reason that military units have a second (or third) in command. You must be prepared to act quickly in high-stress and high-impact situations like a disaster or business continuity disruption.

REAL-LIFE TIP: Succession planning is often overlooked

Testing of BC/DR plans

We reviewed some controls you may want to use to prevent business continuity disruption or limit the damage. However, controls themselves are only part of the equation. Building solid and well-thought-out contingency plans is another essential puzzle piece.

Actors

As stated previously, a contingency plan should identify all the actors. These actors will include your BC/DR team during a disruptive event. Such a team usually consists of an incident coordinator, technical specialist, legal specialist, and communication professional.

The incident coordinator pulls the team together and initiates the plan. Based on the defined parameters, they may also declare an incident a disaster (which may trigger a DR plan in specific). The legal specialist is part of the team to evaluate how and if to approach the situation from a legal perspective. Based on the event, your organization may be required to inform local law enforcement, and contact emergency services or other government agencies.

The communications professional will ensure that the communications are conducted in a pre-defined manner. Your organization may or may not want to give public statements. These statements need to be well-prepared. In some cases, disclosing too much, too little, or the wrong information can be detrimental when fighting an incident or disaster.

The technical specialist in the team will conduct recovery operations as defined in the plan. These operations could include building a new environment in a cold site, restoring backups, conducting forensics, and so on.

Testing

It is essential to determine who is on the BC/DR team and ensure you have all the skills needed to remediate the situation. You must also test the effectiveness and correctness of the plan; by pulling your team together and evaluating the plan, you can establish if your plan will be feasible in an incident or disaster. At the same time, you can also identify shortcomings or room for improvement in the plan. While ensuring everybody fully understands the tasks at hand.

Walkthrough

One easy way to perform testing of a BC/DR plan is by performing a walkthrough exercise. During a walkthrough, the team reviews the document for correctness. In many cases, a walkthrough exercise identifies many shortcomings and possible improvements without significant time investments and impact on the organization. Walkthroughs may even be performed individually.

Table-top

Table-top exercises take the walkthrough a step further. Instead of reviewing the document, you evaluate the plan by discussing the steps as if the incident were occurring. By doing so, everybody becomes more aware of their tasks, and you can identify shortcomings in the step-by-step plan. For a tabletop exercise to work out, you should pull your BC/DR team together physically or virtually. Doing so makes tabletop testing more involved than walkthroughs.

Failover/parallel tests

Failover or parallel tests seek to execute a plan. During a failover test, you perform the actions to switch to your hot site. During a failover test, you can establish if the plan works. Failover tests are often called parallel tests because they may not involve disruption of normal business activities. These tests can usually be conducted in parallel with the regular processing environment. For many organizations, parallel or failover tests are the perfect medium as they do not require disruption of operations but evaluate a plan's technical effectiveness.

Simulation tests

A simulation test is the most involved method to test a BC/DR plan. During a simulation test, all the steps of the plan are executed. One typical example of simulation tests is fire drills. All the actions that are supposed to be performed are executed during such tests. Simulation tests allow you to evaluate your plan and disrupt business activities thoroughly.

For example, your customers may experience downtime while you switch your operations to another DC. In general, you should ensure consensus across the business before conducting simulation tests. You want to prevent, at all costs, that your tests turn into a disruptive event or disaster.

EXAM TIP: The CCSP exam will ask which test type is most applicable. Beware that there is often a cost or organizational impact component included in the question. For example, they may ask which type of test is the cheapest to conduct.

Conclusion

Throughout the chapter, we have discussed the most critical steps (based on NIST 800-34) for creating a BC/DR strategy. By conducting a BIA, your organization can identify critical processes and assets to its business continuity. With business requirements and legal or regulator requirements, your organization will be able to define a strategy that suits its needs.

Standard controls like succession planning, backups, and redundancy are essential in preventing adverse effects from incidents and disasters. By using different backup and redundancy strategies, such as full, incremental, or differential backups and warm, hot, or cold sites, your organization can limit the damage of adverse events or even prevent damage altogether.

Regardless of your organization's controls, BC/DR plans must be created for different scenarios. The plans must identify the BC/DR team, and the plans must be evaluated frequently. Through walkthroughs, table-top exercises, parallel/failover, and simulation tests, your organization can ensure you are ready to fight incidents and disasters when they occur.

In the next chapter, we will learn secure development, awareness and training.

Learning goals

This chapter addresses the following CCSP exam outline learning goals:

Domain 3: Cloud platform and infrastructure security

     3.5 Plan **business continuity (BC)** and **disaster recovery (DR)**

CHAPTER 11

Secure Development, Awareness, and Training

Introduction

The cloud offers new perspectives and tools for security. However, developing insecurely is more dangerous in the cloud than on-premise. This chapter explores common pitfalls, cloud-based vulnerabilities, and development tactics to ensure the software is produced securely within or outside the cloud.

Structure

This chapter covers the following topics:

- Development methodologies
- Secure software development life cycle
- Secure coding
- Threat modeling
- Open Web Application Security Project top 10
- SANS Top-25
- Common security pitfalls
- Security awareness and training

Objectives

This chapter aims to improve your knowledge of secure development (in the cloud). Secure development is essential to the overall security of an organization. After all, insecure software can cause trouble, even when its underlying infrastructure is protected. This chapter will explore development processes and how security can be intertwined. The chapter will review practices like secure coding and threat modeling. We will also examine common application security issues covered in the OWASP top 10 and SANS top 25. At the tail end of the chapter, we will examine common pitfalls and how security awareness and training are essential to prevent them.

Development methodologies

Secure development is an absolute must now. Creating insecure software will lead to vulnerabilities that are exploitable for attackers. We must include security throughout the entire development process from the start. However, to understand how we can embed security, we must first examine how software is developed in the first place. Following, we will look at a standard development methodology that you will encounter.

EXAM TIP: This chapter does not cover the iterative, v-model, and spiral models as they rarely appear on the exam.

Waterfall

The first methodology we must cover is called the **waterfall approach**. This method of software development has been around for many decades. Waterfalling is a very reliable process. It dictates that software is developed in a linear structure. Meaning software requirements must first be gathered. The designs must be created and validated. After the design is made, software development can begin. Once the software is developed, it will be subjected to testing. Only at the time that the software works as designed will the software be released.

Sequentially going through the development steps and only realizing a product, when thoroughly tested and validated against the requirements, has a significant benefit. Waterfalling creates reliable and predictable software. Unfortunately, waterfalling also has a major downside. Because the process is sequential, the next phase can start once the previous one has been completed. That fact can make a waterfall project very time-consuming. You may spend months working on requirements gathering and designs before a single line of code is ever written.

In today's IT landscape, waterfalling may be too slow for an organization. After all, many organizations are releasing new IT products every day. If you want to beat your competitors to market, you cannot spend months or even years on development without a marketable product. That said, you will commonly see waterfalls used in governmental or scientific settings. In these environments, precision and accuracy may weigh higher than time to market.

Agile

In 2001, a group of forward thinkers wrote the **Agile Manifesto**[1]. This Manifesto outlined principles to allow for better ways to develop software. Up until then, waterfall development was the most common approach. However, the Agile Manifesto dictates a rigorously different approach. The Agile approach consists of twelve principles that, in summary, say, let us develop software in a way that allows us to adjust to changing customer demands. While simultaneously limiting the time it takes to get to market while not compromising on quality.

Over the past two decades, many organizations have switched to Agile development, As customer requirements change faster than ever. Common approaches to Agile that you may have heard of are **Kanban** and **Scrum**. In Scrum, you work with teams that commit to completing a pre-defined amount of work over a set (and recurring) limited period called **sprints**. Typically, you keep the work included in a sprint. In Kanban, a team pulls work from a backlog, and once it is finished, they pull new tasks from the backlog. If the priority changes of tasks change, Kanban allows you to pivot straightaway.

Regardless of the specific approach, Agile development works differently than waterfall. In most cases, requirements are quickly gathered, little design work is performed, and instead, the first lines of code are written rapidly. The customer reviews the written code very shortly after functionality is requested. The developer then gathers the feedback from the customer and adjusts the code if needed.

Once the customer has tested and approved the code, it is released to production. Instead of realizing software in large batches with tons of functionality, most Agile approaches attempt to independently remove functionalities, patches, or bug fixes. You might release code to production daily in an Agile development environment. In contrast, you could do one release in a waterfall environment over a much-extended period.

> **EXAM TIP: The CCSP exam does not expect you to know how Agile is implemented in detail. So, you do not have to understand how Scrum or Kanban works.**

Rapid application development

One Agile approach that you must be aware of for the exam is **rapid application development (RAD)**. In RAD, developers build prototypes rather than complex designs. Prototypes allow customers to evaluate if the prototype satisfies their provided requirements quickly. The benefit of this approach is that it may be easier for customers to evaluate a prototype than an (abstract) design document.

---

[1] *https://www.agilealliance.org/agile101/12-principles-behind-the-agile-manifesto/*

REAL-LIFE TIP: Agile is not better than waterfall, per se. Instead, both are suitable for different situations.

DevOps

One of the more recent development methodologies is called **DevOps**. DevOps is an approach where software developers, system administrators, and infrastructure team members combine their skills in a single team. Most DevOps teams work using an Agile methodology, as DevOps' main goal is to enable single teams to release new software and infrastructure quickly. Combining multiple disciplines and responsibilities in one team allows a single team to deliver end-to-end projects without creating additional dependencies on other teams.

DevSecOps

A common variation of DevOps is DevSecOps. In DevSecOps teams, security professionals are also embedded within the team. A significant advantage of this approach is that security professionals can ensure security is in scope from the beginning. Many organizations create functional requirements and develop code before taking the project to their security team. In practice, this can result in significant rework or even complete abandonment of projects. By embedding security at the initial stages of the project, you can capture security requirements and constraints at the project's inception.

EXAM TIP: For the CCSP exam, you must understand the different methodologies and their benefits and drawbacks.

Secure software development life cycle

While you can take many different approaches to software development, Agile and waterfall require the same fundamental steps refer to the following figure, even though they are performed differently. In this section, we will examine these steps and zoom in on the security aspects of these steps:

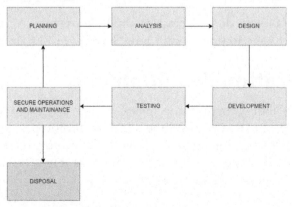

Figure 11.1: *The secure software development lifecycle*

EXAM TIP: You will see the secure software development life cycle (SSDLC) and SDLC acronyms used throughout the exam. SSDLC and SDLC are the same things in this context.

Planning

The first step of the lifecycle is planning. During the planning phase, you will do the following:

1. Determine the scope of the project.

2. Gather functional requirements.

3. Gather security requirements.

4. Gather applicable policies, standards, and guidelines.

5. Gather legal and regulatory requirements and restrictions.

Once you have completed these steps, you will have a comprehensive list of your project's requirements. You will notice that this phase is far more intensive in a waterfall project than in an Agile project. However, regardless of the approach, it is essential to gather these requirements. In Agile teams, this may be a story comprising of tickets or a full-on requirements document in waterfall projects.

Feasibility or requirements analysis

During the feasibility or requirements phase of the SDLC you must ensure the project is do-able. Some of the steps you must complete are:

1. Determining requirements based on the data collected during the planning phase.

2. Evaluating the project's feasibility (technology, personnel, and finances).

While this step may seem silly, it is very important to perform it. Many projects fail because the requirements of a project are not realistic. For example, if you have a need that your application must work without a network connection, but another condition is that all requests are centrally processed in real-time, you may have requirements that clash with each other. Alternatively, requirements may grossly exceed the organization's (technical or financial) capabilities.

Identifying such issues early on is of vital importance to project success. Especially where security is concerned. You may notice that you identify customer requirements that clash with security policies. For example, a customer may want a user to be able to log in without a password, while your corporate policy requires that identities are verified.

It is important to understand some of the common ways in which feasibility, or requirements analysis can be conducted. Helpful tools are a **strengths, weaknesses, opportunities, and**

threats (SWOT) analysis. By categorizing aspects of a project based on these properties, you will quickly see if the project is likely to succeed.

Another example that could help is a **PESTLE**-analysis. This analysis looks at the political, economical, social, technical, legal, and environmental influences on a project or organization. By doing so, you can more easily identify requirements or factors that may greatly hinder your project.

Aside from a SWOT or PESTLE analysis, you may also want to look at the **Project Management Body of Knowledge (PMBOK)**. The PMBOK contains valuable tools for feasibility analysis.

You must communicate such issues to the customers and within the development team. Try to avoid compromising on security because of functional requirements. However, at the same time, ensure that security is possible while still achieving the customer's needs. If you identify potential conflicts or challenges early, you have a better chance of finding a secure and acceptable solution early on.

Designing

During the design phase, you must translate the requirements into a solution. During this phase, you may create architecture diagrams and documents, but depending on your methodology, your design could also be a prototype RAD. The most important thing to keep in mind during this phase is that you must satisfy the requirements in a secure manner that is maintainable in the future. During this phase, you will do the following:

1. Determine system boundaries and dependencies.

2. Make decisions on technologies (cloud or on-premises, low code or not, and so on.).

3. Determine application integrations (logging, monitoring, authentication, and so on.).

4. Create test plans

5. Create logging and monitoring plans

The design phase also plays an essential role in the threat modeling process, which we will cover later in this chapter.

Development

During the development phase, your organization will start building the application. Depending on the chosen approach, this could include building (cloud) infrastructure. Ensuring the development phase includes safeguards and best practices to facilitate secure development is essential. We will review these items later in the chapter.

Testing

The testing phase will include validation and verification of the requirements set for in the planning, analysis, and design phases. Validation is confirming that the requirements meet the customer's needs. At the same time, verification means confirming the software functions according to the requirements.

For example, a customer may have set the requirements for the application to support 1000 concurrent users. During validation, you evaluate if this requirement is still correct. The customer's need may have changed throughout the process. During verification, you would test if the application can support 1000 users.

EXAM TIP: You must understand the difference between validation and verification.

Your organization may incorporate testing after development has finished, but most of the time, testing is conducted throughout the development of an application. Following you see a list of test types your organization may perform as part of the testing phase:

- Unit testing

- Integration testing

- End-to-end (E2) testing

- Regression testing

- Vulnerability and configuration scanning

- Penetration testing

- Functional testing

- Performance testing

Unit tests are designed to test small functionalities within a software package. A unit tests a single function in a piece of software. The benefit of unit testing is that you can ensure a function works correctly without interacting with other pieces of code. Thus, unit testing allows you to identify the origin of errors quickly. The drawback to unit testing is also its scope. Because the tests should be created only to test that functionality, you cannot determine if the code works well with other functions. Let us look at an example code below:

```
1. function applyDiscount (initialAmount: number, discountPercentage:
   number): number {
2.     let discountedAmount = initialAmount * ((100 - discountPercentage)
   / 100);
3.     return discountedAmount;
4. }
```

```
5.
6.  if (applyDiscount(100, 20) === 80) {
7.      console.log('test passed');
8.  } else {
9.      console.log('test failed');
10. }
```

As you can see in the example above, a unit test can be as simple as calling a function with pre-determined values and determining if the code returns the expected result. The unit test above can verify if the code executes exactly as intended. However, as mentioned before, it does not test integration with other functions. Let us look at what this means:

```
1.  function checkout(amount: number, couponCode: string): number {
2.      let discountPercentage = 0;
3.
4.      if (couponCode === '20OFF') {
5.          discountPercentage = 0.20;
6.      }
7.
8.      return applyDiscount(100, discountPercentage);
9.  }
10. // function to apply the discount to the original price
11. function applyDiscount (initialAmount: number, discountPercentage: number): number {
12.     let discountedAmount = initialAmount * ((100 - discountPercentage) / 100);
13.     return discountedAmount;
14. }
15. // run a test to determine if applying an incorrect code fails
16. if (applyDiscount(100, 20) === 80) {
17.     console.log('test passed');
18. } else {
19.     console.log('test failed');
20. }
21. // run a test to determine if applying a coupon works
22. if (checkout(100, '20OFF') === 80) {
```

```
23.        console.log('test passed');
24. } else {
25.        console.log('test failed');
26. }
```

In the example above, the **applyDiscount** function is called by the **checkout** function. The checkout function determines the **discountPercentage** passed to the **applyDiscount** function. However, the **applyDiscount** function expects the percentage to be formatted between 0 and 100. The **checkout** function instead provides the **discountPercentage** as a number between 0 and 1. The result is that the unit test for the **applyDiscount** function works fine, but the test for **checkout** fails.

As you can see in the previous example, unit tests alone are not enough. **Integration tests** can be used to see how your software interacts with other software, systems, or other code. Imagine the checkout function is not just another piece of code but a software program that calls an API to apply the discount. In that case, you must ensure the software and API return the correct value together.

E2E testing expands on the principle of integration tests. In E2E testing, you may test a large chain of applications and actions. For example, an E2E test might verify if an action passes correctly through a front-end application, a back-end application, and the database. As you might have noticed, testing becomes more complex as you increase the scope. It is normal to start with unit testing and expand testing as you go along. In many cases, unit testing occurs as a part of the development process before testing.

Regression testing is a form of testing that seeks to establish if changes do not compromise existing functionality. Especially in Agile development, many changes may be released in a matter of days or even hours. Sometimes, changes can have unwanted side effects on other code. Regression testing is, in essence, a form of E2E testing executed to establish if the unchanged functionality still functions as expected.

Vulnerability scanning has been covered throughout the book several times. In software development, vulnerability scanning can detect the usage of insecure dependencies and software packages. Similarly, it may be used to detect known vulnerabilities in the infrastructure used for the application. Vulnerability scanning should be conducted before release. However, vulnerability scanning must be continuous as new vulnerabilities arise daily. You will notice that vulnerability scanning is also part of the next section, secure operations.

Penetration testing is a special form of security testing during which hackers attempt to breach the application's security. Penetration testing is generally conducted in three different forms. white box, gray box, or black box. Let us examine some of the differences:

Test Type	Documentation available to hackers	Authorized access available to hackers	Security team aware of the test
Black box	No	No	Usually not
Gray box	Partially	No or partially	Limited awareness
White box	Full	Full	Aware of the test

Table 11.1: Forms of penetration testing

As you can see in the table above, the main difference between the test types is who knows about the test being conducted and what access and knowledge hackers have. Black box testing is more like what external attackers would have to do, while white box testing is bound to reveal more vulnerabilities. It is important to note that there is no official definition for what a black, gray, or white box test can or cannot contain. Some white-box tests may exclude specific access or documentation, and so on.

EXAM TIP: You must understand the difference between black box, gray box, and white box testing

Performance testing can be included as part of every other form of testing. This form of testing is used to establish if performance requirements can be met. For example, a performance test may test how much traffic a website can handle or how long a transaction takes to complete. Performance testing is extremely important as it ensures that specific business requirements are satisfied. **Stress testing** is a common form of performance testing used in penetration testing. Stress tests determine which amounts of traffic can be handled until DoS occurs.

Aside from testing the technical facets of an application, you must also test its functional requirements. Functional tests are generally conducted by testers (or stakeholders). These tests usually consist of conducting actions the application users may conduct. For example, an insurance company may conduct functional tests to ensure the user can easily find where to register a policy and determine if they can purchase it as expected. **Functional testing** allows for **edge-case testing** as well. Edge cases are situations that differ from the predicted situation. For example, the author of this book has a last name with spaces in it. Many IT systems in the United States cannot process such names as they do not expect spaces in last names. Functional testing can quickly reveal such shortcomings.

All in all, it is essential to realize that the testing phase consists of various forms of testing that should be used in conjunction with each other. Testing is an essential step to validation and verifying that all requirements (including security requirements) are satisfied.

EXAM TIP: You must be aware of all mentioned test types for the CCSP exam.

Once it has been established that the requirements have been met, the software can be released through a secure deployment process. Such a process should include written approval from a **Change Advisory Board (CAB)** or similar function. We call such approvals release management. A CAB verifies if the correct steps have been conducted for a release to occur. This verification is essential to ensure the software can be released safely.

For example, a CAB may check if a software release interferes with another pending software release. If that is the case, software releases may have to be postponed. A CAB also ensures that software can only be released with the proper authorization. An organization generally does not want software engineers to release software at their will. Instead, management must consent to the release as they are accountable if something goes south.

EXAM TIP: Release management is essential to secure development, especially in organizations that frequently release new software.

Secure operations and maintenance

Once an application is released to production, our work does not stop. An application in production must be monitored and maintained. Maintenance may include bug fixes, configuration updates, credential rotation, and so on. Monitoring should consist of functional logs, performance logs, security events, and vulnerability scanning. New vulnerabilities are, unfortunately, discovered every day. While your application may not have had vulnerabilities at the time of release, this could change over its lifecycle.

Security incidents are another factor to consider during the security operations and maintenance phase. Your organization must ensure you can monitor security events and respond to security incidents. Your application's logs must be available to your **security incident and response team (SIRT)** or **security operations center (SOC)**. You may also have to define parameters for events that constitute an event, such as abnormal behavior, and so on.

Disposal

The last phase of the life cycle is the disposal phase. An application, infrastructure, and data may be decommissioned during disposal. In some cases, data must be archived (to comply with legal requirements); in other situations, it may be deleted or even transferred to another system. In the disposal phase, all disposal actions must be conducted securely. For example, if the data associated with an application must be deleted, you must ensure that deletion is performed securely. In a cloud environment, you may have to employ cryptographic erasure, or if your company has physical devices, destruction or erasure of devices may be necessary.

EXAM TIP: The SDLC phases in this book are based on the CCSLP certification. The CCSP exam may combine some of these phases as the industry has no singular standard.

Secure software development framework

The SDLC is a very extensive process. Every step contains various activities that must be executed consistently and effectively. Depending on your development approach, some steps may be sequential, or they may occur at the same time. For example, you may design, develop, and test simultaneously in an Agile environment. Regardless, it is vital to remember that every development methodology needs to include every step.

REAL-LIFE TIP: Working Agile does not mean you can skip requirements gathering, documentation, design, or testing. If your organization does, you are unlikely to have implemented the Agile methodology correctly.

Luckily, as with many things in IT, the NIST has created the **secure software development framework** (SSDF) (NIST SP800-218[2]. The framework outlines four practice groups:

- Prepare the organization
- Protect the software
- Produce well-secured software
- Respond to vulnerabilities

Every practice group consists of pre-defined tasks that your organization can incorporate within its SDLC. While this document is not covered as part of the exam, it is extremely useful, and reviewing the paper will help you further understand security within the SDLC.

EXAM TIP: The SSDF is not part of the CCSP exam but reviewing it will help you understand the security practices that must be part of the SDLC.

Secure coding and development

Now that we have covered the overall software development life cycle let us continue diving into secure coding and development practices. You will notice that security requires a lot of extra steps to be taken during the lifecycle. If you have reviewed the SSDF, you should already know these practices well.

Shift-left

The first term we must cover is shift-left security. Shift-left security is not a development or coding practice. Instead, it is a term to indicate that security is covered from the beginning of the lifecycle instead of only at the end. An organization that practices shift-left security implements the processes we will cover below throughout its SDLC instead of only minding security once a product has been created. Shift-left has a significant benefit in

---

[2] *https://csrc.nist.gov/publications/detail/sp/800-218/final*

that it is cheaper than bolt-on security. Bolt-on security means that security controls are applied after a product is finished. In practice, that means security measures are poorly integrated and often become very expensive as they may require extensive changes to the application to function correctly.

EXAM TIP: Shift-left security is what we strive for, and bolt-on security is what we try to avoid.

Requirements gathering

The first and likely most skipped step is security requirements gathering. As we discussed earlier in the book, security requirements should be put forth by the business. For example, if the company wants to process highly confidential data, the security requirements for that classification are automatically included. Aside from security requirements based on customers' needs, your organization may have policies, standards, laws, and regulations it must abide by. You must document and incorporate these requirements in your design from the start.

Gathering security requirements is not always easy. There are many factors to consider. For example, you should interview your stakeholders for specific requirements for the CIA of their application. Similarly, you should evaluate which requirements are imposed by local laws and regulations. At the same time, there may be an overarching architecture program that has requirements as well. It is vital that you create a structured approach to gather security requirements from all areas that may influence them.

You need to gather all the security requirements early on to avoid delays, extensive costs, and even a failed project. For example, imagine building a microservice application with 20 different APIs. If your organization requires you to implement a centralized identity provider, but you need to complete this requirement, you may end up with 20 other identity stores. If you must rectify this when your CAB reviews your release, you are guaranteed to exceed your project timeline and budget.

Design

Like the requirements gathering, you must include security requirements in your designs. For example, if your customer wants to store highly confidential data, and your organization requires encryption in transit and at rest, the system must be designed to support this. You must build your design based on technology capable of encryption. Depending on the requirements, you may decide to use a PaaS database solution over an on-premises database solution because the PaaS solution offers native encryption.

Similarly, you must include other facets of security in your design. For example, how does your application integrate with other applications, how is application data logged, and where is it stored?

The design phase also offers vast opportunities to include security controls to help the application throughout its lifecycle. You may elect to use pre-hardened VM images, making it easier for your developers to deploy new secure machines. The design phase allows you to proactively tackle many security issues and help your development team build secure applications more quickly.

Threat modeling

A critical aspect of security is called **threat modeling**. Threat modeling is a process of identifying potential threats to your system. During threat modeling, you identify who might want to attack your application, how likely they are to do so, how they may do so, and what the damage could be if they did. Threat modeling allows you to proactively identify appropriate controls while spending a budget on realistic controls.

For example, a government agency is more likely to be targeted by APTs than the candy store mentioned earlier in the book. So, if the candy store is unlikely to be targeted by APTs, must it implement the same controls as the government agency? The answer is no. Security must be proportional. We must take measures against credible threats to use valuable resources wisely. Threat modeling helps us understand what we should and should not protect against.

In the past decades, security professionals have developed various methods for threat modeling. In the section below, we will review some commonly used techniques.

STRIDE

One of the most used approaches is called **STRIDE**. STRIDE stands for:

- Spoofing
- Tampering
- Repudiation
- Information disclosure
- Denial of Service
- Elevation of privilege

The approach to STRIDE is to identify threats to your application using the attack type. As you can see, the method has six different attack approaches to consider. When you use this approach, you examine your application and identify the possible ways an attacker can achieve every attack type. Doing so lets you determine which controls you may need to implement to prevent these attacks from being successful.

For example, if you are threat modeling a car with STRIDE, an attacker could achieve a spoofing attack by faking the signature of the owner's key fob. An attacker could tamper with the vehicle by deflating the tire. Repudiation could be achieved by attaching a fake license plate. Similarly, hacking the onboard computer could cause information disclosure by providing the attacker access to driving data. At the same time, denial of service may be achieved by putting a wheel lock on the car. An elevation of privilege attack could be performed by attempting to hotwire the car's ignition.

The main appeal to STRIDE is that it can be applied to various actors. The STRIDE approach cares about the method of attack and not the type of actor. The benefit of this approach is that you are unlikely to overlook threats if you fail to identify a specific actor. At the same time, not considering the actor makes it more challenging to determine how likely an attack will succeed based on the actor's capabilities or how likely it is to occur.

For example, a government agency may be more likely to inject code into a car than small-time criminals.

REAL-LIFE TIP: Every threat modeling approach has benefits and drawbacks. Usually, it is helpful to use multiple approaches on a single application.

DREAD

Contrary to STRIDE, the **DREAD** approach focuses on the parameters of an attack. Let us look at the components of the acronym as follows:

- Damage
- Reproducibility
- Exploitability
- Affected users
- Discoverability

As you can see above, the DREAD approach seeks to answer questions about the threat. What damage would an attack cause, is it easy to reproduce the attack, can an attacker efficiently perform the attack, whom will it affect if the threat is realized, and how easy is it for attackers to figure out they can perform the attack? Every category is scored from 0-10, and the overall result creates a risk score.

You may have noticed that the DREAD approach is common to *regular* risk management because it determines impact and likelihood. However, many organizations have found that producing reliable ratings based on DEAD is complicated.

REAL-LIFE TIP: Adam Shostack (former Microsoft employee) has written many publications on threat modeling that cover the usability of different approaches.

ATASM

ATASM stands for **Architecture, Threats, Attack Surfaces, and Mitigations**. This method approaches threat modeling through technical architecture. ATASM dissects systems to identify threats and attack surfaces on an architectural level. The upside to this approach is that it is very in-depth. Architecture analysis lets you gain detailed information about threats and build mitigations more easily. However, the downside to ATASM is that it requires significant technical knowledge (of the application). At the same time, virtually anyone can perform STRIDE.

PASTA

PASTA stands for **Process of Attack Simulation and Threat Analysis**. The PASTA approach is relatively new and aims to incorporate business context within the threat modeling process. During a PASTA threat model, you will involve your developers, testers, and business stakeholders. Because the PASTA approach includes so many sources, you can build a well-defined context for the application.

For example, you may discover that the application is unavailable outside the corporate network by talking to the business. Instead, the application may only be accessible if you are authenticated on the local network. If you performed your threat model with STRIDE, you may have identified that the application lacks authentication. However, you may not have been aware of the context, that the authentication is performed at the network level.

The PASTA approach has seven steps, as shown:

- Define the objective.
- Define the technical scope.
- Decompose the application.
- Analyze threats.
- Analyze vulnerabilities.
- Analyze attacks.
- Rick and impact analysis.

As you can see above, the PASTA approach is more comprehensive than STRIDE. It looks at threats, vulnerabilities, and the actors and the technical details of the application.

EXAM TIP: For the CCSP exam, you do not need in-depth knowledge of the different approaches.

Threat intelligence

Regardless of the threat modeling approach most suitable for your organization, you must understand the threat landscape. Gathering intelligence will help you know threat actors affecting your sector, market, or geographic location. Subscribing to threat intelligence sources who can update you on new, emerging, and existing threats is essential. Many organizations provide (free) threat intelligence services. Depending on your organization's knowledge level and budget, your organization should enlist at least one, but preferably multiple sources. The more threat intelligence you gather, the more effective your threat modeling will be.

Code review

While threat modeling and threat intelligence can be applied at various levels throughout the organization, we also have to implement practices related to development itself. One of these practices is called **code review**.

Code review aims to improve the overall quality of code. It attempts to reduce (cyclic) complexity, prevent bugs, and avoid security mishaps such as hardcoded credentials and vulnerabilities. Generally, we can distinguish two types of code review, manual or automatic.

In a manual code review (sometimes called peer review), a developer (other than the creator of the code) looks at the code and checks it for correctness, complexity, and security. A significant challenge to manual code review is that organizations may write vast amounts of code. Manually reviewing all this code is time-consuming but also error-prone. You will likely miss mistakes if you review thousands of code lines. Similarly, the reviewer may need to be made aware of the context of the code. Hence, the reviewer may need help to spot functional shortcomings. Another essential factor to consider is skill. More issues will be identified if an experienced programmer reviews code than a less-skilled programmer. This is especially true for security issues. After all, only some people that programs understand secure coding.

Automatic code review uses computerized algorithms to vet code for issues. The benefit of this approach is that it is much faster than manual code review. Most of the time, automatic code review is also far more consistent in detecting shortcomings. However, like any algorithm, automatic code review can only detect based on rules. It is entirely context unaware. If your organization has limited or faulty rulesets for automatic code review, the tooling will cause more trouble than good.

Many organizations choose to implement manual code review and automatic code review. The benefit of that approach is combining the strengths of both review methodologies. You can introduce context awareness through a combined study while ensuring a quality baseline.

Code review is often a requirement before code is committed to releasing branches. We will cover versioning and deployment processes (and the role of code review in them) later in this chapter.

> **EXAM TIP:** Manual code review can introduce context awareness, but quality fluctuates based on the reviewer. Automatic code review is consistent but dependent on well-developed rule sets and unawareness of the context.

Linting

Reviewing code is essential, but it is also somewhat reactive. During software development, you want to prevent mistakes from being made in the first place. A valued tool for this is called **linting**. Linting is a broad term for making (enforceable) agreements on how code is written.

For example, linting may determine if function names are written in snake case (**LikeThis**) or camel case (**likeThat**).

Linting can be used to ensure that every developer's code formatting is the same. Not only does this make the code base more uniform, but it also makes it easier to create code review rules or spot poorly written code. Linting can be used to set requirements for items like cyclic complexity, thus preventing programmers from writing hard-to-read code (due to complexity).

Most modern IDEs allow you to import linting standards for different languages. By creating a linting definition for the languages in use in your organization, you can enforce standards across developers. Their IDEs will correct their mistakes or at least point them out.

Code testing

Earlier in this chapter, we talked about testing already. From unit tests to end-to-end testing, everyone is essential for security. Most of the time, tests are only designed to verify functionality. However, if you integrate security functions into your tests, you can ensure your application is more secure. For example, you may want to test your code's protection against code injection attacks. You should view your security requirements as testable, like your functional requirements.

For example, you can use fuzzing, a testing method that enumerates different input options, to detect broken content filtering or injection attacks. During a fuzzing test, the test attempts to enter many different values through user input to observe incorrect behavior.

Version control

Writing code rarely happens in a day or even by a single person. Version control is an essential tool to allow for collaboration without creating significant problems. Imagine if everyone was working on a single text file at the same time. One would overwrite the other's work and vice versa.

Some standard version control software is **Git** and **SVN**. If you have worked in the IT industry, you have likely worked with at least one. Both Git and SVN allow you to track file changes, create branches (different versions of software), and merge various software versions. These features will enable us to collaborate on code efficiently. You can see an example of version control through GitHub below. Note that the example shows when changes were made:

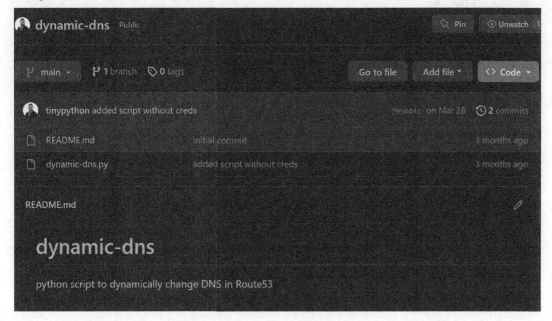

Figure 11.2: Sample GitHub repository

While the CCSP exam does not go deep into version control, it is essential to know that it should be used. Not only for collaboration but also to ensure the correct code versions can be deployed. Especially since version control allows you to perform code reviews more easily by highlighting code changes rather than requiring total check reviews all the time.

Commit signing

Earlier in the book, we discussed how encryption and signatures can prevent non-repudiation. If you encrypt an e-mail with your private key or add a signature, the recipient can decrypt the message or signature with your public key. Because the e-mail or signature was encrypted with the sender's private key, the recipient can verify the sender, as the sender is the only one who should have access to the private key.

A similar concept called **commit signing** should be applied to software. When you incorporate commit signing into your process, code written by developers is signed with the private key of that developer. By signing the commit, the other developers know which developer created the code. The massive benefit is that if an attacker can compromise credentials to the version control system, they cannot make signed commits. After all, getting access to the version control system does not give them access to the developer's private key. Depending on the configuration of your version control system, this could prevent attackers from making any changes to code or, at the very least, allow for the detection of potentially malicious code. Let us look at an example of a verified git commit:

Figure 11.3: Verified commit as listed by GitHub's documentation[3]

Commit signing is a simple yet very effective way to protect your code from malicious changes from outside attackers. However, remember that this control will not stop an inside attacker that can perform code signing.

Open-Source software and dependencies

Another essential factor to consider is the usage of open-source code. For years, experts have debated the security of open-source software. The main reason for this discussion is the software's nature. As the name suggests, open-source software's source code is public to others. Anybody can read the code and make changes depending on the license. Some have argued that public access to the code allows for better detection of security issues, while others state that it helps hackers find and exploit vulnerabilities. Traditionally, many organizations have used closed source code. Such code is proprietary and can only be viewed, used, or altered by the company that holds the copyright of the code.

Unfortunately, the truth about open-source security is not a simple matter of more or less security. Instead, it depends on how it is used. A community of developers often maintains open-source software. These developers may or may not be skilled programmers and may or may not have security knowledge. Depending on the software, your organization should consider whether it has enough community trust to vet the code for vulnerabilities. If your organization does not, it must implement processes to do so itself.

After all, using open-source does not excuse an organization from implementing sufficient security controls. The problem is that many open-source projects are freeware and can be used at no cost. Organizations consider freeware options as an economical way to build IT solutions. However, like any other software, open-source software still requires maintenance and secure development. Suppose your organization pursues the usage of open-source software, including software dependencies (for any language). In that case, it must establish processes to vet the security of the software and implement processes to build and implement security fixes when necessary.

---

[3]*https://docs.github.com/en/authentication/managing-commit-signature-verification/signing-commits*

REAL-LIFE TIP: If you use open-source freeware securely, it is rarely cheaper than closed-source software.

Software Bill of Materials

If your organization does choose to implement open-source software or other (paid) software dependencies, it is essential to maintain a **Software Bill of Materials (SBOM)**. SBOMs have gotten more attention in the past few years after a breach of **SolarWinds** caused organizations across the globe to experience breaches. Many organizations did not even know they had implemented the vulnerable software. Unfortunately, very few organizations document all the software they use within their environment, and even less so, the software they use as part of their own.

An SBOM is, simply put, a list of all the software you use within your organization (or within a system or application). Let us say you have a Node.js application; if you import packages through the **Node Package Manager (NPM)**, you should add these packages to your SBOM. This is because it makes it easy to determine if your software might be vulnerable through its dependencies.

Imagine you use a package like Angular (a front-end framework). Suppose a vulnerability is found in Angular, but you are unaware it is part of your software packages. In that case, you will unlikely take timely action against this new vulnerability. However, if you maintain an SBOM, you can subscribe to threat intelligence services for the software on your SBOM. That way, you will be proactively notified against breaches in your dependencies. Hence, significantly increasing the odds of preventing a breach through compromised dependencies.

Configuration and secrets

A commonly overlooked factor in securing development is the configuration of the application. Often, developers include configuration files within the code. Unfortunately, these configuration files often contain credentials to access other services like databases or APIs. By adding these secrets to the code, anybody with access to the repository can access these services with your application's credentials. Attackers that can access your version control software immediately also gain access to your (production) systems. Another factor to consider is that you may not want developers to have direct access to services, especially since authorized users could use these credentials as part of insider attacks.

So, how do you solve this issue? Software needs configuration to function. The solution lies in secrets management. We discussed how secrets management can be used to distribute secrets to cloud infrastructure. Secrets management can be used in the same way to inject secrets into the software build or deployment process. That way, the code does not need to contain the unknown in the configuration files. Instead, they are injected by your build or deploy tool. The benefit of this approach is that developers do not have to know the secrets, nor are they viewable through version control software.

Deployment, building, and CI/CD

We briefly touched on deployment in the previous sections. Deployments are the process of releasing software to an environment. Releasing software means it is distributed and configured to the system that will run the software. The system is made available for use after the software is in place.

In the past, deployment processes were often manual. A system administrator may have logged in to the version control software, copied the source code to a VM, configured the application on the VM, and updated the networking configuration as needed. However, nowadays, many companies work in Agile and use DevOps. Meaning deployments may occur multiple times daily and can be executed entirely by a single team. For this to be saleable, deployment tooling is needed. These tools automatically release software to a system, configure it, and make any necessary environmental changes. The benefit of this approach is that it is fast, consistent, and less error-prone.

The process of fully building and releasing code on-demand is called **continuous integration/continuous deployment (CI/CD)**. However, deploying software is only half of the puzzle. Most software must be compiled or built to be useable for deployment. CI/CD almost always consists of a pipeline that builds and deploys code. As the CCSP exam is not a software development certification, we will not investigate how this works. However, it is essential to know the following:

You must use secrets management to inject secrets in your build or deployment process rather than using hard-coded credentials. It is also wise to use a process called **code signing**. Code signing is very similar to commit signing. However, instead of only verifying who wrote the code, it is also used to verify that the code being deployed is the same code the developers wrote.

Code signing works by creating a hash of the software and signing the software with a certificate of the build server. By verifying the hash, the deployment software knows the software has not changed, and by verifying the signature, the deployment process knows that the code was built by the build process.

In short, CI/CD is a collection of tools and processes that allows the software to be built and released on demand. It consists of building and deploying software. For security, it is essential to inject secrets during the build process rather than storing them in the code. At the same time, code signing can be used to ensure that the deployed code was built by the build server and that the code was not altered between the building and deployment.

Separating environments

One essential element to secure development is using separate environments for different stages in the development process. Most development processes first release code to a test environment, then a staging environment that mimics the production environment and the production environment. They are in place to ensure the software functions correctly and are often used to conduct various forms of testing before release.

One commonly made a mistake is to allow communications between test, staging, and production environments. The danger behind this is that it can cause service disruptions if the software does not work correctly and can cause information disclosure or even destruction.

For example, your test environment may provide access to all developers in the organization. Developers can access databases, view and edit data, and so on, directly. However, if allowed, an application in the test environment access the production database, the developer may be able to access the databases and view and edit data on production. Through that access, a developer can steal information, modify systems, and cause significant harm to the organization. Similarly, your test environment may have fewer security controls in place (as it should not use accurate production data), which makes a test environment an excellent place for attackers. If an attacker can gain access to a test environment and consequently connect to production services, the damage from a breach can increase significantly.

In short, your organization must ensure separate environments to perform testing that does not affect production. Each environment must be entirely separated from the others, and access to each environment should be restricted to the absolute minimum. Ideally, only CI/CD tooling (and select administrators) should have access to your production environment.

Monitoring and logging

An essential part of secure development is monitoring and logging. The development process, including version control, build and deployment tooling, and infrastructure, must be monitored during development. It is essential to log and monitor during the development process, as developer devices can be used to breach version control systems or application environments.

Aside from monitoring and logging the process, it would be best if you also worked to implement (security) logging within your application. During the analysis and design phases, a plan must be created on what events should be logged and when and where they must be logged.

OWASP

We already discussed the importance of threat modeling and the role of threat intelligence. One crucial source to discuss more in-depth is the **Open Web Application Security Project (OWASP)**. The OWASP has identified the top 10 most common web application security flaws. The first top-10 was published in 2017; the most recent version was released in 2021.

Throughout the industry, the OWASP top-10 is regarded as essential knowledge for attackers and defenders alike. Let us look at the current OWASP top 10:

1	Broken access control
2	Cryptographic failures
3	Injection
4	Insecure design
5	Security misconfiguration
6	Vulnerable and outdated components
7	Identification and authentication failures
8	Software and data integrity failures
9	Security logging and monitoring failures
10	Server-side request forgery

Table 11.2: 2021 version of the OWASP top ten

EXAM TIP: You should memorize the OWASP top ten

As you can see in the table above, the ten most common web application, attacks are all highly related to poor security during the SDLC. Let us briefly examine these common pitfalls and how we can prevent them.

Broken access controls can be prevented by adequately testing your access control mechanisms before release. Writing tests to ensure actions require proper authentication is vital. It would be best if you tried to access the application and integrations with other services. Many broken access controls are caused by a complete lack of access controls or by assumptions. These assumptions are often related to considering internal networks secure.

Cryptographic failures are usually caused by organizations improperly implementing secure algorithms, using insecure algorithms, or designing their algorithms. During your development process, you must follow company policies and standards regarding encryption. However, you should also verify if the encryption algorithms and policies are suitable for your application and if they are still secure at the time of development.

Injection attacks stem from a lack of input validation. Input validation is the process of evaluating if user-provided input meets the expected data. For example, input validation may check if a user entered a valid `zip` code in the `zip` code field. However, it can also be used to detect negative values. In general, you should ensure that your code verifies the correctness of every user-provided value. You should check for formatting, and incredibly validating free text fields for known attacks such as **SQLi** and **XSS**.

Insecure design is caused by not including security in the planning, analysis, and design phases. Common examples of insecure design may be building services that do not require service-to-service authentication, providing users with excessive privileges, using insecure communication channels and so on.

Security misconfiguration often results from a need for more configuration testing and security baselining. We discussed baselining earlier in this book. Like baselining systems, software configuration baselines should be followed where possible. Such a baseline may be provided by the vendor or developed internally. Another issue with security misconfiguration can be caused by needing more threat intelligence and vulnerability scanning. If an organization does not update its configuration during the application's lifecycle, it will likely become insecure.

Vulnerable and outdated components can be prevented by adequately maintaining an SBOM and performing vulnerability scanning (more about this later).

Exposed credentials, poor session handling, and a general lack of testing often cause identification and authentication failures. However, they can easily be prevented by implementing code review (automatic or manual), enforcing adequate session lifespans, and validating authentication and identification processes.

As discussed earlier, code and commit signing can prevent software and data integrity failures. At the same time, security logging and monitoring failures result from poorly designed (or implemented) logging and monitoring plans during the design phase.

The last item on the list, **Server Side Request Forgery** (**SSRF**), is a complicated attack that can be easily defeated by performing input validation and preventing server-side software from calling external applications based on user content. The technical details of this attack go beyond the scope of the CCSP exam.

SANS Top 25

Like the OWASP top 10, the SANS Institute has published a list of the Top 25 Most Dangerous Software Weaknesses. Contrary to the OWASP top 10, the SANS top 25 includes weaknesses across software types and not only web applications. If you examine the top 25[4] you will notice that it is mainly in line with the OWASP top 10. The SANS top 25 dives deeper into the flaws behind the items in the OWASP top 10. Another difference is that the SANS list is based on **common weakness enumeration** (**CWE**) data. While the OWASP top 10 uses a combination of different resources for its ranking. The top 25, at the time of writing, are included for your reference:

Rank	Name
1	Out-of-bounds write
2	Improper Neutralization of Input During Web Page Generation ('Cross-site Scripting')

---

[4] *https://cwe.mitre.org/top25/archive/2022/2022_cwe_top25.html*

Rank	Name
3	Improper Neutralization of Special Elements used in an SQL Command ('SQL Injection')
4	Improper Input Validation
5	Out-of-bounds Read
6	Improper Neutralization of Special Elements used in an OS Command ('OS Command Injection')
7	Use After Free
8	Improper Limitation of a Pathname to a Restricted Directory ('Path Traversal')
9	Cross-Site Request Forgery (CSRF)
10	Unrestricted Upload of File with Dangerous Type
11	NULL Pointer Dereference
12	Deserialization of Untrusted Data
13	Integer Overflow or Wraparound
14	Improper Authentication
15	Use of Hard-coded Credentials
16	Missing Authorization
17	Improper Neutralization of Special Elements used in a Command ('Command Injection')
18	Missing Authentication for Critical Function
19	Improper Restriction of Operations within the Bounds of a Memory Buffer
20	Incorrect Default Permissions
21	Server-Side Request Forgery (SSRF)
22	Concurrent Execution using Shared Resource with Improper Synchronization ('Race Condition')
23	Uncontrolled Resource Consumption
24	Improper Restriction of XML External Entity Reference
25	Improper Control of Generation of Code ('Code Injection')

Table 11.3: The SANS top 25 most dangerous software weaknesses

EXAM TIP: You do not have to memorize the SANS top 25

During your development process, you should utilize the SANS top 25, the OWASP top 10, and the SSDF to ensure your team incorporates protections against common attacks.

SAFECode

Another institution that is involved in improving application security is SAFECode. This organization offers a platform for security engineers and managers from technology companies to design solutions to some of the most pressing software security issues. SAFECode often publishes blogs, white papers, and other helpful information on secure development.

ASVS

Aside from the OWASP top-10, the OWASP has also published the **Application Security Verification Standard (ASVS)**. The ASVS is extremely useful for organizations to guide the implementation of secure development. Additionally, it offers an easy way for parties to share the extent of their security controls. The ASVS has three different certification levels, each with its subset of controls and practices. While you cannot certify against the ASVS verification levels, it offers insight into an organization's security. Like the OWASP top 10, SANS top 25, and SSDF, the ASVS can be a helpful tool for your organization to shape secure development.

Vulnerability scanning

Establishing an SBOM is essential to ensure you know what software your application is built on. However, maintaining an SBOM alone has limited effects. Instead, you should ensure your application is scanned for vulnerabilities in the software listed in the SBOM. Automatic vulnerability scanning tools can detect if code is exploitable by searching for vulnerable packages and dependencies. At the same time, vulnerability scanning can detect vulnerabilities in live code.

For example, your application may utilize a library known to contain vulnerabilities. A vulnerability scanner may look at your application and try to verify if the specific library is patched or configured to prevent abuse. If not, a vulnerability scan report will be created that contains details on how to fix the vulnerability.

Vulnerability scanning must be continuous, as new vulnerabilities are released daily. Your organization should execute them daily in an automated fashion but also embed them in development processes.

Penetration testing

We know that testing is essential, from unit to regression tests and even complete scope e2e testing. As you are aware, these tests focus on functional requirements. They answer whether the software functions and how it should achieve a business goal. However, we must also test software to ensure it meets security requirements. We already touched on penetration testing a bit in this chapter. Penetration tests simulate an attacker attempting to breach a system or environment. As discussed, pentests can be executed as white, gray, or black box tests.

Many organizations conduct yearly penetration tests on their applications. While this approach is practical, organizations should evaluate if including pen testing in their development process is feasible. If you choose penetration testing as part of the process, you should conduct tests before releasing the software. Depending on the size and nature of the change, consider pen testing before releasing code updates, bug fixes, or new features.

It is important to note that your organization should strive to conduct pen tests externally. This is because external pentest agencies (generally) have more specialized knowledge and different skills and are impartial to the organization's goals. It would be best if you avoided situations where internal testing teams hide vulnerabilities to enable insecure software releases to take place to meet a deadline. Especially in organizations where security is embedded as part of the IT team, impartiality must be safeguarded during pen tests.

SAST and DAST

We already covered that application security testing is essential. In general, we can group the different forms of testing into two forms, static and dynamic. **Static testing** means the code is available to the tester and tools, but the application is not running. Dynamic testing means that tests are executed against a running application.

For example, code review is a form of **Static Application Security Testing (SAST)**, while pen-testing is a form of **Dynamic Application Security Testing (DAST)**. In some cases, like vulnerability scanning, the testing may be SAST and DAST. If a vulnerability scanner reads the application's code or configuration to find vulnerabilities, it is a SAST test. While if it scans for vulnerable ports on a live server, it is DAST. Let us look at some examples:

Static Application Security Testing	Dynamic Application Security Testing
Code review	Vulnerability scanning
Threat modeling	Penetration testing
	Performance testing

Table 11.4: Examples of SAST and DAST

There is no hard all-in definition for SAST or DAST. However, you must understand that both are names to group various security testing approaches.

EXAM TIP: You should always strive to implement SAST and DAST.

Security awareness and training

As you understand, secure development is a very involved process. An organization must embed security development practices throughout the entire software development lifecycle. Every phase relies on security processes, from requirements gathering to design, development, testing, operations, and disposal. Unfortunately, knowing how to develop securely is not the same as doing so. Many organizations understand the SDLC process. Only some organizations have built skills and raised awareness around the general need for security and secure development. The section below will discuss security awareness and training and how they are vital to an organization's effort to work more securely.

Awareness versus training

Firstly, let us establish the difference between awareness and training. Awareness means that people understand the existence (and hopefully) significance of something. For security an organization with security awareness realizes that it must strive for security. As evident as this seems, many organizations have lacked awareness. In some cases, senior management may not be aware of the threats their organization faces and the risks for the organization (and them personally). In other organizations, you might find a senior management team that is fully aware of security but without awareness of the tactical and operational layers of the organization.

Learning that security awareness should live throughout the organization may be familiar to you. From the executive level to the managers, team members, temporary employees, and vendors. As you saw during the sections about the SDLC, adequate security requires it to be embedded throughout the software development lifecycle. However, security really must be included in every process.

For example, data breaches can occur if your archival department does not destroy paper records properly. If your cafeteria personnel leave the door to the outside open for a smoke break, a physical breach can occur that results in data breaches.

So, let us come back to the difference between security awareness and security training. As we discussed, awareness is knowing its existence and why it matters. Security training is about understanding how to operate securely. For example, knowing that phishing attacks target your organization is part of security awareness. However, training personnel to recognize phishing e-mails is security training.

Your organization must create security awareness and train its employees to operate securely. As with most things, humans are reluctant to perform tasks they experience as bothersome. You may have noticed that many security practices could be more practical or may be experienced as excessive or time-consuming. As a security professional, it will be your task to help build awareness about why these security practices are necessary. Within an organization, it is helpful to hold employee briefings explaining the threats that your organization faces and the impact of these risks.

For example, you could brief your employees about the threat of phishing attacks. Meanwhile, you can explain to the employees that a phishing attack can lead to a data breach and result in diminished customer trust and significant fines. If your employees know the impact on the organization and their job security, they are more likely to be willing to operate securely.

Aside from raising awareness, you must offer (mandatory) training in the shape of workshops or training videos that explain to employees how to securely perform their work duties. For example, you should have employees complete training videos or workshops on recognizing phishing attacks. Similarly, you may want to conduct more specific training for employees that handle sensitive data, and so on. Especially IT personnel will require specific training on the security policies and standards they are supposed to implement.

REAL-LIFE TIP: Do not assume that employees read policy documents and standards. Facilitate them with mandatory training on these internal standards.

Recurrence

Once you have established a baseline for security awareness within your organization, it is essential to keep building on it. Research has shown that awareness training's effectiveness starts to diminish six months after it has been conducted quickly. Therefore, your organization must organize recurring (mandatory) awareness sessions. At a minimum, security awareness and training should be addressed at least yearly, but preferably more frequently.

Positivity

One essential thing to mention is the way your organization conducts security awareness efforts and security training. Over the past years, many organizations have taken a punitive approach to security training. For example, they send out phishing e-mails within their organization and make employees retake training by clicking a link or replying to the e-mail. Such efforts are suboptimal. By singling out employees who could not execute the secure practice, you create a culture of negative reinforcement. This will demotivate employees and impact their willingness to adapt to secure processes.

Instead of that approach, try to approach security with positivity. Reward personnel that securely execute their work. Praise employees who act as security champions within their organizations and highlight the impact of secure behavior as a positive trait.

Some organizations add secure work as a job requirement and include it in yearly evaluations. Such an approach may be very effective; however, you must ensure that you provide employees with ample training if you choose to do so.

Conclusion

Secure development is an often overlooked element of security in organizations. Suppose your organization strives to include security throughout the software development lifecycle. In that case, you will find that it improves security and ultimately saves costs, as shift-left security is always more economical than bolt-on security.

Organizations develop software in different ways, they may approach projects with a waterfall approach or an Agile methodology. The secure software development lifecycle follows the same phases regardless of the approach. They are executed differently based on your development approach.

Throughout the SDLC phases: planning, analyzing requirements, designing, developing, testing, securely operating, and disposing, you must embed security at every step. From gathering security requirements, designing secure architectures, performing code reviews, linting code, and executing penetration tests, every aspect is vital to maintaining a secure SDLC. Common pitfalls during development can be prevented by proper threat modeling and embedding the SSDF, OWASP top 10, and SANS top 25 as part of your development processes.

Remember that your organization must raise awareness about security throughout the organization. With awareness, an adaptation of secure processes, like the ones in the secure SDLC, will be satisfactory. Aside from raising awareness, training your employees to perform their jobs securely is essential. You must ensure that employees are provided with regular training on how they must translate policies and standards to secure day-to-day tasks.

In the next chapter, you will learn about the processes involved in the testing and verification of software.

Learning goals

This chapter addresses the following CCSP exam outline learning goals:

Domain 4: Cloud application security

      4.1 Advocate training and awareness for application security

      4.2 Describe the **secure software development life cycle (SDLC)**

      4.3 Apply the **secure software development life cycle (SDLC)**

Join our book's Discord space

Join the book's Discord Workspace for Latest updates, Offers, Tech happenings around the world, New Release and Sessions with the Authors:

https://discord.bpbonline.com

CHAPTER 12

Security Testing and Software Verification

Introduction

Secure development is essential in creating a secure (cloud) ecosystem. However, while we aim to develop securely, we must verify that we did so. This chapter explores the role of security testing methods such as static and dynamic code analysis, code review, pen-testing, and functional and non-functional testing. This chapter also highlights how APIs can be secured and vulnerabilities within dependencies or open-source software can be detected.

Structure

This chapter covers the following topics:

- Functional and non-functional testing
- Security testing methodologies
- Quality assurance
- Supply-chain management and vendor assessments
- Third-party software management
- Validated open-source software

Objectives

This chapter aims to dive deep into the methods used for testing in the cloud. This chapter will provide more in-depth knowledge about various testing methodologies and how they relate to the cloud. This chapter will also help you understand risks surrounding the supply chain, third-party software, and open-source software in specific. At the end of the chapter, you will understand how testing and verifying software are essential to a secure environment in the cloud.

Functional and non-functional testing

In *Chapter 11, Secure Development, Awareness, and Training*, we discussed various forms of testing as part of the SDLC. In this chapter, we will dive deeper into the forms of testing we perform and what they entail. Before we dive into security testing methodologies, it is important to re-iterate the difference between functional and non-functional testing.

Generally, functional testing is considered every form of testing that evaluates if the software functions per applicable requirements. This form of testing evaluates if the application delivers the functionality needed to provide business value.

For example, a functional test may verify if a user can purchase a product from a webshop. The web shop has a functional requirement to allow for online sales of products. The test to establish if the requirement is met should be an end-to-end test that verifies the customer side of the transaction and the subsequent processing in any related systems.

Non-functional testing considers factors not directly described in the project's requirements. In many cases, non-functional testing may involve security, performance, and CI/CD functionality. It is essential to remember that security and performance should always be requirements. If an application or system is built using the secure SDLC, you can also consider the security and performance part of functional testing. However, most applications have limited applicable requirements for security.

For example, a new application should be resilient against DoS attacks. However, only some applications will have a specific functional requirement about how much traffic an application and its infrastructure must be capable of serving. If such a definition is not given, you should still test the resilience of the application and infrastructure, but it would be considered a non-functional test.

It is essential to realize that functional and non-functional tests can be executed using the same means. For example, you may conduct functional and non-functional tests using penetration tests. The difference between functional and non-functional testing depends on the requirements of your project. In many projects, you will see the following differentiation for tests:

Functional tests	Non-functional tests
Unit testing	Security testing
Regression testing	Performance/stress testing
E2E testing	CI/CD testing
Database testing	

Table 12.1: Common division of test types

Security testing methodologies

In many projects, security testing is considered a form of non-functional testing. However, it would be best if you strived to include hard security requirements in your project requirements. That way, you can more easily (and quantifiably) verify if your application meets your security requirements.

For example, your functional requirements may include that your application should detect and prevent **cross-site scripting (XSS)** attacks. Or your webserver must withstand a **distributed denial of service (DDoS)** attack by 10.000 concurrent attackers.

Reality teaches us that many projects need to have well-defined security requirements. Nevertheless, we must ensure that we properly evaluate the security of a system or application. The answer to the need for measurable requirements is the implementation of comprehensive and generalized testing of all security facets of an application. A major downside to this is that the time needed for testing is significant, while the results can be more challenging to measure or trace back to a specific cause.

Abuse case testing

One of the tests we can use in security testing is abuse case testing. Remember that we talked about threat modeling in *Chapter 11, Secure Development, Awareness, and Training*, threat modeling is a practice that allows us to determine threats to our systems and applications so that we can create security controls to minimize them. Well, abuse case testing is relatively similar. During this form of testing, we define ways in which an application can be misused or abused. Let us look at an example of an abuse case, as follows:

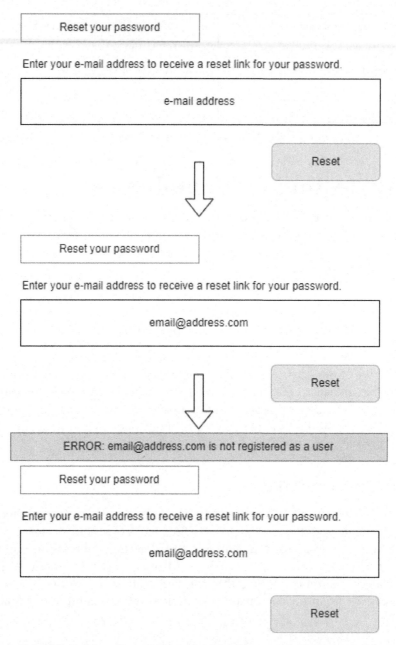

Figure 12.1*: Abuse of password reset functionality to enumerate usernames*

The figure above shows a website with a password reset functionality. As you can see, the form invites the user to enter their e-mail address to receive their password reset e-mail. In the second step, the user entered their e-mail address: **email@address.com**. In the third step, you may have noticed that the form returns an error stating that **email@address.com** is not registered as a user. This functionality will perform exactly what you need if you are a legitimate user. If you enter your e-mail address, it sends you a reset e-mail so you can regain access to your action.

However, there is also a clear case for abuse here. If you are an attacker, you can use this form to determine what e-mail addresses have an account on the website. You could exploit the form to tell you whether an e-mail was sent. By collecting information on the e-mails associated with an account, you could target the e-mails with a phishing attack or use them in a brute-force attack.

As you saw above, abuse cases are scenarios where functionality is used contrary to its purpose. The sample above is a very common example of an abuse case. If you look at some of the websites you use, you will likely notice that some have neglected to test for this abuse case.

Another exciting example targets video streaming platforms—many websites load videos using the HTML5 video element. The video element loads a video file from a web location to display to the user. Many companies have an access control system to prevent unauthorized access to the resource. However, they do not realize you can download the video file directly from the HTML5 video element link. This structure sometimes allows you to bypass authentication entirely or download video files to gain ownership of the video.

Of course, abuse cases can get a lot more dangerous than this, especially if abuse would lead to financial obligations on behalf of others or massive information disclosure. Whenever you conduct abuse case testing, using threat modeling to identify potential abuse cases and build tests from there can be helpful.

Black, gray, and white box penetration testing

Throughout the book, we discussed black, gray, and white box penetration testing. As you now know, the main difference between the tests is how much knowledge and access the tester has.

Penetration tests are one of the most in-depth security testing at our disposal. Regardless of the form of testing, it can have a real-life impact on the organization. Because penetration tests seek to identify vulnerabilities in a system (or organization as a whole), tests should be conducted in a production environment or as close to production as possible. The need for production (like) testing sets penetration testing apart from the other test forms we have discussed. You can conduct code reviews, unit tests, performance tests, and abuse case testing on a staging environment without many problems. Whenever you test production environments, there are other considerations to consider.

The first consideration is the **rules of engagement** (**RoE**). The RoE defines what penetration testers can do and to which system. For example, some penetration tests may enable the testers to inject malicious code into software to see if they can breach the underlying machine. In contrast, other tests may allow for service disruption if an attacker finds such an attack vector. In essence, the RoE helps define the scope of the penetration test. Whenever you test on production systems, you should attempt to balance business needs with the effectiveness of the penetration test. For example, if you prohibit testers from pivoting to other systems, you remove part of the test scope. However, banning these actions prevents other systems from experiencing downtime due to testing activities.

EXAM TIP: The more restrictive the RoE is, the less practical a penetration test will be. In return, the chances of disruption of the business continuity are generally lower as well.

Perhaps the most crucial facet of penetration testing is the resulting report. Most penetration testing companies provide their customers with a comprehensive report outlining all vulnerabilities. Some organizations also offer an executive summary in addition to the full report. These executive summaries are essential to convey the pentest information within the organization. After all, your senior management is unlikely to have the in-depth technical knowledge needed to interpret the full report. Whether you are using an external organization or an internal team, you must report and record the results of penetration tests. The correct actions will only be taken with proper briefings to the management team. Remember that risk scoring is an essential component of the briefing.

EXAM TIP: Remember that external pentest is regarded as impartial, whereas internal pentests may not be considered as such.

The CCSP exam is not a comprehensive pentesting exam. For the CCSP exam, you must understand the difference between black, gray, and white box testing, the impact of RoE, reporting, and the choice of internal versus external testers. Please refer to *Chapter 11, Secure Development, Awareness, and Training* for more details about the test types.

Static application security testing and dynamic application security testing

In *Chapter 11, Secure Development, Awareness, and Training*, we also briefly covered SAST and DAST. As pointed out there, the main difference between SAST and DAST is that DAST is performed on a running application, while SAST is performed on code and configuration files only.

It is essential to understand that SAST or DAST is not a testing method. Instead, they are a name to describe a form of security testing collectively. For example, a black box penetration test executed against a live application is considered a form of DAST. However, a white box penetration test with code review can be considered SAST and DAST.

During the exam, it is vital that you understand the difference between the two categories and can differentiate various forms of testing. Please refer to *Chapter 11, Secure Development, Awareness, and Training*, for an overview of standard tests per category.

Software composition analysis

Software composition analysis (SCA) is a form of SAST that automatically scans code to identify (open-source) dependencies. SCA is an extremely valuable tool for building your SBOM. Through consistently performing SCA, you can ensure your SBOM remains up-to-date. Which, in turn, allows you to respond more quickly to new vulnerabilities that may exist in your dependencies. SCA should be used as a verification tool. It would be best to rely on something other than SCA to tell you your dependencies. Instead, your organization should carefully consider and pick which dependencies it includes. SCA can then be used to confirm that these are the (only) dependencies in use.

Interactive application security testing

We already talked about the difference between SAST and DAST. However, there is another new testing methodology that we must discuss. We call this method **interactive application security testing (IAST)**. Whereas SAST only examines static code and DAST only performs testing on the running application, IAST combines both components.

When you perform IAST, you can use SAST to uncover vulnerabilities in code and then use DAST techniques to see if they are exploitable. As you can imagine, IAST testing takes more skill and knowledge to implement. After all, IAST requires that you corroborate findings from various testing methodologies. Let us see how the methodologies line up:

Form of testing	SAST	DAST	IAST
Code review	Yes	No	Yes
Vulnerability scanning	Yes, but only in the code	Yes, but only on running apps	Yes
Penetration testing	No	Yes	Yes

Table 12.2: Common security tests per testing methodology

Quality assurance

An essential part of (secure) development is called **Quality assurance (QA)**. QA determines if a software application or infrastructure meets its requirements. In many cases, an organization's building software or infrastructure will need a test and proven method to assurance customers of the quality of their product. After all, many governmental agencies or certain private corporations may have strict requirements for their software.

One of the most common processes to establish quality assurance is through the **Capability Maturity Model Integration (CMMI)** model created by the **Software Engineering Institute (SEI)** at Carnegie Mellon University. The CMMI model allows you to determine a maturity level for software. The maturity or capability level is a measurement of the quality of an application. Specifically, it provides information about the processes used throughout the development and testing process to ensure quality.

The CMMI has five different capability levels, as shown:

CCMI maturity levels
Initial
Managed
Defined processes
Managed quantitatively
Optimizing

Table 12.3: CCMI maturity levels

The first level of the maturity model, initial, means that the development and testing process needs to be more reactive and well-defined. The organization that developed the software or infrastructure needs more processes to safeguard the product's quality. They are not defined or managed if they do have processes in place.

The next level, managed processes, means an organization has processes to ensure quality. Such processes can include project planning, quality testing, management of requirements, and so on. While the methods are in place, they must be more broadly developed. For example, they are not measured for success, or they might need to be improved continuously.

When an organization reaches the third maturity level, defined processes, they actively review their procedures and improve on shortcomings in these processes. They likely have processes like risk management, validation, and verification as part of their development. Contrary to an organization operating at levels one and two, an organization at maturity level 3 is far more likely to produce higher quality products as they have clearly defined their processes.

At the fourth level, managed quantitatively, an organization has extensive processes to measure its operations' effectiveness. At this level, the organization has well-defined processes but uses data to make decisions throughout a project.

In the last level, optimizing, an organization takes the data it collects about its well-defined processes, actively uses it to improve processes, and identifies new opportunities for improvement. Organizations that work at levels four and five can be considered mature and are likely to deliver high-quality products continuously.

When you select an organization to purchase software, asking about the CMMI maturity level is helpful. Organizations can obtain certificates of CMMI maturity level that impartial third parties provide. If your organization develops software or systems, pursuing a CMMI certification for your products may be beneficial. The process of obtaining certification will allow your organization to not only improve its processes but also allows you to prove its maturity to (prospective) customers.

Of course, the CMMI is one of many models that can be used for QA purposes. Organizations may adopt their own QA processes or use other industry-specific models.

EXAM TIP: The CCSP exam expects you to understand the five CCMI maturity levels. It also expects you to understand the need for QA processes in general.

Supply-chain

We just talked about the need for quality assurance. Whenever an organization purchases an application (in the cloud or otherwise), it must know it was developed well. The same is true for an organization's supply chain in general. In the land of cloud computing, applications often rely on dozens of other software packages and vendors.

For example, if you build a SaaS service on a CSP platform and serve the platform to customers, the CSP is part of your supply chain. In turn, the CSP relies on many vendors in their supply chain. If you build your application on a cloud platform that is not built with security in mind, a breach in the platform can severely damage your organization even though your security may be substantial.

In some cases, attackers may even deliberately attempt to attack a party that is part of your supply chain, aiming to breach your organization's systems. For example, attackers could target a producer of microchips, install the malware in the chips after intercepting them during shipment, and ultimately hack the cars in which the chips are used.

Currently, it is impossible to provide all services by yourself. Organizations must gain the knowledge, money, or expertise to do so. So, how do we ensure that an organization in the supply chain does not compromise our security? Unfortunately, there is no perfect answer. Including organizations within your supply chain always creates the risk of security problems on their side. However, we can take various steps to limit the supply chain risks.

EXAM TIP: Generally, you should only work with suppliers with a similar or higher level of security than your own organization.

One of the most critical steps is ensuring that a vendor or partner has security processes that align with our organization's requirements. Requiring a vendor to approach security at the same level means we must verify if they have policies, standards, and processes to safeguard security. Sometimes, vendors may be willing to share this information with you. It allows you to determine if their security practices align with your own. However, vendors will be reluctant to share such information in many situations.

Because of the general reluctance to share security policies, standards, and processes, you must evaluate the vendor's security practices in other ways. One common way to do so is by requiring vendors to be certified against a specific standard. Alternatively, you can perform audits or require vendors to share audit information to ensure their processes are in place and effective.

Regardless of your chosen approach, you must realize that you will not wholly understand an organization's security. While security certifications are helpful for organizations, they do not guarantee adequate security controls. Instead, they outline policies and processes that are in place. Similarly, audits produce results at a specific time. While an organization may pass an audit with flying colors, practices could change and deviate from the required level of security.

EXAM TIP: Certifications and audits are commonplace to verify an organization's security level.

It is essential to vet vendors in-depth before acquiring new services. Of course, this applies to CSPs and more conventional services like garbage collection, payrolling, and so on. If your organization does determine that a vendor meets the security bar to work with your organization, you should periodically re-evaluate their security level. At the same time, you must ensure you include security requirements as part of any contract. That way, if a vendor is in compliance with your security requirements (in the future), you have legal means to address the issue.

REAL-LIFE TIP: Always include security requirements in contracts before signing them.

SOC II type II

One typical audit report you can request from a vendor is a SOC 2 report. A SOC 2 report can be found in two types, namely type 1 and type 2. The SOC 2 type 1 report evaluates the design of security processes. A SOC 2 type 2 report evaluates if the implemented controls within the organization are adequate. The SOC 2 type 2 report also can provide in-depth information about those controls and how they function.

Suppose you need more capabilities to audit an organization. In that case, it is wise to request that the organization shares its SOC II type II report with your organization (if they have one). The type II report will provide the most detailed information for your organization to evaluate its security. Beware, however, that SOC reports are scoped, meaning a report might only sometimes include all vendor activities. It is essential that you verify if the scope of the report is in line with the services they will provide to you.

You will find that most CSPs have SOC II type II reports available for download on their website.

ISO 27001 certification

Another commonly sought-after certification to evaluate a vendor's security is the ISO 27001 certification. The ISO 27001 certification is given to organizations that can prove that the controls outlined in the ISO 27002 standard have been successfully implemented. While the ISO 27001 certification provides a decent idea of the security maturity of an organization, it is by no means a guarantee of secure processes. Many organizations achieve the ISO 27001 certification but still have vulnerable software and services due to missing, incomplete, or ineffective processes.

You will find that most CSPs are certified against ISO 27001.

REAL-LIFE TIP: An ISO 27001 certification is an excellent minimum baseline. However, you must evaluate an organization's security practices more in-depth.

Third-party and open-source software

Throughout this book, we have talked a bit about third-party and open-source software. By now, you know that including any third-party (open-source) software in your software, infrastructure, or services creates risks.

In many cases, using existing software as part of our development processes makes more sense. Simply because it saves time and, as a result, money as well. There needs to be more sense for re-inventing the wheel. However, using third-party software means we must ensure the software adheres to the exact security requirements of the rest of our organization. After all, these third-party applications will likely gain access to (some) of the organization's data. Like supply-chain management, we must conduct security evaluations on third-party software, especially open-source software. After all, community-maintained software may not be vetted for security.

Whenever an organization decides to use 3P or open-source software to satisfy a business need, it must carefully weigh the risks. For example, you must evaluate the security level of a vendor as part of the acquisition process, like the processes used for supply-chain management. An organization should also weigh if the increased risk from working with another organization is worth the software's benefits. For example, open-source software can be free. Still, if your organization would have to secure the software or perform rigorous security testing, it may be cheaper to purchase closed-source software.

EXAM TIP: Subject third-party and open-source software to the same processes/standards as internally developed software.

You have already learned that maintaining an SBOM, code review, and vulnerability scanning are essential parts of the secure development of your software and systems. Whenever you use third-party software, secure development practices still apply. Open-source software should (ideally) be vetted the same way internally developed software is. At the same time, third-party (closed-source) software should be subjected to similar checks as other supply-chain providers.

EXAM TIP: Open-source software requires security processes from your organization.

Conclusion

From internal applications to vendors to third-party (open-source) software, every application and system requires security testing. Whether you choose to use SAST, DAST, or IAST testing methodologies, it is essential to perform every test needed to ensure the quality of your software or system meets your organization's requirements. QA processes like the Capability Maturity Model Integration can help organizations build reliable strategies to verify and validate software and systems' quality.

While internally developed systems and infrastructure can be thoroughly vetted, we may have different abilities to verify and validate applications developed by third parties. Sometimes, these systems may be part of our supply chain or can even be integrated into our systems and software. Regardless of what role a third-party plays, we must evaluate the security of the third-party and their products. After all, their systems will process our data and affect our business continuity. Therefore, it is essential to require vendors to subject themselves to (security) reviews like audits and that they provide security certifications and reports where applicable on an ongoing basis. After all, a vendor that is secure today may not be secure tomorrow.

In the next chapter, you will learn about the specifics of cloud security architecture.

Learning goals

This chapter addresses the following CCSP exam outline learning goals:

Domain 4: Cloud application security

      4.4 Apply cloud software assurance and validation

      4.5 Use verified secure software

Join our book's Discord space

Join the book's Discord Workspace for Latest updates, Offers, Tech happenings around the world, New Release and Sessions with the Authors:

https://discord.bpbonline.com

CHAPTER 13

Specifics of Cloud Security Architecture

Introduction

Cloud computing allows us to look at security from a different perspective. This means that we also have to use security tooling in different places and in different ways. This chapter explores supplemental cloud security components such as web applications firewalls, API gateways, and database activity monitoring. Moreover, the chapter dives into encryption in the cloud, security of virtualization through containers, microservices, and sandboxing

Structure

This chapter covers the following topics:

- Web application firewall
- Database Activity Monitoring
- API Gateways
- Virtualization and orchestration

Objectives

This chapter will let you understand how non-traditional security components like web application firewalls, database activity monitoring, virtualization, cryptography, sandboxing, and API gateways are valuable tools in a cloud environment. At the end of the chapter, you can define these controls and understand when and how they can be applied within a cloud environment to improve security.

Web application firewall

The first control we need to examine in more depth is the **web application firewall (WAF)**. In previous chapters, we know the importance of firewalling within a cloud environment. Specifically, how ACLs and SGs act as cloud-native firewalls. We also discussed that firewalls could be virtualized appliances within the cloud. The main benefit to virtualizing firewalls is that you can use the same appliances in the cloud as you use in your on-premises network. However, we also covered how virtualizing any appliance in the cloud brings more maintenance and configuration work.

We also discussed the usage of WAFs as part of security architectures. WAFs are advanced firewalls capable of inspecting requests at the OSI model's highest layer, the application layer. Simply put, a WAF understands the context of a request. Before diving further into WAFs, look at the firewalls you must know.

The most straightforward firewall is called a **stateless** or **packet filter firewall**. A stateless firewall knows where a data packet is coming from and where it is going. Such a firewall can enforce simple rules like **Alice** can send a packet to **Bob**, but **Bob** is not allowed to send a packet to **Eve**. A stateless firewall examines packets by itself. It is not aware of any conversations that are going on between the two parties. For example, if **Bob** requests **Alice** and the protocol requires **Alice** to respond, the stateless firewall will not know the packet exchange was a conversation based on a protocol. Let us look at this as follows:

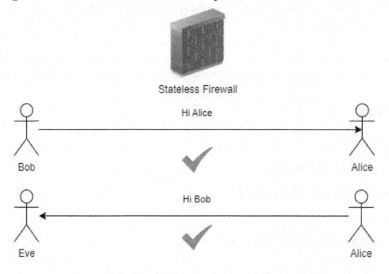

Figure 13.1: Simplified example of a stateless firewall

The figure above shows a simplified example of what a stateless firewall does. In the example above, the firewall rule has been that talking using a specific protocol is allowed.

Initially, **Bob** sent a message to **Alice**, **Alice** replied with a message but sent it to **Eve** rather than **Bob**. The stateless firewall does not know what **Alice**'s response meant for **Bob**. After all, the firewall does not understand that **Bob** and **Alice** are conversing. It merely checks if the packets used for the conversation are allowed. Stateless firewalls are incapable of recognizing malicious traffic patterns and hijacking conversations.

A stateful firewall has more capabilities than a stateless firewall. It can determine if packets are sent as part of an exchange. Because a stateful firewall can follow a conversation, it can determine if packets should be allowed to go to a specific destination. It is essential to understand that a stateful firewall understands the communication protocol used in an exchange.

For example, in *Figure 13.2*, a stateful firewall would determine that the request sent by **Bob** requires a response from **Alice** sent to **Bob**. Because the packet marked as the response was sent to **Eve** instead, it would be blocked, as shown:

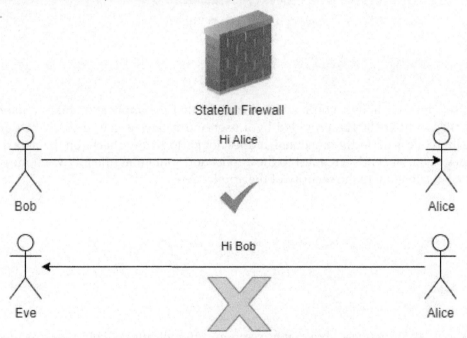

Figure 13.2: Simplified example of a stateful firewall

As you already know, a much more complicated family of firewalls exists called **next generation firewalls** (**NGFWs**). These firewalls can examine traffic more in-depth at the protocol level, like a stateful firewall, but some can also inspect traffic at the application level. NGFWs may use heuristics (user behavioral patterns) to determine if traffic fits normal user behavior.

For example, an NGFW might detect that allowed traffic occurs outside business hours. Because the traffic is outside the typical pattern, the firewall determines it may be malicious and blocks it. Especially in the cloud, heuristics play a significant role, for example, in **attribute based access control** (**ABAC**).

A web application firewall can inspect packets and understand the underlying protocol used for the communication. But most importantly, a WAF can understand the actual content and context of a request. This deep understanding of the contents of a packet is what makes a WAF so extremely powerful. Let us look at an example below:

Let us assume we have a serverless application running in our cloud environment. Whenever users want to create an account, they send a request to our serverless application, and a function is triggered to create a new user. The code for the function looks like the code, as shown:

```
1.  function createNewUser(request: any) {
2.
3.      const username = request.username;
4.      const password = request.password;
5.      const birthDate = request.birthDate;
6.
7.      addUserToDatabase(username, password, birthDate);
8.  }
```

If you see the code above, you may have noticed that the application takes a **username**, **password**, and **birthDate** provided by a user and creates a new user in the database. While this code is perfectly functional, it does not perform any checks on the data the user provides. If a user sends a request to the application containing the following message, it could be detrimental to the security of the application:

```
1.  {
2.      "username": "'; DELETE FROM users;",
3.      "password": "",
4.      "birthDate": "<script>window.location.replace('http://malicious.
    site')</script>"
5.  }
```

If you look at the request above, you see two different attacks could be executed. The username contains an SQLi attack that could erase all users from the database. At the same time, the **birthDate** field contains XSS that would redirect any user who visits a page containing this user's birth date. Of course, the examples above only work if no other security controls exist. Regardless, the examples are valuable for demonstrating the power of a WAF. While a stateful firewall would not mark the request in *Figure 13.2* as malicious, a WAF could.

A WAF can determine if a request's contents are valid or malicious. If you configure the WAF correctly, it could even determine if the data is formatted correctly. For example, it could detect that the birth date is not only malicious in nature but could also highlight that a birth date written as 1995-05-05 was using the wrong format.

So, a WAF can help us with multiple things. Firstly, it can detect common attacks like XSS, SQLi, or XML-based attacks (amongst other OWASP top 10 attacks). Secondly, it can ensure that requests that do not contain malicious entries meet the formatting requirements we may have for requests. The massive benefit of employing a WAF is bringing some of our security controls early in the process. If a WAF detects a malicious request, it will be blocked. The result of this is that the malicious request never reaches the code, because the code is not reached, poor or lack of security in the code will not directly lead to a breach.

A WAF is a fantastic tool; in many cases, it integrates seamlessly with API gateways or other cloud-native tools. It helps us secure our code even with little security built in. However, using more than a would be best. Code and databases must still include security controls. It would be best if you tried to establish layered defenses. Nevertheless, a WAF can be an effective way to introduce security controls to insecure code. Just keep in mind that WAFs are always expensive.

EXAM TIP: NGFW (and WAFs) can inspect packet content and context. Stateful firewalls examine conversations (the protocol), while stateless firewalls only inspect single packets.

Database activity monitoring

Another exciting security available to us in the cloud is **database activity monitoring (DAM)**. As the name suggests, DAM monitors the activity of database usage. DAM tools apply heuristics or rule-based checks to evaluate if database queries and modifications are legitimate. For example, if a database is only used during work hours, DAM would mark hundreds of queries extracting data at night as malicious. It would, in turn, block these queries to prevent data exfiltration.

DAM solutions are offered as integrated features with many PaaS database cloud solutions. DAM fits perfectly in a layered defense strategy. For example, a WAF may block malicious requests, but what if the requests themselves are not malicious, but the purpose for which they are used is? A WAF might not detect such abuse, while DAM (based on its configuration) may detect the queries themselves as malicious. When compromised credentials are used to access a database, DAM can effectively prevent data exfiltration.

Once again, more than DAM is required. However, when used in conjunction with other security measures, it can deepen an application's resilience by detecting malicious behavior at various points of the data flow.

EXAM TIP: DAM should be used as part of a layered defense

API gateways

Earlier in the book, we discussed how API gateways can reduce an organization's attack surface. They can do so by allowing on-premises applications to be reached through the cloud. An API gateway can function as a reverse proxy for your on-premises environment. By doing so, the API gateway can bring cloud-native DDoS protections to your cloud and on-premises environment. However, most API gateways also directly integrate with cloud-native WAFs, meaning you can profit from both the proxy mechanism (and other benefits) of an API gateway and the WAF simultaneously.

Even if you choose to implement an API gateway without a WAF, it can yield security benefits. For example, an API gateway can force authentication on specific endpoints (even if the application does not natively have access control). Like a WAF, an API gateway can also be used to check requests for correct formatting and can even perform rate-limiting to reduce denial-of-service chances.

In an ideal world, you could use a WAF to prevent malicious traffic to your API gateway and use the API gateway to provide access control and request validation before forwarding requests to your cloud-based on-premises applications. The applications would only require to be reachable by the API gateway, thus preventing direct access to your application.

API gateways are an extremely easy way to quickly create new APIs, manage existing APIs, and implement security controls. Paired with a WAF and DAM, API gateways can create an excellent start to a layered defense in the cloud.

Virtualization and orchestration

Throughout the book, we have covered virtualization and orchestration of virtual environments in depth. Regardless of what you are virtualizing, workstations, servers, or even network appliances, virtualization provides security benefits but also requires specific security controls. Hardening hypervisors, preventing escape from virtual machines, and virtual machine sprawl are all concerns that come with virtualization.

While we have looked at what is required to virtualize securely, we have yet to examine how virtualization can be used in favor of security. One of the main reasons to use virtualization for security is that it is flexible. Using virtualization, we can quickly create and destroy instances on demand. In on-premises environments, we may need to build new environments using manual tasks; in some cases, you may even be required to purchase more hardware. However, we can spin up new environments in the cloud in seconds.

So, how is this relevant for security? Well, there are a couple of benefits. Firstly, virtualization allows us to create production-like environments that can be started easily and shut down quickly. Such environments can perform security testing, such as penetration tests.

Secondly, virtualization allows us to quickly test new configurations by spinning up a new instance, applying the updates, and seeing if the instance still functions correctly. Virtualization allows you to quickly test if new security controls (such as hardening) are adequate.

Sandboxing

Another valuable tool of virtualization is called **sandboxing**. Sandboxes are the process of creating a new (blank) virtual instance. In that instance, you can develop code or configuration and examine how it works. One common application of sandboxing is for testing malware. For example, you can create a sandboxed machine (that has no connectivity to other systems), deploy (presumed) malware on it, and observe how it works. By observing malware, defenders can more easily understand the threats they are dealing with and, at the same time, test if their controls are adequate to defeat the malware. The process of sandboxing malware is an example of malware analysis.

Honey potting

The fourth example of using virtualization for security is creating honey pots (or honeynets). Honey pots are systems that are designed to be vulnerable to attackers. The systems function as bait by exposing vulnerabilities. When an attacker attempts to breach the system, they might even find falsified evidence (such as fake user records) on the machine. Meanwhile, your organization's defenders have time to trace the attackers, understand their attack methods, or even involve law enforcement. You might even opt to create honey nets, networks of vulnerable machines, and infrastructure in more elaborate environments. Aside from allowing your organization to observe attackers, it may also prevent attackers from pursuing your existing systems. After all, why would an attacker keep going once they get their hands on their target data?

While honey potting can be extremely useful, it is a tricky business. Your organization needs extensive security skills and knowledge to create properly segregated honey pots and honeynets. Remember that you are running these machines within your cloud or on-premises network and making a breach outside your *honeyed* systems very dangerous. It is essential to ensure you have alerting in place on honey pots or honey nets to make sure you catch attackers.

REAL-LIFE TIP: Leave honey potting or honey netting to governments and organizations with high security maturity.

In short, virtualization allows us to create separate environments on the same physical devices easily quickly, effectively, and reasonably cheaply test security controls, and examine security threats.

EXAM TIP: For the CCSP exam, you must understand the benefits of malware analysis using sandboxing and the applications for Honey potting and Honey netting.

Conclusion

This chapter expands on some of the security concepts you reviewed throughout the book. While you know why firewalling is essential within or outside of the cloud, you now understand that a WAF as an NGFW plays a vital role in preventing abuse of your applications. A WAF can prevent common attacks like SQLi, XSS, and XML-based attacks (and other OWASP top-10 attacks).

Of course, a WAF by itself is not sufficient to secure your environment. By employing DAM, you can ensure that malicious actions on your database are not only detected but can also be stopped before leading to data disclosure.

With a WAF and DAM, an API gateway creates a solid basis for a secure cloud environment. API gateways integrate directly with cloud WAFs, offer an easy way to enforce authentication and check formatting requests, and can bring cloud-native DDoS to on-premises applications by acting as a reverse proxy.

Of course, virtualization is an essential tool in the cloud. While it requires significant effort to be used securely, it also introduces new possibilities. Sandboxing allows us to inspect malware and test security controls and configurations. At the same time, honey potting allows us to securely bait attackers into revealing their skills, techniques, and potentially even their identities.

As you know, none of these measures alone create a secure environment. But, by layering these various defenses throughout your environment, your organization will be more resilient to attacks in the cloud.

The next chapter will dive deep into IAM, **single-sign on (SSO)**, **multi-factor authentication (MFA)**, and other authentication and authorization technologies.

Learning goals

This chapter addresses the following CCSP exam outline learning goals:

Domain 4: Cloud application security

> 4.6 Comprehend the specifics of cloud application architecture

Join our book's Discord space

Join the book's Discord Workspace for Latest updates, Offers, Tech happenings around the world, New Release and Sessions with the Authors:

https://discord.bpbonline.com

CHAPTER 14
Identity and Access Management

Introduction

Broad access is one of the characteristics of the cloud. However, we must manage identities effectively and securely to have broad access and be secure. This chapter explores how **single sign-on (SSO)**, **identity providers (IdP)**, user federation, secrets management, multi-factor authentication, and **cloud access security brokers (CASB)** form the puzzle pieces of secure access in the cloud.

Structure

This chapter covers the following topics:

- Identity and access management
- Identity providers
- Single sign-on
- Multi-factor authentication
- Cloud access security brokers
- Secrets management

Objectives

This chapter aims to build an understanding of identity and access management as a concept. Throughout the chapter, we will review various aspects of an IAM program and how it should be implemented within the cloud. The chapter will explore the role of identity providers and the power (and drawbacks) of single sign-on while examining how multi-factor authentication adds to layered defenses. At the end of the chapter, the concept of cloud access security brokers will be explained, and the student will learn to understand how a CASB can be used in current-day distributed environments. Lastly, we will examine what role secrets management plays within an IAM program and how it ensures secure communication.

Identity and access management

Throughout this book, we have talked extensively about identities, authentication, authorization, and access in general. Throughout this chapter, we will dive deep into some of the concepts we reviewed. Identity and access management, as you know, is an essential facet of security in the cloud (and on-premises).

It is essential to realize that effective IAM is more than just dependent on technology and tooling. Instead, IAM consists of policies, standards, procedures, and tooling that allow us to manage identities and access.

One of the most essential facets of IAM consists of policies. These policies can be shaped as authorization standards, authorization matrices, and other documents. However, regardless of the document title, we must ensure that we formalize how we deal with identities and access.

> **EXAM TIP: IAM is more than technology. It includes policies, standards, and procedures, as well as tooling.**

For example, every organization must maintain standards and procedures about the lifecycle of identities. If an employee is onboarded, a new identity must be created; if an employee changes roles, attributes about the identity must be changed. And finally, if an employee leaves the organization, an identity may have to be disabled or removed. We call this process an identity lifecycle or a joiners, movers, and leavers process.

Every organization has a different maturity level for its processes, some organizations may execute the identity lifecycle as a set of manual processes. At the same time, other organizations may fully automate their processes. As you can imagine, manual processes are often time-consuming and prone to errors.

For example, what happens if Margo changes jobs within her organization? If her role changes from programmer to system administrator, her identity may still have access to programmer resources. If the organization uses an imperfect process and her former access is not revoked, her privileges increase to encompass two roles. We call that situation **privilege creeping**. Privilege creeping can have severe consequences. Privilege can sometimes allow internal actors to stage complicated attacks due to broad access, especially when an employee is disgruntled.

Of course, we must prevent privilege creeping from occurring and making de-provisioning access for movers an essential part of the identity lifecycle. However, there are more issues we can encounter during the identity of a live cycle. If we onboard a new employee but provide adequate access, they may be able to perform their jobs. You can harm your organization by incapacitating employees by providing too few privileges. On the converse, overprovisioning access during onboarding will increase the chances of extensive systems compromise. After all, a highly privileged account may access many systems and execute complex attacks.

One effective way to battle privilege creep at the time of joining and moving is by ensuring roles have clear authorization matrices. Such matrices tie roles (or attributes) to system access. Let us look at some sample matrices for an API, as follows:

Role/Production API Privileges	Developers	System administrators	Customers
Read		X	X
Write		X	X
Delete		X	X

Table 14.1: Example matrix for a production API

Following are some example matrix for a text API:

Role/Test API privileges	Developers	System administrators	Customers
Read	X		
Write	X		
Delete	X		

Table 14.2: Example matrix for a test API

As you can see in the matrices above, an authorization matrix ties roles to access. Once you provision an identity, you like to assign a role (or other attributes to the identity). In some cases, a role may be the business role of an employee; in other cases, it may be a functional role. However, look at the difference between the production and test matrices. Developers have full access to the test environment but need access to the production environment. If an employee transitions from the developer role to the system administrator role and their developer role is not disassociated from the identity, they can still access the test environment even though the test environment must not be available to system administrators according to these matrices.

The point of the example above is simple. Whenever you perform IAM in your organization, you must consider when to provide access to an identity and when to revoke it. In general, the more complicated your authorization model becomes, the more difficult it will be to implement a process to provision or restrict access properly. Your organization should attempt to limit complexity while still ensuring identities are assigned only to provide the least number of privileges needed to perform their work.

In the cloud, your organization could choose to use **cloud infrastructure entitlements management (CIEM)**. CIEM is an evolution of regular IAM tooling that allows you to secure cloud infrastructure and services using the principle of least privilege. CIEM tools do this by monitoring identities, permissions, and activity. CIEM tools allow you to use concepts like **Just-In-Time (JIT)** access to resources across your cloud platforms. Making them very suitable in multi-cloud deployments.

EXAM TIP: Always limit privileges to the minimum needed to perform a job function. Revoke old privileges and assign new privileges if employees change jobs.

We already discussed the dangers of over or under-provisioning access tied to identities. You must also remember that identities are part of the lifecycle. For example, when employees resign or are laid off, their privileges should be revoked. Your organization should revoke privileges from identities as soon as possible. If an employee resigns, this is usually their last workday.

However, if an employee is laid off, you should revoke access while the employee is informed of the lay-off. The reason for this is that an employee who is laid off is likely to be less than pleased with the employer. Allowing such an employee to access corporate systems after becoming aware of the lay-off could allow the employee to conduct malicious actions. Revoking access before informing the employee could alert the employee of an impending lay-off and further sour the relationship between the employee and the employer.

EXAM TIP: Revoke access as soon as possible. If an employee is laid-off, revoke access at the same time as informing them.

You may have noticed that the text mentions revoking privileges rather than deleting the identity. Whenever an identity reaches the end of its lifecycle, your organization must consider several factors before deleting the identity. For example, are accounts or data tied to the account that must be maintained? Your organization may want to retain the e-mails stored in the e-mail account tied to the identity. Similarly, the identity may be used to sign into a work computer containing valuable project data. In some cases, log files may even be dynamically linked to an identity. This means deleting the identity would remove valuable information from the log files.

Because of the factors above, many organizations decide to archive or de-activate identities. That way, valuable information can be accessed if needed, and if an employee comes back to the organization, their identity could be re-instated. Of course, retaining identities also means storing information about the former employee that must be protected. Your organization will have to determine the benefits and drawbacks of either approach.

Let us summarize some of the essential factors of IAM. Firstly, we must define policies, standards, and procedures that outline how we deal with the lifecycle of identities. The facets you must include are:

- When and how we provision an identity
- When and how do we assign which privileges to an identity
- When and how do we modify privileges when employees change jobs
- When and how do we remove privileges if an employee leaves the organization
- When and how do we archive or remove identities

It is important to note that special consideration should be given to identities with extensive privileges (such as admins or senior managers). These accounts can be classified as (highly) privileged accounts. Your organization must define policies, standards, and procedures for dealing with these accounts. The practice of dealing with such accounts and associated risks is called **privileged account management (PAM)**.

PAM is part of IAM and is especially important. Privileged accounts may be treated with more scrutiny than regular accounts. For example, if you use automatic processes for PAM, consider periodic manual reviews to ensure the processes work correctly. Similarly, an organization may require MFA or other attribute-based checks before accessing privileged accounts.

EXAM TIP: Privileged accounts are especially powerful in the cloud because of their on-demand self-service nature.

Identity providers

As mentioned in the previous section, IAM is comprised of multiple facets. One of these facets is tooling. As organizations scale, it becomes more and more challenging to use manual administration. Mainly because most organizations heavily rely on technology in their day-to-day operations. At the core of IAM lies the fact that we must maintain identities. Identities are the core of IAM as they assign roles, store information, and ultimately provide access.

Historically, many organizations used on-premises identity stores, like Active Directory Domain Services. Organizations commonly rely on Microsoft active directory or similar directory technology to create a database of users and administrate information about them. However, with the rise of cloud computing, many organizations use applications hosted outside their on-premises environment or even entirely switched to applications in the cloud.

One of the main issues this presents is that only some applications may be capable of connecting to the directory that stores your identity. Some applications or systems may even maintain their directory of identities. Having multiple identity stores creates a couple of significant issues. Firstly, maintaining identities in various systems using various formats is very time-consuming. Secondly, having multiple different identity stores invites room for error.

For example, if an employee changes jobs but the process used to restrict privileges does not include all identity stores, only part of the privileges will be restored. In practice, this happens frequently, allowing employees to retain access to systems they should not have access to.

In an ideal world, an organization would maintain a single directory of users, their information, and their roles. By doing so, an organization only needs to grant or revoke privileges in a single system. Similarly, any updates to the user's information would be contained in a single source of truth. Unfortunately, many of the user directories of the past do not allow for integration with cloud or web-based applications.

Luckily, a technology called an **identity provider (IdP)** comes to the rescue. An IdP can be a company, external, or internal software package. An IdP can perform similar activities to any regular directory tool. Meaning it offers a place to store identities, attributes, and roles. An IdP tool can be used for user federation, which is covered in-depth in chapter two. However, IdP providers (often CSPs) have built tools that integrate easily with existing directory tooling and offer easy integration options with other platforms.

In many cases, an IdP can import information from an on-premises directory (on an ongoing basis). The benefit of this is that your organization may be able to use the directory tooling that they host on-premises but allow integration with the data from this service through the IdP. An IdP can allow you to use your on-premises identities with other tools that might not typically integrate with your on-premises directory.

Aside from options to integrate an IdP tool or provider with an existing directory, most IdP tools also allow you to maintain a new user directory. Companies transitioning to a cloud-first or cloud-native environment should highly consider using their CSP IdP. The IdP tooling provided by CSPs is often profoundly integrated with the cloud environment. This integration can allow you to provide identities with direct access to certain services. Similarly, these CSP IdPs still allow integration with other 3rd party tools.

Regardless of your organization's situation, finding a way to maintain a single source of identity is essential. Whether you devise a way to allow your on-premises identities to be used by other applications or if you choose to build and maintain identities in a (cloud-native) IdP platform is mainly dependent on your organization's capabilities.

You may have heard of some IdP tools . One thing these IDPs have in common is that they provide a store for identities and perform authentication. An IdP that performs authentication is highly valuable as you can use it as a central authentication source (we will discuss this more in the SSO section). Allowing authentication through a single source is powerful, but it also requires something important, standardization.

Most IdPs support standard authentication like the **Security Assertion Markup Language (SAML)**, **OpenID Connect (OIDC)**, and authorization protocols like OAuth 2.0. Using these standard protocols (which we will dive into more detail) allows IdP tools to easily integrate with other applications and systems that use these standards. Configuration is often the only thing needed to integrate an IdP with an application when adequately implemented.

Single sign-on

One of the main benefits of an identity provider is that it offers a single source of truth on identities. But, as mentioned previously, IdP tools can offer additional benefits. Whenever an IdP can authenticate, it can also serve as a single authentication source (and sometimes authorization). Now, this is where using IDPs becomes especially interesting. When you have a central database of identities and a tool to authenticate the identity, you can allow your user to log in once and prove their identity to multiple applications. We call this process **single sign on (SSO)**.

To understand single sign-on, let us first look at how we authenticate ourselves in an environment with applications that use different identity stores. Let us take a look at an example as follows:

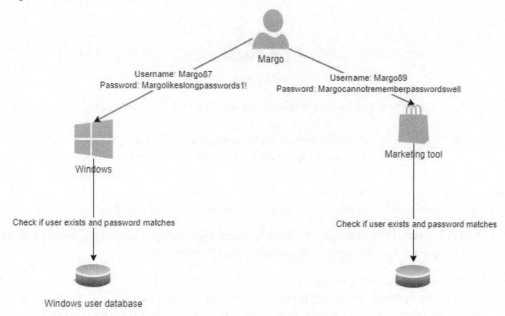

Figure 14.1: Authentication using multiple user directories

In the example above, you can see that employee Margo has two different usernames and passwords. One username and password combination is used to log in to her Windows environment, while the other is used to log in to a marketing tool. Both tools verify if the information provided by Margo is correct (they authenticate her). After that, they also allow her (or prevent her) access to the system (authorizing her). Margo only has two accounts now, but what if the organization used 20 different tools with its identity stores? Margo would have to remember 20 sets of credentials, and if Margo left the organization, every single identity store would need to be updated.

Now, let us look at what authentication looks like if we use a single on-premises directory:

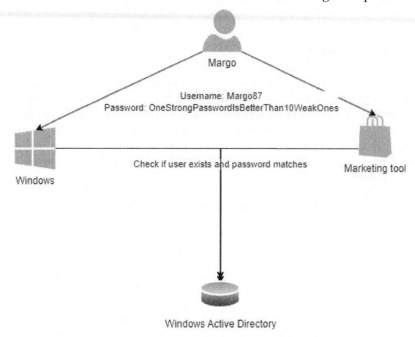

Figure 14.2: Using a single identity directory to authenticate users

As you can see above, if you use a single identity directory that allows you to authenticate users, they only have to remember one set of credentials. Limiting the amount of credentials employees need is essential for security. After all, if you must remember many different passwords, you are likelier to choose weaker passwords or even write them down. Both factors can significantly increase the chance of password compromise.

EXAM TIP: Centralized storage of identities can be more secure, significantly, if they reduce the number of passwords employees must remember.

Remember that cloud computing offers us broad access? Broad access means we can easily access our systems from anywhere. However, in many cases, our systems are also dispersed. For example, one application may be hosted on-premises, another may be hosted by one CSP, and a third one may be hosted by another CSP. The dispersion of these systems causes complications for the figure above. After all, every system must be able to connect to the identity directory to perform centralized authentication. Unless you have an IdP that is reachable through public (or private networks live VPNs), applications outside your IdPs network will not be able to use your directory information.

This is where the benefits of many modern-day IdP tools and providers come in. Instead of having an on-premises identity directory, they may offer an identity store with broad access, which means that your applications can access the identity provider from various places. Because of this broad access, regardless of the location, an application can use its central identity store to gather information and authenticate (and authorize users).

Now that you understand the role of an IdP, we must look at how SSO works. As mentioned, you want to ensure that users have to remember as few passwords as possible. However, users will get frustrated if they have to authenticate with every application every time they require access. This is where single sign-on comes in. SSO technologies allow a user to log in (authenticate) once and be able to authenticate and authorize other applications without further user action.

REAL-LIFE TIP: SSO is essential if your employees use many different applications.

Let us look at how this works using the OAuth 2.0 redirect flow. When you use OAuth, you have three main parties in the exchange. Firstly, the service provider. In the context of OAuth, the service provider is the application you are trying to use. For example, the service provider could be a website like amazon.com. The second party is the identity provider. The identity provider is the entity that stores your identity and authenticates you. The last part is the user trying to gain access to the application.

Whenever the user accesses the service provider, the service provider redirects the user to a page hosted by the identity provider. This page is usually a customized login page. At this point, the user provides their username, password (and other information like MFA codes if needed). The login page then sends the user's data to the authentication server part of the identity provider. Which then verifies if the user provided the correct information to authenticate. If so, the identity provider redirects the user to the service provider's website. But, as the user is redirected, the IdP also passes a token (secret code) back to the service provider. The service provider then uses the token to ask the IdP if the token is still valid and requests information about the user. Once the service provider receives the user info, it determines if the user can use it, the flow is shown as follows:

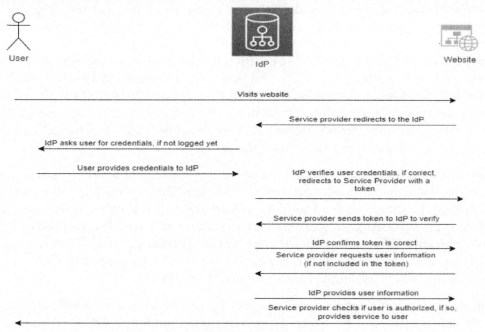

Figure 14.3: OAuth 2.0 redirect flow

It is essential to mention that the diagram above is one of the ways the OAuth framework prescribes authentication can take place. The CCSP exam does not expect you to be familiar with these implementations.

Now that you understand the flow of using an IdP to authenticate your identities and provide access to a service provider, it is essential to understand SAML and OIDC's role. As mentioned, for an IdP to be functional, it must integrate with as many platforms as possible. After all, every platform that does not integrate might require a separate identity store. While OAuth flows dictate how flows should occur (to be secure and convenient), SAML and OIDC offer protocols to make this exchange happen. Ergo, you can see OAuth as the blueprint for modern authentication on the web, while SAML and OIDC offer the means to perform it.

EXAM TIP: You must understand that OAuth 2.0 is a framework that outlines authentication exchanges. SAML and OIDC are protocols that are used to build these exchanges.

If you have an IdP that supports SAML as a protocol but not OIDC, you should ensure you use applications that at least support SAML. In general, it is wise to attempt to implement an IdP that supports both SAML and OIDC, as that significantly improves compatibility between your IdP and service providers.

Alright, there are some important factors we have to consider for SSO. As mentioned, we want as little number of credential sets as possible. Which, as you can, can be achieved by federating identities through an IdP. However, we also want to limit frustration for employees. Having to provide credentials every time you log in is frustrating and may compel users to fight against MFA (more about this later) and complex passwords. You may have noticed that the OAuth 2.0 redirect flow mentions it makes the user log in if they still need to log in. The beauty of using an IdP is that it can store a session in your browser (using a cookie). Every time you visit an application that authenticates users through your IdP, the IdP can check if the session owned by the user is still valid. If so, it can redirect the user to the service provider immediately, negating the need to authenticate again. Instead, the service provider will be provided with the token and continue gathering user information from the IdP and authorizing the user.

Simply put, single sign-on is possible whenever we implement the same authentication provider as the authenticator for our service providers. Because the IdP authenticates the user and provides them with a token, it can skip the authentication steps if the token is valid. Next time you use your work computer, consider how your browser behaves when accessing an application. If you open the application, you see a redirect and a white screen quickly, and then you get access to the application you witnessed the OAuth redirect flow while still logged in. Meaning you just benefitted from SSO.

While SSO is very pleasant for users and generally more secure, some essential security considerations exist. You may have to perform authorization inside your application, depending on your protocol. You may have noticed that the IdP authenticates the user.

However, the application must establish if the user should have access. The service provider must use the information it requests about the user to determine if the user has the correct role or attributes to gain access to the application.

Whenever you implement SSO, you must realize that you may have to perform authorization on the application side. Because of this, you may need to build different rule sets in every application to determine if the user should gain access after being authenticated by the IdP.

Imagine the following scenario. Margo is a IT manager and has the IT manager role assigned to her. When Margo logs in to the HR tool, the role of the manager may authorize her to access the data of her employees. However, when Margo logs in to a finance application, the role of IT manager may not give her any access. Each application will have to interpret Margo's attributes to decide what she is authorized to do.

It is good to note that some IdPs are capable of including authorization information as part of SSO. These IdPs can be used to create a more centralized authorization model.

EXAM TIP: SSO is for authentication, NOT for authorization

Another essential consideration for SSO is that it can also introduce risk because we allow a user to authenticate once and then use that session for a prolonged period, increasing the chance of compromise of the session. For example, if an attacker can steal the session token provided to the user by the IdP, the attacker could you the token to impersonate the user until the session expires. Of course, this is true for authentication mechanisms without SSO as well. However, we need to be more concerned with protecting these sessions because SSO often offers access to many (if not all applications). Your organization should establish a session lifespan that minimizes user frustration while, at the same time, limiting the potential for compromise of the session.

One of the approaches you can use is to limit the session lifespan. Try to limit session lifespans to the length of the workday (at most). Depending on your organization, you may want to invalidate sessions if the same session is used from another IP address or geographic location where it was created, as this could be a sign of a stolen session.

Multi-factor authentication

While SSO allows us to authenticate with multiple applications easily, we must also pay close attention to user authentication. For example, what happens if someone's password is stolen through phishing, shoulder surfing, or a simple accident? If an attacker gains access to credentials, they can easily access corporate systems, mainly if SSO is used. As an organization, you should protect yourself against abuse of stolen or lost credentials. The primary way to do this is by requiring MFA, sometimes called **two factor authentication**. (**2FA**). We already discussed MFA as part of physical security requirements.

For example, an organization may require a user to provide a username, password, and keycard. If the user's keycard is stolen, one can only use it if they know the username and password (and vice versa).

When we talk about MFA, we try to achieve authentication by verifying multiple factors (2FA only requires two factors). Can I give users a set of two passwords and verify both to achieve MFA? Well, not exactly. There are different ways to prove your identity. To implement MFA, you must require your user to prove their identity using methods from different categories. Let us look at these categories:

Category	Examples
Something you know	A password or a pin code
Something you are	Fingerprints, palm scans, iris scans, retina scans, and voice scans
Something you have	Keycards, e-mail account to receive emails, phone to receive text messages, security tokens (physical or digital), and keys

Table 14.3: Categories of authentication factors

As you can see above, using two different passwords only uses a method from the *Something you know* category. However, we would need a combination of the categories to achieve MFA. For example, you could require a password and a fingerprint. Or a code sent to the user by test message and a pin code the user knows. The reason behind using methods from different categories is that compromising methods from multiple categories is much more challenging.

For example, if someone steals your badge, they do not automatically gain access to the password in your memory. However, if they were able to steal your badge, there is a decent chance they could also steal your key or phone.

For those who have seen or read *Dan Brown's Angels and Demons*, the adversaries in this book/movie use physical violence to get a retina scan of an employee to gain access to a facility. As you can imagine, if you can force someone to provide a retina scan, you can probably force them to provide a fingerprint as well.

EXAM TIP: MFA requires at least two methods from different categories to authenticate a user.

An important consideration when you implement MFA is that the more factors you require, the higher the level of security is. Unfortunately, requiring more factors also raises the level of inconvenience. Imagine you were required to unlock a door by entering a key on a keypad, providing a fingerprint on a scanner, and then scanning your badge. While this has made it more challenging to gain authorized access, it will likely cause frustration. As always, you must balance the need for security with ease of use.

Aside from ease of access, it would be best if you also considered the properties of every factor you require. For example, a 4-digit pin is weaker than a 15-character passphrase. Similarly, a code sent by text message is less secure than an authenticator app. You are implementing more secure factors like authenticator apps over texts or e-mails.

However, you must consider the type of tools at the disposal of your employees. Requiring the wrong type of factor can have detrimental effects on availability. For example, if you have remote workers, requiring them to use a password and a physical key to access a server would make remote work impossible. However, requiring a fingerprint, authenticator app, digital keycode, or even a badge (if you offer a badge reader) would work well.

REAL-LIFE TIP: Think carefully about the factors you require. Try to enable multiple factors to facilitate different types of employees (if needed).

Cloud access security brokers

IdPs, MFA, and SSO all significantly influence how we perform IAM. As we discussed, cloud computing has also significantly impacted IAM. Over the past decades, many organizations have moved from strictly on-premises networks to networks that span multiple CSPs. While IdPs, MFA, and SSOs help us authenticate in such environments, the increased remote work from outside networks still poses risks we must address.

For example, traditional on-premises networks may include network-based intrusion detection, malware prevention, monitoring, logging, and so on. However, if employees work remotely through cloud-based tools, none of their network traffic may pass through a company-managed network. This is especially true if an organization relies mainly on SaaS tools and needs to maintain its cloud network with VPNs or applications within complete control of the organization.

In the past, **network access control** (**NAC**) could only provide corporately managed devices with access to the corporate network. Access to the corporate network is necessary for most applications to be available. However, in the world of cloud environments, broad access means anyone can access our application from anywhere. Without further security measures, employees could use their home computers to navigate to corporate environments in the cloud and use their valid credentials to authenticate and gain access.

Once an employee gains access from an unmanaged device, it becomes possible to store data on their machine without being able to apply the appropriate security measures. For example, the computer may be infected with malware; the employee may lose their laptop and its data if the laptop does not have full disk encryption. Many horror scenarios could severely compromise an organization because we allow broad access.

Sometimes, you can provide additional security measures like mutual certificate authentication to ensure that only corporate devices can access an application. However, building consistent and effective security policies can become challenging if you use dozens of SaaS applications.

A new type of product has been developed to combat the problems of broad access and the difficulty of managing various environments. This product/service is a **cloud access security broker** (**CASB**). Let us examine the way a CASB works using the illustration as shown:

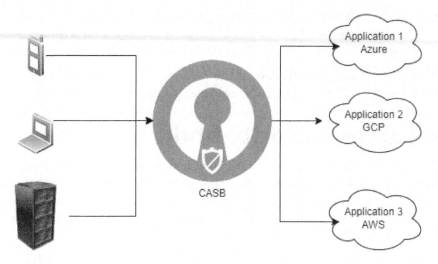

***Figure 14.4**: Cloud access security broker to implement security across providers.*

As you can see in the figure above, a CASB functions as a gatekeeper between users and cloud applications. In essence, a CASB works like a proxy. Instead of sending your traffic straight to the cloud environment, the traffic is routed to the CASB. The CASB then evaluates if your device can access the environment, has applied the correct security controls, and may perform advanced security scans (such as malware scanning and intrusion detection). If you pass the security checks, your traffic is forwarded to the cloud, and you can use the application. The strength of a CASB is that it can be implemented in various ways. For example, a CASB may be used to brokerage traffic to the cloud from an on-premises network. However, it might have agents on mobile devices like laptops, phones, or even servers. A CASB can be used to broker traffic and apply security controls, even from a network connected to a non-managed network.

Of course, many other tools, like endpoint security tools, can also perform some of these tasks. The main benefit of CASB is that CASB providers built their tools to be useable across different cloud platforms. The CASB provider may allow direct integration with the CSP. In other cases, the CASB tooling may present a solution that can be used across platforms.

Using a CASB can help your organization secure access to its resources. However, it does not secure access to infrastructure and other resources per say. A **secure access service edge (SASE)**, in contrast to CASB, uses a combination of zero trust tools to create a zero-trust cloud-native network. It combines tools like **secure web gateways (SWG)**, **Firewall as a Service (FWaaS)**, and **Zero Trust Network Access (ZTNA)**, and **Data Loss Prevention (DLP)** tooling to create a highly secure network that can be used to access resources securely from any location.

EXAM TIP: CASB uses a proxy mechanism to enforce security controls across different cloud platforms. CASB is especially useful if you use many different cloud providers.

Secrets management

Throughout the chapter, we have talked in detail about identities. You know that identities should be tied to a singular person. Suppose we create generalized identities for entire teams. In that case, it becomes impossible to trace who did what, which is detrimental to incident response efforts, digital forensics, and legal recourse after an attack. However, not every identity has to belong to a physical person. In some cases, identities can represent services, applications, or infrastructure. Especially in the cloud environment, a service might be an entity that you can use to provide or deny access to. In most IdP tools you will find in the cloud, you can let your services function as an identity.

Whenever your services authenticate within the cloud environment, their authentication can often be handled by the native IdP. The benefit is that you are not required to create credentials for these services. Instead, the CSP takes care of the authentication process for you. Using the built-in IdP lets you create rules that allow one service to talk to another without worrying about how they authenticate (usually through roles or rules).

However, it is likely, that within your environment, you will have system-to-system or service-to-service communication that cannot be authenticated through the native IdP tooling. For example, you may host a VM that runs a database. The DB may be accessed by a software application running inside a container. Your software must be able to authenticate itself to the database to be able to gain access. Throughout the book, we have already discussed the need for secret management. Most CSPs offer cloud-native solutions to store secrets like API keys, database credentials, or other forms of authentication information.

It is essential to determine how your services will communicate whenever your organization defines its environment. It would be best if you strived to use your regular IdP where possible. However, when your services communicate through any secret, you should employ secrets management tools within the CSP's toolset or provide your own secrets management technologies.

Conclusion

This chapter taught us that IAM is not a matter of tools alone. Policies, standards, and procedures are the foundation of effective and secure IAM. Every organization must define processes for their joiners, movers, and leavers process. Using an IdP can be a great way to centralize your identities and enable simplified identity management while also allowing you to authenticate users through a single source.

Implementing IdP tooling will also allow your organization to implement single sign-on to reduce employee effort while at the same time helping users abide to secure credential management practices. Aside from SSO, your organization should consider implementing MFA. Using MFA, your organization can reduce the risk of abuse of (accidentally) disclosed credentials. For MFA to be effective, you should use different methods to prove the user's identity. For example, when you use a password (something you know), you should combine it with something you have (like a keycard) or something you are (like a fingerprint).

An IdP can ensure your organization can authenticate through a single source when using multiple applications, even when hosted in different clouds. Unfortunately, broad access still means employees can easily access loud resources from non-managed devices. Implementing a CASB tool can allow your organization to uniformly implement security controls and policies regardless of the network (or device) the user originates from. CASBs function by proxying the traffic to your cloud environment, performing checks, and applying security controls on that traffic.

Aside from IdPs, SSO, MFA, and CASB, it is essential to remember that highly privileged accounts are an important facet of IAM in the cloud. By implementing PAM, your organization can stay on top of these powerful accounts and ensure they are not exploited for evil. Similarly, your organization should be mindful of authentication between systems and services. Avoid always using generalized accounts and store any secrets you need in a secret management tool.

In the next chapter, you will learn more about infrastructure security through **hardware security modules (HSMs)**, **Trusted Platform Modules (TPMs)**, hypervisor, and operating system security.

Learning goals

This chapter addresses the following CCSP exam outline learning goals:

Domain 4: Cloud application security

> 4.7 Design appropriate **identity and access management (IAM)** solutions.

Join our book's Discord space

Join the book's Discord Workspace for Latest updates, Offers, Tech happenings around the world, New Release and Sessions with the Authors:

https://discord.bpbonline.com

CHAPTER 15
Infrastructure Security

Introduction

Logical isolation and data encryption are the most important ways to ensure that multi-tenancy is secure. Encrypting data requires storage of keys; without secure key management, data can easily be decrypted or, on the flip side, may remain indefinitely encrypted.

This chapter will explore how infrastructure security is vital in enabling confidentiality while maintaining availability. We will discuss how you can secure common cloud infrastructure components such as containers and virtual machines. At the same time, we will look at the security of other important infrastructures such as hypervisors and the technologies used for securely storing keys and certificates. Moreover, we will look into isolation at the hypervisor level and security inside virtual guest operating systems.

Structure

This chapter covers the following topics:

- Infrastructure and multi-tenancy
- Hardware security module
- Trusted platform module

- Hypervisor security

- Guest OS security

Objectives

This chapter dives deeper into security measures that are needed for cloud infrastructure. Throughout the chapter, you will learn how physical components like a **hardware security module (HSM)** or **Trusted Platform Module (TPM)** are essential to data encryption (even within virtual environments). Aside from securing the physical infrastructure, the chapter also dives into the role of hypervisor and guest OS security, as they are vital to ensuring a secure cloud environment. At the end of the chapter, you will understand how these components are building blocks for secure computing throughout every service model in the cloud.

Infrastructure and multi-tenancy

Security in the cloud always comes back to the characteristics of cloud computing. You have already seen that broad access, on-demand self-service, and resource pooling have extensive security impacts. General access requires us to consider who will access our environments from where. At the same time, on-demand self-service creates unprecedented risks by allowing attackers to develop complicated environments and sustain a foothold after a successful breach. Resource pooling presents risks because it only works by allowing a vast number of customers to access a shared set of computing resources dynamically.

It is essential for a CCSP to fully understand the risks that come along with the cloud characteristics. However, knowing how to minimize these risks to fully benefit from what the cloud offers is even more critical. In this chapter, we need to look deeper into the impact of resource pooling in conjunction with on-demand self-service. Resource pooling is an essential building block of the cloud. Resource pooling allows us to quickly scale our environments without breaking the bank. After all, pooling resources allows a CSP to keep costs low but offer scalable on-demand computing.

Unfortunately, the pooling of resources means that these resources are assigned and released based on customer demand. For example, if your application is sustaining significant traffic, you may have created policies to automatically spin up new instances of your application to distribute the load. These resources are allocated to your organization on demand. Once traffic to your application slows down, you can start rereleasing the help. Once resources are released, they can be assigned to other CSP customers.

Let us think of this concept in the sense of on-premises computing. Imagine Elliot and Alice both need to perform calculations for a science project. Their university has a science lab containing five computers. Elliot likes to get up early in the morning and decides to perform calculations from 08:00 a.m. until 01:45 p.m. To conduct his analyses, Elliot needs three computers. Alice had classes in the morning and decided to start running her calculations at 02:00 p.m. Alice's calculations are more time-consuming and require all five computers. Luckily, Elliot's calculations are already completed. This means Alice can use all five computers.

Now, in the example above, the computers are physical workstations. The workstations use hard drives to store data. As such, Elliot's calculations are stored on the same hard disk that holds the measures that Alice will perform. Because both parties use the same physical machines to complete the math, gaining access to the other person's estimates would be pretty straightforward. For example, Alice could physically access the hard drive and copy the drive's data. Alternatively, Alice may be able to logically access the industry through the operating system on the computer. Depending on the setup, she may be able to access the files through the operating system directly. As you can imagine, this is detrimental to the confidentiality, integrity, and availability of the data produced by Alice and Elliot.

While it is clear-cut why data may be at risk in the example above, the same concept occurs in cloud computing. However, rather than accessing a machine physically, you are gaining access to a computer remotely. If the computer does not store your data separately from other customer data, others could easily access it. Similarly, your data could be accessed by CSP personnel with physical access to the storage devices.

You could employ full disk encryption to prevent physical access to the drive from compromising confidentiality. Similarly, you could use virtualization as a measure of isolation and encrypted virtual hard drives to ensure customers cannot access each other's data in the virtual environment. But remember, encryption only works if you can access the encryption key. Similarly, isolation is only effective if it cannot be broken. In the sections below, we will dive into some of the tools we have at our disposal to allow resource pooling (or multi-tenancy) without compromising our data.

Hardware security module

Encryption and key management go hand in hand. You cannot rely on encryption to protect your data without a secure way to store keys. Instead, it may even render your data useless. As we talked about, many devices need encryption keys.

For example, a machine might have encryption at the disk level, encryption for virtual disks, and encryption at the database level. Whenever you store keys, you must ensure you do not keep them inside of the encrypted media. After all, if you do, you cannot retrieve/ recover the key when you need it, especially if the key has to be used programmatically. Let us look at the difference:

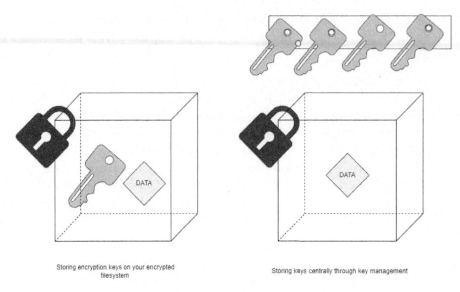

Storing encryption keys on your encrypted
filesystem

Storing keys centrally through key management

Figure 15.1: *Proper key management is essential to data availability*

So, you now know that you should store encryption keys on a separate system. However, if you have multiple encryption keys for different systems, you may not want them all to be accessible to everybody who has system access. This is where the concept of a **hardware security module (HSM)** comes in.

An HSM is a hardware device (a computer, really) that can store encryption keys. At the same time, an HSM can securely provide access to specific keys to specific users, as shown:

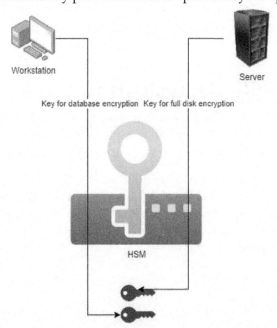

Figure 15.2: *HSMs can store keys for different systems and users (virtual or otherwise)*

An HSM can hold many different encryption keys for other customers without compromising the confidentiality of the keys. HSMs are also specially produced. For example, an HSM can store encryption keys for various customer virtual machines. The HSM will only provide access to the customer's encryption if the customer can authenticate.

The beauty of an HSM is that it can also perform cryptographic operations. So, rather than sending sensitive encryption keys throughout the environment, an HSM can encrypt or decrypt the data with the HSM and share the result with the user. There are some profound benefits to this. For one, HSMs are built for cryptographic operations, which can improve performance. Secondly, performing cryptographic operations within the HSM limits the potential for crucial compromise. Aside from performing cryptographic operations, it can also securely create, destroy and rotate keys.

Let us summarize what an HSM can do. An HSM creates, stores, archives, and destroys keys. In short, an HSM manages a key's lifecycle. Secondly, an HSM can perform cryptographic operations and authenticate and authorize users of keys to ensure keys are only used by authorized users. However, these features still do not protect the keys from being physically compromised. If a CSP employee gains access to the HSM, they could attempt to access its hard drive and obtain the keys. It is essential to store HSMs in areas that limit physical access to the device as much as possible.

EXAM TIP: The physical security of HSMs is essential. They should be stored in the most restricted areas of a DC.

Fortunately, HSMs are designed to be tamperproof. A tamper-proof design means the HSM is designed to prevent illegitimate (physical) access. One of the ways this can be guaranteed is by self-destructive mechanisms. If the system detects physical damage to the device, it may erase the stored keys or render the system unusable. Many laws and regulations have specific requirements that force organizations to employ HSMs within the environment. Also, rules and regulations may impose conditions on the HSM's level of security and tamper-proofness.

EXAM TIP: HSMs are tamperproof, meaning they have controls to prevent tampering and can render themselves unusable if tampering is detected. It is essential to realize the role of HSMs in cloud environments. As you know, a CSP may offer functionality to encrypt data. Whenever you use built-in encryption technologies or request a new certificate in your cloud environment, the CSP has to be able to safely generate, use, and distribute certificates and keys. By using HSMs, CSPs can ensure the key materials they generate for their customers are generated and stored securely. HSMs also play an essential role is isolating key and certificate material for each customer.

FIPS 140-2 and FIPS 140-3

One of the standards to evaluate the security of an HSM is the **Federal Information Processing Standard (FIPS)** 140-2 and 140-3. The NIST created the FIPS 140-2 in 2001, which is mandatory for US governmental agencies and their contractors. In 2021, the NIST switched to a new iteration of the standard in FIPS 140-3, now the applicable standard.

EXAM TIP: The CCSP exam may mention either FIPS 140-2 or FIPS 140-3.

The FIPS 140-3 details specific requirements for HSMs, such as the cryptographic algorithms permitted, how keys should be generated, how anti-tamper mechanisms should work, and how they must be protected against **electromagnetic interference** (**EMI**).

It is important to note that the FIPS standard recognizes four levels of security. The higher the level, the better the security measures a HSM provides. It is important to note that the security level also determines what the HSM can be used for. Let us look at the levels, refer to the following table:

Level 1	Production grade equipment and externally tested algorithms
Level 2	Level 1 + Protection against physical tampering and role-based authentication.
Level 3	Level 2 + additional physical tampering protection and identity-based authentication
Level 4	Level 3 + self-destruction of data if tampering is detected

Table 15.1: Broad overview of the FIPS 140-2/140-3 levels

For example, an HSM with security level 1 cannot be used for the same applications as a level 4 HSM. For the CCSP exam, you do not need to know the FIPS 140-2/140-3 standards' various levels. However, you should be able to recognize that HSMs have different levels of security depending on their level.

It is essential to know that HSMs can be certified against the FIPS and **Common Criteria** (**CC**). If your organization is required to comply with FIPS, you must verify that your CSP uses HSMs that comply with these standards.

PCI-DSS

Aside from US governmental agencies, any organization under **Payment Card Industry-Data Security Standard (PCI-DDS)** has specific requirements for HSMs. PCI-DSS is a self-regulated industry standard for the credit card payments industry. Self-regulated means it applies only to the members of that industry, and enforcement and accountability are organized within the industry.

For the CCSP exam, you do not need to know the PCI-DSS requirements for HSMs. Nevertheless, you should be aware that they exist. If your organization is subject to PCI-DSS, you should evaluate CSPs based on compliance with PCI-DSS.

Trusted Platform Module

As you can imagine, an HSM is a costly appliance. While many cloud providers have seamlessly integrated them within their cloud-based critical management systems, they may need to be more affordable for on-premises deployments. Even more so, HSMs are only useable for some types of deployment.

For example, if your organization uses mobile devices like phones and laptops, these devices cannot connect to an HSM to encrypt their disks. The machines may only sometimes have network access and most need to be physically connected to the HSM in your data center (or the cloud).

Nevertheless, these mobile devices still require encryption and thus require access to keys. Remember that we discussed not storing encryption keys on your encrypted media? In the case of a mobile device, we need somewhere to keep our encryption keys other than its internal hard drive. After all, the internal hard drive is what needs to be encrypted.

Instead of storing the keys on the internal storage media, we can use a **Trusted Platform Module**. A TPM is a tiny HSM that is placed inside your device. A TPM is a small chip on the device's motherboard. It stores the encryption keys and ensures they cannot be accessed without the proper authentication and authorization.

In practice, you have likely worked with devices fitted with a TPM. For example, Windows 11 requires a device with a TPM to run the operating system. The beauty of a TPM is that it offers a more secure way to store your keys without them being held on the device's hard drive. Let us look at a simplified version of **Microsoft Bitlocker** encryption:

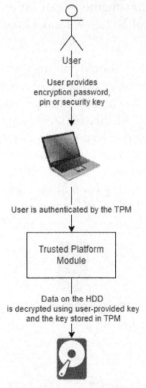

Figure 15.3: Simplified representation of full-disk decryption using Microsoft Bitlocker

Like an HSM, a TPM can perform certain cryptographic operations. Because of this, a TPM can also help speed up certain cryptographic operations on your machine. Additionally, TPMs can be used for digital rights management (such as software license management) and even to store device certificates.

While TPMs offer a different level of security than HSMs, they are essential for (mobile) devices that do not have access to HSMs. The difference between HSMs and TPMs is listed in the following table:

TPM	HSM
Made for end-user devices	Made to be used by many machines and servers
Secure, but not as advanced as an HSM	Very secure
Limited cryptographic capabilities	Massive cryptographic capabilities

Table 15.2: Differences between TPMs and HSMs

Hypervisor security

Encrypting data is essential to ensure unauthorized users cannot access it. We must encrypt entire disks of physical machines, virtual storage devices, and application-level data like databases. While these encryption methods can help us protect against data exposure stemming from physical or logical access, we must take more actions to ensure the secure isolation of infrastructure.

As discussed throughout the book, resource pooling means sharing our cloud infrastructure with other customers. The CSP must virtualize environments on top of physical hardware to do so. After all, we cannot all use one operating system on a single physical computer and have isolated environments. At this point, you have already learned that to create virtualized environments, we need a hypervisor. A hypervisor is a specialized piece of software that can create multiple virtual instances of one physical computer. The cases use the physical computing resources by virtualizing them. This virtualization allows us to split processor cores, RAM, networking capabilities, and storage devices between different environments. In most cases, a single CPU can power many other virtual machines this way, as shown in the following figure:

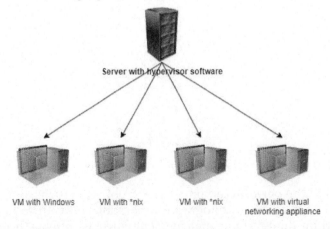

Figure 15.4: One physical machine can create many virtual machines that share its resources

We already looked at the impact of shared storage devices on a single physical machine. Unfortunately, using other computing resources like CPUs, networking cards, and RAM presents additional challenges to isolating the environments. After all, if multiple virtual machines have access to the same CPU, they could gain access to the data being processed. Similarly, sharing RAM modules between virtual environments could allow one virtual machine to access data created in RAM by another domain.

As you can imagine, providing isolation on every shared resource is essential. We must ensure that each VM can only access its part of the CPU, RAM, and another networking device, especially in cloud environments where many organizations that change at a moment's notice may share a physical machine. While complex drive data can be easily isolated by encryption, data used by processors or stored in RAM does not have this luxury. While encryption is possible, it would tremendously require significant computing resources and harm performance. At the same time, data would still have to be decrypted when processed anyway, once again opening up the data for exposure.

While the CCSP exam does not expect you to understand or name the processes used to isolate the compute resources, isolation is essential. Similarly, you must understand the different types of hypervisors we can use and how they affect security.

EXAM TIP: For the CCSP exam, you must understand that (logical) isolation of resources is necessary for secure virtualization.

Let us take a deeper look at the different types of hypervisors. If you read the book in order, you are already familiar with type 1 and 2 hypervisors.

A type 1 hypervisor is a specialized hypervisor. The hypervisor functions as an operating system and is installed directly on the physical hardware (like a standard computer running Windows, MacOS, or Linux). Rather than offering an extensive operating system with many applications, a type 1 hypervisor is a minimalistic OS that is specialized in virtualization. Any unnecessary software is stripped from a hypervisor. Because of its lean nature, type 1 hypervisors are generally fast and less prone to vulnerable software. After all, software that is not there cannot break or be hacked.

Typical **Type 1** hypervisors you may have heard of are Microsoft **Hyper V**, **VMWare vSphere**, **Proxmox**, and others. However, large CSPs might use in-house hypervisor software unavailable to other companies. Understanding that the hypervisor's security is paramount to secure virtualization is essential.

Type 2 Hypervisors perform the same actions as **Type 1 Hypervisors**. However, the main difference is that a **Type 2 Hypervisor** does not run directly on the underlying hardware, as shown:

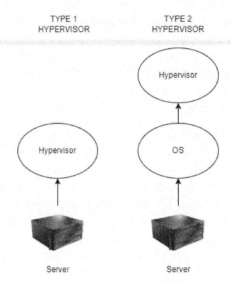

Figure 15.5: The difference between a type 1 and type 2 hypervisor

Instead, it runs as software on top of another operating system. The benefit to this is that you can use a Type 2 hypervisor on a computer that does not have the sole purpose of virtualization. After all, you can start or stop the hypervisor when needed and use the computer for other purposes while it is off. Unfortunately, running on top of another OS makes a hypervisor less efficient. The OS consumes valuable computing resources, meaning fewer resources are available for the hypervisor to assign to virtual environments. Another downside is that the underlying OS is usually not built to be minimalistic and security oriented. Because of this, it may be easier to breach the OS of a **Type 2** hypervisor to gain access to than to breach a **Type 1** hypervisor itself.

Regardless of the hypervisor type, attackers may compromise your hypervisor if its underlying OS contains vulnerabilities. Such a compromise would allow attackers to access every virtualized environment within the hypervisor. This means the attacker can spread malware, as shown below, or take other adverse actions against your virtual environment, refer to the following image:

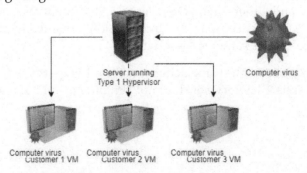

Figure 15.6: Hypervisor compromise can compromise all virtual machines

As you can imagine, any hypervisor must be hardened to prevent misconfiguration and vulnerable software. Similarly, a hypervisor should be protected by security measures such as anti-virus/anti-malware and **Data-loss Prevention (DLP)** tooling. Aside from active and passive security controls, a hypervisor should also be configured to send its log files to your centralized logging platform, and the logs should be examined for breach indicators.

In short, when evaluating a CSP for security, you should carefully examine how they harden, test, and secure their hypervisors. Poor hypervisor security will likely lead to a compromise of your virtual environments over time. However, as with anything in the cloud, responsibilities are shared between the CSP and the customer. While a vulnerable hypervisor can compromise VMs, a vulnerable VM might also compromise the hypervisor.

Remember that Type 1 hypervisors are generally more secure than Type 2 hypervisors. However, you may not always have the need or capability to dedicate a machine to being a hypervisor. In case you want to run a small number of VMs or if you simply want to virtualize from time to time, a Type 2 hypervisor may be more suitable. In the next section, we will look at security inside virtual environments.

Guest OS security

We just talked about security on the side of the hypervisor. However, attackers may only sometimes attempt to attack this layer of the virtualization infrastructure. Instead, it may be simpler to attack the virtualized environments themselves. In some cases, attackers might target these environments to gain access to the data and applications contained within the environment. However, they could also try to use a virtual environment that runs on top of a hypervisor to break into the hypervisor. We call this practice **virtual machine escape**, pictured as follows:

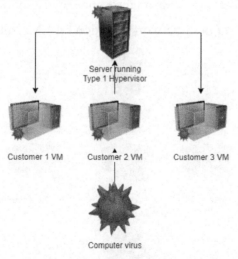

Figure 15.7: Example of VM escape

EXAM TIP: You must understand that VM escape occurs through a VM and affects the hypervisor and, consequently, all other VMs on the hypervisor.

A virtual machine escape is usually possible because of a lack of security on the side of the hypervisor. However, it may be possible to use vulnerabilities or misconfiguration on the guest machine in some cases. A successful VM escape attack allows an attacker to interact directly with the hypervisor. The attacker can access all the virtualized environments and even change the hypervisor through this access. An attacker could stop, start, and delete virtual machines or even exfiltrate data.

While it is the CSP's responsibility to ensure your hypervisor is secure and your communications are isolated (through network controls), your organization must ensure that the virtual environments you create are safe. Depending on your organization's policies, your VMs (and containers) should be subjected to similar security controls.

For example, if your organization requires workstations to be fitted with anti-virus software, you should ensure that your VMs have similar software. Likewise, if your workstations use DLP solutions, your VMs and containers should too. One of the most essential factors is hardening machines within your environment. If you use pre-hardened Windows images for your on-premises servers, apply the same hardening to virtual environments (in the cloud or otherwise). While virtual machines can be quickly created, you must remember that they are part of your environment. Allowing VMs to have lesser security controls than other components of your environment could compromise much more than the VM.

Earlier in this book, we talked about network isolation. Isolating resources on the network level is essential to ensure your systems can only access the help they need. The same concept should apply to your virtual machines. You should seek to limit any access your VMs have within your broad environment to an absolute minimum. Even if your VMs run on the same hypervisor, you should prevent them from accessing each other on the network. Some (more advanced) virtualization tooling like VMWare NSX or other cloud platforms will allow you to limit communications between VMs on the same hypervisor quite easily.

Let us look at an example of poor network isolation for VMs, refer to the following figure:

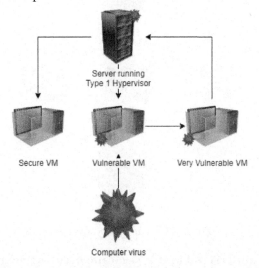

Figure 15.8: *Pivoting between VM to achieve VM escape*

In the figure above, you can see that a server runs three different VMs. The first VM is secure and runs as intended. The second VM is vulnerable and has been infected by an attacker. In the figure above, the vulnerability in the VM does not allow the VM to escape. However, it does grant the attacker a foothold on the VM itself. Because the vulnerable VM allows network access to the other VMs, the attacker can exploit the vulnerable VM on the right side. Unlike the vulnerable machine, the very vulnerable device can be used to achieve VM escape. Hence, the attacker can compromise the hypervisor itself. Now, let us look at another example:

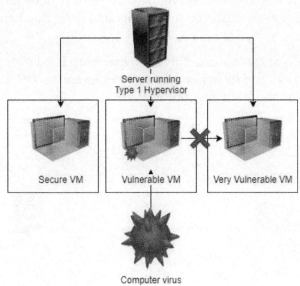

Figure 5.9: *Pivoting is not possible when VMs are isolated*

As you can see above, the figure contains another three virtual machines. The first machine is, once again, secure and running as expected. The second VM is vulnerable and has been compromised by an attacker. Luckily, the machine's vulnerability cannot be used to achieve a VM escape. When the attacker attempts to pivot to the very vulnerable VM, network segregation or isolation (through a VNet or security group) prevents the attacker from gaining access to the very vulnerable VM. Because the attacker cannot access the very vulnerable VM, she cannot achieve VM escape from that machine and thus cannot compromise all three VMs.

You cannot always isolate virtual machines. Sometimes, one VM might contain an API, and another might have a database. The API might need to talk to the VM that runs the DB. While you cannot wholly isolate these machines, you should strive to prevent all traffic that is not necessary. In this example, you could only allow DB traffic from the API to the DB but deny every other protocol.

Securing a virtual environment is not more complicated than connecting regular devices. Hardening, anti-virus/anti-malware, DLP, secure configuration, logging and monitoring, network isolation, and IDS/IPS might still be required. However, because physical infrastructure is shared to create these environments, we must ensure that the hypervisor cannot be breached directly or through a virtual machine.

Now that you know what actions should be taken to secure a hypervisor and the guest operating systems running on the hypervisor, we should take a quick look at a complicated situation that might occur in the cloud. Firstly, you must remember that many organizations might use a hybrid cloud. Meaning they may have an on-premises data center and a cloud data center. Each of these environments might make use of virtualization. In some cases, an organization may want to virtualize environments across the cloud and their on-premises DC.

In those cases, an organization can run its hypervisor inside an already virtualized environment in the cloud and its hypervisor in the on-premises DC. Let us take a see how that could look, refer to the following figure:

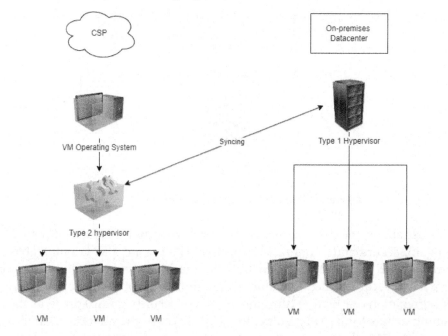

Figure 15.10: *Virtualizing across cloud and on-premises environments*

In the figure above, you see a setup of a cloud environment. In this cloud environment, an organization runs a VM. On top of the VM, it runs a **Type 2 hypervisor**; on top of the hypervisor, it runs three more VMs. What you see in this environment is nested virtualization; environments are virtualized within a virtual environment. On the right side, you see an on-premises DC that uses a **Type 1 hypervisor** to create various VMs. In this figure, the **Type-1 hypervisor** on-premises and the **Type-2 hypervisor** in the cloud can communicate. They can move virtual machines from one hypervisor to another, clone them, or even shut them down.

The massive benefit of this approach is that your organization can use a single control interface for virtualization. For example, if your organization uses VMWare vSphere, it could use that interface to move VMs from on-premises to the cloud without requiring separate environments. It is important to note that your on-premises and cloud network, of course, would need to be able to communicate with each other.

REAL-LIFE TIP: Stretching virtual environments from on-premises to the cloud has many benefits. But remember, you remain responsible for everything running on top of the CSP hypervisor.

While the example above is not mainstream, many organizations with hybrid clouds and existing virtualization software might opt for such a model. Ease of management, knowledge of the virtualization software, and easy expansion of the virtual environment without purchasing additional equipment might make it a desirable solution.

However, suppose your organization chooses to adopt such an approach. In that case, you must understand that your organization is responsible for the security of the Type-2 hypervisor in the cloud and the guest operating system used to run the hypervisor. Your organization is still responsible for the Type 2 hypervisor in this scenario. The CSP remains only accountable for the hypervisor running the guest OS that contains the Type-2 hypervisor.

Conclusion

Securing the infrastructure of our environment is essential. You must ensure your environment's data remains confidential, even when you share the physical infrastructure to host it. Hardware security modules and Trusted Platform Modules offer us a secure way to store key material. That key material can then encrypt and decrypt our valuable data while ensuring it remains secure. HSMs (and TPMs) have varying levels of security. The PCI-DSS industry standard and FIPS 140-2/140-3 define requirements for these devices. If your organization must comply with either standard, you must vet your CSP (and internal network) for compliance.

Aside from encrypting data, your organization must also ensure that your (virtual) environments are secure. With implementing sufficient security controls at the hypervisor level, your virtual environments will likely be protected. Whenever you pick a hypervisor, you should realize that Type 1 hypervisors are generally more secure than Type 2 hypervisors because they contain minimalistic operating systems and are designed with security in mind.

Regardless of the hypervisor type and the security controls you implement, you must also secure the guest OS. The guest OS runs on top of the hypervisor and can be abused to gain access to the hypervisor. As you have learned, once an attacker gains access to the hypervisor, all virtual machines running on it are compromised. Whenever your organization has a hybrid cloud and chooses to virtualize across environments, you must ensure your organization lives up to its responsibility to secure everything running on top of the CSP's hypervisor

To conclude, hypervisor and guest OS security are the same controls as any other machine. Harden the device, configure it securely, and implement security controls like logging and monitoring, IDP/IDS, anti-virus/anti-malware, DLP, and any other measure required based on your organization's needs.

In the next chapter, you will learn about secure configuration. The chapter will review important practices like baselining, hardening, patching, and more.

Learning goals

This chapter addresses the following CCSP exam outline learning goals:

Domain 5: Cloud security operations

  5.1 Build and implement physical and logical infrastructure for a cloud environment.

Join our book's Discord space

Join the book's Discord Workspace for Latest updates, Offers, Tech happenings around the world, New Release and Sessions with the Authors:

https://discord.bpbonline.com

CHAPTER 16

Secure Configuration

Introduction

Security tooling and complex cloud architectures can improve security. The configuration powering the tools and systems ultimately decides if an ecosystem is secure. This chapter explores the different security policies that must be in place to create a secure environment. It dives into secure network configuration, network security controls, OS hardening, patch management, **Infrastructure as Code (IaC)**, **high availability (HA)**, monitoring of performance and hardware, and backup/restore.

We will also look at the process side of secure configuration. We will examine how problem management, deployment management, change management, and other management processes are essential to secure configuration. Another factor we will examine is the complexity of a cloud environment. As you can imagine, hybrid multi-cloud environments are more difficult to configure uniformly than a regular cloud environment.

Structure

This chapter covers the following topics:

- Technology and service hardening
- OS hardening

- Infrastructure as Code

- Patch management

- Change management

- Continuity management

- Incident management

- Problem management

- Release management

- Deployment management

- Configuration management

- SLA management

- Availability management

- Capacity management

Objectives

This chapter aims to help you understand the necessity of secure configuration in the cloud. While many CSPs offer various security features, configuring them securely is vital to adequate security controls. This chapter will teach you some standard protocols and technologies and how they should be configured and secured in the cloud. At the same time, this chapter will take you on a journey through some vital management processes. You will gain insight into the need for managing changes, continuity, incidents, problems, release, deployments, SLAs, availability, and configuration. These management processes are necessary for our once-secure design to become secure fast.

Technology and service hardening

As you know, CSPs offer various services that operate at varying levels of the cloud service models. CSPS needs to ensure that these services can be used securely. They invest significant amounts of time into providing these secure services. However, the CSP does not secure how you use their services.

For example, if you use an object-storage tool, you can encrypt the data using native encryption functionality. However, you will still have to enable the encryption. Without making conscious decisions to securely configure cloud services, the CSP's security efforts on their side of the shared responsibility model are quickly negated.

The section below will look at standard services and technologies you will likely use in the cloud. We will examine what secure configuration steps you should take to ensure your data will remain closed. As the CCSP exam is vendor agnostic, beware that you do not need to have CSP-specific knowledge for this exam.

Access control technologies

By now, you know that broad access presents terrific opportunities and has implications for an environment's security. One of the most critical steps that we must take to limit the risks associated with broad access is adequately configuring access control technologies. You know that a cloud environment can be accessed through a cloud console, CLI, or even through APIs. Depending on the maturity of your organization, you may use one or even every one of these options.

Whenever we seek to gain access to the cloud environment through a CLI, we often use the **Secure Socket Shell (SSH)** protocol. SSH allows us to transfer commands (or files) from a local command line interface to a target machine. Once the target machine receives the command, it executes it and returns the output to the sender. By using SSH, we can perform a wide variety of operations on a remote machine. As you can imagine, SSH is beneficial but can also be used for evil.

For example, what happens if an attacker can access a machine in your cloud environment through SSH? Depending on the user they gain access to, they may be able to wipe your device, infect it with malware, and even pivot throughout your network.

So, while SSH is beneficial, we must take several measures to ensure the chance for abuse is negated where possible. Let us look at some essential configurations below. Firstly, it is crucial that you only install SSH servers on machines that need to be managed with SSH. The SSH service should be exposed to as few other machines as possible. In some cases, your organization may choose to use a single stepping stone that reveals SSH externally and can then be used to reach other hosts in your cloud environment through SSH, as shown:

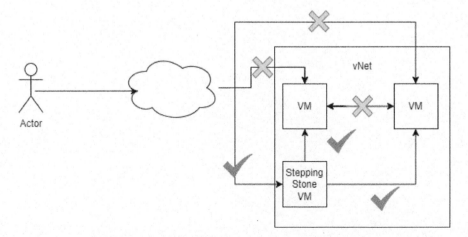

Figure 16.1: Accessing cloud VMs through an SSH Jumpbox

Using the approach above, attackers can only see an SSH service running on the stepping stone VM. Because the attacker is unaware of the other machines running SSH, the attack surface is smaller, which limits the attacker's opportunities. Nevertheless, the stepping stone must be secured extremely well to prevent breaches.

Another important measure to take is ensuring the authentication methods used for an SSH server are secure. For example, you should consider requiring public key authentication rather than just a username/password. By using public key authentication, you require the identity to have the private key, and the password to use the key. That way, stealing a user's username and password will not lead to unauthorized access without access to the private key. Ideally, SSH connections require a form of true multi-factor authentication. Most SSH servers require a special plugin to facilitate this.

REAL-LIFE TIP: Public key authentication may be seen as MFA, but it can be used without a password to decrypt the private key. This means public key authentication is not always a form of MFA.

Aside from limiting the number of servers that run SSH servers and limiting their exposure to the internet, they must also be configured to stop attacks. One of the easiest ways to do this is by blocking machines or users that fail to authenticate multiple times. For example, you can configure your SSH server to (temporarily) block an IP address from connecting if it fails to authenticate five times within a certain period.

Similarly, you should ensure that user authentication with an empty password is impossible on your server. SSH services may allow users to authenticate with a blank password by default. An attacker may quickly gain access if a user account is improperly configured.

At the same time, consider requiring key-based authentication for users (and machines). Let us look at the following figure to see how this works:

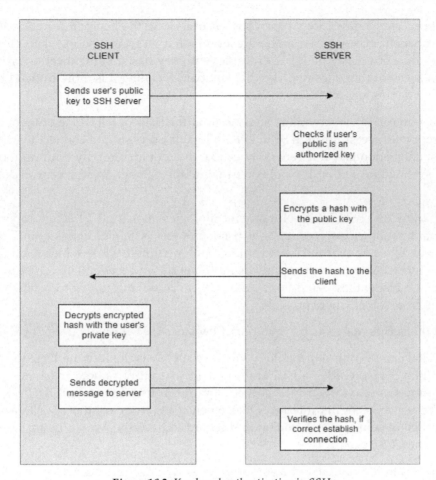

Figure 16.2: *Key-based authentication in SSH*

As shown in the figure above, key-based authentication requires two things. The client must have a private and public key pair, and the server must add the public key to its authorized keys database. Once these prerequisites are fulfilled, the client can exchange its public key with the server. If the server recognizes the key, it will send an encrypted hash to the client. The hash is encrypted using the public key of the client. The client then decrypts the hash using its private key. The result is then sent back to the server. The server can then validate that the decrypted hash does or does not match the original hash. If the hash matches, the server knows the connecting client has the private key associated with the authorized public key, and the connection can start. After this step, it will negotiate a key used to encrypt the traffic for the session.

EXAM TIP: For the CCSP exam, you do not need to understand the SSH protocol and its handshaking mechanisms.

The considerable benefit of key-based authentication is that it is more difficult to compromise a private and public key than to obtain a username and password. Your organization can even require a password for unlocking the key pair for added security. An added benefit of key-based authentication is that you can also use it to verify if the device has the correct key pair. For example, with key-based authentication, you cannot sign-in on a device that does not have the key pair. Meaning it is more difficult to use an unmanaged device to authenticate.

Of course, you can take many more steps to limit the risks of SSH. One of them can be to prevent root user access through SSH. After all, your users should connect to an SSH box with personal credentials, not general ones like the root account. By limiting root access, reducing session lifespan, and so on, you can limit the damage an attacker can do through SSH.

You may know that SSH is one of many technologies allowing CLI access to your cloud environment. Another very commonly used protocol is telnet. One significant benefit of SSH over telnet is that SSH connections are encrypted while telnet commands are sent as plaintext. As you can imagine, using telnet to send credentials can easily lead to compromised credentials. So, if your organization is looking for a protocol, ensure you steer away from telnet where possible.

EXAM TIP: SSH is more secure than telnet because SSH encrypts traffic by default.

Another vital access control technology we must review is the **Remote Desktop Protocol (RDP)**. While SSH provides a CLI environment to control remote machines, the RDP protocol allows you to forward the server's **graphical user interface (GUI)**. So, you can control the server using its interface, like when using your computer. While SSH also supports this (to some extent), you should regard RDP as the way to go for remote GUI access for the CCSP exam.

Having access to the full GUI of a server gives you a level of access that is not possible through SSH. For example, you can use desktop applications like a word processor or other GUI-based applications that may not be accessible through SSH. Because of this, RDP is ideal for remote computing that requires more elaborate ways of interacting with a computer.

For example, your organization may virtualize employee computers in the cloud. The employees may be provided a simple laptop that connects to the cloud using RDP, as shown:

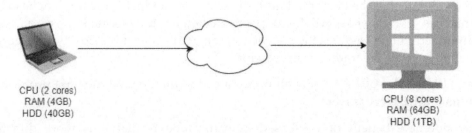

CPU (2 cores)
RAM (4GB)
HDD (40GB)

CPU (8 cores)
RAM (64GB)
HDD (1TB)

Figure 16.3: *Accessing virtual compute resources in the cloud*

That way, the employee can access vast computing power without carrying a big, heavy laptop. At the same time, the company can save money by shutting down these expensive VMs when employees are not working. As you know, cloud computing is based on metered service, meaning your company will not have to pay for these resources when they are not being used. Using RDP to access cloud resources can save your company from purchasing expensive, non-upgradeable hardware. Instead, your company only pays for these virtual machines when employees use them.

Aside from cost-saving considerations, using VMs for employee computing can have other significant benefits. Because your VMs are part of your cloud environment, you can uniformly implement security controls. After all, the computer used in the cloud stores all the data and software. You can implement any security control you want on the cloud side. A user may be able to connect to the cloud VM from any device (even unmanaged devices), but it must be able to circumvent the security controls in the cloud.

Aside from the easy and broad application of security controls (regardless of the user's location and connecting machine), using RDP to access cloud VMs can allow your users to access company resources securely. Rather than providing direct access to your cloud resources, you could require users to access them through cloud VMs. That way, you can ensure that users have the proper security controls before accessing the application. Similarly, you can use these VMs to allow users to connect to your on-premises network if your cloud and on-premises network are connected.

However, RDP could be better. Your users may still be able to exfiltrate data by taking screenshots, copying data, or other specific RDP attacks. It is essential that you carefully decide what to use RDP for. If you let your employees use RDP to access cloud resources, it is vital to secure the devices they RDP in with as well. For example, you could use key authentication (like SSH) to ensure the employees connect from a corporate device rather than a personal device.

At the same time, you should ensure that machines that can be accessed through RDP have the proper OS hardening and network segmentation in place. For example, if an employee uses a cloud VM as a desktop environment, it should only have access to other cloud resources required to perform the user's job. So, if the user is an HR employee, the VM should not have access to systems not used by HR. In short, you should still operate under a zero-trust model when you use RDP to provide user access.

Network security

We have talked about network security extensively in this book. You know that your networks must be configured to encrypt data in transit and that network access should be limited to the bare minimum. However, your responsibilities in this domain may only sometimes be clear. For example, if you use SaaS applications, your CSP may ensure your connections are encrypted through TLS or your DNS queries are secured through DNSSEC.

Unfortunately, your organization will still bear some responsibility for these items. Let us look at an example:

Figure 16.4: A cloud consumer must ensure encryption throughout the chain.

In the example above, the CSP offers a load balancer that can be reached through TLS. Once the traffic reaches the load balancer, it is propagated within the organization's cloud network to an application server. However, as you may have noticed, the load balancer directs the traffic of an HTTP connection to the application server. Meaning the traffic within the cloud network is not encrypted. You may think this is irrelevant as it is within the organization's cloud environment. But what if an attacker or employee listens for network traffic from their VM in the cloud environment? They would be able to listen in on all the traffic sent by the user through the load balancer.

The point in the example above is simple. It would be best if you did not assume all communications are encrypted by default whenever you consume cloud services. Especially when using IaaS, you will likely have to configure encryption in transit. Ensure that your traffic flows are encrypted end-to-end, and refrain from using services without encrypted communication channels (even within your cloud).

EXAM TIP: Only TLS 1.2 and TLS 1.3 are considered secure by the CCSP exam.

Another aspect of network security we need to review is the **Domain Name System (DNS)**. DNS is an address book (if you will) that links computers to domain names. For example, whenever you type in google.com in your browser. A DNS query is made to a DNS server. The DNS server tells your computer what the IP address of the **google.com** domain name is. In essence, it translates a domain name into an IP address that your computer can use to connect.

Your organization likely manages so-called **DNS records**. These records specify what IP addresses are associated with the domain names owned by your company. For example, if your company website lives in your cloud environment, a DNS record is needed to ensure that a user who types in your domain name is sent to the correct server in your environment.

Most of the time, as a user, you will not even notice that DNS exists. However, DNS has some serious risks. For example, an attacker could perform a DNS poisoning (or spoofing) attack. During this type of attack, an attacker illegitimately replies to a DNS query sent out by a machine. The attacker acts like it is a valid DNS server. The danger is that an attacker can send fake information to respond to the query. Because DNS determines what machine is associated with a domain name, an attacker can use DNS spoofing to make your computer connect to a machine under their control and not associated with the DNS name. let us look at the result of the attack:

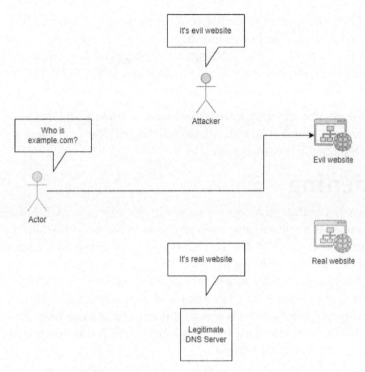

Figure 16.5: Simplified example of a DNS Spoofing attack

Elliot asks what server **example.com** is associated with (a DNS query) in the example above. In the figure, both the attacker and a legitimate server respond to his request. Elliot will believe the attacker over the actual DNS server, depending on the situation (for example, if the attacker replies faster). Because of this, Elliot associates the DNS name **example.com** with the wrong, dangerous website.

The attack in the figure above targets the user, but attackers can also target the DNS server. If a DNS server does not know whom a domain name is associated with, it will perform a query to the authoritative server. In some situations, the attacker can spoof the authoritative server's response. The local DNS server then caches that response, providing the wrong information to all users that send a DNS query to that server. This approach is called a DNS cache poisoning attack.

EXAM TIP: You do not need to understand the mechanism behind DNS spoofing or DNS (cache) poisoning attacks for the CCSP exam.

As you can imagine, an attacker can achieve significant damage if it can trick your machines into believing domain names are associated with malicious servers. Users may send confidential data to these servers or worse. In the cloud, you will be using DNS servers as well. In many cases, the CSP may offer managed DNS services, or you may create your own DNS server. Regardless of your approach, you must be aware of this type of attack.

Luckily, many CSPs offer you the ability to stop these attacks through something called **DNSSEC**. DNSSEC uses public key authentication to ensure the user knows the legitimate DNS server. At the same time, the DNS server uses public key authentication to ensure that any authoritative server it uses is also legitimate. DNSSEC prevents attackers from spoofing the DNS server or the authoritative servers a DNS server asks for information.

> **EXAM TIP: You do not need to know the inner working of DNSSEC for the CCSP exam. However, you must understand that DNSSEC can be used to prevent DNS spoofing and DNS cache poisoning attacks.**

OS hardening

Hardening networks and access control technologies are essential. However, in a zero-trust environment, we must assume these controls have been breached. Therefore, it is vital that we implement security controls on the level of individual compute elements as well. One aspect of this is applying OS hardening. OS hardening has frequently been a subject in the chapters prior. You know that many (industry) hardening standards exist. STIGs are required for government agencies and subcontractors, while CIS benchmarks are a good starting point for non-governmental entities. At the same time, your specific industry (such as the payment card industry) may have requirements for OS hardening that your organization must implement.

Regardless of your approach, you should take some essential steps and follow best-practice steps for OS hardening in the cloud and on-premises. Let us look at some of these steps in the following section:

Updates, patches, and immutable infrastructure

The first and foremost step is to ensure your operating system (and the software running) are frequently updated. New security vulnerabilities are discovered daily, meaning that what was secure yesterday may not be secure today. You must ensure your organization establishes processes to monitor vulnerabilities in your operating systems and software packages. Once your organization finds vulnerabilities, it should update the system after updates have been validated and tested (you want to be careful to prevent updates from breaking your system).

Now, you may be used to updating your system by using a centralized patch management tool, built-in update tools, or even manually downloading updates from the internet and installing them on the computer. In the age of cloud computing, we can take a better approach. Using immutable infrastructure ensures that our systems can be updated without error-prone manual intervention on the (virtual) machine in a way that reduces down-time and is easily tested.

Immutable infrastructure means that you do not make changes to live systems. Instead, you build a new version of your infrastructure component and replace the old one (in its entirety) with the latest version. The benefit of this approach is that you do not need direct access to the machine to perform management tasks. Instead, you use the organization's deployment pipeline to deploy a new version of a virtual machine or container (or another infrastructure component). To understand the benefits of immutable infrastructure, let us take a quick look at traditional update and patch processes as follows:

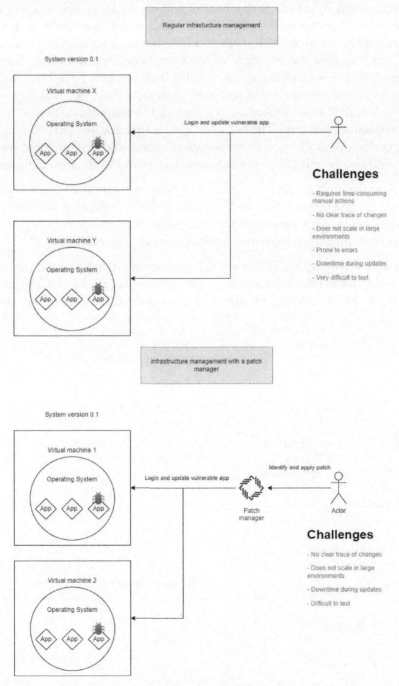

Figure 16.6: Infrastructure management through patch management and manual processes

As you can see in the preceding figure, manual patching and even patch management have some downsides. Firstly, manual processes are very error-prone. To perform manual updates, an engineer must log in to every device and perform an update sequence. It is likely (especially) in large environments that mistakes will be made. At the same time, manual processes require broad access on the side of the engineers that update the systems. In turn, these engineers might have access to data they should not have access to. In essence, manual updates go directly against the principle of least privilege. Another huge downside to a manual process is that it is challenging to establish if all systems have been appropriately updated. Maintaining a current list of software versions would be challenging, meaning tracking new vulnerabilities in the future requires significant administration and is likely to become less effective over time. The last downside is that any system being updated will likely experience downtime. The downtime negatively affects the availability of your systems. Sometimes, the downtime might be very extensive (for example, during OS updates).

Updating systems through a patch management system is better than manual processes. It is far more scalable, less error-prone, and provides better verification and documentation of updates. However, in many cases, patch management tooling does not negate downtime during updates. Meaning your systems' availability will still suffer.

Now that you understand (globally) how patch management and manual updating work, let us look at how **Immutable infrastructure** can tackle some of the challenges associated with this approach. In the following figure, you can see the difference in approach refer to the following image:

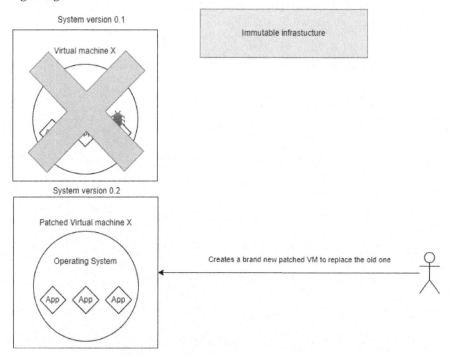

Figure 16.7: *Patching in immutable infrastructure*

In the previous figure, you can see that rather than making changes to the VM with vulnerable software, the engineer now replaces the entire VM with a new one. The new VM is already patched. Because the VM is replaced, there is no need to log in to the old VM and perform manual actions. Instead, the regular deployment process can be used to roll out the new VM. It is important to note that immutable infrastructure is often combined using infrastructure as code. The definition of the VM is stored as a configuration file, which is then dynamically created and deployed. There are some significant benefits to this approach.

EXAM TIP: Immutable infrastructure is more secure and stable because it limits access requirements, lowers the chance of errors during updates, and prevents downtime during updates and patches.

Firstly, the configuration file defines how the system is built and what software versions are used. Because of this, it is easy to detect if a system is on the correct version. At the same time, it becomes simpler to detect new vulnerabilities.

The second benefit is that IaC-based systems can easily be tested before roll-out. Testing patches and updates before production release is essential to prevent issues during and after deployment. Immutable infrastructure also works well with a blue-green deployment strategy. During a blue-green deployment, a new version of a system is deployed, and once it is up and running, traffic is switched to the new system, after which the old one is shut down. By doing this, end-users will always be able to reach the system, even though you are deploying a new one. Of course, there are some caveats. It would be best if you waited to shut down the old server until all open sessions with that server are terminated. Nevertheless, when implemented correctly, immutable infrastructure in combination with blue-green deployments can negate downtime during updates and patches. Let us see what this looks like in the following figure:

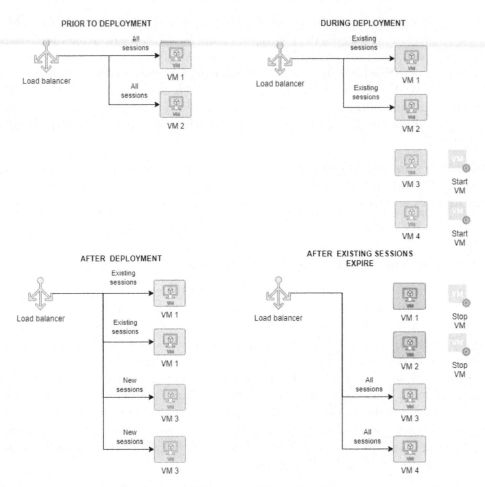

Figure 16.8: Blue-green deployment of VMs

As shown in the figure above, a blue-green deployment goes through different phases. Initially, a load balancer directs traffic to two application VMs. Once the patched VMs are built using IaC, they are deployed to the cloud environment. Currently, there are four running application VMs (two unpatched and two patched). Once the patched VMs are up and running, the LB directs all new traffic to the new VMs. Doing this ensures that new sessions no longer use the (insecure) unpatched VMs. Existing sessions are still directed to the old VMs, as they likely contain important session data for the users. However, remember that you can end existing sessions if application availability is not your highest priority. Once all old sessions on the unpatched VMs have been completed, those VMs are shutdown and cleaned-up. Leaving us with two patched VMs.

The beauty of the approach above is that it is very scalable and has minimal effects on application availability. While setting up blue-green deployments using IaC in the initial stages can be complex, your organization will significantly benefit from this approach over time.

EXAM TIP: Immutable infrastructure is usually realized through Infrastructure as Code deployments.

Of course, immutable infrastructure also presents some challenges. For example, it may be difficult for an organization to transition to this way of working. System administrators may be used to conducting changes on live systems and may not be able to read or write code. Similarly, immutable infrastructure requires processes for developing IaC securely. At the same time, the code must be stored an deployed securely. Switching to immutable infrastructure and IaC in general will take time an effort.

Monitoring and logging

Aside from ensuring your OS and its applications are hardened following baselines and patched or updated when needed, you must also configure security controls on the OS level. One prime example of such controls is monitoring and logging. Even in a cloud environment with virtual servers, it is essential that you perform logging and monitoring. As discussed throughout the book, your operating systems and applications should carefully log actions performed within the application, from authentication (success or failure) to privileged activities and other events of value. While your system must perform logging, it is essential to ensure that the log data is not stored on the machine the logs are about. Instead, log files should be stored centrally.

The benefit of storing logs centrally is limiting attackers' opportunity to tamper with log files. As you can imagine, an attacker could destroy or modify logs once they gain (administrative) access to a machine. If the attackers are knowledgeable, they will attempt to erase their steps. If logs are shared to one central storage space, it becomes much more difficult for the attacker to remove records. Unfortunately, the attacker can still (relatively easily) create false log data. Nevertheless, aggregating logs centrally also allows for more straightforward analysis by security systems such as SIEMs or security teams like SOC.

However, more than logging performed on the OS and application level is required. Logging should always be combined with different forms of monitoring. Monitoring can occur on the security side and other factors such as availability. For example, a VM may log failed and successful authentication actions to a central log aggregation tool. At the same time, it may also report information about its CPU utilization ratio.

By sharing data about the (virtual) hardware usage of the VM, your organization can gain valuable insights. Imagine if your VM reaches a CPU utilization ratio of 99%; at that point, your users are likely already experiencing performance problems. You should ensure that you have monitoring tools to (at least) detect these situations. Most cloud providers provide standard logging tools that can be installed on the VM (or are natively installed) that report metrics such as CPU utilization, RAM consumption, and storage utilization.

These metrics can then be monitored in a cloud native dashboard or reporting tools. Such data can help your organization determine if your cloud environment's capacity is sufficient. If you notice you have a pool of VMs that are consistently at low utilization rates, consider horizontally or vertically scaling down these VMs. At the same time, if you notice your machine running at max capacity, you may need to scale horizontally or vertically. The difference between horizontal and vertical scaling is shown below (as a reminder) refer to the following figure:

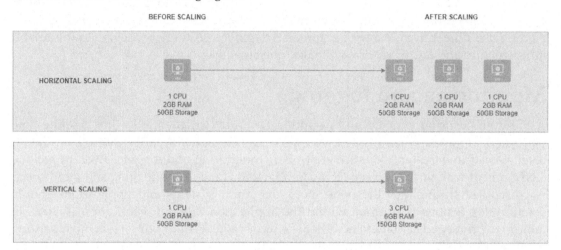

Figure 16.9: Horizontal and vertical scaling

As you can see in the figure above, horizontal scaling means you create more instances of the same capacity. In contrast, vertical scaling means increasing the capacity of your compute instance by increasing its resources. Of course, you can also use a combination of horizontal and vertical scaling. In many cases, your scaling strategy depends on the applications you are running and the cost considerations for your organization.

Regardless of how you scale your machines, logging and monitoring are vital to determine when (and if) you need to scale up and down. Some organizations may require different computation needs based on business patterns.

For example, a web shop may require more computing capacity when it launches a store-wide sale. Similarly, the IRS may experience increased traffic when taxes are due.

Monitoring and logging can help you identify such patterns. By doing so, your organization can prepare for high amounts of traffic (and even attacks) by scaling environments through set scheduling or dynamic optimization and scaling whenever necessary.

Host-based security controls

Aside from hardening your machines by using secure configuration, patching, monitoring, and logging, you may want to take additional security measures on the OS level. For example, your organization could implement IDS, IPS, or DLP technologies in virtual environments. We must assume that any network-based controls have failed whenever you operate from a zero-trust perspective. Hence, every single server, laptop, or phone must be able to defend itself against attacks. By implementing IDS, IPS, DLP, and anti-virus, you can ensure your VMs (and containers) can protect themselves more effectively against attackers. Many CSPs even offer agents you can install on your VMs that provide such security controls without much configuration work.

Infrastructure as Code

You already know that **Infrastructure as Code (IaC)** can be an essential tool for easy and scalable deployments. However, in this chapter, you have also learned that deploying through IaC has security benefits. After all, if our infrastructure is defined in code, we can easily trace if it has vulnerabilities. By defining infrastructure as code, we can also negate the need for manual intervention on running machines. Reducing manual actions on running hosts negates the need for broad access to production systems (for updates) and lowers the chance of human errors. You have also learned that IaC plays a vital role in effective blue-green deployments to ensure users are not negatively affected by downtime during deployments.

At this point, you may think that IaC has no downsides. For the most part, this is true. However, we must be cautious when using IaC as well. In most cases, IaC allows developers to build infrastructure through code that can then be deployed at will. As you can imagine, IaC is powerful not only to our organizations but also to attackers. After all, if an attacker can control the source code used to build infrastructure, they can introduce new vulnerabilities or even gain complete control of a system. Another point at which IaC is very vulnerable is during the deployment process. If an attacker somehow influences the IaC during the deployment, they could alter the code and achieve the same effect outlined above.

As you can imagine, building safeguards in the development and deployment processes of IaC is essential. Earlier in the book, we discussed code signing and hash validation for regular code commits. Whenever you use IaC, these practices are essential to prevent large-scale, high-impact breaches. Your developers should sign their code to establish that legitimate engineers created them. Similarly, IaC code should be verified during deployment. We must ensure the IaC we intend to deploy is the correct artifact.

Aside from validating the engineers' identity and the code's integrity, we should also closely monitor IaC deployment processes. Especially in blue-green deployment situations, you must establish that your newly deployed infrastructure is deployed correctly and functions before switching traffic to your new instances. Of course, you should test your IaC in development and test environments like any other deployment. However, your IaC deployments must also verify that the execution of the deployment was successful and that the systems function as expected.

Ultimately, it is essential to remember that IaC should also be subjected to regular secure software development lifecycle controls. For example, IaC should be subjected to (manual or automatic) code review, vulnerability scanning, testing, and so on. It is good to remember that unauthorized access to IaC will likely have a very detrimental effect on your environment.

Information Technology Infrastructure Library and ISO/IEC 20000

Throughout this chapter, we have talked extensively about the technical controls and aspects of secure configuration. However, secure configuration (and operation) requires a complex set of processes that span the entire lifecycle of an application or service. Your organization will have to embed these processes throughout the lifecycle of any IT resource to be secure.

We already talked about SDLC, and the specific steps required in the software development process. However, for the CCSP exam, you must also be familiar with the **Information Technology Infrastructure Library (ITIL)** and the ISO/IEC 20000 standard. ITIL is a framework that outlines the lifecycle of an IT service. The lifecycle drives continual process improvement but also encompasses many actions that we must take that directly affect the security of our services. ITIL is closely aligned with the ISO/IEC 20000 standard for service management. Because ITIL is not a standard like ISO/IEC 20000, it does not offer certification. In short, ISO/IEC 20000 sets requirements for certification, while ITIL provides guidelines.

Throughout the following sections of this chapter, we will explore the ITIL framework and the ISO/IEC 20000 standard and relate them to secure configuration.

Firstly, let us quickly look into the five stages of the ITIL service lifecycle. This lifecycle represents the lifecycle of a service from its inception through its use, the phases are listed as follows:

ITIL Phases
Service strategy
Service design
Service transition
Service operation
Continual service improvement

Table 16.1: *ITIL Lifecycle phases*

EXAM TIP: The CCSP exam does not expect you to know every phase of the ITIL lifecycle.

Contrary to ITIL, the ISO/IEC 20000 standard has no lifecycle. Rather it uses a **plan-do-check-act (PDCA)** methodology to implement every part of the standard. PDCA means establishing policies, standards, plans, and processes first. After establishing these formal documents, you can work on designing and implementing your service. Once the service has been built and implemented, you can perform monitoring and testing to evaluate service effectiveness. Based on the results of your checks, you then take action to improve your service. You may notice that a PDCA cycle is closely related to the approach of SDLC.

EXAM TIP: Remember the order of the plan-do-check-act cycle (PDCA).

Change management

While the CCSP exam does not require you to thoroughly understand the ITIL framework nor memorize the ISO/IEC 20000 standard, it is essential to understand some of their components more in-depth. One of the most critical items we must discuss is change management. Change management is a collection of processes that support the safe, secure, and practical application of changes.

While change management may sound vague, most organizations already implemented some version. For example, if your organization has a ticket system for software development or IT helpdesk tickets, you are inadvertently conducting change management. Ticketing methods are used to document the need for change. An engineer then uses the key to document a plan, execute work, and test and verify the result. If your organization does not use any form of tracking for changes to its environment, it is severely at risk. Ad hoc changes without documentation and well-established processes are a guarantee for issues and security vulnerabilities. After all, conflicting changes could be executed that break underlying systems, applications, and infrastructure.

An essential part of change management is documenting the need for change and the actions used to perform the change. However, approval is an equally important part of change management. Most organizations (whether they work Agile or not) require customer consent before launching a change. Without such consent, changes could be launched that disrupt business and cause all sorts of damage.

For example, a development team is working on a change to alter how insurance prices are calculated on a health insurance website. The difference is completed before the due date. The developers have tested the change and function correctly. The team feels motivated to get the change in production and decides to push the change to show ahead of schedule. In such a scenario, the price adjustments would take effect without the businesses' consent. This could cause legal issues if the new prices go against customer communication or can even prevent insurance policies from going through if the back-end systems cannot yet handle the new prices.

In short, an organization must carefully track a change and require explicit consent before publishing a change to production. Your organization can prevent unauthorized changes that disrupt the business by doing so.

Another essential component of change management is documentation around the change after completion. Changes should be evaluated for effective implementation but can also provide valuable data about a team's throughput or issues that arise throughout the change process.

Continuity management

Managing changes is essential, but regardless of change, we must ensure our environment's availability is on par with the business requirements. We already discussed the need to determine MTD, RTO, and RPO. Continuity management builds on these numbers by defining processes to ensure continuity.

For example, continuity management addresses recovery tasks such as backup/restore processes. However, it could also include processes for disruption in an organization's supply chain. Continuity management is about anticipating, preventing, and remediating any issues with business continuity.

As you can imagine, continuity management includes creating a **business continuity plan** and **disaster recovery plans**. However, continuity management can also apply at an application level or specific environment. For example, you can develop plans to maintain your application's continuity. Such plans can include processes to auto-scale environments in cases of increased traffic to full-on recovery processes when an application's source data is rendered unusable due to a ransomware attack.

The continuity of IT environments is vital to ensure an organization can thrive; as you can imagine, continuity management should be a high priority. Mainly if your organization is dependent on CSP or other downstream partners, continuity management (of your supply chain) can mean the difference between success and failure of your business.

Information security management

Information security management is another essential component of ITIL and ISO/IEC 20000. As you know, Information security management focuses on defining policies, standards, guidelines, and processes to ensure the organization's security is on par with its requirements. ISM seeks to ensure that the organization is secured to a level that corresponds to the organization's goals and legal/regulatory obligations. As we have extensively discussed information security management throughout this book, this chapter will not further elaborate on it.

Continual service improvement management

Continual service improvement is a collection of processes focusing on improving services. Of course, any organization should consistently evaluate itself and its services to its customers. During continual service improvement management, an organization identifies areas for improvement (sometimes captured in problem management). It then identifies a way to improve the process itself.

For example, if your organization is confronted with underperforming VMs, your organization can set out to implement dynamic vertical or horizontal scaling of these VMs.

Once an organization has determined how an improvement will occur, it is essential to define the measurement used to evaluate the improvement.

For example, if we consider the scenario from the previous example, a measure of success could be the percentage of users that experience application timeouts. Alternatively, you could use a measure based on the application performance or VM utilization.

Regardless of the measurement you choose for evaluation, you must make sure it correctly measures if the improvement has taken place. If your improvement is to lower the amount of timeouts users, experience, measure something that accurately reflects that. While measuring VM utilization may be a good indicator, it does not measure if your improvement has been achieved. You must attempt to establish clear metrics that measure precisely what the results are. Of course, you can use supporting metrics to support your conclusions.

For example, if you measure the number of timeouts users experience, you can correlate the reduction in timeouts with the VM utilization. That way, you can find an optimum between cost and user experience.

The next step is to collect the data needed for your measurements. Once you have gathered enough data, you can process and analyze the data. Now, you will know if your improvement has had the expected results. Based on these results, you can identify new opportunities for improvement or correct courses where necessary.

Once you have gathered the data needed to clarify the need for improvement, you can go ahead and implement the changes and measure their effects.

Incident management

Unfortunately, things do not always go the way we expect. An organization can be faced with many different types of incidents. For example, an organization may be hacked, devices can be stolen, permissions may be abused, and so on. Incident management defines processes that dictate how an organization will respond when an incident occurs. Regardless of the nature of the incident, it is essential to create policies, standards, processes, and guidelines to ensure your organization can act timely and effectively during an incident.

Once an incident occurs, like a disaster, you must have established processes to ensure the correct actions are taken. Incident management requires that an organization prepare for incidents (including defining how to detect them). Once the organization has taken its preparation tasks, it must be able to identify incidents when they happen effectively.

In the case of a hacker, this could be a SIEM registering a security event and determining it may be malicious. However, it could be counting office inventory to detect employee theft.

Once an incident is identified, it must be contained. In the case of a cyberattack, that may mean that systems have to be isolated from others, and logs must be extracted. However, an incident could also be a fight between two employees. Incident containment in that scope may be for a manager to break up the fight and send the employee home.

Once an incident is contained, it must be eradicated. Meaning the situation causing the incident must be resolved. In the case of cyberattacks, that could mean that a computer virus would have to be removed from a server. In the other example, this could mean mediation between the employees in the conflict.

Once the incident has been stopped, it is time for the organization to focus on recovery. In cyberattacks, this could mean restoring affected systems by reinstating backups. In the employee conflict situation, it could be making an announcement to your team explaining that the problem has been remediated using mediation.

At the very end of incident management, we should ensure we cover the lessons we learned throughout the incident. For example, if your organization was hacked and did not notice the hack timely enough, it can update its incident management processes to enable earlier detection. In the example of the employees, you may identify that the closed-in office space is causing friction between the employees. As you can imagine, lessons learned are essential to the incident management process.

REAL-LIFE TIP: Incident management processes are similar for cyber and non-cyber incidents.

EXAM TIP: Incident response consists of Preparation, identification, containment, eradication, recovery, and lessons learned. Incident management defines how to take these actions.

Problem management

You may have noticed that almost every management process includes room to identify failures and opportunities. Problem management is a useful tool to address these lessons effectively. Problem management seeks to identify broadly/commonly occurring issues. These issues may be spread throughout the organization but have a similar cause.

For example, an organization may need help deploying the wrong software versions on production and issues with insufficient or incorrect licensing. The cause might be that the organization needs to practice configuration and change management. Hence, the organization needs to know what current software versions are running on systems and allow for incompatible versions to be deployed and incorrect licenses to be purchased.

Regardless of the problem and its cause, problem management defines processes to help your organization identify such common issues. Once a problem is detected, it should be logged, categorized, and prioritized. Once this is done, problem management can define processes to find workarounds or solutions to implement a fix. A problem is often transferred to the organization's change process. Once the change is completed, the problem should be re-evaluated and closed if mitigated.

The power behind problem management is that it is designed to detect issues that may affect large parts of your organization. It focuses on problems in underlying processes and practices. Of course, problems can also have a technical nature. For example, using outdated operating systems can cause different related issues throughout the organization that need mitigation. Through problem management, OS updates can be logged, categorized, and prioritized.

EXAM TIP: Problem management goes hand in hand with change management

Release management

Whereas change management focuses on defining, building, and implementing a change, release management goes further. Release management is a set of overarching processes, including change management, deployment management, and other management processes. Rather than focusing merely on the change, release management encompasses the whole lifecycle of a release. It includes planning releases, the change process, testing and deployment, and support and monitoring after changes are completed.

If you are familiar with software development, it makes sense that release management contains and expands on change management. After all, a single software release may contain many different changes.

Generally, release management consists of the following lifecycle:

1. Request for release

2. Planning and design

3. Change execution

4. Change review

5. Change testing

6. Change deployment

7. Post-deployment support

8. Issue reporting and collection

As you can see, release management adds planning, post-deployment support, issue reporting, and collection the change management. This is because a release requires coordination over the various changes included in the release. At the same time, release management must ensure the entire release works correctly. Therefore, it is essential to establish if all changes work together and as expected. If issues arise, release management dictates how to respond to them (new changes, rollbacks, and so on). In the following figure, you can see how release management relates to some other management processes:

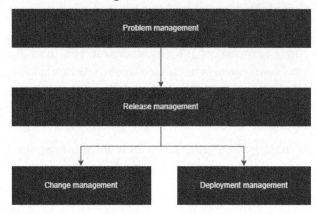

Figure 16.10: *Relation of release management to other management processes*

Deployment management

Release management encompasses change management, however, deployment management is also a part of release management. As you saw in the previous section, the deployment of a change is the 6th step of release management. Deployment management defines policies, standards, and processes for deploying changes.

For example, deployment management defines how changes are propagated from one environment to another. It might also detail how the technical deployment should take place. Are changes made manually on a device by an engineer, or must they be pushed through CI/CD tooling using blue-green deployments?

Deployment management also defines the need for test, acceptance, and production environments. For example, an organization may have to deploy its software to a test and acceptance system to conduct (security) testing before releasing it to a production server. Deployment management defines when and how this is needed.

Another facet defined by deployment management is scheduling. In some cases, deployments may take significant amounts of time and might even render systems unusable. Deployment management might dictate that deployments are only allowed on specific dates and times. It can even define if deployments must meet criteria (such as deployment speeds and sizes). Similarly, deployment management may dictate that multiple releases are not allowed to be released at the same time.

It is essential to realize that deployment management also includes the processes needed to build, test, and deploy releases. This means that security controls like artifact validation are essential to deployment management.

Configuration management

Configuration management is critical and can be executed in many ways. Configuration management may only track application names and versions in its most basic form. However, in some cases, organizations may use configuration management processes to log application, system, and device configuration in detail. Configuration management defines policies, standards, processes, and guidelines on how configuration is documented and used within an organization.

The more detailed configuration management takes place, the easier it is to detect security problems, comply with audits, and baseline devices. Configuration information can allow you to detect if the software is vulnerable quickly. At the same time, it can make detecting issues due to new changes easier. Configuration management almost always dictates the use of a **configuration management database** (**CMDB**); an example is shown as follows:

CMDB	
System Name:	Application server
OS:	*Nix
OS Version:	19.12
Kernel Version:	5.4
Installed applications:	Bash, DropBear
Last deployed:	01-01-1971
Created:	01-01-1970

Figure 16.2: Example of a CMDB record

It is important to note that any form of change management requires an initial baseline. Your organization must put in significant effort when it is initially adopted to create a baseline of all configurations. Afterward, your organization should embed configuration management within your release and change management processes. Doing so can ensure that changes to your environments also require configuration management. If your organization does not do this, its configuration management will quickly become ineffective, and configuration baselines will deviate from reality.

REAL-LIFE TIP: Configuration management is not integrated into the release and change management is not helpful.

It is essential to realize that configuration management can be highly time-consuming. It is recommended to adopt methods of configuration management that are easy to automate. For example, you can implement deployment processes that automatically update your configuration databases once a new deployment has been executed. That way, you can avoid extensive manual update work and frustration amongst engineers while ensuring reliable data.

Another interesting note is that IaC has a significant impact on configuration management. If your organization uses immutable infrastructure and IaC, your code is part of your configuration management. After all, your code contains all the information you need about your system. IaC can negate the need to administrate configuration outside of your code.

Service level management

Cloud computing uses metered services. Meaning you only pay for what you use. To do so, CSPs have service levels that they agree on with their customers. If an SLA is breached, the customer is entitled to financial compensation. While your organization may not be a CSP, it likely does have service levels it must manage internally or with partners or customers. Service level management is a practice that defines which service levels an organization must meet, how they are measured, how they are reported on, and how to take actions to act if SLAs are missed.

Service level management requires that you define SLAs with internal customers and any external parties that require SLAs. After which, you define how these SLAs will be delivered and how they can be managed. Once all parties agree on the SLAs and the way they are measured, it is essential to document and agree on how these SLAs are monitored and how reporting on them is performed.

For example, CSPs often provide (monthly) SLA reports to their customers. If they have breached an SLA, they provide the customer with credit against cloud services. Similarly, your organization may have to (proactively) report to internal customers or external parties on the SLAs you have in place.

Once your organization has measured and reported on service levels, ensuring SLAs can be met in the future is essential. In many cases, failing SLAs may result in a problem that is then documented in problem management. Measures can then be taken to translate the situation into a change, included in a release that is then deployed. As you can see, service-level management is an essential driver/input for many other organizational management processes, as shown:

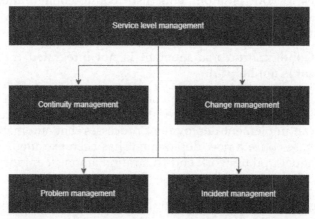

Figure 16.11: Service level management as a driver for other management processes

Availability management

Availability management is part of continuity management. Where continuity management seeks to ensure that the organization stays available under any circumstance, availability management focuses on ensuring the organization can stay available.

For example, availability management may define policies, standards, processes, and guidelines to ensure an organization can remain reachable to customers. Imagine an organization with a website to handle insurance claims. Due to a storm, the internet connection between their on-premises data center and the internet has been disrupted. Availability management policies could dictate that the organization must be capable of switching to another data center so that its services remain available. However, it could also dictate that the organization has a phone number available to help customers who need help to reach the website.

Depending on the organization and the situation, availability management can be highly technical or not technical at all. For example, if a store has a website and a physical store, it may not need to implement fail-over measures to ensure its website always stays available. After all, the store is still open to customers in the physical world.

Most organizations use availability management to define what their needs for availability are. Does the organization require immediate fail-over by using multiple availability zones in the cloud or only need a cold site to slowly transfer their online services if their environment is no longer available? The answer to those questions depends highly on the organization and its business requirements. Regardless, your organization should use availability management to determine its needs and define the processes needed to ensure availability in case of adversity.

EXAM TIP: Availability management is about fail-over and recovery.

Capacity management

Like availability management, capacity management is a part of continuity management. Where availability management focuses on the policies, standards, processes, and guidelines to keep a business available to its customers, partners, and employees, capacity management ensures the organization is open to the correct level.

For example, an organization may have a public website that is reachable to customers. However, because of large traffic volumes, the server may not have enough capacity to handle every customer request. Meaning some customers may experience poor service.

Capacity management dictates how the organization can ensure its dependents get the level of service they need. As you can imagine, capacity management is thus also highly related to service-level management. After all, capacity is essential to ensure service levels can be met. At the same time, the service levels are likely part of the organization's business continuity needs. Availability and capacity management form a large amount of continuity management and thus form the basis for service-level management, as shown:

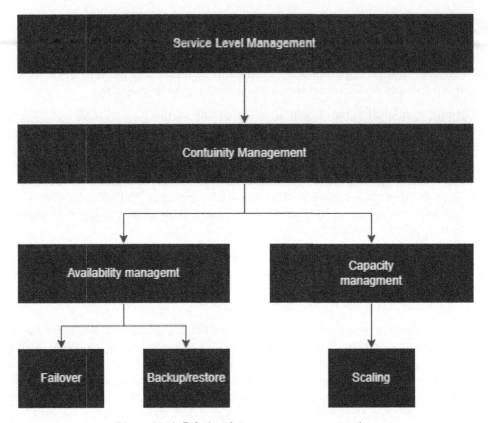

Figure 16.12: Relations between management practices

Conclusion

Throughout this chapter, we have covered a wide variety of subjects. We have looked at access control protocols like RDP and SSH. You now know these protocols hold immense power and allow us to manage our environments. However, they can easily be exploited without proper configuration and additional measures like stepping stones. We also covered security needs for common protocols like TLS and DNS. Implementing DNSSEC and using TLS throughout your landscape will help you keep your data confidential.

Aside from protocol security, we have also looked at hardening operating systems. Aside from implementing baselines like STIGs and CIS benchmarks, you must ensure your OS is properly patched and updated. Using immutable infrastructure and IaC, you can significantly reduce the risks of your systems being breached, enabling your organization to anticipate vulnerabilities in the future.

We also reviewed how endpoint security measures like logging and monitoring play a vital role in keeping your environment secure. Remember that logging should always be done to a central location, when possible, to prevent tampering and erasure of logs. At the same time, logged data must be monitored. Without monitoring for performance (and security), your organization's environment will not perform as needed.

In the last section of the chapter, we briefly looked at some of the supporting management processes surrounding secure configuration and operation of your environment. We walked about the ITIL framework and the ISO/IEC 20000 standard. ITIL and the ISO/IEC 20000 define standard management processes such as change management, configuration management, release management, service level management, and continuity management.

You now know that every management practice seeks to define policies, standards, processes, and guidelines on how your organization can ensure the respective goals of every practice are met. You have also learned that every practice is deeply related to another. For example, you could not perform continuity management without availability and capacity management. Your organization must fully understand and implement these management practices to ensure your organization is resilient, now and in the future.

Lastly, I must remind you that while ITIL is a framework and does not offer certification, the ISO/IEC 20000 standard can be certified against. Whenever your organization selects partners, it can be beneficial to establish if they are certified against that standard to ensure they have these management processes in place.

In the next chapter, you will learn about secure operations within an organization. The chapter will review security operations centers, policies, monitoring, AI, and more.

Learning goals

This chapter addresses the following CCSP exam outline learning goals:

Domain 5: Cloud security operations

5.2. Operate and maintain physical and logical infrastructure for cloud environments.

5.3. Implement operational controls and standards (for example, **Information Technology Infrastructure Library (ITIL)**, **International Organization for Standardization/International Electrotechnical Commission (ISO/IEC) 20000-1**).

Join our book's Discord space

Join the book's Discord Workspace for Latest updates, Offers, Tech happenings around the world, New Release and Sessions with the Authors:

https://discord.bpbonline.com

CHAPTER 17

Security Operations

Introduction

Policies and configuration are essential to create a secure baseline within your environment. However, security processes and operations ensure your environment stays secure over time and adapts to emerging threats. This chapter further expands on security policies, digital forensics, security operations like SOC, SIEM, incident management, and how to communicate to customers, vendors, partners, and others if our controls prove to be ineffective.

Structure

This chapter covers the following topics:

- Security policy and operations
- Security processes
- **Security operations center (SOC)**
- **Security incident and event monitoring (SIEM)**
- **Artificial intelligence (AI)**
- Incident management and disclosure

- Vulnerability assessments

- Forensics

Objectives

This chapter aims to create an understanding of common security policies and how they relate to their supporting operations. Every organization requires a basic combination of security processes to ensure their environment stays secure over time. In this chapter, you will learn the role of a **security operations center (SOC)** and the place of **security incident and event monitoring (SIEM)** within the organization. Throughout the chapter, we will also review how **artificial intelligence (AI)** plays an important role in security operations. We will learn about the practices surrounding digital forensics and vulnerability assessments. Lastly, the chapter will explain incident management and disclosure.

Security policy and operations

Throughout this book, we have discussed the need for security policies. Policies, standards, guidelines, and process documentation are essential elements of any security program. However, as you can imagine, putting policies and standards on paper does not automatically apply them to your organization. In some situations, your organization's policies may even be too ambitious for your organization. It is essential to ensure the gap between policy and reality can be bridged.

For example, if your organization requires that every application integrates with your identity provider, you can easily work on implementing the IdP within your new applications. Legacy applications may require more significant rework and investment to allow for integration with the IdP. It is important to set your goals realistically. If your organization is not planning on investing significant resources in revamping old applications, you should include exceptions to your IdP policy. Otherwise, the paper world of policies has a completely different reality than the organization.

Company culture is also an important factor to consider when establishing policy. Some organizations may have extensive knowledge of security and its necessity (like companies that manufacture planes). While other organizations may be focused on fast innovation in a quickly changing market. As you can imagine, the ability of an organization (and the need) to apply security policies effectively is largely influenced by its culture.

For example, if your company has a culture of an informal organization in which people communicate largely verbally, creating policies that require extensive documentation may be difficult to exercise.

EXAM TIP: Gaps in policy and reality can be dangerous to an organization's security posture.

Such a disconnect is dangerous for various reasons. Firstly, your senior management is likely to have an unrealistic expectation of your security posture. Secondly, you know that at the time of audits, your organization's policies will not hold up against inspection. Failing audits can put your organization at risk of losing certifications and reputational damage. However, the most important point is that your organization as a whole will likely become demotivated towards security. Just like any goal-setting exercise, your goals should be timely and realistic.

Simply put, when you design policy, build policy to set attainable goals for the near future. Realize the impact of policy on your organization. For example, if you require MFA for all corporate applications, it will impact not only users but also the organization's finances and ability to produce new functionality (as old apps might need to be revamped).

You get the point. Policy and reality should be within reach of each other. The reason to bring this up is simple. As said, policy alone does not make an organization secure. Your organization will have to build secure processes and operations. Policies need to set realistic and clear expectations for your operational organization. The engineers (and other employees) that build and use systems should be able to comply, understand, and act in compliance with the corporate policies.

Whenever you draft any policy, make sure to research your current (security) operations. Talk with engineers and other stakeholders to establish if the new policy is realistic and implementable. At the same time, you should make sure that policies are sufficiently clear to allow for process creation and operational implementation. Let us take a look at an example below:

If an organization creates a cryptography policy that states the following: *All data in transit must be encrypted* do you think this policy would be sufficiently clear for your operational teams? Most likely it will not be. The policy wording is broad and not specific. It leaves much room for interpretation. For example, an engineer could enable encryption in transit using insecure or proprietary algorithms. At the same time, engineers may actually encrypt data that might not need encryption.

On the other hand, a policy that states the following: All names, birthdates, and social security numbers must be encrypted using TLS 1.3 may actually be too specific. The problem with this policy text is that it sets rigid boundaries for what types of data must be encrypted in transit. If your organization starts handling new data that requires encryption, you would have to revise the policy. Revising policies always requires senior management approval and should not be excessively performed. Contrary to the previous policy, this policy does specify what encryption method should be applied. Unfortunately, encryption algorithms become insecure as well and not every form of encryption may be applicable for every technology. In short, the policy example above is too specific to be applied easily on operational side of your organization.

So, how do you create a policy that is easily implantable, specific enough but not limiting or in need of constant revision? The trick is to reference other (lower) policy documents while using broad definitions.

Let us take a look at an example: *All data, as required by the data handling standard, must be encrypted in transit using algorithms and key lengths as defined in the cryptography guideline.* In the prior text, the data that must be encrypted is defined in the data handling standard. Such standards are often subject of frequent revisions and may have an expedited approval process. The benefit is that your policy does not become obsolete if your organization changes its requirements for specific data types. At the same time, engineers can find in-depth information to help guide them in a more specific document.

The same concept applies to the encryption algorithms. Rather than outlining the approved algorithms and key lengths in your policy, it is more helpful to reference a guideline document. That guideline document can be updated frequently and can include common situations your organization encounters. For example, if your company uses object storage, it may dictate a specific approach for that storage type. The huge benefit of this approach is that engineers can develop secure operations that match organizational policy but support their specific operations rather than impeding them by setting rigid constraints.

If you are afraid that engineers will develop guidelines that include insecure algorithms, you can also maintain a list of prohibited algorithms and technologies. That way, you can easily add and remove algorithms and technologies when needed. Let us look at the two different policy set-ups:

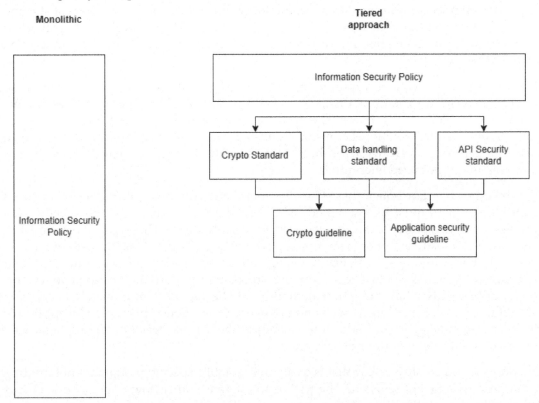

Figure 17.1: *Monolithic policy versus a tiered policy structure*

A tiered structure to your policy allows your organization to integrate security in your operations in a more accessible way, without requiring constant policy revision. However, it is important that you include your operational teams in creating more specific guidelines and policies, so that these are maintained and reviewed. After all, no policy should ever exist without a (yearly) mandatory review. As you can see above, a monolithic policy structure would create a single very large policy document. Any time a change has to be made, the whole document would have to be revised and re-approved. That process is generally cumbersome and time-consuming. It also makes it more difficult to have operational teams contribute to policy, standards, and guidelines.

EXAM TIP: Tiered policy structures are more adaptive to organizational change, without requiring constant senior management approval.

Security processes

Policies, standards, and guidelines form the constraints for our security processes. Without these constraints, our organizations could easily inconsistently execute processes throughout the organization. The danger of this is that our processes may contradict each other.

For example, if our networking team implements new network structures that prevent external access to our (cloud) environment, but our application team requires external incoming API communication, we will experience functional breakdowns. It is of vital importance that we consistently implement the correct security controls throughout all of our processes.

On the other hand, we can also see more subtle differences. For example, if our authentication standard states that applications must be built to use an **IdP**, but they do not sufficiently dictate which protocols should be used, we could easily experience compatibility issues later on in a project. Let us take a look at this example:

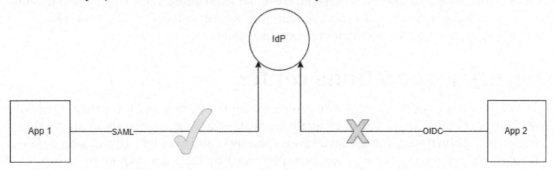

Figure 17.2: *Security compliant applications but functional issues due to inconsistent policy application*

As you can see in the figure above, two applications both have the capability to connect to an IdP. However, each application uses a different protocol to do so. Because the authentication standard only dictates that IdP connectivity must be included developers can implement a protocol of their choosing to be compliant with policy. Unfortunately, in the example above, the organization's IdP does not support OIDC. Meaning, the application is compliant, but it does not add to the organization's security as the integration with the IdP is not possible.

The point here is, we must think about the effects of our policies on our security processes. In the example above, policy ambiguity directly affects our (secure) development process. If the policy was more explicit, or a guideline was in place, the incompatibility issue could easily have been avoided.

Now that you understand the direct impact policies have on our processes it is of vital importance to review some of the common types of security processes found in organizations.

First of all, an organization must have processes in place to gather threat intelligence. As we discussed throughout the book, these processes may be heavily automated or can even be managed by external providers. Threat intelligence is essential for an organization to be able to anticipate its future security needs and to be able to anticipate new and emerging threats.

At the same time, an organization must also have processes in place for security testing. Depending on the company's needs, these processes can range from simple code review practices all the way to internal and external penetration testing.

Aside from testing, your organization is likely to need processes for secure development, secure deployment, and so forth. Any team in your organization that produces, maintains, or uses any internal or external processes should define processes that include security components.

Of course, our security controls may not always prove effective. Meaning, we may need processes to monitor for security events, detect and respond to incidents, but also to conduct forensics, and communicate with customers and authorities. Throughout the next parts of this chapter, we will examine common security processes that take place in a security operations center and incident response teams.

Security operations center

One of the most important areas where security processes take place is called a **security operations center (SOC)**. A SOC generally consists of a team of security analysts, threat researchers, security engineers, incident responders, and incident coordinators. These different disciplines may or may not be represented by different people. In many cases, senior analysts may also be incident coordinators and analysts with programming experience may be engineers and so on.

The purpose of a SOC is to continuously monitor security events that occur throughout the organization. The SOC monitors these events to establish patterns or signs that may indicate that a security event is actually an incident. Once the SOC discovers a potential incident, it initiates incident response procedures.

The NIST recognizes four distinct phases to incident response. The first step is preparation. During the preparation phase an organization gathers threat intelligence, inventories assets, classifies data, builds systems with detection capabilities, places sensors within the network, determines what classifies as an incident and so on.

The second phase, detection and analysis, exists to collect and analyze the data that is now collectable through the steps in the preparation phase. Meaning, that during this phase, we collect security events, correlate them with security events throughout the organization and link them to any threat intelligence we may have. Additionally, we perform analysis on events to determine if they qualify as incidents or regular security events.

The third phase, containment, eradication, and recovery, starts taking place when a security incident is discovered during detection and analysis. To begin, containment means that we must ensure that the danger coming forth from the incident does not spread further and to limit the damage it can still cause.

For example, containment in a ransomware attack may mean disconnecting an afflicted device from the network. Isolation of a machine can (most of the time) prevent the ransomware from spreading to other systems. In some cases, the machine can even be shutdown to limit the damage the ransomware can cause to the affected machine itself. Shutting down a machine affected by malware (such as ransomware) has some negative effects for digital forensics which we will review later this chapter.

The second step of the third phase is eradication. Contrary to containment, eradication seeks to fully eliminate the threat. For example, if an attacker has installed malware on a VM, eradication means to remove the malware (in its entirety) from the system.

The last step of the third phase is recovery. Recovery can have a broad scope, it may mean restoring data that has been lost, restoring webservices for customers, and so on. Many security professionals also feel that taking measures to prevent such a breach in the future should be part of the recovery steps.

Let us take the example of the infected VM above. If you remove malware from the machine, and then bring it back online the chances of re-infection are quite high. Recovery should therefore include steps to ensure that the breach does not re-occur prior to recovering services. In the case of the VM, that could mean implementing hardening or installing/ updating anti-malware software prior to updating.

EXAM TIP: Recovery tasks should include protecting the system from the breach that just occurred.

The last phase, post-incident activity, takes place after the incident situation has been resolved. Ideally, post-incident activity follows quickly after an incident. The activities include conducting lessons learned (about the incident but also the incident management process itself), re-training, policy adjustment, security testing, and so on.

Now, it is important to know that the NIST incident response lifecycle is not the only commonly used model. The SANS institute also has an incident response model. Let us look at the two models:

SANS	NIST
Preparation	Preparation
Identification	Detection and analysis
Containment	Containment, eradication, and recovery
Eradication	Post-incident activity
Recovery	
Lessons learned	

Table 17.1: Incident response steps by the NIST and the SANS institute

As you can see above, the NIST and SANS institute incident response models are very similar. The main difference is that the SANS institute has split the steps into more individual items. The identification phase of the SANS model and the detection and analysis phase of the NIST model also closely resemble each other. For your exam, you should be familiar with both models and broadly understand the activities that are part of each model.

A SOC plays an important role in every step of the incident response lifecycle. However, there are other parties that also play a role in incident response. For example, the organization's legal team, senior management, and the public relations team are likely to be part of this process as well.

EXAM TIP: Incident response teams can include SOC employees but also legal teams, PR teams, and even senior management.

Let us circle back to the role of a SOC. As you now know, a SOC plays an important role in the incident response lifecycle. They help prepare for incidents, they perform detection and analysis, and in many cases, also perform containment, eradication, and recovery activities. As you can imagine having a well-trained and capable SOC is quite important for fast and effective incident response.

Unfortunately, having a SOC is not realistic for many organizations. First off, a SOC requires extensive and specific experience. Your organization will need to hire and train skilled cybersecurity professionals to ensure your detection and analysis takes place correctly. At the same time, your team will have to be able to handle a variety of tools and systems for containment, eradication, and recovery activities. Even more so, your SOC will need specialists who can investigate emerging threats, perform (forensic) investigations, and even analyze malware.

As you can imagine, building a SOC is time-consuming and extremely expensive. Especially if you take into account that incidents can happen any time. This continuous nature of incident response makes it so that a SOC should (ideally) be operated 24 hours a day, every day. Of course, this makes it even more difficult to find suitable professionals and even more expensive to payroll them.

This is why many organizations implement **security operations center as a Service (SOCaaS)** or a managed SOC. A managed SOC is operated by a third-party service provider (sometimes a CSP). The third party maintains a 24/7 SOC staffed with well-trained professionals. Their SOC will review log data and security events from your organization and (depending on the service model) notify your internal incident response team or even handle incidents themselves.

The big upside to this approach is that you do not have to hire and train specialists in an already understaffed market. Another benefit is that SOC employees at a managed SOC handle incidents from a wide variety of organizations. Meaning they likely have more practice and experience with a wide variety of threats and systems than an internal SOC would. This extended exposure means a managed SOC may be able to detect more incidents and respond to them more effectively than an internal SOC.

So, why does not everybody use a managed SOC? Well, managed SOCs are very expensive. Sometimes, they can be more expensive than hiring and training your own teams. At the same time, a managed SOC needs to gain access to your security events and logging to detect events. That means you must share sensitive information (in real-time) with an external party. Some organizations may not be allowed to share such data or simply decide it does not fit their risk appetite. In some cases, a managed SOC may also not be able to handle the log types or **security incident and event monitoring (SIEM)** system your organization uses. We will dive a bit deeper into SIEM and SIEM systems in the next section of this chapter.

Regardless of your approach, an organization seeking a strong security posture will need a SOC in one shape or another. Incident response can mean the difference between the organization failing due to a hack or recovering without (unnecessarily) large damage. As a CCSP you may play an important role in determining how a SOC is created, which data they will have at their disposal, and how/if your cloud environment is integrated and accessible to your SOC.

Whenever your organization decides how it will create a SOC, remember that attackers are cunning. Many organizations are attacked outside of business hours or on holidays to capitalize on limited SOC operation times.

EXAM TIP: 24/7 SOCs are ideal, but some organizations choose to limit SOC operation times.

Security incident and event monitoring

Throughout this book, we have talked about **security incident and event monitoring (SIEM)**. The term SIEM stands for security incident and event monitoring and is often synonymous for software that performs aggregation, correlation, and analysis of log data. In current-day IT environments, many organizations have implemented logging throughout their environments. Every sign-in, application action, IP-lease, and so on is logged. As you can imagine, that means millions (or even billions) of log records are created every day. While SOC analysts are often very skilled professionals, it would be impossible to manually review all these events.

That is where SIEMs come in. SIEMs are capable (often) capable of ingesting millions of log records, correlating and analyzing them in near real-time. Most CSPs now offer SIEM solutions as part of their cloud offerings. In some cases, cloud SIEMs may even be directly integrated in the environment to automatically receive logs from other cloud services you use through that CSP.

However, especially in hybrid environment, setting up SIEM can be challenging. You may be gathering network and VM logs in the cloud, but also gathering logs from your on-premise IdP. For a SIEM to perform the best, it should be fed with logs from as many different areas of your environment as possible. After all, the task of a SIEM is also to correlate events with each other.

For example, if your IdP logs a new login from an unknown IP-address, and your cloud application registers a purge of database records from the same unknown IP-address, a SIEM could correlate these separate logs and indicate an incident may be taking place. Of course, the SIEM must have access to these logs to make such analyses. It is important that your organization carefully evaluates if the SIEM of your choosing can process the log files that your environment creates and if log augmentation can be used to make incompatible log files readable to the SIEM, as shown here:

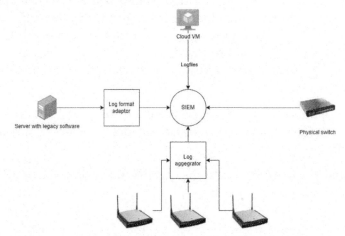

Figure 17.3: A SIEM can be provided with logs in various different manners

The power of a SIEM is that it can analyze many records much faster than a human could. Linking two events from different log files could take hours, days or weeks if done by hand. A SIEM may be able to correlate such records in seconds. Your organization should be aware that maintaining a SIEM is not an easy task. Similarly, maintaining a SIEM requires expertise, training, and lots of optimization. After all, like a firewall or IDS/IPS, a SIEM works basic on rulesets and/or heuristics (behavior patterns). Let us look at an example:

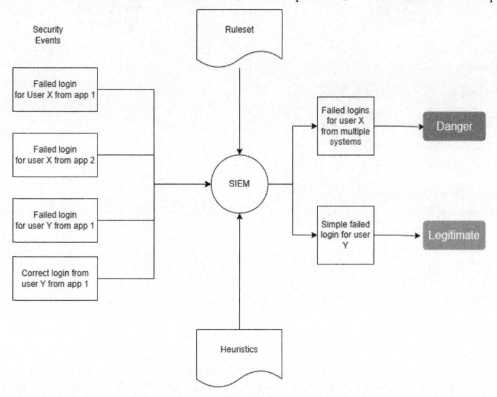

Figure 17.4: *Sample detection flow for a SIEM*

In the figure above, you can see that the SIEM processes events from different sources (namely applications 1 and 2). Because users may sometimes mistype their password, the SIEM rules that the failed login followed by a successful login for user Y on app 1 is legitimate. While the failed logins coming from different apps for user X are a potential incident. The SIEM uses a combination of rules and normal user behavior to make its assertions.

A SIEM must be *trained* to function correctly. Your organization will have to build rulesets to optimize detections for your environment. At the same time, you may need time for the SIEM to be able to establish normal usage patterns to be able to detect incidents. On the other hand, many SIEMs come with default rulesets. Some of these rulesets may be useful, while others may create false positives (or known-positives). Meaning the SIEM flags events as incidents even though they may be legitimate or may represent an accepted risk.

The danger of false positives is that they can create something called **alert fatigue**. Alert fatigue means that operators become overwhelmed by incident notifications. Because of that, they may not be able to determine effectively which incidents actually need their attention. This will likely result in true-positive incidents not being handled in a timely manner, effectively putting your organization at risk, as depicted in the following figure:

Figure 17.5: Sample of an untrained SIEM causing alert fatigue versus a well-trained SIEM

Imagine you are the SOC analyst looking at the dashboard on the left depicted in the figure above. There are 200 reported incidents, of which 190 have been ruled false positives. Your screen in filled with new incident information. Would you know where to start addressing incidents? Probably not. This is exactly the problem of a poorly trained/configured SIEM. If your SIEM creates many incidents that turn out to be false positives your analysts waste time.

At the same time, they will no longer be able to prioritize, which could result in actual incidents being handled too slow. Now, take a look at the dashboard to the right, you are probably feeling much more comfortable addressing the situation in this dashboard. The interesting thing, is that either dashboard could be based on the same data set. Depending on the rules and training of the SIEM it could ensure false positives are not flagged as incidents.

REAL-LIFE TIP: Remember that alert fatigue also has an equally dangerous opposite. If your SIEM is too forgiving, you may miss out on true positive notifications as well.

In short, your SIEM must be trained and optimized to increase detection capabilities but, at the same time, prevent alert fatigue. Because of the extensive experience and knowledge required to do so, your organization may consider using a managed SIEM solution or even letting your SOCaaS setup and manage a SIEM for you. Please be careful to consider if your SOC party supports the SIEM solution of your choice if you choose to implement your own SIEM but use a managed SOC.

EXAM TIP: A SIEM is rarely a plug-and-play solution.

Security orchestration, automation, and response

Earlier in this chapter, we talked about the role of a SOC. They detect incidents and respond to them. If you think back on *Figure 17.5*, you may have thought with that little incidents or events, alert fatigue is not realistic. Of course, organizations indeed vary in size. Large organizations are bound to have more security events, more incidents, and a higher potential for alert fatigue.

However, SOCs do not always scale with the size of the organization. For example, an organization with 1000 employees may have a SOC consisting of 5 individuals, while a company with 200,000 employees may have 50 people. While their SOC is ten times bigger, their organization is 200 times bigger. Meaning, the SOC at the large organization probably not only handles more events and incidents in absolute numbers, but also per SOC analyst.

If your organization deals with a couple dozen events in a week, you may be able to handle each incident manually. However, if you deal with hundreds or thousands of incidents, it is unlikely that you can scale your SOC to manually handle all of these incidents. This is where our next topic comes in, **security orchestration, automation, and response (SOAR)**.

SOAR is a name for a wide variety of technologies that can be used to respond to security incidents in an automated fashion. An example of SOAR could be a script that runs as a serverless application in your cloud to block a user account when too many failed logins (across applications) are identified. SOAR can also be a full application that automatically analyzes incidents found by a SIEM, logs in to affected systems, isolates them, patches them, reconfigures them, and brings them back online.

It is important that you understand that SOAR is not just a single technology. An organization's implementation of SOAR can consist of simple shell scripts or fully automated pipelines. Many organizations (including CSPs) advertise their SOAR solutions that often integrate with their own (or other) SIEM platforms. While SOAR is extremely useful and powerful (especially in organizations of large scale) it requires a fairly mature organization.

For example, if your organization decides to purchase a SOAR solution while it does not have a SIEM, it will likely not help you. Similarly, if you purchase a SOAR platform, but you have not optimized your SIEM, you are likely to experience outages due to SOAR intervention.

At the same time, like SIEM, any SOAR technology has to be built and applied with purpose. You must ensure any SOAR solution has correct access, is triggered only when needed, and so on.

If your organization is just looking to implement SOAR, try to automate low-hanging fruit prior to purchasing complex and expensive solutions. In many cases, you can automate incident response without much cost (for example through serverless applications). Especially when you organization has many recurring incidents, SOAR will help you get these under control without requiring vast numbers of extra SOC analysts.

Let us take a look below at a common use-case where SOAR can greatly improve response time to incidents, with little cost and effort. Imagine your SIEM gathers information from endpoint security agents on various virtual machines in your cloud. The endpoint agents report sudden high processor usage, high write operations, and high volumes of outgoing network traffic. The SIEM you use flags the logs as a potential ransomware attack (high CPU usage and high writes can be indicatives of these) especially when large amounts of data are sent out of your network.

Your organization could easily build a serverless function triggered by an incident warning for ransomware generated by the SIEM. By using a webhook, the SIEM triggers the function and provides information about the VM the issues take place at. The function uses a role to move the VM to a quarantine vNet, the vNet has no internet connectivity.

The beauty of a simple solution like the one above is that you can easily stop data exfiltration in near real-time. The VM is isolated so the data can no longer be extracted to the attacker. Of course, this function does not stop the ransomware from encrypting the storage attached to the VM. However, your simple serverless function may have just reduced a large-scale data breach to a much more manageable situation. This SOAR solution costs a one-time fee for running the serverless function (we are talking less than a cent).

You can build a collection of such functions that address very serious security incidents automatically and instantly without much cost or work at all. Of course, you need to ensure your SOAR operates in a way that does not disrupt your functional environment. But you can also go much further than the example above.

For example, you could shut down the VM entirely, freeze it, detach the storage volume, and so on. The point is, SOAR can be simple, cheap, and effective. It is highly advisable to experiment with simple SOAR applications like the example above, prior to purchasing high cost, complex SOAR solutions.

EXAM TIP: SOAR can be realized in many different ways; SOAR can even be achieved through simple automation.

As your organization matures and better understands the threats it faces, and the incidents it will need to handle more mature SOAR products can be very helpful. Many SOAR products seamlessly integrate with SIEMs, allowing simple to very complex automation. In most cases, SOAR tools will also have a library of automatic interventions that can be tailored to your environment. Currently, SOAR is not a viable alternative to replace all manual SOC interventions. Simply because a SOAR has to be trained on how to act, it cannot (yet) completely make up new fixes on the go for incidents it has not encountered before.

Artificial intelligence

As stated in the last section, SIEM and SOAR require significant training and configuration. Luckily, **artificial intelligence (AI)** is quickly accelerating this process and making SIEM and SOAR tools even more effective. Many SIEM and SOAR vendors utilize AI to detect (pattern-based) attacks that would be difficult, if not near impossible, to detect with basic rule-based detections.

At the same time, AI will start to play in increasingly important role in allowing SOAR tools to divine new interventions on the fly. AI can allow the SOAR tools to act differently depending on the development of an incident.

For example, an AI powered SOAR tool could choose to isolate all machines in an entire vNet once multiple hosts show signs of compromise. A simple SOAR tool would likely have to isolate every different machine separately, allowing for more machines to become infected and a higher potential for data exfiltration. Let us look at an example of this, refer to the following figure:

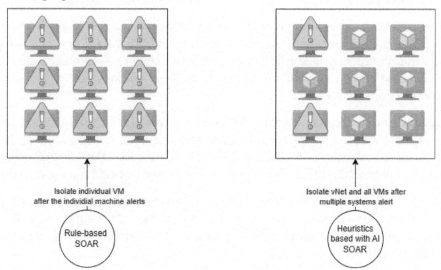

Figure 17.6: *AI can improve SOAR effectiveness by adapting to the incident as it evolves*

As you can see in the figure above, a SOAR solution with AI, might be able to act more adaptively. While the simple SOAR solution isolated a machine once it showed signs of compromise, an AI-based SOAR could use a pattern of compromise to pre-emptively isolate an entire vNet and all the systems within. By doing so, in the example above, the AI would prevent seven additional machines from being compromised. Of course, this example is theoretical, and may even be achievable through rule-based automation. However, it is intended to show that SOAR tools could be more adaptable during incidents using AI (like a SOC analyst would be), of course, using AI as part of SIEM or SOAR can also pose risks. If the AI is acting on malformed or even compromised data, attackers may be able to bypass detections by targeting the AIs dataset itself. Similarly, attackers will likely start to employ AI in increasing numbers to stage more complex attacks and create malware that can implement evasive techniques based on the defenders counter-measures.

As with anything AI, it brings significant benefits but presents new (often unknown) challenges. If your organization is considering using AI, you must evaluate if the benefits outweigh the drawbacks. One of the drawbacks you must consider is that AI and other **machine learning** (**ML**) applications need access to data to function. Meaning, for your AI to be effective, it needs access to large amounts of your data. Most CSPs that offer SIEM and SOAR already use AI and ML to train their systems with (anonymized) data from all their customers. You must consider how AI/ML will use your data and logs before you decide to implement such technologies.

EXAM TIP: AI improves SIEM detection capabilities and SOAR intervention capabilities.

Incident management and disclosure

You now understand some of the most important tasks and duties of a SOC. You know a SOC uses SIEM and sometimes SOAR to ensure they can scale their operations efficiently, effectively, and timely. As you know, incident response encompasses more than examining technical data and performing technical fixes. In many cases, incidents adversely affect an organization's operations.

For example, an incident causing denial of service may disrupt critical business operations, cause damages to clients and the organization, and so on. So, it is vital that an incident is managed in more ways than just the technical. In many cases, the internal organization, customers, and potentially the authorities may have to be notified during an incident.

Especially in cases where an incident leads to a data breach, your organization may be required by (local) law to notify customers and authorities. At the time of writing, every state in the US already has requirements for data breach notifications. Similarly, countries in the EU do as well.

You may remember that an incident response team comprises more than technical personnel. These teams often include lawyers and public relations professionals. The reason is that your organization must quickly evaluate what types of communication are necessary during an incident. A legal team can help evaluate if the incident requires the organization to disclose information to authorities or customers. At the same time, public relations can determine how external communications are performed. Your organization may want to hold off communicating publicly until the incident is resolved. You must ensure communications are run through official channels. The last thing your organization needs during an incident is employees posting information on social media about your organization being hacked.

Imagine if your organization is a bank, such social media posts, could quickly cause a run on your bank. This means your customers attempt to withdraw their balances. If this happens in large volumes, your organization could experience financial trouble, or in the worst case, even collapse.

Throughout the book, we have touched on the need for incident response planning. These plans must include a communication strategy and (ideally) also include pre-written statements that can be publicly released. Of course, that means your organization must carefully prepare for various incidents that can occur and tailor the communication strategy to these situations. While this is a significant amount of work, you want to avoid making up a communications strategy while an incident occurs.

Incident situations are often high stress, high impact situations. Important matters are likely overlooked if your organization is in the middle of such an incident. As we covered earlier, your incident response planning should provide as much information and clear guidance as possible. The same concept of course applies to legal implications. Your organization should prepare for various incident situations and pre-emptively determine if a breach warrants notification, and if so to whom.

Your organization can prepare for these situations by making boilerplate decisions based on data classification. For example, if your organization requires that all data that is confidential or a higher classification is encrypted, your lawyers can determine what actions have to be taken if a breach takes place involving encrypted data. The ideal end result is a step-by-step playbook that your organization can use to quickly determine what actions have to be taken. Let us take a look at an example:

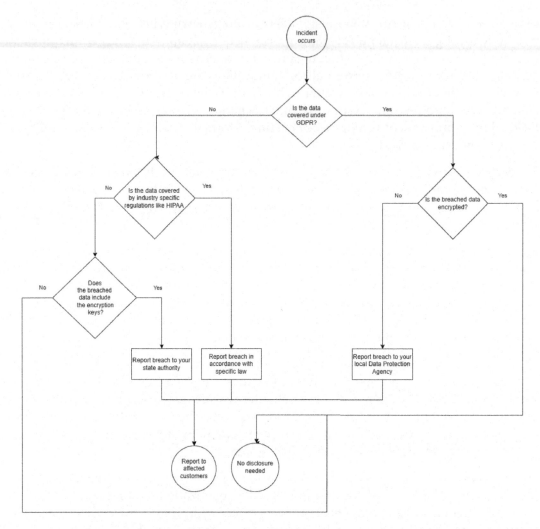

Figure 17.7*: Sample decision tree for legal disclosure requirements during an incident*

As you can see in the sample decision tree above, your organization should prepare itself by asking some important questions. Which type of data is breached, under what jurisdiction does the data fall, is data covered under specific laws, how many records were breached, were they encrypted, were encryption keys also compromised, and so on. Based on the answers to these questions, your incident response plan, should quickly reveal if disclosure of an incident is required, and if so, in what capacity and to whom.

Please remember that the sample diagram above is not a diagram you can copy and paste into your organization. Rather, it gives an example of factors your organization will likely have to consider as part of their incident response planning. Remember that your organization may be bound by rules and regulations that are specific to the locales in which your organization operates, or even the industry it operates within.

Aside from notification of authorities and customers, you may also need a communication plan for your internal organization. Once again, it is vital that your communication provides useful information to impacted employees, however, it should be sufficiently vague to prevent employees from publicly disclosing information about the ongoing incident. Let us look at two examples:

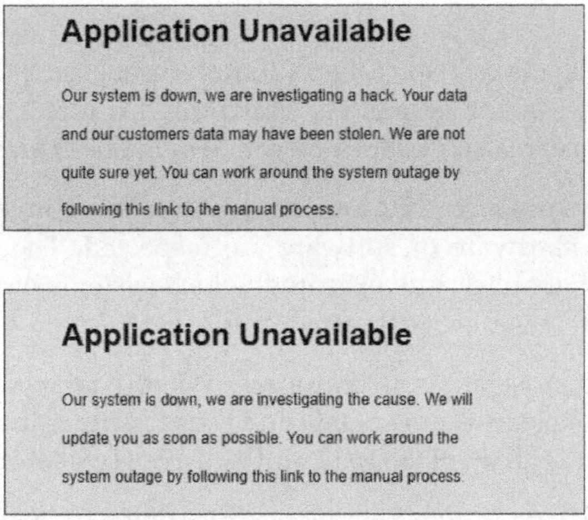

Figure 17.8: Samples of internal communication strategies

As you can see in the figure above, there are two sample notifications to internal employees. Both notifications attempt to tell the user their application is currently unavailable. The example on the top, mentions a hack has taken place and data may or may not have been stolen. The example on the bottom speaks in general terms. It informs the user the application is down and that they will be informed as soon as possible. Both notifications provide documentation for a workaround procedure. Which example do you think is best?

While being transparent with your organization is good, the top example is more likely to elicit an erratic response from employees. For example, they may post this notification in social media, which would disclose the hack publicly. While your policy may prohibit such actions, the fear of their data being stolen may cause people to ignore the policy.

The second message is ambiguous about the cause. The employee does not have reason to expect a hack. Your employees need to stay calm while your incident response team investigates the cause and extent of the incident. Think of an evacuation when the fire alarm goes off. Would it be helpful to state *the building is on fire, people may not make it out, evacuate now* or is it better to calmly notify employees that the building must be evacuated? Whenever your organization develops its incident response plans, and communication plans (both internal and external) pay close attention to how you inform your target audience.

EXAM TIP: Like other components of an incident response plan, a communication and breach notification plan should be established before an incident occurring.

Forensics

As you know, the incident response lifecycle includes detecting, eradicating, and recovering from incidents. However, to prevent incidents from happening in the future or to support legal claims against attackers it is important to understand who attacked you and how they did it.

One important tool to achieve this is called (digital) **forensics**. You may be familiar with forensics in a law enforcement setting. As shown on TV, forensic analysts may inspect evidence to link evidence to a suspect or determine if an object was used for a crime.

Digital forensics is very similar to this. During digital forensic investigations, digital files, computers, and other hardware or software are inspected. The inspection may reveal valuable data about what attack was executed, which systems were breached, what files were stolen, and in some cases who the attacker is.

As with any evidence, it must be handled properly. Without taking proper care of evidence, it may become inadmissible in a court of law and thus lose its value in legal action. As part of this, we will review the chain of custody and e-discovery later in this chapter.

For the CCSP exam, we have to dive a bit deeper into digital forensics, what it can uncover, how it is performed, and when it is legal to conduct. First, let us take a look at how digital forensics works and what challenges you may experience with forensics in the cloud.

As you can imagine, digital forensics is mostly concentrated around inspecting files and live systems. Log files, malware, and even user-created files can all be subject of forensic analysis. In many cases, forensic analysts will also attempt to recover files that may have been previously deleted (more about this later). So, an important question is how and when can we provide an analyst with files to inspect?

Well, let us take a look at an example. Imagine a situation where an employee is suspected to have used their work computer to alter the company's payment software with malicious code that steal small amounts of money from customer payments (we call that practice salami slicing). Forensic analysis could be used in this situation to establish if the employee indeed built this malicious code, and embed it with the payment software.

Now, because the employee has allegedly used company equipment to execute this attack, the organization that owns the device may execute forensic analysis on the device. If the employee allegedly used his personal computer to inject the code, the company would have no right to perform forensic analysis on the employee's personal computer. Rather it would have to file criminal charges, and the police would have to obtain a warrant to gather evidence from the device.

So, first things first, you can only conduct forensic analysis (as a company) on assets that you own or pay for. Forensic analysis used in a criminal prosecution may be conducted on non-company-owned assets, but only by law enforcement agencies and only after the correct warrants are obtained.

EXAM TIP: You can only legally conduct hardware forensics on company owned assets.

Now, because forensics cannot be executed on devices that are not owned by your company, using cloud computing can make digital forensics more difficult. After all, resource pooling means that you use shared computing resources amongst many different customers. If you were to conduct forensics on the physical devices used to power your cloud services, you would potentially gain access to other cloud consumer data.

As you can imagine, digital forensics on physical devices in cloud environments is rarely legal. Only in very select cases, can a CSP be compelled into allowing forensics on their physical devices. Those cases are (almost) always criminal investigations by law enforcement agencies. Simply put, as a private organization, using cloud computing means that your options for digital forensics will be limited. You will not be given physical access to devices, meaning your forensic options will be limited to your virtual environment.

EXAM TIP: Cloud computing greatly limits opportunities for hardware forensics.

So, let us take the example earlier. Because the employee allegedly used a company computer, it can be subjected to digital forensics. If the employee used a cloud VM, the physical device hosting the VM could not be subjected to forensics. However, the company could investigate the virtual storage device and logs associated with the VM. If the employee used their personal computer for an attack, a company would have no options for forensic investigation, short of criminal prosecution and investigation by law enforcement agencies. Let us look at an overview of where forensics can be conducted, refer to the following figure:

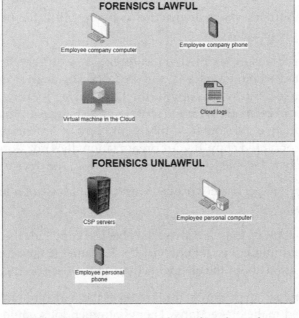

Figure 17.9: Forensics cannot be conducted anywhere

EXAM TIP: law enforcement agencies, with the proper warrants, may be allowed to conduct forensics on your organization's devices as part of criminal or regulatory investigations.

Now that you know when forensics can be applied. Let us take a deeper look at how they are executed. In general, we can distinguish two different forms of digital forensics. The first type is called **live forensics**.

Live forensics is executed on a running machine. During life analysis, a capture can be taken of the RAM of a machine. The RAM might contain valuable data about the last/ongoing actions executed on the machine. In some cases, captures may also be taken of incoming and outgoing network traffic. Similarly, if the interface of the machine is available, images can be taken of the user interface. Live forensics can only be conducted once a device is still running. If a machine is shutdown, the RAM (which is volatile storage) which be cleared and network traffic will be released. In short, shutting off a machine destroys evidence that could be gathered through live forensics.

During live forensics, the analyst should also take a *live* image of the machine. This means a copy is made of the machine in its running state. The process of taking an image for forensics is very similar to the process of taking a live image of a VM. Forensics requires evidence to be pristine, so it is essential to prevent any alteration of the evidence using write blockers (more about this later). Live forensics provides the most information you can gather during forensics as the volatile memory of the computer is accessible.

EXAM TIP: Live forensics is only possible if the investigated device has not been shut down

EXAM TIP: You should not *use* a device that is being subjected to a live investigation as it tampers with the evidence

The second form of forensics is called **static forensics**. Contrary to live forensics, static forensics is conducted when a device is powered off. The analyst uses a device called a **write-blocker** to make a bit-by-bit copy of the hard drive. Because of the write blocker, the bit-by-bit copy can be made without writing any changes to the drive, ensuring the evidence remains pristine. Of course, a bit-by-bit copy of an encrypted hard drive will simply result in an encrypted copy. If your organization does not store fallback decryption keys, you are unlikely to be able to recover any data from the device.

EXAM TIP: Encryption can largely prevent forensic analysis of a hard drive if the data cannot be decrypted

Once the bit-by-bit copy of the hard drive has been completed, the forensic analyst can examine the copy (assuming it is not encrypted). The analyst then looks for files and logs that provide information about the alleged actions of the user or attacker.

For example, the forensic analyst may find traces of the malware or log files that show an attacker has executed malicious actions. There is tremendous value to such information because it can reveal what specific attack was used, how the attacker was able to breach the system, what data has been compromised, and sometimes where the attack originated from.

EXAM TIP: Drive images must be made using a write-blocker to prevent modification of evidence.

Of course, skilled attackers will do everything in their power to erase their traces. Malware may erase (or encrypt) itself after execution, log files may be purged, and botnets can be used to stage attacks. Nevertheless, attackers may not always take these measures, or may not take them effectively. Especially in situations where an attack was staged by an employee, there is a high chance of finding valuable information.

Now, let us circle back to the challenges of cloud computing to forensics. As you know, if you use cloud service, you will not be permitted to conduct digital forensics on physical devices. Meaning, you are unlikely to be able to capture RAM, you are unlikely to be able to create a bit-to-bit copy of a hard drive, and you may not even be able to capture and inspect network traffic.

So, what can you do in the cloud? The main forensics you can conduct in the cloud pertains to inspecting log files. If you set up in-depth logging within your cloud environment, you may be able to gather the data you need from there. Every CSP will have different levels of support for forensics.

At the time of writing, some large CSPs (like Microsoft) provide tooling to conduct cloud native forensics. Using such tooling you will be able to maintain digital evidence and even get access to some (scoped) logs that may not normally be accessible.

On the other hand, some CSPs may be willing to conduct limited forensics on your behalf, while others may offer built-in tools to conduct limited forensics within your own cloud resources. In any case, your organization must take the limited opportunity for forensics into account when it decides to use cloud services.

EXAM TIP: Before you use cloud services, evaluate if the limited options for forensics are acceptable to your organization.

Chain of custody

We already talked about the necessity of evidence to remain pristine. If your organization is conducting a simple internal investigation, you may not need to produce evidence in a manner that is admissible in court. Unfortunately, there are many circumstances during which a forensic investigation may need to be used to gather evidence to support a lawsuit. In other cases, a simple investigation may lead to more shocking findings that require legal steps anyway.

In any case, it is highly advisable to operate in a way that always maintains a proper chain of custody. That way, any evidence that is produced is likely to remain admissible in a court of law if needed. So, what does a chain of custody mean? The specific requirements for a chain of custody may differ per jurisdiction. For the CCSP exam, it is important to be familiar with the chain of custody requirements as used in the United States.

Chain of custody requires two basic things. Firstly, it requires that evidence is handled correctly. We call this evidence management. Evidence management means that the evidence must be stored correctly so that it cannot be tampered with or be damaged. You may have seen examples of this on TV when a forensics employee doubles an evidence bag, labels it, and assigns an evidence number with it. Aside from specific storage requirements, it is mandatory to note who collected the evidence, when it was found, and what case or investigation it is related to.

In digital forensics, evidence management still applies. For example, if you conduct evidence on a computer, the computer should be wrapped, stored, and labeled following the legal requirements. However, when you are dealing with digital files, evidence management can become more ambiguous. For example, when you create a live image from a machine, how do you label that file and store it? You must use digital alternatives, such as file names, timestamps, digital evidence lockers, and so on.

Aside from evidence management, we must also ensure an evidence log is in place. An evidence log is an overview of the evidence gathered in an investigation. The log should include descriptions of the collected evidence, but it also outlines who handled which piece of evidence when, and for what purpose. In essence, an evidence log must detail every action that is performed with a piece of evidence. The purpose is to ensure evidence is not illegally entered, altered, or even removed. Let us take a look at a sample of an evidence log:

SAMPLE EVIDENCE LOG					
Evidence ID	Description:	Purpose:	Collected or deposited by:	Time:	Date:
1	Harddrive	Enter into the evidence locker	Deposited -IT department	10:10	01/08/2023
1	Harddrive	Create bit-to-bit image	Collected -Forensics	12:00	01/08/2023
1	Harddrive	Return to the evidence locker	Deposited - Forensics	14:00	01/08/2023

Table 17.2: *Sample of an evidence log*

As you can see in the preceding figure, an evidence log specifies who handled evidence, for which purpose, and at what date and time. If an evidence log shows gaps or actions that could compromise the evidence, it may not be admissible.

Cryptographic technologies such as hashing can also be used to ensure the integrity of evidence. Similar to code integrity, hashes should be created of digital evidence at the time of collection. The hash can then be verified at the time the evidence will be processed as part of legal proceedings. By ensuring the hash of the data matches the original hash integrity of the data can be confirmed.

Whenever you want to present evidence to a court of law, you must prove evidence management was performed correctly, and the evidence log is established and correct. If you cannot prove these two items, a judge will likely deem your evidence inadmissible. In the case of digital forensics, this could easily mean that any case you were building could be thrown out.

Types of evidence

While every type of evidence requires evidence management and a solid chain of custody, we do distinguish different forms of evidence. Some types of evidence hold more value than other types. It is important, to understand what role the different types can play in your cases.

Firstly, we have real evidence, this type of evidence includes actual objects. For example, physical hard drives, thumb drives, and even computers. It is important to note, that real evidence part of these items is only the device itself and not the data on it.

Secondly, there is direct evidence, usually testimony from an eyewitness. For example, in the IT sphere, this could be a witness that sees an attacker tamper with physical equipment.

Aside, from real and direct evidence we also have circumstantial evidence. Circumstantial evidence provides support for other types of evidence. For example, it could provide information about the circumstances of an attacker.

Lastly, there is hearsay; hearsay is likely not admissible in a court of law. An example of hearsay is that a witness claims to have heard another person was going to attack your organization. It is important to know that this type of evidence has little value.

Alright, now that you understand some of the different types of evidence. Let us look at the priority a court gives to evidence. Firstly, we have the best evidence rule. Meaning, a court will prefer the best form of evidence. For example, a written contract will always overrule a verbal contract. Simply because the written contract can be verified, while the verbal contract probably cannot.

EXAM TIP: You must understand the best evidence rule for the CCSP exam but do not need in-depth knowledge of the legal process.

E-Discovery

E-discovery is the last element of forensics you must understand for the CCSP exam. In the United States, e-discovery refers to discovering digital forms of evidence. Whenever a legal case is brought to court, evidence must be produced to support the case. The e-discovery process is a nine-step process for data collection, preservation, and presentation. Once your organization is requested to produce evidence, you must ensure your organization abides by the rules of e-discovery to avoid destroying valuable evidence.

The first step of e-discovery is called **information governance (IG)**. IG is a collection of policies and processes in an organization to handle information/data. IG includes data retention policies, data handling, and so on. Regardless of pending litigation, your organization should always have a clear IG.

The second step, identification, is triggered once your organization becomes involved in (pending) litigation. During this phase, your organization will have to identify which data is required to be preserved. In some cases, if your company is facing charges, your organization may be told which data it must preserve (if not all data).

The preservation step starts once it is clear what data must be preserved. During this step, your organization is strictly forbidden from destroying or altering the data. In many cases, this can lead to business impact. For example, your organization may have to halt automated deletion processes, stop manual/physical destruction of files, and so on.

Once your organization has taken steps to preserve data, it must be collected. During collecting, data must be collected using proper processes such as evidence management and chain of custody. We call this phase collection.

After data is collected, we enter the processing phase. During the processing phase, the collected data must be processed to ensure only relevant data is collected. Processing is often done through automated tooling, as manual processing is far too time-consuming.

When processing has concluded, the evidence must be reviewed. During review, useable evidence is selected, and evidence irrelevant to the (pending) case will be removed. At the same time, your legal team will have to decide what data can be withheld as part of client-attorney privilege. Your company should establish clear policies on communication to ensure your exchanges with your attorneys qualify under privilege.

Once the review has concluded, evidence is analyzed further during the analysis phase. Evidence is evaluated for patterns and will be linked to other evidence and testimony to build a case.

After analysis, physical versions of the evidence must be produced. As you can imagine, this is a rather comprehensive task. After all, digital files can lead to vast numbers of physical files. Nevertheless, this is essential to ensure the evidence can be handed to the court.

During the last phase, presentation, the evidence is used in the legal process. In the following table, you can find an overview of every step of the e-discovery process:

1	Information Governance
2	Identification
3	Preservation
4	Collection
5	Processing
6	Review
7	Analysis
8	Production
9	Presentation

Table 17.3: The nine steps of e-discovery

EXAM TIP: Most organizations will have to purchase digital forensic services (on retainer) as there are few digital forensic investigators. Especially small organizations are unlikely to start their own forensics team.

Conclusion

Throughout this chapter, we have reviewed the need for policy and processes. Policies alone do not change an organization. We must translate policy into actionable standards and guidelines. Policy dictates how an organization should do things, the reality is often different. Whenever we write policy, we must ensure the policy set goals for the future but is not disconnected from the status quo. If policy is too stringent, adaptation will likely be poor. At the same time, policies that do not reflect the security level of an organization can create a false sense of security.

A security operations center or SOC is an important place for security processes in an organization. A SOC can perform incident response and management. Using advanced tooling such as security incident and event management, they can collect a wide variety of security events throughout the organization. SOC analysts and the SIEM tooling then aggregate and cross-reference these events to identify malicious patterns and rule-based violations. A SOC requires highly trained personnel. Unfortunately, not every organization can acquire and retain these types of professionals.

Like a SOC, a SIEM needs to be trained to detect incidents. By optimizing rule-sets and training the SIEM to understand your organizational patterns you will be more effective in detecting incidents and false-positives. Limiting the number of false positives to lower the chance of alert fatigue within your SOC is essential.

Of course, a SOC and SIEM may be faced with large numbers of incidents daily. **Security orchestration, automation, and response (SOAR)** can help them to automate incident response processes. By using SOAR, your SOC can scale its operations significantly and ensure the response is timelier. The advent of AI plays a huge role in the capabilities of both SIEM and SOAR tools.

Whenever an incident occurs, we also may need to take legal steps. However, legislation requires evidence to ensure a favorable outcome. Digital forensics can be a tool for an organization to produce evidence that resides on their IT-resources. Log files, work files, chat history, emails, and so on. can all be part of the evidence. However, your organization must understand how to recover this data using evidence management while maintaining a chain of custody. Failing to do so, will result in evidence being inadmissible in court.

In the next chapter, we will learn about the legal and regulatory requirements in the cloud.

Learning goals

This chapter addresses the following CCSP exam outline learning goals:

Domain 5: Cloud security operations

       5.4 Support digital forensics

       5.5 Manage communications with relevant parties

       5.6 Manage security operations

Join our book's Discord space

Join the book's Discord Workspace for Latest updates, Offers, Tech happenings around the world, New Release and Sessions with the Authors:

https://discord.bpbonline.com

CHAPTER 18

Legal and Regulatory Requirements in the Cloud

Introduction

Cloud computing has many benefits, for example, it offers better availability. Some of these characteristics have drawbacks. When talking about legal requirements, the dispersion of data can complicate the scope of regulations your organization must adhere to. This chapter explores, various legal requirements and risks associated with computing in the cloud.

Structure

This chapter covers the following topics:

- Conflicting international legislation
- **California Privacy Protection Act (CPPA)**
- **General Data Protection Regulation (GDPR)**
- **Payment Card Industry – Data Security Standard (PCI-DSS)**
- Evaluation of legal risks specific to cloud computing
- Legal frameworks and guidelines

- Intellectual property

- E-discovery ISO/IEC 27050

- Forensics

Objectives

The purpose of this chapter is to build an understanding of the complex legal and regulatory environment in which security professionals operate. Especially in cloud environments that are physically dispersed, organizations are faced with numerous differing, and sometimes conflicting laws and regulations. This will prepare you to understand common challenges and solutions for ensuring regulatory and legal compliance. The chapter teaches you about some of the common laws and regulations that may apply to your organization.

At the same time, the chapter provides you with information on legal frameworks and guidelines that can aid your organization. Specifically, this chapter reiterates some of the e-Discovery and requirements surrounding forensics. At the end of the chapter, you will understand how laws and regulations influence the choices your organization will have to make, especially when operating in the cloud.

Conflicting international legislation

Imagine the following scenario: You work for a large organization in Brazil. Your organization intends to bring their business to a new market, namely the south of Europe. Your company has conducted extensive market research, and it feels that its products would be well received. Because you operate in a new business segment, there are barely any contenders.

When your organization is done researching the new market, it establishes a plan to open a new office in Europe. The new office will be in Lisbon. Your organization has procured an office, hired staff, and even transferred employees to work in Portugal.

At the same time, your company is rolling out the IT infrastructure for your organization. Because your company wants to limit overhead (expansion is risky after all), they decided to manage the IT infrastructure remotely from Brazil. All employees will be using cloud desktop environments running in the company's existing cloud. Your application development team has put in much hard work to ensure the client-facing website and applications are ported to a version optimized for Portugal.

Your legal team has done extensive research on laws and regulations in Europe. The organization has taken actions to ensure the product complies with EU regulations, and is manufactured by companies that can ship to the EU. Everything seems to go well.

Several months after your organization started operating in Europe, they have generated a large revenue stream. However, shortly after the first quarter, your organization received a letter from the data protection agency in Portugal. Stating that your organization is violating the **General Data Protection Regulation** by storing customer information at your CSP located in Brazil.

As you can imagine, such a scenario can be very dangerous to an organization. Large fines, orders to cease and desist, or worse, can halt a business or even destroy its reputation. Unfortunately, such scenarios occur frequently.

The advent of cloud computing, while extremely powerful, presents some unique challenges. Because of cloud computing, it is extremely easy to roll out services across the globe and manage them centrally. However, as with every aspect of business, operating in different jurisdictions presents legal challenges.

Many countries (and sometimes even states or provinces) have widely varying laws and regulations regarding IT security and data privacy in general. For example, the European Union protects the data of its residents using the **General Data Protection Regulation (GDPR)**. While the US does not have comprehensive data protection laws and regulations. Rather, many states have specific requirements for data protection. At the same time, different sectors of industry within the same jurisdiction may be subject to different laws and regulations.

For example, in the US, health providers and brokers are subject to the **Health Information Portability and Accountability Act (HIPAA)** as well as the **Health Information Technology for Economic and Clinical Health (HITECH)** act.

While HIPAA only applies to US organizations, there are also laws and regulations, like the **Payment Card Industry Data Security Standard (PCI-DSS)** that apply globally. Unfortunately, there are few laws and regulations with such a large span. Rather, most countries have their laws, and some industries have their regulations.

The complexity of the legal and regulatory landscape is not new to cloud computing. International companies have been confronted with these complexities for many decades. However, when organizations use on-premises computing, they normally rely on data centers in the country where the data originates. Meaning, that their on-premises environment may only store data from residents in that country. At the same time, the laws and regulations that pertain to that environment are likely limited to the local laws and regulations.

Now, you know that the cloud offers availability zones and regions. You can use availability zones and regions to ensure your services remain available regardless of disaster or outages. However, using them has some significant implications.

For example, if you replicate data between regions, you now may be subjected to the laws and regulations that apply to both regions. For example, if you store your data in an EU region and decide to replicate the data to a region in the US, you could be violating EU laws and regulations (such as GDPR) as well as US regulations.

Similarly, your organization may offer centralized services that are available globally. Like in the example at the beginning of the chapter, you may offer services in the EU through an application that is hosted in a South American region. Inadvertently, you may be breaching EU laws and regulations as the CSP may not have implemented sufficient security controls to protect EU resident data in their South American data centers.

Whenever you use cloud computing you are bound to introduce some legal and regulatory complexity. Whether your CSP does not provide services directly in your country, or whether the services you use share data across country lines. Your cloud services may even operate across different regions without your specific knowledge (especially in the case of SaaS solutions), let us look at an example:

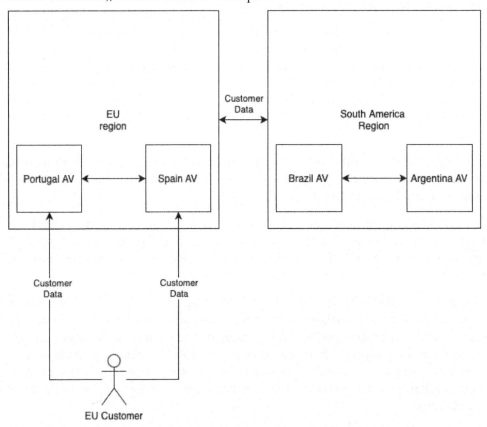

Figure 18.1: *Data duplication across regions and Avs*

As you can see in the figure above, your services are likely to use some form of data duplication. Whether that means duplicating data between Avs or regions, there is a chance data will be copied across different countries. For example, duplicating data across **AV**s in **South America** could result in data being stored in **Argentina** and **Brazil**. Each country has specific laws and regulations. Similarly, duplicating data across regions could result in EU resident data ending up in **South America**.

Whenever you choose a CSP or cloud service, you must thoroughly understand how data travels through a cloud environment. Many SaaS services take care of data duplication for you. Meaning, your organization might be presented with laws and regulations of countries your organization does not even operate in, just by using a SaaS tool.

Similarly, your engineers may activate duplication amongst regions and Avs and as a result expose your company to laws and regulations that are applicable within the localities of the AV.

These laws and regulations may have far-reaching consequences for your organization. For example, data stored in the US, may under certain circumstances by used by the US government and law enforcement agencies. At the same time, data stored in other countries may allow governmental agencies to conduct forensics or even appropriate your data as part of government investigations.

While compliance with all these different laws and regulations is difficult on its own, some combinations of laws and regulations make it impossible to be compliant all around. For example, some of the laws a country has may inherently violate the laws of another country. Imagine a situation in which a country, by law, requires encrypted data to be decrypted as part of law enforcement investigations. If that data concerns citizens of another country, that strictly prohibits decryption of its citizen's data for foreign law enforcement investigation you are presented with a tough situation.

Whenever you operate in multiple countries, there is a significant chance that your organization will have to deal with conflicting laws and regulations. Sometimes, this may result in fines, sanctions, or even dissolution of your business in the country in which you violate the laws and regulations. In the following figure, you can see an example of conflicting laws you could encounter:

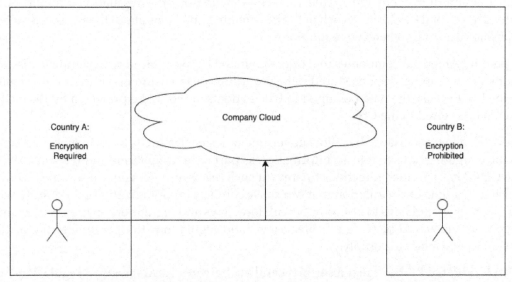

Figure 18.2: Laws in different countries may directly conflict each other

It is essential, that your legal team and technical teams work together to investigate with laws and regulations apply to an environment. In many cases, it may be worthwhile to create separate environments for different countries that can comply with different laws and regulations. Whenever you do this, you may be presented with additional costs, increased maintenance workload, and even lower availability (as you might not be able to replicate environments).

Throughout the chapter, we will look at common laws you may encounter and some tactics to attempt to limit the implications of the complex legal and regulatory environment.

General Data Protection Regulation

One of the most well-known security-related (data protection really) laws is the **General Data Protection Regulation (GDPR)**. GDPR has been instated by the European Union and its member nations. The regulation seeks to control and limit the processing and storage of data of EU residents. The reason that this regulation is so well known is that it was rather controversial at the time of its inception. Many organizations were not (well) prepared to become compliant with its stringent requirements.

At the same time, every country in the EU has its data protection agency (DPA) with limited jurisdiction. During the early phases of this regulation (and even until the time of writing) this means that there is also much uncertainty about how and by whom the regulation will and can be enforced. Especially in situations where organizations operate throughout or outside the European Union.

One of the most challenging components of the regulation is the fact that it was created to apply to EU residents irrespective of their location. Meaning, the regulation even protected EU residents living outside of the EU. For that reason, the regulation's applicability extended beyond the normal reach of the EU, creating questions about the EU's jurisdiction to create such comprehensive regulations.

Especially American companies that operated in the EU were faced with significant issues. Many of these organizations stored data about European customers in their data centers in the US. Because the data belonged to EU residents, it would be protected by the GDPR even when stored in the US.

The US has extensive laws that allow governmental agencies and law enforcement agencies to force organizations to release information as part of investigations and lawsuits. While the GDPR has specific protections to prevent such disclosure. As you can see, the GDPR is a prime example of a regulation that can cause conflicts for organizations. To comply with GDPR, they would have to not comply with local laws and regulations in the US. Meaning, organizations would be forced to break laws and regulations to operate internationally, even if they wanted to comply.

EXAM TIP: GDPR has caused serious conflicts between local laws and regulations.

To understand the effects of GDPR on the landscape of laws and regulations, it is essential to understand the regulation in more detail. *Chapter 19, Privacy*, will zoom in on the technicalities of this law. For now, you must simply understand that this law is a good example of conflicting laws and regulations in the international landscape.

California Customer Privacy Act

GDPR is only one example of a regulation that can cause conflict. Another interesting law to look at in this scope is the **California Customer Privacy Act (CCPA)**. California has followed in the footsteps of the EU and issued an act that aims to protect the privacy of its residents. In broad strokes, the CCPA implements some of the same mechanisms as found in GDPR. However, the applicability of the act is relatively limited. Whereas the GDPR applies to EU resident data. The CCPA only applies to for-profit organizations with more than 25 million USD in annual revenue or organizations that buy, sell, or share data from more than 100.000 Californians.

As you can see above, the CCPA does not apply to non-profit organizations, or governmental organizations, but it also does not apply to some organizations covered by industry specific laws and regulations. For example, HIPAA-covered entities are excluded from having to comply with the CCPA.

As you can imagine, it can be difficult for companies that operate within different areas across the globe, but even in the same country to select the proper controls for data protection. For example, an organization that operates in California and is covered by the CCPA, but also stores data from EU residents may have conflicting requirements or might be required to implement excessive security controls in some of their operating areas.

Excessive in this context only means that it exceeds the legal requirements. For example, to comply with GDPR you are likely required to implement more stringent controls than for CCPA. If your organization stores or processes data using the same technology, applications, or databases, it should be configured to meet the strictest requirements. The result of this is that you may have controls in place to comply with GDPR, that are not required by CCPA. Strictly speaking, this means you may be incurring more costs (and work) as an organization than required to operate within the local law and regulations.

Especially in the US, where local laws and regulations vary widely between different states, it can be worthwhile to separate data stores, applications, and so on. on a state-by-state basis. That way, you can ensure compliance with local laws and regulations without wasting resources. Your organization will have to choose an approach, in some cases, it is better to apply more stringent security requirements across environments. Especially if there are no direct conflicts in applicable laws and regulations. However, in other situations, it may be better to separate environments and tailor them to the local requirements.

EXAM TIP: CCPA has limited applicability. It does not apply to non-profit, governmental, or HIPAA-covered entities (amongst others).

Payment Card Industry: Data Security Standard

Aside from complexities related to the physical locale of your operations (or data), issues can also arise from the industries you operate in. For example, if your organization is a hospital in the US, it will have to comply with HIPAA and HITECH. If your organization is part of a university, some data will also be covered under the **Family Education Records and Privacy Act (FERPA)**. Aside from providing care and teaching students, your organization is also likely to perform billing to customers. As credit cards are a common form of payment, your organization is also likely to be subjected to the **Payment Card Industry – Data Security Standard (PCI-DSS)**.

While HIPAA, FERPA, and HITECH are all federal laws, PCI-DSS is an industry-based self-regulated standard. Meaning, any organization that wishes to take part in the payment card industry, be it to issue cards, perform payments, and so on. will have to comply with their requirements. One well-known PCI-DSS requirement is that payment data must be stored encrypted. However, what if your organization is prohibited from using encryption by other local laws and regulations? Well, the answer is simple, you will not be able to comply with the standard. Meaning, you may incur fines or other measures as dictated by the standard.

EXAM TIP: PCI-DSS applies across the payment card industry, regardless of your locality.

Evaluating legal risks in cloud environments

Now that you have been briefly introduced to some of the common laws and regulations that can cause complexity in the compliance landscape, let us look at how we can evaluate legal risks, specifically in cloud environments.

As an organization that operates or aims to operate in the cloud, it is essential to determine under which jurisdictions you operate (or are willing to operate). For example, if your company operates in the US and Luxembourg, you will have to comply with their laws and regulations. However, if you choose a SaaS solution operated by a company that stores your data in the people's republic of China, you are likely to become subject to the local laws and regulations that apply there as well, as shown:

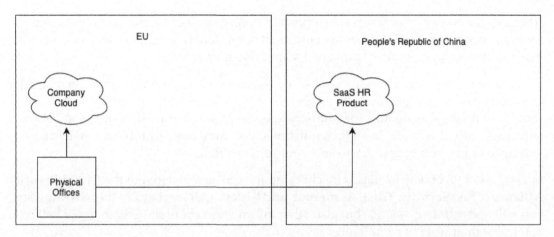

Figure 18.3: Choosing a vendor, partner, or product hosted in another jurisdiction can complicate compliance.

To ensure your organization is not presented with unwelcome surprises, you must decide which jurisdictions apply to you (due to your area of operation) and which jurisdictions you would be willing to include through IT operations, vendors, and partners.

For example, if you only want to operate in the EU and US, you must ensure that any (SaaS) solution you purchase does not store your data outside these regions. So, your organization must evaluate the location through which (managed) services are running.

REAL-LIFE TIP: Determine which jurisdictions your organization is willing to deal with.

Once your organization knows which jurisdictions are acceptable, you must ensure your environment stays within these jurisdictions. For example, you may have to choose a different AV to replicate your environment. In some cases, limiting jurisdictions can mean that normal mechanisms to preserve availability are not available to your organization. For example, if your country only has one AV, you may not be able to replicate another AV at all without getting involved in another country's legal and regulatory framework.

At the same time, your organization must ensure it properly vets vendors, partners, and products to establish if they process your data outside of your preferred jurisdictions. If so, you may have to negotiate about specific requirements for your organization or work with another party or product.

At the same time, working with products, partners, and vendors in your chosen jurisdictions does not mean that they are compliant with local laws and regulations. Therefore, evaluating which laws and regulations may apply to you and your vendors and partners is essential. Ideally, you can have these parties prove their compliance with applicable laws and regulations through certifications or attestations. However, in some cases, organizations may not be able to prove their compliance that easily. You may need to ask for more in-depth audit reports, external investigations, and so on, to ensure these parties are compliant.

After all, if you use a SaaS service to process your customer or employee data and the company behind the SaaS tool has not ensured it nor its tool is compliant, your organization may face fines and reputation damage if something goes wrong.

Many larger CSPs will provide proof of compliance (even publicly). However, smaller CSPs may not be compliant at all. At the same time, large CSPs are unlikely to want to comply with small regulatory or industry-specific requirements. If your organization is regulated with all specific laws or regulations, you may have to rely on smaller parties willing to tailor their operations to suit your organization.

In any case, a great way to start is by checking if a CSP is registered in the **Cloud Security Alliance (CSA) Security, Trust, Assurance, and Risk (STAR)** registry. In the STAR-registry, you will find self-assessments, but also other information about the CSP that will help you determine their level of compliance.

In the worst case, compliance issues may be a cause for your organization to steer clear of cloud computing, as it may pose too high a risk, might be too costly, or there may be no products or vendors that are compliant with all the rules and regulations that apply to your organization.

EXAM TIP: if you choose to operate in the Cloud, ensure you establish a way to verify vendor and product compliance repeatedly.

Legal frameworks and guidelines

What laws dictate is not the only thing that differs between jurisdictions. The legal system itself can even vastly differ from one country to the next. Understanding some of the common legal frameworks and systems to navigate legal and regulatory compliance is essential. The section below will examine some important aspects and differences in the legal world.

Firstly, let us examine the word jurisdiction. You may have noticed that this is a key word throughout this chapter. Jurisdiction may be a familiar term to you, it is often covered in police shows, for example. The meaning of jurisdiction is that it defines which court, law enforcement agency, or regulatory body can prosecute and/or convict.

For example, in the United States, there are many different law enforcement agencies. City police have jurisdiction within city limits, county police within a county, state police within a state, and federal agencies throughout the country. Similarly, different courts are used to try different cases in different areas. It is vital to know that an agency with jurisdiction in one area might not have jurisdiction in another. For example, while a federal agency may have jurisdiction in the US, it likely does not outside the country.

Aside from jurisdictions, there are also different forms of law. There are broadly two different forms of law. Firstly, there is civil law. In civil law, laws are written on paper. They dictate what is and what is not allowed. Often, these laws also predicate the punishment if you violate a law.

Now, the alternative is common law. Common law is built on previous rulings by courts. These types of laws are not written out like civil law. Rather they are interpretations made by courts. For example, if a court rules one way in a certain case, the next time a case with the same parameters is tried, the court should consider the decisions made by the court in the previous situation. Many countries across the globe utilize a civil law system; however, the US and the UK are some of the countries that use a common law legal system instead. Let us look at the difference between common and civil:

EXAM TIP: Common law is not codified (written) and changes with time.

	Codified	Based on precedent	Changes by court decisions
Common Law	No	Yes	Yes
Civil Law	Yes	No	No

Table 18.1: Characteristics of common and civil law

Most legal systems, irrespective of their nature as common or civil law also recognize different areas of law. One of these areas is criminal law. Criminal law is an area of the law that the government enforces against other people, groups, or organizations. In criminal cases, a government agency charges another party with a criminal complaint (which is called **prosecution**). Criminal law can be used to sanction one to jail sentences or other more severe forms of punishment.

Aside from criminal law, there is also civil law. Civil law regulates the violation of the law between two parties (not being the government). For example, a violation of a contract, and the subsequent legal action from the affected party against the violator is an example of civil law. Civil cases can result in financial compensation, but do not result in jail sentences.

The example above, is also called **contract law**. Contract law applies to violations of the terms of a contract. For example, contract law can be used if a CSP does not meet the agreed-upon SLAs.

Aside from contract law, we also know tort law. Tort law is used to remedy a situation where one party takes tortuous acts against another (without an agreement). For example, posting on social media to damage someone's reputation is an example of defamation. Which is a tortuous act and would fall under tort law.

The last two forms of law we must examine are administrative law and international law. Administrative law are laws that are created by governmental agencies as part of the execution of their tasks. For example, tax laws are a form of administrative law.

International laws, as the name suggests, are laws that span multiple nations. Common examples of international laws can be cross-country agreements, conventions (like the **Geneva Convention**), trade laws, and treaties.

It is important to understand that different forms of law have different priorities. For example, a constitution supersedes (lower) laws in a country, while federal laws may supersede state laws. It is important to understand the hierarchy of laws in the jurisdictions you operate in.

EXAM TIP: There is a hierarchy in law, the constitution is often the supreme law of the land (the most important law).

Intellectual property

A specific set of laws you must be familiar with is intellectual property laws. In general, we distinguish four different ways to protect intellectual property.

Firstly, there are copyrights. A copyright protects an expression of ideas. For example, an idea for a game or movie could be copyrighted. Copyrights mostly apply to artistic works and created works such as software. While copyright law is different in every country, the US allows copyrights to be established for 70 years after the author's death or 120 years after the work was published. Copyrights do not have to be registered to be enforceable. However, the author must be able to prove the originality of their idea.

Secondly, there are trademarks. Trademarks protect the identity of brands and organizations. A trademark registration can be used to protect logos, slogans, sounds, and so on. Trademarks must be registered to be enforceable.

Aside from copyrights, and trademarks, you can also use patents to protect your intellectual property. Patents are used to protect inventions. For example, if your organization develops a new electronic device for a certain purpose, your organization could register a patent. By registering a patent, you can prevent others from using your idea.

The last way to protect intellectual property is called **trade secrets**. Trade secrets are usually organization-specific ways of working, which may include best practices, formulas, and business ideas. While copyrights, patents, and trademarks are all enforceable, trade secrets have no enforceability. A trade secret means your organization keeps information secret to prevent competition from gaining access to the ideas. Whenever you register a patent, trademark, or copyright, you must divulge your ideas. Otherwise, you would not be able to register them. Inherently, that creates the risk of other companies exploring the same ideas or even stealing your ideas and hoping to not get caught.

Your organization can decide not to register a patent or copyright and instead keep your ideas a secret. However, it is up to your organization to ensure they do not leak. Here is an overview of the different IP protections:

Intellectual property protection mechanisms	
Copyrights	Expressions of ideas, videos, photos, software, arts
Patents	Ideas, formulas, and so on.
Trademarks	Logos or unique identifiers of a brand
Trade secrets	Company secrets that could hurt the organization if leaked to a competitor

Table 18.2: Intellectual property protection mechanisms

Cloud also presents some unique challenges to protection intellectual property. As you know, data is cloud environments may be accessible from the internet. This means that data may be viewed, shared or created by devices that your organization has no or limited control over. Because of this, your organization may have to take additional measures to ensure the intellectual property is not shared in ways that could damage the company.

For example, if your organization has a BYOD policy, a developer may be able to use their device to produce or read code. The code is the intellectual property of your organization. However, your company has no direct control over what the developer does with the code that is stored on their device. Meaning the developer could easily copy and distribute the data and thereby compromise the intellectual property.

In most cases, an organization will have to take additional measures using information protection tools or digital rights management tools to ensure their intellectual property in the cloud stays in the cloud. Or, at the very least, that data that is taken out of the cloud can only be viewed by authorized individuals. Many CSPs have introduced capabilities that provide IRM tools that allow you to encrypt files that can only be decrypted by authorized employees. That way, files can be distributed by employees externally but they will remain unreadable to authorized parties. A great example of such a tool is **Azure Information Protection (AIP)**.

EXAM TIP: Copyrights, patents, and trademarks provide enforcement options while trade secrets do not.

E-discovery (ISO/IEC 27050)

In this chapter, security processes, we discussed e-discovery and forensics. You know that using cloud computing has a big impact on an organization's ability to gather evidence through forensics. At the same time, using cloud environments can make it more challenging (or easier) to collect data per e-discovery best practices and regulations.

As you know, collecting evidence following e-discovery requirements is vital to be able to support legal actions. The **International Organization for Standardization (ISO)** / **International Electronic Commission (IEC)** has developed a standard to allow for proper e-discovery on an international level. The ISO/IEC 27050 standard, information technology, electronic discovery, outlines important parties and processes needed for e-discovery.

Your organization must evaluate its e-discovery processes to ensure compliance with local laws and regulations to prevent evidence from becoming inadmissible in a court of law. The ISO/IEC 27050 can offer a useful framework through which your organization can create a set of controls to ensure an effective e-discovery process. The standard will need tailoring to ensure compliance with local laws and regulations. However, it provides a solid starting point.

Forensics

Similar to e-discovery, forensics has legal and regulatory requirements. These requirements also differ heavily depending on your jurisdiction. For example, in the US, the US PATRIOT act may allow extensive forensic investigation by US government agencies. While other countries may not have such provisions or even more extensive laws and regulations.

Whenever your organization works on setting up procedures (or procuring services) for forensics, you must ensure they are compliant with local laws and regulations. If you want more information about forensics, please check *Chapter 17, Security processes.*

Conclusion

As organizations scale and expand across different states, countries, and regions the legal and regulatory framework in which they operate becomes more complex. Organizations may be subjected to many different jurisdictions, which means many different rules must be followed for compliance. In some unfortunate cases, the laws and regulations in one area or industry may directly contradict laws and regulations in another applicable jurisdiction. Such conflicts can put an organization in a difficult situation. Sometimes, it means an organization cannot comply with all applicable laws and regulations, even if it wants to.

Whenever an organization operates in the cloud the risks of complexity in the legal and regulatory landscape increase, simply replicating an environment from one AV or region to another could subject your organization to a whole new set of laws, your organization may never have heard of.

It is essential that an organization clearly defines in which jurisdictions it is willing to operate. By determining which applicable laws and regulations it is willing (and capable) of dealing with, your organization can prevent non-compliance and the consequences that it brings. Without proper screening of vendors, partners, and products, your organization faces the risk of reputational damage, fines, and even rulings to cease operations in certain areas.

Your company should evaluate if the products they use fit within the chosen jurisdictions, and if so, if these partners and products comply with local laws and regulations. It is important to attempt to verify their compliance through certifications and attestations on an ongoing basis.

Conflicting law is a problem, but your organization must also understand that the legal system does not work the same everywhere. Some laws use a common law system, while others use a civil law system. While a civil law system is based on codified laws, new court rulings change common law over time. Aside from differences in the legal system, there are also different forms of law. Criminal law is enforceable by governments and can lead to jail sentences or worse. While civil law pertains to cases between two non-governmental agencies.

Both civil and criminal law have many subsections of law. For example, contract law, tort law, and so on. These types of laws have a large impact on how cases are tried and what legal options are available.

Your organization is also likely to have intellectual property. Various legal systems offer different ways to protect intellectual property. In many countries, you can register copyrights, patents, trademarks, or maintain trade secrets. In a cloud environment, you will likely have to take additional measures to ensure data that is taken outside of the cloud remains confidential to your organization. IRM or DRM tools will be essential to achieve this.

As with anything, your organization must also ensure that operations like forensics and e-discovery comply with local laws and regulations. The ISO/IEC 27050 outlines some valuable best practices for the e-discovery process that your organization can leverage.

The legal and regulatory domain is extremely complex in a world with various laws and regulations. Using cloud computing makes this puzzle more difficult and requires effective and in-depth analysis on the part of your organization.

In the next chapter, you will learn more about the specifics of auditing a cloud environment.

Learning goals

This chapter addresses the following CCSP exam outline learning goals:

Domain 6: Legal, risk, and compliance

   6.1 Articulate legal requirements and unique risks within the cloud environment

Join our book's Discord space

Join the book's Discord Workspace for Latest updates, Offers, Tech happenings around the world, New Release and Sessions with the Authors:

https://discord.bpbonline.com

CHAPTER 19
Privacy

Introduction

Similar to legal requirements, privacy issues can become more complicated in the cloud. It is essential to approach privacy with a well-thought-out approach. This chapter zooms in on country-specific legislation, data categories, jurisdictions for privacy, standard privacy requirements, and data privacy impact assessmentsEnsuring that you have a clear image of all matters of privacy will help your organization safeguard the privacy of its customers and employees. Being privacy-minded will allow your organization to stand out positively within your industry. Compliance with applicable laws and regulations will also ensure your company does not suffer steep fines and reputational damage from non-compliance in the future.

Structure

This chapter covers the following topics:

- Privacy
- Contractual and regulated data (PII, PHI)
- Country-specific regulations
- Jurisdictional differences in data privacy

- Standard privacy requirements

- Generally Accepted Privacy Principles (GAPP)

- General Data Protection Regulation (GDPR)

- Data Privacy Impact Assessments (DPIA)

- Data breach notification laws

- Safe harbor agreements

Objectives

After reading this chapter, you will have more in-depth knowledge of common privacy regulations and the challenges that they pose to cloud computing. The chapter will help you understand how PII and PHI require different levels of protection (by law or by choice). At the same time, we will reexamine some of the problems jurisdictional differences create in the privacy landscape. Throughout the chapter, you will learn about standard privacy requirements and the accepted privacy principles. Understanding these standards and principles, will help you understand the need and approaches used to ensure privacy.

Privacy

Before we dive into some of the most important aspects of privacy in the cloud. Let us take a quick look at privacy itself. Many people have different definitions of what privacy means to them. For some it means being able to do what you want to do in private, while for others it may mean the freedom to decide who knows what about you. Regardless of the strict definition, in the scope of the CCSP exam, privacy refers to the right of persons to control how and if your personal data is collected.

As society digitizes more and more, many parties are very concerned with the privacy of their data. For example, through social media, large amounts of information are freely available about a huge part of the population. That information can be abused for a wide variety of purposes. Attackers may use data to circumvent authentication controls (such as recovery questions) or they may leverage information to blackmail or impersonate others.

As an organization that collects data, you must protect that data. However, data protection and privacy are not the same. For example, your organization may collect data from employees or customers that harms their privacy, but at the same time offer sufficient data protection.

For example, if your company uses advanced tracking methods to observe user behavior, this could be experienced as a violation of privacy. At the same time, you can store the data securely through encryption, a well-defined data lifecycle, and other controls.

Whenever your organization deals with data, it should assess the impact of data collection, processing, storage, and sharing on privacy and assess how you can ensure sufficient data protection is in place.

EXAM TIP: Data protection and privacy are not the same. Data protection is about sufficiently protecting data from being exposed or abused. While privacy is about what the information can tell us. Insufficient data protection can easily lead to privacy concerns.

REAL-LIFE TIP: Data protection and privacy are often used synonymously.

Contractual versus regulated data

Whenever a business operates, it requires data to do so effectively. In the IT landscape, it is common for partners to exchange large volumes of information. For example, your organization may use an external company to process credit card transactions, or you may use external recruiters that use their system to track applicants.

Regardless of the reason or structure for sharing data with other parties, we must document what data we will share, when, for what purpose, and how the data sharing takes place. Especially, within cloud environments, it is vital to closely examine data sharing. Using cloud computing means that you are inadvertently sharing your data with the CSP.

Imagine a situation where your organization does not specify its data sharing with another party. Let us say your organization shares employee data with a company-provided benefit provider. If your organization does not specify what data is allowed to be used, they can resell your employee data, target employees with unsolicited ads, or worse.

You already know that you should define why you collect data, how you store it, and how you process it. However, sharing data is an important part of the (cloud) data lifecycle. Of course, not all data will be shared with other parties, but in the current landscape of cloud computing, most of it may be shared (even without your organization realizing it). You must contractually limit what the recipient of your data is allowed to do with it. Can they process, read, or merely store an encrypted version of it? You must also define the standards that should be applied to their data handling.For example, if your company has an internal policy that all customer data must be encrypted, any party receiving that data from you should abide by the same rules. As you can imagine, such requirements make data sharing difficult. Not all vendors or parties may have the necessary controls to satisfy your requirements. In reverse, you may want to receive data from other parties while your security controls are not sufficient.

By defining strict agreements on data handling and data protection your organization can better prevent data exposure and all the adverse effects it brings. Aside from contractual clauses about data, there may be legal or regulatory requirements for protecting data and maintaining privacy.

Your organization must ensure it includes safeguards like data sharing and data processing agreements in its contracts. That way, your organization can ensure the CSP is contractually obligated to handle data in a compliant manner. While contracts are essential, they are not foolproof. You must ensure your CSP reports on their compliance and that you monitor (and audit) the CSP.

In the next section, we will examine some specially protected types of data.

Personal identifiable informationThe first type of regulated data that we must explore is called **personal identifiable information (PII)**. As the name suggests, PII consists of data that can be used directly or indirectly to identify a person. In the US, PII is also data that can identify names, addresses, social security numbers, unique identifiers, phone numbers, or e-mail addresses. Exposure of PII can compromise an individual's privacy and requires more extensive protection than non-PII data. Let us look at some examples of PII:

Data type	Type
Full Name	Direct PII
Address	Direct PII
Social Security Number	Direct PII
Passport number	Direct PII
Driver's License number	Direct PII
Credit card information	Direct PII
Date of birth	Direct PII
Username and password	Direct PII
IP addresses	Direct PII
MAC addresses	Direct PII
Gender	Linkable data
Race	Linkable data
Age	Linkable data
Job position and company	Linkable data

Table 19.1: Data than can qualify as (direct or indirect) PII

As you can see above, many different pieces of data can constitute as PII. You know that data like a full name is considered PII. However, did you expect an IP-address to be PII? The difficulty with PII is that some data can be used to identify a person in conjunction with other data as well. For example, if you know a person's job title, company, and age, that data together is likely to be identifiable. While each piece of information on its own may not be. Please be aware that the figure above is not a complete list. Data that is considered PII differs per area.

At the same time, some data that is considered PII, like a MAC or IP address may not always be traceable to a person. Regardless of the practical useability of PII, we must ensure this data is protected well. Many laws and regulations even have specific requirements for these types of data (more about this later).

As you know, protection data can be costly. It is important that your organization carefully considers if it should collect such data in the first place. If PII collection is necessary, your organization should apply data anonymization tactics. For example, when collecting IP addresses, you could hash the Ips to make them unidentifiable while maintaining a unique value. By doing so, your company can reduce the amount of sensitive data it stores, thus reducing the need for costly protections (in some cases).

If some data is classified as PII, some data is not. In broad strokes, you can say that the following data will not qualify as PII:

- Aggregated data

- Statistics

- Mased or anonymized data

So, if you were to collect the names of 1000 persons and create an overview of how many people have the same first name, the source data would be PII, but the overview would not be. This is important to know, because your organization could decide to use source data to create statistical overviews or aggregated overviews. If your organization deletes the PII used for the overviews, it could still use the overviews without requiring protecting them like PII. Once again, smart data processing will help your organization limit the amount of sensitive data it must protect.

Protected health informationAside from PII, we also distinguish **protected health information (PHI)** as a regulated form of data. PHI data (in the US) is data about the personal health of an individual. PHI is protected by the **Health Insurance Portability and Accountability Act (HIPAA)**. HIPAA requires covered entities to take measures to ensure the confidentiality, integrity, and availability of PHI data is maintained as part of its security rule. At the same time, it mandates that covered entities protect against anticipated threats, disclosure, and impermissible use.

As you can imagine, the requirements for PHI are even more stringent than for PII. PHI can contain medical information that could not only compromise the privacy of individuals but could also result in adverse effects surrounding their health, work, and social status.

Imagine that a person suffers from a severe condition, medical laws in certain countries preclude employers from inquiring about this information. If the information is exposed due to poor data protection or misuse, a company might take adverse action on an applicant's job candidacy.

It is important to note that not every country or jurisdiction has laws regulating PHI. Some jurisdictions may have more stringent requirements than those covered in HIPAA, while others may not have any further regulations for PHI. However, as an organization, you should carefully weigh the value of PHI, the need to collect, process, and store it and contrast it with the adverse effects disclosure would have on your organization.

It is important to note that in the US, HIPAA preempts other regulations that cover data regulated under HIPAA. For example, the CCPA in California has data protection requirements, however, these do not apply to data covered by HIPAA. Regardless of your jurisdiction you should verify if there are special legal or regulatory requirements for PII and PHI. Let us take a quick look at some data that is considered PHI in the US:

Data type
Photos
Address
Social security number
Medical files
Driver's license number
Surgery reports
Health plan numbers
IP addresses
MAC addresses

Table 19.2: Data that can qualify as PHI

As you can see above, PII and PHI have some significant overlap. It is important to understand that PII as it relates to health information is covered by HIPAA and thus PHI. The HIPAA privacy rule identifies a total of 18 identifiers that are PHI.

Data privacy and jurisdictions

In the previous chapter, we talked about the challenges in the legal and regulatory domain. As you know, many different jurisdictions have varying laws and regulations. In some cases, laws and regulations may even directly contradict each other. Unfortunately, the field of privacy deals with a similar challenge. Some jurisdictions protect privacy extensively, while others may not have any requirements for privacy.

For example, the European Union has the **General Data Protection Regulation (GDPR)** that outlines requirements for data protection that play an important role in maintaining privacy for EU residents. At the same time, other countries may not have any data protection or privacy regulations.

Just like other laws and regulations, your organization must carefully evaluate which requirements it must meet for privacy and data protection. Your organization must ensure it can be compliant with all applicable laws and regulations. In many cases this means your organization may not be allowed to operate the same way in different jurisdictions.

Take cookies stored by web browsers, in the EU, your organization must request consent to store (non-functional) cookies. While in many other countries you are not required to request consent at all, or you may be allowed to let users opt-in instead of consent. In the next part of this chapter, we will take a look at standard privacy requirements, the accepted privacy principles, and several important privacy and data protection laws your organization must be aware of.

Standard privacy requirements

As you know, the ISO has created standards relating to information security. The ISO 27001 standard is one of the most used examples of this. However, the ISO has extended their work to the privacy domain as well.In the ISO 27701 standard, ISO details the components of a **Privacy Information Management System** (**PIMS**). You can view the ISO 27701 as the ISO 27001 variant for privacy. An important aspect of the ISO 27701 standard is that it can help your organization comply with relevant privacy and data protection standards. As it provides a framework that takes international privacy and data protection requirements into account.

Generally Accepted Privacy PrinciplesAnother organization that works on preserving privacy is the **International Association of Privacy Professionals** (**IAPP**). The IAPP provides various certifications in the privacy field, and also provides training. However, one of the most important IAPP works to know for the CCSP exam is the **Generally Accepted Privacy Principles** (**GAPP**).

EXAM TIP: Implementing the GAPP helps your organization in becoming compliant with laws and regulations.

The GAPP are comprised of ten privacy principles. An organization that incorporates these principles within their organization, is likely to do a much better job of protecting their employee and customer privacy. Let us look at the principles below:

The first principle, management, dictates that an organization must define, document, and communicate privacy policies and procedures. Management ensures that privacy is formally established (and prioritized) in an organization. At the same time, management means that the company's personnel understand how privacy affects the processes they are involved in. More importantly, as part of management, your organization must also assign accountable parties for privacy within the organization. Just as security, accountability is necessary to drive, evaluate, and improve privacy practices.

The second principle is called **notice**. Notice means that an organization must notify its data subjects of its privacy policies and procedures. In practice you see this happen often by company's posting privacy policies on their website. When your organization notifies its data subjects, it should also inform them about the reasons for collecting their data. At the same time, it must provide insight into what data is collected and for what purpose.

The third principle is called **choice** and **consent**. An organization should provide its data subjects with a choice on if data is collected, and if so, what data. A practical application of choice and consent could be cookie consent mechanisms on a website.

The fourth principle is called **collection**. The collection principle states that your organization must ensure it only collects data for the purposes it provided notice about. For example, if you state to your data subjects you collect only their ages, but secretly also store their names you are not adhering to the principle of collection.

The fifth principle, use, retention, and disposal dictates that an organization must only use data for the purposes it has notified its data subjects about. Additionally, data subjects must have provided consent (implicitly or explicitly) to the processing. Once an organization no longer needs the data, it should ensure the data is disposed of as quickly as possible.

The sixth principle, access, states that an organization must provide its data subjects with access to their own data. Meaning, an organization must disclose what data they store about an individual when that individual requests insight. At the same time, the organization must offer the opportunity to the data subject to have corrections made to their data.

The seventh principle, disclosure to third parties, dictates that data should only be shared with third parties for purposes disclosed to the data subject. Once again, data sharing should only take place after the data subject has provided consent for the data sharing.

The eighth principle, is security for privacy. This principle states that an organization must take technical measures to prevent unauthorized access to data. Ergo, an organization that stores data, should take reasonable data protection measures.

The ninth principle, quality, states that an organization must ensure data integrity. Simply put, the data it stores about data subjects must be complete and accurate. At the same time, the data should be relevant to the data collection purposes that the subject was notified about.

The tenth, and last principle, monitoring and enforcement wants organizations to monitor internal compliance. An organization must evaluate if its policies, standards, and procedures are executed properly. Organizations should also address complaints and disputes surrounding their privacy practices.

As you may have noticed, there are a couple recurring motives in the GAPP. Firstly, data subject consent is essential. Organizations must get consent before collecting, storing, processing, and sharing data. At the same time, organizations must notify data subjects of their actions, and only use the data in accordance with their notification.

You may have noticed that the GAPP also includes the CIA triad. Data must only be accessible to authorized entities (Confidentiality), data must be correct, relevant, and complete (integrity), and insight into the collected data must be provided upon request of the data subject (availability).

The power of the GAPP is that they provides a framework that, if followed, provides practices that are compliant with laws and regulations like the GDPR and CCPA. For example, the GDPR has the right to access, which is closely resembled by the principle of access in the GAPP. At the same time, you also see close resemblance to laws that are not directly privacy laws. For example, the quality principle can also be found in the **Fair and Accurate Credit Transactions Act (FACTA)**.

Regardless of the laws and regulations that apply to your organization, following the GAPP will provide your organization with a well-established baseline for privacy. Following you can find an overview of the principles:

1	Management
2	Notice
3	Choice and consent
4	Collection
5	Use, retention, and disposal
6	Access
7	Disclosure to third parties
8	Security for privacy
9	Quality
10	Monitoring and enforcement

Table 19.3: The accepted privacy principles

General Data Protection RegulationThroughout this book we have talked about the **General Data Protection Regulation (GDPR)** several times already. The GDPR is one of the most well-known data protection laws and has a huge privacy component. The GDPR applies to EU residents and has caused many organizations compliance issues, and even fines.

The GDPR considers a couple different parties in the data protection landscape, firstly, you have the data subject. A data subject is an entity (usually an individual) that the data is collected about. Secondly, you have a data controller. The data controller is the party that wants to collect the data subjects data. Usually, the data controller is the organization that has a purpose for collecting and processing the data. The third party is called a **data processor**. Many data controllers do not actually collect, store, and process the data themselves. They use a third party to do this for them. That third party is a data processor.

In some cases, the data controller may perform (parts of) the role of data processor. For example, if a company has a website that collects data, it may store it in the cloud. From the cloud environment the data may be processed by on-premises application. In such a situation, the cloud provider is a data processor, while the company collecting the data is the data controller and a data processor as well.

EXAM TIP: It is important to understand that a data controller can use many different data processors.

Now that you know what parties the GDPR considers, it is important to understand the rights the GDPR provides to EU residents. The GDPR has 8 rights that we will review below:

Firstly, the right for information, meaning the subject has the right to be informed about data collection and processing as well as its purpose.

Secondly, the right to access. This means, the data controller must provide insight to the data subject about all data that is collected about them.

Next, there is the right to withdraw consent. Meaning the data subject can revoke the consent it gave to the data controller. Thus, the data controller would have to stop processing data and remove it.

Fourth, the right to object to automated processing. Automated processing can cause decisions to be made with bias. The GDPR protects EU residents from being subjected to automated processing if the data subject has an objection against this processing.

Fifth, the right for data portability. Similar to cloud computing, data portability means that the data subject must be able to request their data and move it to another service or provider. The data controller must ensure this is possible.

Further, the sixth right is the right to be forgotten. The right to be forgotten states that a data subject must be able to request the deletion of their data. The data controller must then remove all such data within a set time period. It is important to note that the right to be forgotten does not apply outside of the EU due to a 2019 decision of the European court of justice. Even if the data subject is a EU resident. Meaning, a company does not have to remove data they collected or stored outside of the EU. However, many companies do offer the ability to delink your EU based data from the US data.

The next right is the right to object. The right to object pertains to the collection of data. Similar to the right to object to automated processing, this right protects EU residents from being subjected to processing they do not want.

The last right, the right to rectification, states that a data subject must be able to request correction of data a data controller has collected about them.

As you may have noticed, the rights covered in the GDPR are very close to the principles outlined in the GAPP. As you can imagine, implementing the GAPP will already provide your organization with a solid basis to become compliant with the GDPR. Your organization may have to implement specific requirements not covered within the GAPP to become fully compliant.

A brief overview of the data subject rights under the GDPR is shown:

1	Right to information
2	Right to access
3	Right to withdraw consent
4	Right to object to automated processing
5	Right for data portability
6	Right to be forgotten
7	Right to object
8	Right to rectification

Table 19.4: Data subject rights under the GDPR

It is very likely that you have seen some of these rights in action. For example, cookie consent on a website is part of the right to object. While privacy policies and statements are often examples of the right to information. The right to be forgotten is the most difficult of all rights to honor as a data controller. After all, many organizations do not have an easy way to purge all data of an individual throughout a broad landscape of applications.

Whenever you are involved in projects, you should attempt to design them with security by design, as well as privacy by design. If you include the GAPP and applicable laws and regulations from the design phase, you are more likely to become compliant in a cost-effective manner.

Data privacy impact assessmentAn important part of the GDPR is called **data privacy impact assessments** (**DPIA**)s. A DPIA is a process that identifies privacy risks for data collection and processing. If your organization uses automated decision-making, processes PHI (or other highly private PII), or processes criminal records, your organization should conduct a DPIA on the collection, processing, and storing of these data.

It is important to note that while you must conduct DPIAs you do not have to publish them. Especially because DPIAs can contain sensitive information about your organization's internal security. However, it is advisable to publish a summary of your DPIA findings publicly. That way, you are ensuring your data subjects can be informed properly.

If your organization does not execute a DPIA it can face fines if your organization's practices are reported to the local **data protection agency** (**DPA**). Your organization can enlist other companies to perform DPIAs for you. DPIAs should be repeated regularly to reevaluate risks and practices (even if the data processing does not change).

California Consumer Privacy ActOne of the most well-known privacy laws (aside from the GDPR) is the **California Consumer Privacy Act** (**CCPA**). The CCPA was the first state privacy law in the US and is closely modelled after the GDPR. While the CCPA is modeled after the GDPR, it also has some differences.

For example, the CCPA requires implicit consent for processing, while the GDPR requires explicit consent. One way you can see this difference is in cookie notifications. Websites under CCPA may show a banner stating that they use cookies and giving a button to opt out, while websites regulated under the GDPR must ask for explicit cookie consent.

It is important to re-iterate that the CCPA does not apply to governmental agencies and non-profit organizations. Some other US states, and countries are following in the footsteps of the GDPR and CCPA. For example, Canada has the **Personal Information Protection and Electronic Documents Act (PIPEDA)**, while Brazil has the **Lei Geral de Protecao De Dados (LGPD)**. There are other laws that are not listed here, the CCSP exam does not require you to know the contents of these laws.

Data Breach Notification Laws

Aside from GDPR, CCPA, PIPEDA, and other privacy laws there is also something called data breach notification laws. In the US, every state now has such a law. In the EU, data breach notification is part of the GDPR. Data breach notification laws require companies (and sometimes governments) to report data breaches. These reports are often made to a government agency. However, in some cases, data breach notification laws may require your company to inform law enforcement, public media, and affected data subjects.

Your organization should investigate which data breach notification laws are applicable to your organization. These laws differ between jurisdictions. For example, some laws may require notification within 15 days, while others require notification within 60 days. At the same time, different laws also have different definitions for what constitutes a data breach.

For example, some laws include encrypted data (but often only if the encryption key is also breached). While others explicitly exclude any encrypted data. Due to the high variance in data breach notification laws per jurisdiction it is difficult to provide a one-size fits all guideline for data breach notification.

EXAM TIP: You do not need to know the details of all the different data breach notification laws in the US.

Safe harbor agreements

The last item we must review in this chapter is safe harbor agreements. Whenever parties exchange data between different jurisdictions, the legal and regulatory environment can become extremely complicated. To allow (international) organizations to operate globally, there have been so-called safe harbor agreements. These agreements outline requirements that, when followed, allow data transfer between countries. One of the most well-known safe harbor agreements was the EU-US Privacy Shield agreement.The Privacy Shield facilitated data exchange between the EU and the US. The agreement set requirements that allowed companies to exchange data between the two regions while ensuring compliance with EU and US standards for data protection. The Privacy Shield agreement has been invalidated by the Schrems II case by the Court of Justice of the European Union. The invalidation of the EU-US Privacy Shield meant that many organizations had to halt the exchange of data from the EU to the US, because the court ruled that EU data would not be sufficiently protected in the US.

Since the invalidation of the Privacy Shield, a new framework, namely the EU-US Data Privacy Framework has gone into effect (July 2023). The Data Privacy Framework once again provides a way for EU and US companies to exchange data in a compliant manner. It is important to note that the DPF will be enforced by the Federal Trade Commission. Incompliance or false claims can lead to steep fines.

EXAM TIP: To comply with the EU-US Data Privacy Framework, companies can self-certify that they are compliant with the framework.

EXAM TIP: It is illegal to transfer EU data to US parties that are not certified under the EU-US Data Privacy Framework.

The EU-US Privacy Shield and the EU-US Data Privacy Framework are examples of an adequacy decision. An adequacy decision means that a jurisdiction determines that other jurisdictions laws and regulations are like their own. This means that compliance with one jurisdiction means compliance with the other. The adequacy decision of the EU-US Data Privacy Framework only applies to organizations that certify under the framework.

Conclusion

While privacy means something different to everyone, it revolves around having the decision who knows what about you. Whenever an organization collects, processes, stores, and shares data, it should carefully consider the implications to the data subject's privacy. At the same time, it is the company's responsibility to ensure proper data protection measures. Privacy and data protection go hand in hand as a data protection failure often results in compromised privacy.

Whenever an organization collects data, it should have a purpose for collection. In some cases, the purpose may be sharing data with other parties. It is essential to ensure data sharing is properly outlined in contracts. Aside from documenting what data is shared, an organization must also consider special requirements that may apply to regulated data. Two important examples of regulated data are **personal identifiable information (PII)** and **Personal Health Information (PHI)**. Both types of information could have significant privacy impacts on the data subject if not properly protected. Most jurisdictions have special requirements for collecting, processing, storing, and sharing PII. As with laws concerning security, privacy laws and regulations differ vastly between different jurisdictions. Unfortunately, this makes it more difficult for companies to comply with all applicable laws and regulations when operating in multiple jurisdictions. Luckily, the ISO has created a standard, the ISO 27701, that outlines the requirements for a Privacy Information Management System. Like an ISMS, a PIMS helps an organization handle data with great attention to privacy.

Aside from the ISO 27701, your organization can also leverage the **Generally Accepted Privacy Principles (GAPP)**. The GAPP are closely aligned to common laws and regulations like the **General Data Protection ACT (GDPR)**. By following the ten principles outlined in the GAPP, your organization will create a solid foundation for compliant privacy practices.

Aside from privacy and data protection laws and regulations, many jurisdictions also have data breach notification laws. Every US state now has such a law, requiring organizations to report data breaches. Because of the wide variety of data breach notification laws, your organization should investigate which type of breaches must be reported, to whom, and within what time frame. Failure to comply with data breach notification laws can lead to significant fines and lengthy investigations. Notification to governmental agencies, law enforcement, customers, and even the public media may be required for your organization.

Privacy and security are intertwined. Without security, we cannot achieve privacy. As a CCSP, you must understand the challenges of the privacy environment and include data protection (and privacy) requirements within your security requirements.

In the next chapter, cloud auditing and enterprise risk management, you will learn about the challenges of auditing a cloud environment. At the same time, you will learn more about the challenges and approaches to managing risk at the enterprise level.

Learning goals

This chapter addresses the following CCSP exam outline learning goals:

Domain 6: Legal, risk, and compliance

6.2 Understand privacy issues

Join our book's Discord space

Join the book's Discord Workspace for Latest updates, Offers, Tech happenings around the world, New Release and Sessions with the Authors:

https://discord.bpbonline.com

CHAPTER 20

Cloud Auditing and Enterprise Risk Management

Introduction

There are many reasons for an organization to implement security controls. An organization may need to implement controls to sufficiently protect its business processes from being disrupted. On the other hand, an organization may need to protect its data about internal processes, employees, and customers. In some cases, organizations may also be required to implement security controls by applicable laws and regulations.

Regardless of why an organization implements security controls, it should do so based on risk. Implementing (expensive) controls to thwart non-existent risks would save resources. Managing risk is a complicated process that involves determining the organization's willingness to take risks, evaluating the threat landscape, and gaining a thorough understanding of the organization's assets. Luckily, risk management framework and risk management can help data owners and processors secure their data better.

Once an organization has implemented controls, it is of vital importance to evaluate these controls. In some cases, an organization does so solely to improve its program; in other cases, it may have to prove its security efforts to external parties like customers or regulators. Through audits, an organization can evaluate its current state, determine the gap between the present and future situations, and assure customers.

This chapter will take you through the challenging worlds of risk management and auditing and help you understand the impacts of cloud computing on both.

Structure

This chapter covers the following topics:

- Risk appetite
- Risk management frameworks
- Metrics for risk management
- Assessment of risk environment
- Data roles
- Audit requirements
- Logs and auditability
- Internal and external audits
- Audit challenges in the cloud
- Audit scope
- Stakeholder identification
- Audit planning
- Audit execution
- Audit reports
- Audit process follow-up
- Audit process summary
- SOC
- SOX
- CSA STAR
- Gap analysis
- Information Security Management System
- Information Security Controls
- PCI-DDS
- HIPAA
- HITECH
- NERC/CIP

- GDPR
- Legal and regulatory landscape

Objectives

After reading this chapter, you will be able to understand how organizations can perform risk management by determining risk appetite and employing a risk management framework. You will also be able to score risk through quantitative and qualitative assessments. At the end of the chapter, you will also understand the different types of audits in the security domain. You will be able to determine which audit, scope, and report is most suitable to provide assurance within and outside of the organization.

Lastly, you will understand how audit reports form a basis for a gap analysis and thus can help your organization determine which steps to take to comply with legal, regulatory, and customer requirements.

Risk appetite

As mentioned in the introduction, there are many reasons for an organization to implement security controls. One important one is to limit the amount of risk an organization is exposed to. For most people, risk-taking has a reckless or negative undertone. However, risk-taking is successful in life, especially in the business world. Organizations need to take risks to create and invent new products or launch in new markets. Risk-taking allows organizations (and people) to get the most out of themselves.

While risk-taking allows businesses to achieve their full potential, it can also have an adverse effect. For example, launching a new product may not result in the expected revenue, starting a new business may not yield the desired results, and so on.

Whenever you decide to take a risk, you should determine if the potential yield and the potential damage generated by taking the risk make sense to you.

The concept above is (in short) the concept of risk appetite. How much risk are you willing to take to achieve a specific goal? While we do not have to fight dragons in business, this concept is very relevant. An organization must determine how much risk it will take to stay in business. Some companies are willing to take significant risks in exchange for high rewards, while some may be compelled to err on the side of caution and take the more predictable gains.

Before an organization determines which security controls it implements, it must assess its risk appetite, as the risk appetite of the organization may lead to a different level of security. For example, highly regulated organizations may be less willing to take risks. Thus, they have to ensure they put more effort into reducing risks, which leads to implementing more security controls. At the same time, companies that are pioneers in their industry may be built on the fact that they are willing to take risks. Some of these organizations may decide not to implement controls.

It is important to note that risk appetite can differ at various levels in an organization. For example, a company may be willing to take enormous risks in a business concept but may have a small risk appetite in developing products. You must understand that risk appetite can differ throughout an organization, even within teams or between projects.

Regardless, your organization must determine some overall risk appetite related to information security. For example, is your company willing to take risks in compliance with local laws or regulations to launch a product, or is your organization the type to ensure security controls are in place at every level and step of a product launch? Formally establishing an organization's risk appetite will help justify costs, capacity, and time for implementing and operating security controls.

EXAM TIP: Highly regulated organizations usually have a lower risk appetite than pioneers or front-runners of an industry.

REAL-LIFE TIP: Many companies must establish a formal risk appetite, making it challenging to justify security measures and expenses.

Risk management frameworks

Understanding how much risk your organization will take to achieve its business goals is only the start. As you know, your organization must perform risk management. Identifying, evaluating, and treating risks is vital to ensure your organization takes only a few or too few risks.

In chapter eight, risk management in the cloud, we covered some risk management essentials. For example, you must understand how to express risks (quantitively or qualitatively). Luckily, the NIST has designed a **risk management framework (RMF)** framework that can help your organization manage organization, system, and application risks more quickly.

The NIST RMF is an iterative process that consists of seven steps; let us take a more in-depth look below:

The first step, prepare, includes activities for the organization to understand how to manage security and privacy risks. For example, identifying processes for risk management, identifying important stakeholders, determining the risk appetite, and so on.

The second step, the categorize system, is an important point of the risk management journey. Before determining what controls an organization, application, or system needs, you must understand the environment in more detail. One good way to do so, is conducting a **Business Impact Analysis (BIA)** on the organization, system, or application you are trying to manage risks for. By conducting a BIA, you will learn how essential your assessment scope is. For example, the questions: does an application support critical business functions, or does a system process sensitive information influence the impact that risks can have.

During the next step, select, you pick security controls to apply to your system. These steps should not be chosen at random. Instead, you should conduct a risk assessment to identify relevant risks within the scope. Once you have determined which risks exist, you should relate them to the application category and evaluate them against the organization's risk appetite. You can now decide which controls should be applied based on these factors.

Once you have decided on a set of controls, you should implement them during the next step of the RMF, named implement. As you may suspect, the implement step requires you to document controls, document the success criteria, and actually implement the controls. You must establish measurements to evaluate the control effectiveness prior to continuing to the next step.

The following step, assess, ensures that controls are effectively implemented and functioning as intended. Implementing security controls is important, but you must establish their function. For example, if your organization implements rate-limiting to prevent DoS, it must verify that the rate-limiting can prevent the DoS. If you do not assess the control effectiveness, there is a high likelihood that some of your controls will prove ineffective, with negative consequences.

Once controls have been assessed, authorization of the application or system is needed during the authorization step. The authorization step requires a manager to authorize the operation of an application officially. Based on the results of the assessment step, a manager should determine if the controls function well enough to allow an application or system to be used. In some cases, the output of the authorizing step may be that additional controls must be implemented or adjustments to existing controls must be realized prior to authorization.

Once management has signed off on your system or application, it must be monitored closely. Security controls must be evaluated on an ongoing basis, risks must be re-evaluated over time, and new threats to the system must be identified. While the journey to the last phase, monitoring, is long, it is one of the most critical steps of the RMF. Without continuous and effective monitoring, your controls will quickly prove to no longer be sufficient. Following, you can find an overview of the NIST RMF steps:

Prepare
Categorize
Select
Implement
Assess
Authorize
Monitor

Table 20.1: Steps of the NIST RMF

Metrics for risk management

As you just read, monitoring and assessment are essential for risk management. Monitoring and assessment are required for controls used to reduce risk, but this also applies to risk management in general. An organization should establish **key risk indicators** (**KRIs**). KRIs are metrics that represent the organizations' risk landscape and trends within that landscape.

For example, a valuable KRI is the month-to-month residual risk. If the residual risk of an organization has increased over time, it is taking more risks. At the same time, you should track how many risks of a specific category your organization has accepted. An increase or decrease in risk acceptance (as part of risk treatment) can provide valuable information about the actual risk appetite of an organization. Both metrics are valuable indicators of risk in an organization.

Data roles

The roles in the data landscape are also essential as part of risk assessments. In general, we distinguish three role types when it comes to data.

Firstly, we have the data owner or data controller. The data controller is the party that wants to collect data. The data owner is always accountable for securing their data. Another party is the data processor or data custodian. The data custodian is the party that actually manages, processes, or even stores the data. In the cloud, the CSC is often the data owner, while the CSP is the data owner. The last role in the data landscape is the data subject; this is the entity the data is about.

As you can imagine, risk management is quite different for each party. As the data owner, you are accountable. This means you should also address risks that are part of risk processing. The data owner often transfers responsibility for these risks to the data processor. However, as the data owner, you must verify that the data processor adequately addresses the risks.

It is important to note that the data controller and data processor can be the same party. This is often the case in on-premise environments. In the cloud, the CSC is often the data owner while the CSP performs (some) data processor tasks.

> **EXAM TIP: Data owners and data processors can be the same entity**

> **EXAM TIP: Data owners are accountable, while data custodians are responsible**

Audit requirements

As mentioned earlier in this chapter, companies have many reasons to implement controls. Risk management is a great tool to determine which controls are essential for your organization based on the risks your organization faces. At the same time, you may have to implement rules specific to your organization's role concerning data.

However, there is also a possibility that your organization is required to implement controls as part of the laws and regulations that apply to your organization. If your organization is mandated to implement security controls, you have to prove the implementation and the effectiveness of said controls.

Similarly, if you provide services to other companies, you may be required to implement specific security controls by your customers and partners. For example, as a CSP, you may implement controls to ensure your customers can comply with applicable laws and regulations (even if they do not directly apply to your organization).

Regardless of why an external entity requires you to implement controls, they always need you to prove that you did. In many cases, such a requirement is expressed by requiring your organization to perform audits. In the rest of the chapter, we will dive into the processes for the audits, the outputs you can expect, some of the challenges during these audits, and some of the laws and regulations that can require an audit.

Internal and external audits

First, it is essential to understand the different types of audits conducted. We know two different types of audits: **external** and **internal**.

The organization itself conducts internal audits. When an organization performs an internal audit, it usually has an auditing staff to do so. The team may be trained to perform audits at various organizational levels. For example, some auditors may be able to verify financial practices, their practices, or even systems. Whenever your organization decides to conduct internal audits, it is crucial to ensure your internal auditors have the skills and knowledge to perform the audits. Secondly, you must ensure the auditors can operate with as little bias as possible.

For example, a conflict of interest can arise if your IT auditors report to your CIO. Imagine a situation in which a CIO is tasked to deploy a new product to the company's customers. The CIO must conduct an internal audit to ensure the product is safe to release. The CIO might receive a bonus tied to this new product. His auditing team might have difficulty reporting findings that would jeopardize the product. Such results would negatively reflect on the CIO. As the CIO is the auditor's boss, they could experience adverse action from the CIO if they raise such findings.

While only some organizations may experience conflicts of interest in such a direct manner, internal auditors are paid by the organization to perform the audit. So, in some shape or form, the auditors have a stake in the results. For example, if a new product release is pending an audit, and a product launch delay would cause financial damage, the auditor's jobs may be in jeopardy if they report findings.

The combination of a lack of knowledge and skill and potential integrity issues makes internal audits unsuitable for all audit purposes. For example, most regulatory audit requirements require an external rather than an internal audit. Similarly, many customers should consider requiring external audits over internal audits. In many cases, certification boards also need external auditors to confirm compliance with standards used to certify (like ISO 27001).

EXAM TIP: Internal audits are primarily helpful for assurance within an organization. It is less suitable for assurance towards external parties.

Contrary to internal audits, external audits are conducted by specialized parties. These parties have auditors with various backgrounds and skill sets. Because of this, external agencies can provide well-prepared auditors to audit specific organizations, systems, or compliance requirements.

External auditors are not paid directly by their customers and rely on their impartial status to get work, so they are considered more reliable than internal auditors. Reporting negative findings about compliance or security does not put the auditor's job at risk. As a cloud service consumer, you should request external audit reports about the activities of your CSP. After all, internal auditors at a CSP likely have a conflict of interest as negative audit results would damage the CSP and could have negative results for the auditor.

Similarly, it would be wise to consider hiring external auditors to conduct audits on your own organization. After all, you are also more likely to get realistic audit reports from external auditors. Please remember that external auditors need to gain more knowledge about your organization. External audits may require significant time, documentation, and interviews. Whereas internal auditors likely have. A higher level of knowledge about your internal organization.

EXAM TIP: External audits require significant time investment, interviews, and documentation sharing, as external auditors likely need to learn your organization.

It is also advisable to rotate the companies you use for external auditing. If you continuously work with a single external auditor, they may develop a conflict of interest to obtain or hold on to your continued business.

Let us compare some of the benefits and drawbacks of internal and external auditing:

	Internal	External
Expensive		X
Potential conflict of interest	X	
Useable for certifications		X
Auditors know the organization	X	
Auditors require extensive interviews, documentation, and time		X

Table 20.2: The characteristics of internal and external auditing

Logs and auditability

The process of auditing seeks to ensure that controls function in the way they are intended. That means auditors will likely require evidence of control effectiveness. Depending on the scope of an audit (more about this later) an auditor may simply require seeing a policy or standard that outlines the control. But often, an auditor will want to see evidence (established over time) that confirms a control is effective.

As you can imagine, proving control effectiveness can be difficult. If your organization has followed secure development practices, metrics or tests should be defined to establish control effectiveness. Meaning your organization has gathered data. If this is the case for your organization, you will simplify the auditor's life. If you can provide data that quickly establishes and proves control effectiveness, an auditor is more likely to have confidence in your control implementation.

Conversely, if you cannot provide an auditor with any data supporting the effective implementation of a control, they will have little confidence in your implementation. At the same time, they will have to invest significant efforts into evaluating control effectiveness. For example, they may have to review large numbers of log files.

Imagine the following scenario: your organization has implemented a control to block the enumeration of user accounts. The control is a mechanism to block an account after five failed login attempts. If your organization practiced secure development, you likely collect log data about login attempts; you may even have reported on the number of failed and blocked accounts. Providing such data in an organized, easy-to-understand format will help the auditor establish control effectiveness. If the auditor can access statistics or the log files tracking your blocking actions, you are likely to prove control effectiveness.

If you design controls, ensure you include methods and metrics to evaluate your control effectiveness. Consider how you could prove control effectiveness to external parties and ensure you collect evidence. Doing so will enable your company to successfully prove control effectiveness during audits without requiring significant amounts of work to gather data during an audit and significant work (and thus costs) on the auditor's side. Let us take a look at the difference proper control effectiveness reporting can make, refer to the following figure:

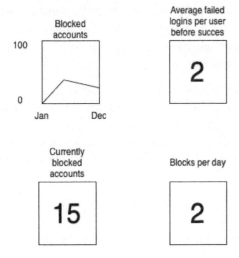

Figure 20.1: Data is essential in proving control effectiveness

In the figure above, you can see two examples of how you can prepare audits. The example on the left uses clear metrics representing control effectiveness. The metrics are based on log data (that should still be given to the auditor), but they are represented in a way that is easy to understand and verify. The example on the right is a log file containing insufficient information for the auditor to assess control effectiveness. The data and time need to be set correctly in the log, and there is no reference to which user logged in successfully or not. The auditor cannot assess control effectiveness based on the log files on the right.

REAL-LIFE TIP: How you present data to an auditor matters a lot. Present your data in a well-prepared and easy-to-understand fashion.

EXAM TIP: Tools like security incident and event monitoring can provide valuable insights for auditors.

Audit challenges in the cloud

Forensic analysis in the cloud is challenging because you may need access to all the data you need. The same can be said for auditing in the cloud. Unfortunately, the shared responsibility matrix means that you only get access to some data on the side of the CSP even though some of that data may be needed to prove compliance with laws and regulations or to prove control effectiveness.

In the cloud, you must rely on the right to audit (established in a contract) or on audits provided to you by the CSP. It is unlikely that your own auditor will have direct access to all the data it needs from the CSP. However, an auditor will still have to evaluate if you have met the requirements, you are accountable for. Instead of the data, the auditor can be provided with (external) audit reports or can sometimes be provided access to (some) data to perform an audit herself.

Whenever you select a CSP, partner, or vendor, ensure you include the right to audit them in the contract. Or, at the very least, ensure they will provide you with audit reports that cover the scope of your accountability.

Audit scope

While auditing can be more challenging in the cloud, it depends on an audit's scope. For example, an audit may only concern the customer responsibilities of the cloud. In most cases, audits conducted for legal and regulatory requirements are scoped toward establishing compliance. This means these audits may be scoped only to controls required by these laws and regulations. Similarly, for comprehensive certifications and attestations, the scope of an audit may far exceed the technical. ISO 27001 audits, for example, heavily focus on an organization's Information Security Management System. Meaning it focuses more on policies, standards, and their implementation. At the same time, a PCI-DSS audit may rely more heavily on evaluating technical controls.

It is essential to understand that the purpose of an audit heavily influences the scope of the audit. If your organization is undergoing an audit, it can be helpful to adjust the scope. For example, consider extending an audit's scope to increase the assurance level. At the same time, if you are being audited for compliance, you should consider scoping the audit only to include the bare minimum required for submission.

Scoping audits can significantly affect the audit process and results. As you can imagine, audits with an extensive scope may take more time and involve more of your organization's resources. Comprehensive audits can significantly impact an organization's capabilities to perform day-to-day activities.

Similarly, it can be more difficult for an auditor to properly assess everything in an audit with an enormous scope. After all, auditors are humans and have limited capabilities for processing information. Conversely, introducing a more extensive scope also increases the chance of negative findings. If your company is going through an audit for compliance purposes, increasing scope may make it easier to prove compliance.

Beware that CSPs, vendors, and partners may use audit scoping to hide organizational deficiencies. Many organizations publish audit reports publicly to assure their customers. However, it is wise to read these reports and examine the scope of the audit before putting too much value into the findings.

EXAM TIP: Audit scoping can increase your organization's chances of proving control effectiveness. However, it can also be used to hide control deficiencies.

Stakeholder identification

Every type of audit has something important in common. Every audit has stakeholders. These stakeholders can include customers, partners, management team, employees, and so on. Stakeholders may have a vested interest in the organization's audit. For example, customers may need a vendor to be compliant with laws and regulations that apply to themselves. Management and employees are often involved in a different capacity. Based on the type of audit, auditors may have to interview employees and management to evaluate control effectiveness.

A typical example of this is that an auditor may interview managers and employees to ask them about their knowledge of internal policies and standards. While also asking them to attest to how they are executed within the organization.

It is important that your organization carefully examines who the stakeholders are for an audit. The auditor must be provided a list of stakeholders that they can contact to conduct interviews and request evidence.

The fact that an auditor needs to work with the organization's stakeholders also means it impacts them. For example, stakeholders may be required to produce evidence and documentation or conduct interviews. In some cases, auditors may even need to examine live systems or perform testing on such systems. Meaning audits can impact stakeholders in more ways than one. It is vital that your organization communicates (internally) and to the auditor who will be available to work with the auditor. That way, stakeholders can prepare and ensure the auditor receives all needed data and evidence.

EXAM TIP: Identifying stakeholders should happen before an audit or early in the process.

Audit planning

Once the scope of an audit has been defined and stakeholders have been identified, it is vital that audit planning takes place. As mentioned, audits require significant amounts of effort by the audited organization. The organization must collect data, provide documents, prepare for interviews, and arrange time and facilities to perform testing.

Ensuring all stakeholders know what to expect during the audit process will help your organization prevent delays. At the same time, planning an audit will help an auditor ensure the process goes smoothly. The auditor can schedule interviews with different stakeholders in a logical order while reserving sufficient amounts of time.

Because audits take significant effort, it is wise to plan audits during a time when your organization can work with the auditor. For example, scheduling an audit during vacation season or a new product release may make it more difficult for an auditor to work with all the required stakeholders.

Audit execution

Once all the preparation and planning for an audit has taken place, the time has finally come for the audit to be executed. During an audit, the auditor may visit your organization in person, or they may review evidence digitally. During most audits, interviews with employees and managers will be conducted, policies and standards will be reviewed, and files such as log files, records, and financial data may be reviewed.

During the audit process, the auditor works within the pre-defined scope and ensures the identified stakeholders are approached following the planning of the audit. However, during an audit, it may come to light that the audit scope needs to be adjusted or that additional stakeholders exist. If this is the case, the auditor will work with you to do so.

Audit reports

After an auditor has conducted all her investigations, she will analyze the evidence and produce an audit report. An audit report contains typically the following components, as shown:

Executive summary
Scope
Planning
Stakeholders
Findings
Recommendations
Conclusion

Table 20.3: Common elements of an audit report

As you can see above, an audit report usually contains an executive summary. Such a summary provides a high-level overview of the audit results for the management of an organization. The summary outlines the most critical findings and usually includes a conclusion summarizing the audit's outcome.

Aside from the executive summary, an audit report should also cover the scope of the audit, the planning of the audit, the stakeholders involved, the processes used to audit, the findings identified, and, in some cases, a list of recommendations to address the results. At the end of the report, you may also find a conclusion or statement of compliance that indicates if the audit has seen the organization to have passed or failed the audit.

The audit report is often considered one of the most essential parts of the audit. A good report can clearly and concisely convey the state of an organization and provide practical recommendations to remediate findings. Once again, if you request an audit report from a vendor or partner, you must ensure that you understand the audit's scope to understand the result fully. In practice, many companies scope audits to provide a positive image of the organization, yet it may reveal only some relevant information about an organization. Aside from the scope of an audit, you should also evaluate (to the best of your ability) if the auditor is impartial.

Audit follow-up

An audit report can be a precious asset to an organization. However, an audit report can only help an organization if it is appropriately reviewed and given follow-up. Once an audit has concluded, it should be distributed to various organizational stakeholders. At the same time, the management team should decide which findings will be addressed (audits rarely do not have findings).

Audit findings should be remediated (using the advice provided by the auditor), especially if the audit's purpose was to confirm or deny compliance to laws and regulations. Your organization should plan to remediate findings in a way that provides evidence so that future audits can quickly identify and evaluate the remediations.

Whenever an external audit reveals findings, it can be helpful to use an internal audit to verify remediation actions taken in response to the audit. That way, your organization can be more assured that the findings will not reappear in the following external audit. The benefit of such an approach is that your organization may save the costs of multiple extra external audits. At the same time, your company could also scope a follow-up audit only to evaluate the remediations.

Audit process summary

In the previous sections, we have taken a more detailed look at the activities that are part of the audit process. A CCSP should fully understand how audits are conducted and what the value of audit reports can be to an organization. After all, you are likely to play a role in auditing one way or another. You may have to evaluate audit reports about a CSP or provide input to audits of your organization. An overview of the steps of the audit process is as follows:

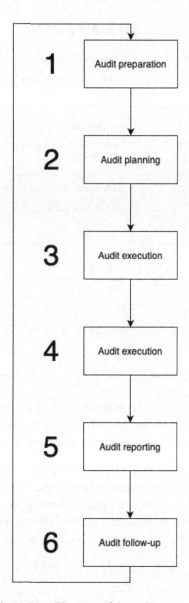

Figure 20.2: The steps of the audit process

Systems and Organization Controls

As discussed, different audits have different purposes. One type of audit that is commonly conducted for security is a **Systems and Organization Controls (SOC)** audit. The SOC audits have been created by the **American Institute of CPAs (AICPA)**. There are three different categories of SOC audits. The first and second categories also have different types the audit can follow. Let us take a look at an overview as follows:

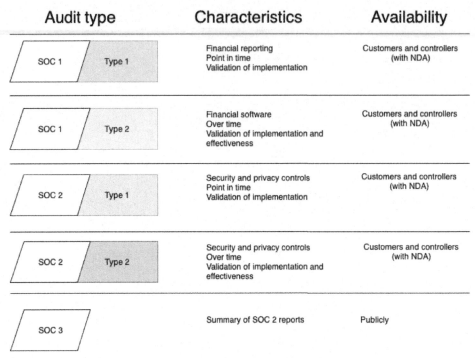

Figure 20.3: *Overview of SOC audit types and their properties*

As you can see in the figure above, there are a total of five different SOC audits. The **SOC 1 Type 1** and **2** report on an organization's financial reporting. The **Type 1** audit checks if controls are implemented but do not verify if they work correctly over time. Whereas a type two audit does.

A **SOC 2 Type 1** or **2** examines an organization's security and privacy controls. Like the **SOC 1** audit, **Type 1** is used to check for implementation of controls but does not verify effectiveness. The **Type 2** audit does verify control effectiveness. Because of this, the **SOC 2 Type 2** audit is a very suitable one to verify a CSP's security and privacy.

EXAM TIP: Use SOC 2 TYPE 2 audits to verify security and privacy controls implemented by a vendor.

It is essential to understand that a **SOC 2 Type 2** audit provides in-depth information about a vendor's security and privacy controls. That means a vendor may be reluctant to share **SOC 2 Type 2** audits, without having a **non-disclosure agreement** (NDA) in place. At the same time, a vendor may advertise their **SOC 2 Type 2** audit publicly if they feel their security and privacy controls can withstand outside threats (many CSPs do so). Whenever you evaluate a CSP, try to obtain a **SOC 2 Type 2** report over a type 1 one. If you do obtain a report, make sure to evaluate the scope of the audit to establish all the services and controls your organization needs are covered. Many organizations scope **SOC 2 Type 2** audits in a favorable way to the audited company. SOC 2 reports are also known as **International Standard on Assurance Engagement (ISAE)** 3000

Sarbanes-Oxley Act

Another important and frequent audit is part of the **Sarbanes-Oxley Act (SOX)** (in the US). An external auditor conducts a SOX audit to review an organization's financial statements. It is essential to understand that all publicly traded companies, subsidiaries, and foreign publicly traded companies that are traded or operate within the US must undergo audits yearly. SOX audits aim to reduce fraudulent activities and make executives personally accountable for such actions. SOX audit reports that follow the **Statement on Standards for Attestation Engagements (SSAE)**.

Many companies are not regulated by the SOX act. However, some countries may have similar requirements, especially for companies operating within the financial sector.

CSA STAR

Another relevant audit type within the security industry is the **Cloud Security Alliance Security Trust Assurance and Risk (CSA STAR)** program. The CSA STAR program has different certification levels. The first level requires an organization's self-certification (and thus an internal audit). The second level has three audit types and can be integrated within SOC 2 or ISO/IEC 27001 audits. For example, the Level 2 STAR attestation can be reached through a SOC 2 audit that includes the CSA **Cloud Controls Matrix (CCM)**. Similarly, the STAR certification can be achieved by conducting an ISO/IEC 27001 audit that includes the CSA CCM.

Companies can register their CSA compliance levels, attestations, and certifications online in the CSA STAR registry. The CSA registry, as such, is a great place to start your CSP or vendor evaluation process, as STAR certifications and attestations can provide valuable information for assessing a CSP or vendor.

Gap analysis

Regardless of the nature of the audit that has been conducted, an audit report can provide handy information to an organization. For example, it can serve as a basis for a gap analysis. Such an analysis is often used to determine the steps needed to reach a desired future state.

A gap analysis determines what is needed to get from the current state to the desired state. In the figure above, the current state is a house, while the desired state is a castle. To get from the house to a castle, several changes are needed. An audit report provides information about the current state of an organization.

It is important to compare the scope of an audit report to the scope of your gap analysis. For example, if you are conducting a gap analysis on cloud controls and use a SOC 1 type 1 report as a basis, it will likely provide little helpful information. If you had a SOC 2 type 2 or CSA STAR audit report, it could be a solid starting point for your gap analysis.

It is essential to understand that the reason to conduct a gap analysis often is the outcome of a **Business Impact Analysis (BIA)**. After all, a BIA can reveal that the compromised availability of a process or system might significantly impact your organization. A gap analysis can help determine the steps to protect such vital assets.

REAL-LIFE TIP: Even audits required for compliance can provide essential information to an organization that can be used to determine growth strategy.

Information security management system

As you may have noticed, different audits address different areas of an organization. ISO 27001 audits focus on implementing an **information security management system (ISMS)**, while CSA STAR attestations concentrate more on the implementation and effectiveness of security controls themselves.

Whenever you establish an ISMS within your organization, it can be valuable to model your ISMS towards common audit standards. For example, if your company seeks to certify against an ISO standard, it is wise to build your ISMS in a way that is compliant with the standard. Your organization should create policies based on your organization's needs. However, you can ensure that your policies at least cover the requirements of a standard or an audit. Doing so will make it much easier for your organization to prove compliance.

Information security controls

Implementing an ISMS by certification requirements or applicable standards (or even regulations) is a smart way to prove compliance in the future easily. If your information security controls must be validated through external audits or certifications, you should take the same approach for these controls. For example, your organization could use the cloud controls matrix as a baseline for developing cloud security controls within your organization. That way, your organization will have a significantly easier time certifying within the CSA STAR program later. Like an ISMS, you must still ensure your tailor controls based on your organization's needs. However, using control baselines, standards, or audit requirements as the basis for your control landscape will also ensure that you have covered some of the most common (and important controls).

PCI-DSS

Throughout this book, we have talked about the **Payment Card Industry – Data Security Standard** quite a few times. PCI-DSS is a significant standard for a couple of reasons. Firstly, the standard covers payment data for the credit card industry. Such data is precious to data subjects and data owners alike. Secondly, the PCI-DSS is a textbook example of a successful self-regulating standard. The concept of self-regulation means that an industry creates its own rules and mechanisms to enforce compliance within the industry. By doing so, they large negate the need for jurisdictions to create their laws and regulations.

The big benefit of self-regulation, especially in international industries, is that it naturally causes some law harmonization. Meaning it prevents different jurisdictions from needing to impose specific (and sometimes conflicting) laws and regulations. Instead, it produces a single, easy-to-follow ruleset for every party within an industry to comply with.

Self-regulation requires more than creating a common set of standards. Rather it needs mechanisms for enforcement. After all, jurisdictions are likely to develop their own laws and regulations when they see industry parties are not complying with self-regulated standards.

In the case of PCI-DDS, this means that PCI has set forth requirements for auditing compliance with the standard. Merchants that process over a million or more credit card payments or service providers that retain, transmit, or process more than 300,000 transactions yearly must undergo a yearly PCI-DSS audit.

If an organization fails to prove compliance with PCI-DSS, it will be fined by the industry governing body. Fines under PCI-DSS are not a pay-once type of fine. Instead, a company found to be incompliant will be fined a recurring fee until they prove they are fully compliant. Such fines can range up to 100.000 per day depending on the nature of the incompliance and the number of processed transactions.

As you can imagine, companies regulated under PCI-DSS face substantial financial impact if they cannot prove compliance. Thus, they will usually try to design their controls to comply with the PCI-DSS naturally.

HIPAA

As you know, PCI-DSS is hardly the only law or regulation organizations are subjected to. In the United States, healthcare organizations and other covered entities must comply with the **Health Insurance Portability and Accountability Act (HIPAA)**. HIPAA is an act, meaning it is enforced by the US government rather than the industry itself.

To ensure compliance with HIPAA, yearly audits are conducted by the **Office for Civil Rights (OCR)**. During these audits, covered entities are chosen at random. In some cases, entities may be audited after reports of suspected non-compliance, breaches, or complaints.

If an organization is non-compliant with HIPAA, it can be fined following the law. This means an organization may be fined between 100 and 50000 USD for every violation. As you can imagine, failing a HIPAA audit could have significant and severe consequences for a covered entity. As such, HIPAA-covered entities should conduct (internal) audits. That way, your organization can fix compliance issues before being audited by the OCR (and thus prevent fines).

HITECH

Like HIPAA, the **Health Information Technology for Economical and Clinical Health (HITECH)** act regulates healthcare organizations and other covered entities. The HITECH act is an expansion or amendment to HIPAA. HITECH improves patient data access, allows for greater penalties for non-compliance, and so on. Similar to HIPAA, audits may be performed on covered entities under HITECH.

NERC/CIP

The **North American Electric Reliability Corporation (NERC) critical infrastructure protection (CIP)** plan provides a set of standards that power companies and other critical infrastructure companies must follow. NERC/CIP seeks to ensure essential infrastructure (and its users) are adequately protected. NERC/CIP only applies within the US and is auditable, like HIPAA and HITECH.

As NERC/CIP pertains to critical infrastructure, fines for violating the standards can be severe. The maximum penalty is 1 million USD per day the violation endures.

GDPR

Companies that collect data of EU residents may also be audited for their compliance with the **General Data Protection Act (GDPR)**. Throughout this book, we have talked extensively about the requirements of GDPR and the complicated landscape it governs. While the GDPR does not need audits, a **Data Protection Agency (DPA)** within the EU may decide to investigate or audit a company after it receives complaints or suspects non-compliance.

Companies can consider using external audits to prove compliance to customers and partners and improve their implementation and internal assurance. Non-compliance with GDPR can result in hefty fines calculated based on a company's turnover. The maximum penalty is 20 million euros or 4% of the preceding year's turnover.

Legal and regulatory landscape

As you have been able to read throughout this chapter, companies may face a wide variety of audit requirements based on laws and regulations in their jurisdiction and industries. In some cases, audits are mandated by the law or regulation and will have to occur every year. Other laws and regulations may only audit parties suspected of non-compliance, while some laws and regulations have no formal audit requirements.

Regardless of the audit requirements that apply to your organization, conducting internal and external audits can be helpful even if it is not required. Internal and external audits can provide valuable information to your organization about its compliance and help direct the company's efforts toward compliance. Especially if your organization can face severe (financial) consequences for non-compliance, it is highly advisable to pre-emptively audit your organization to prevent incurring fines or penalties.

Conclusion

Risk appetite represents an organization's willingness to take risks to achieve its business goals. As such, risk appetite forms the basis for risk management. Without understanding how much risk is acceptable, it becomes tough to determine how risks should be treated. After all, a company with a large risk appetite might accept a risk, whereas a company with a smaller one would choose risk mitigation.

Regardless of your organization's risk appetite, choosing a risk management framework to implement within your organization is crucial. A framework like the NIST RMF can help your organization address risks in an organized manner. At the same time, risk management metrics can help your organization evaluate the effectiveness of your risk management program while ensuring your company operates within its risk appetite.

Your organization's role within the data landscape is important to the amount of risk your organization should be willing to take. At the same time, it also greatly influences what controls your organization should implement.

No matter your risk appetite, risk management framework, or role in the data landscape, your organization will likely be required to participate in audits. Whether these audits are mandated by applicable laws, regulations, or self-initiated, they can provide valuable information to an organization. Whenever you conduct audits, you must evaluate if internal or external audits are more suitable. But, regardless of the audit type, audits should be carefully prepared, planned, executed, reported about, and followed up.

Audits can serve solely to prove compliance to regulators and customers, but they can also serve a role in the organization's future. Audits can form a solid basis for a gap analysis that helps an organization determine the steps it must take to reach a future desired state.

Audit reports exist in many shapes and forms, from SOC 2 type 2 audits that are suitable for evaluating CSPs, SOX audits to prevent fraud to CSA STAR audits, HIPAA audits, or audits for critical infrastructure. Each audit has its scope, purpose, and end goal.

Suppose your organization is required to comply with laws or regulations. In that case, it is wise to audit your organization pre-emptively to ensure compliance and allow your organization to address any issues.

The next chapter dives into the ins and outs of managing contract in the cloud.

Learning goals

This chapter addresses the following CCSP exam outline learning goals:

Domain 2: Cloud data security

> 2.8 Design and implement auditability, traceability, and accountability of data events

Domain 6: Legal, risk, and compliance

> 6.3 Understand the audit process, methodologies, and required adaptations for a cloud environment

> 6.4 Understand the implications of cloud to enterprise risk management

Join our book's Discord space

Join the book's Discord Workspace for Latest updates, Offers, Tech happenings around the world, New Release and Sessions with the Authors:

https://discord.bpbonline.com

CHAPTER 21

Contracts and the Cloud

Introduction

When your organization decides to use cloud computing within its ecosystem, it must be prepared for the contractual challenges of cloud computing. Because cloud services are delivered, used, and paid for differently from other IT services, your organization needs to understand how to use **service-level agreements (SLAs)**, **master service agreements (MSAs)**, and **statements of works (SoWs)** to ensure the cloud service provider delivers the service your organization needs.

You must ensure the services you purchase meet your organization's expectations. This chapter explores how you can use service-level agreements, master service agreements, and statements of work to ensure you get the services you need. While vendor, contract, and supply chain management ensure you can prevent issues now and in the future.

Structure

This chapter covers the following topics:

- **Service-level agreement (SLA)**
- **Master service agreement (MSA)**
- **Statement of work (SOW)**

- Vendor management

- Vendor assessments

- Vendor lock-in risks

- Vendor viability

- Escrow

- Contract management

- Right to audit

- Metrics

- Definitions

- Termination

- Litigation

- Assurance

- Compliance

- Access to cloud data

- Cyber risk insurance

- Supply-chain management

Objectives

After reading this chapter, you will understand how SLAs allow an organization to carefully specify what the requirements a (cloud) service must satisfy. You will be able to understand common ways in which SLAs are defined and will be able to create SLAs for your own organization. At the same time, you will understand how **master service agreements (MSAs)** and SoWs play an essential role in defining the scope of a contract.

Throughout the chapter, you will also learn how vendors and contracts should be managed. You will learn how to prevent vendor lock-in risks and assess vendor viability through vendor assessments.

At the end of the chapter, you will also understand the essential components of contract management. You can evaluate and define contracts based on their definitions, metrics, and other factors to ensure compliance and obtain certain assurance about the services you purchase.

Service-level agreements

As you know, cloud computing can be conducted in various ways. For example, you can use private, public, or hybrid cloud environments. At the same time, there is a large variety of service levels, from standard models like **Infrastructure as a Service** to **Identity as a Service**; every service model delivers value differently.

In on-premises computing, most external services are simple to understand. For example, your organization may buy licenses to use hypervisor software. The vendor supplies the licenses, and your company sets up the environment. Sometimes, your organization may also purchase technical support or consultancy services. In such a situation, the expectations between customer and vendor are often easy to manage. After all, providing a license does not require extensive effort on the vendor's side; it is a simple transaction.

The customer and vendor relationship in the cloud may not be as clear-cut as in the example above. For example, whenever you purchase an Infrastructure as a Service offering like a VM, the CSP is responsible for ensuring your IaaS service remains secure and operational. Because of this, purchasing (any kind) of cloud services from a CSP creates more than a customer-vendor relationship between the CSP and CSC. Instead, it creates a situation that resembles a continued partnership.

As with any partnership, its success depends on managing expectations. The same is true for cloud services. If you purchase IaaS computing, you expect that compute to be available, sufficiently fast, and secure. But, in this context, available, sufficiently fast, and secure are very broad terms. Without further defining them, the CSP or the CSC likely has different expectations from the other party.

One way to create clarity between two parties that engage in a contract is by defining **service-level agreements** (**SLAs**). SLAs are measurable agreements that reflect what level of service is provided from one party to another.

For example, an SLA can define the uptime of a virtual machine that a vendor will provide. By establishing an SLA for uptime, both CSC and CSP can ensure they fully understand what they can expect of each other.

Defining SLAs is essential to any contract, especially between a CSC and a CSP. When you define SLAs, you should ensure they are clear, concise, and measurable. Without room for discussion, the SLA should define the service level and present how the SLA will be measured and reported on and what consequences failing to meet an SLA has. Let us look at different ways to create an SLA, as follows:

SLA 1	SLA 2
The CSP will provide an uptime for virtual machines of 99.7%. Uptime is the amount of time the machine is reachable from the internet. For every percentage point of underperformance, the CSP will refund the customer 5% of the charges related to the virtual machine in the month the underperformance occurs.	The CSP will ensure virtual machines are useable by the CSC.

Table 21.1: Samples of SLA definition

In the examples above, you can see two different ways of creating an SLA. The first example attempts to define clearly what the customer can expect. It attempts to specify what the SLA relates to and discloses the consequences if the SLA is not met. The second example vaguely defines what the CSP will deliver to the CSC. It does not define what useable means, nor does it specify the consequences of underperformance.

Now, ask yourself, which SLA would you be more comfortable with as a CSC or CSP? Would it be the SLA that outlines clearly what it entails, or would it be the vague SLA? In any case, your organization should sign contracts with well-defined SLAs that make it easy for your organization and the CSP to understand what must be delivered. At the same time, adding consequences to underperformance on an SLA (sometimes called an **SLA breach**) will make enforcement of the contract much more straightforward. If a CSP cannot deliver the promised SLA, you can make them liable. Both of the SLA examples above could be better. You should define more in-depth SLAs that outline reporting requirements and other factors. However, remember that the more effort you put into an SLA, the better it will be for the CSC and CSP.

Large CSPs offer standardized SLAs to all their customers, meaning you cannot negotiate the service levels with the CSP. Instead, their (public) cloud offerings have a standard SLA that comes with the product and applies to everyone who purchases their service. Whenever your organization picks a CSP or cloud service, you must verify if the SLAs tied to the offering suit your organization.

For example, an SLA could define that your data will be backed up every week, but if your organization needs to obtain daily back-ups to satisfy its RPO, more than that SLA may be required. Your organization may have to look for another service provider or purchase a service with a higher SLA. When you deal with smaller CSPs or SaaS companies, you may be able to negotiate the contents of SLAs. Your organization should consider this whenever it selects a CSP.

EXAM TIP: Good SLAs are specific, measurable and define the consequences of underperformance.

Master service agreement

SLAs are often specific and may be different for various services. However, in many cases, a customer might engage in more comprehensive agreements with a vendor. For example, a company contracting a vendor to manage their internal IT might need more comprehensive terms to define their partnership. A **master service agreement** (**MSA**) broadly defines agreements between customer and vendor. Such contracts can pertain to the manner of service delivery, timeframes, and so on.

Contrary to SLAs, MSA attempts to define the terms of a partnership at a broader (more abstract level). MSAs can be useful when organizations have many (prospective) agreements or contracts. For example, if your company works with a vendor to manage its IT environment, they will work together on other projects.

A company may use the vendor to purchase licenses or perform migration projects. An MSA can create general terms that can be applied to multiple contracts (that may be signed in the future). By creating an MSA, the customer and vendor can make high-level agreements that can be established only for some specific contracts.

A common example of something covered in an MSA may be a (mutual) **non-disclosure agreement** (**NDA**). Similarly, an MSA can provide pricing, billing, warranties, intellectual property information, and so on.

Let us compare SLAs and MSAs:

	SLA	MSA
Broad and high-level		X
Specific and measurable	X	

Table 21.2: *Differences between SLAs and MSAs*

Statement of work

A **statement of work** (**SoW**) is an essential partnership component. A statement of work is a document that outlines the scope of a project. A SoW is far more specific than an MSA. It defines details about a project, such as the purpose, scope, milestones, and deliverables. Other factors usually included in a statement of work are the project schedule, testing requirements, success criteria, and details like when the customer will pay for the rendered services and when the project is concluded.

Now that you know the purpose of SLAs, MSAs, and SoWs, you should know they are not mutually exclusive. An MSA can lead to an SOW, and an SOW can include SLAs, for example. Your organization should use (a combination of) these documents to define what your partnership with a vendor should entail clearly.

Vendor management

Throughout this book, we have discussed some of the challenges of dealing with vendors. Organizations need help determining which vendor would be best suited to collaborate with. Some vendors may not comply with laws and regulations that apply to your organization. At the same time, other vendors may need the scale or security to work with your organization. In other cases, one vendor may be far more expensive than another.

You could produce hundreds of factors that may influence an organization's decision for a specific vendor. Many of these factors may not even relate directly to the product your organization is interested in purchasing. So, how can your organization determine what vendor is suitable for it? Let us look in the next section:

Vendor assessments

One effective way to determine the suitability of a vendor is called a **vendor assessment**. Generally, a vendor assessment starts with a questionnaire sent to a vendor. The vendor is asked to provide information about the organization. For example, what do their processes like, what resources does the organization have, and how much capacity it has? In the cloud, other commonly considered factors are privacy and security practices.

Once a vendor returns the questionnaire, your organization should evaluate the answers. For example, if your organization needs a vendor to provide services internationally, but they only operate in a small area, that vendor may need to be better-suited.

Similarly, a small company may need help to offer the support a large multinational organization needs. At the same time, your vendor may not be able to provide sufficient security or privacy controls to ensure your data is protected to the extent your organization desires.

Regardless, your organization should attempt to evaluate multiple vendors that deliver similar services. That way, it can pick the organization that aligns the best with your organization's needs. Aside from using a vendor questionnaire, you can also use external proof as part of your evaluation. External audits and certifications can provide relevant information and assurance to your organization.

Once your organization has found a vendor that aligns with its requirements, it can continue drafting the necessary agreements and contracts.

Vendor lock-in risks

One essential item to consider is the risk of vendor lock-in. As we covered in several other chapters, vendor lock-in means that your organization has a (dangerous) dependency on one organization that cannot easily be remedied. For example, suppose your organization hosts all its data in a proprietary format. In that case, you may not be able to move this data to another organization quickly if your agreement with the vendor ends (on bad terms).

It would be best to attempt to achieve sufficient data portability whenever you pick a vendor. Aside from data portability, you can work with vendors that use open standards over proprietary standards as they make transitioning to another vendor more straightforward.

Vendor viability

While lock-in can be a significant risk, the viability of a vendor is also an essential factor to consider. For example, if your vendor has a precarious financial situation, it may need help to meet its future obligations. At the same time, a company facing significant legal action may not be allowed or able to provide services if the legal case does not work out in its favor. Another factor may be that an organization may be operating in an industry facing (new) impacting legislation, such as trade bans or similarly influential measures.

Escrow

Sometimes, an organization may seem viable, but you never know the future. Events like a global pandemic or war could easily affect the viability of an organization. If your organization doubts the risk of vendor lock-in or viability, it may consider utilizing escrow services. Escrow services can range from data escrow to more specific services like key escrow. Escrow essentially uses another third party to store your data or your keys to protect it in case your vendor can no longer fulfill their obligations. For example, key escrow can ensure your key material remains available even if your vendor goes bankrupt.

Of course, if you decide to use any escrow service, you should ensure your escrow service is more reliable than the vendor you are using escrow for.

Contract management

Managing vendors has many different aspects. Vendors must be assessed for viability, lock-in, and other factors such as security and privacy (compliance). SLAs, MSAs, and SoWs can be used to set expectations with vendors whenever you have found a suitable one. Sometimes, vendor selection can be based on the vendor's ability to satisfy SLA, MSA, or SoW requirements.

In any case, once your organization has deemed a party suitable to partner with, it must establish a contract between the vendor and itself. A contract includes terms that outline the services to be rendered by the vendor to the partner and the costs that will be involved. However, many other factors must be carefully considered when establishing a contract (for cloud services). Let us look at some critical components in the sections ahead.

Right to audit

Throughout the book, we have discussed some of the challenges you can encounter in the cloud regarding auditing. Shared responsibility means that your organization will also have limited accessibility to data for audits. This means your company can do two things: trust that a vendor is speaking the truth about their practices, policies, controls, and so on. Alternatively, your organization can embed a right to audit in the contract.

A right to audit is an extremely powerful clause that every vendor may only sometimes accept. The right to audit gives the customer the power to force the vendor to submit to an external audit. In some cases, your organization may conduct the audit. However, not every organization has auditors; even fewer companies have auditors suitable to audit various vendors. So, in most cases, the right to audit is executed by an external company instead of the customer. This independent third party can conduct an audit to evaluate if the vendor complies with SLAs, security and privacy requirements, and other relevant parts of the contract.

You must carefully define the terms whenever you include the right to audit in a contract. For example, does the right to audit apply to the vendor or only to the services you have decided to purchase? As you can imagine, a vendor is likely to have differing views on an extensive audit scope, especially if the value of a contract is not very large. In many cases, vendors will only agree to a tightly scoped right to audit, for example, only with audits on specific laws and regulations rather than comprehensive audits of an entire organization.

Ensure that your organization weighs the value of the right to audit, the audit scope, and how the audit is conducted. These factors greatly influence the viability of the right to audit and the value the audit provides your organization.

In many cases, a vendor may also provide third-party audit reports (on request) to customers rather than agreeing to every customer having an individual right to audit. As you know, audits can be impacting and costly, making it very difficult for a (large) CSP to support the right to audit for its many different customers if they all want to be able to conduct their audits.

EXAM TIP: You should always include some form of a right to audit in a contract.

REAL-LIFE TIP: Many vendors will only provide third-party audit reports to customers and not agree to a right to audit executed by the customer.

Even when your vendor does agree to let your organization perform audits, you should be wary. After all, if they allow your organization to audit, they are likely to allow others to do so as well. Extensive audit scopes and poorly trained auditors at other companies can potentially be a risk to your data.

Metrics

Aside from the right to audit, other important factors should be part of a contract. One of these is metrics. Whenever an organization creates a contract, it has expectations about the level of service that will be delivered. As you know, many of these are expressed as service-level agreements. However, for SLAs to be useable, they need to be measured.

After all, what is the point of an SLA if you cannot evaluate if the vendor is providing services in agreeance with the SLA? Metrics allow your organization to measure a variety of things. For example, your organization can define **key performance indicators (KPIs)**. KPIs are metrics that provide valuable information about the performance of a system or service. Tying KPIs to SLAs is a great way to evaluate if the SLA is being met.

Your organization and the vendor should determine metrics to track, monitor, and report. For example, your organization may want to receive daily, weekly, or monthly information on your KPIs. By frequently checking these metrics, your organization can act more quickly if SLAs are breached or the service needs to meet expectations.

Aside from KPIs, it may also be good to introduce another type of metrics called **key risk indicators (KRIs)**. While KPIs represent performance, KRIs express a measure of risk. For example, a KRI can track the number of vulnerabilities within an environment. Similarly, a KRI could represent the time to complete failover processes. By combining KPIs and KRIs in your contract, your vendor and your organization will be able to react to changes in the environment quickly.

Similarly, KPIs and KRIs allow the partners to analyze trends, adjust their working methods, create additional SLAs, or even invoke the right audit.

EXAM TIP: Ensure to include KPIs and KRIs in your contract. Also include agreements on how and when the vendor reports on KPIs and KRIs.

Definitions

For a contract to be executed properly, it is vital that all parties properly understand each other. You have already read in this book that some words mean different to everybody. For example, privacy has different meanings in different jurisdictions and can even be interpreted differently by other people.

To avoid confusion, the customer and the vendor must create a list of common definitions. These common definitions ensure that each party fully understands the terms. Let us look at a situation where the lack of definitions could play a huge role:

	Vendor	Customer
Privacy	Protecting the customer's data	Limiting what data we collect and process about employees and customers

Table 21.3: Differences in definitions can cause issues.

In the example above, the vendor and the customer look at privacy differently. The vendor views privacy as data protection only, while the customer focuses on data collection. If you formulate the terms of a contract with this mismatch in definition, you can guarantee issues in the future.

Let us look at the following example of contract text:

The vendor will be responsible for controls to ensure the privacy of customers and employees.

When you consider the text above, you quickly realize that the customer needs to be better, not be well aligned. Based on the text, the vendor will implement controls to protect data. For example, it may implement encryption or data loss prevention controls. However, the customer is likely expecting the vendor to implement controls to limit the collection of (unnecessary) data from data subjects. Hence, it expects the vendor to implement measures like data anonymization, data retention controls, and so on.

Privacy is a common example of a definition that differs between parties. However, many technical and non-technical definitions may not be as clear-cut as you might think. Creating a list of definitions included in the contract is highly advisable. Beware that the list of definitions should be agreed on between all parties; otherwise, the vendor may be unable to offer the services you expect for the quoted price. Establish definitions early on to prevent confusion, price changes, and frustrations between the customer and the vendor.

Termination

Whenever you choose to contract with a vendor, the last thing you think about is terminating that contract. After all, you contract for a purpose; your organization purchases valuable services, hardware, and so on, to satisfy business needs.

Unfortunately, not all partnerships will last forever. Especially in the cloud, where services and customer needs evolve quickly, it is not unthinkable that what seems to be a good partnership now may not be suitable later. Whenever you sign a contract, you should build in clear terms surrounding the termination of a contract in the future.

For every contract, you should define how long the contract lasts, what grounds can lead to termination (for example, prolonged failure to meet SLAs), and how the termination process will occur.

That last item, the termination process, is essential (especially in the cloud). Imagine the following scenario: an organization has purchased a SaaS package for human resource management. Over the past few years, the vendor has performed poorly; it has frequently failed to comply with SLAs, has not reported per the defined metrics, and has charged excessive costs. Your organization has found a new vendor to provide another cloud-based HRM system.

Your contract states you can cancel it every month after the first two years. Because you are in the third year of service, your company purchases the new product and provides notice to the old vendor. Because your company is an essential asset to the vendor, they are angry that your organization has canceled the contract. Due to poor definitions, the vendor feels their organization has not underperformed at all. In response to the termination, the vendor decided not to comply with your company's request to provide an export of the system's data.

While your company has legal grounds to terminate the contract, it may not be able to force the vendor to share the data export. As a result, your organization may lose all its data because it cannot import it from the old system.

As you can imagine, such a scenario could be highly damaging to an organization, especially if the data involved is critical to the customer. To prevent situations like the scenario above, you should clearly define the duties of the customer and the vendor upon termination. For example, should the vendor allow the customer access to their data, provide a data export proactively, or even assist in a data migration project to another vendor?

All these factors will significantly influence your organization's ability to transition from one vendor to another or from a vendor to an internal environment. Even if you are not aiming to reuse the data, the termination clauses should dictate what the vendor must do with your data once the contract ends; for example, must they delete your data or archive it and make it available on request?

EXAM TIP: Termination clauses are to a contract what a prenup is to a marriage. You can engage in it without defining them, but it may cost you in the long run.

Litigation

Like the termination clause, the litigation clauses of a contract are essential to prevent damage if a partnership does not go as expected. As part of the litigation clause, you should define under which jurisdiction the contract falls and what rights each party has to engage in litigation against each other.

For example, a vendor may limit the customer's ability to engage in legal action against the vendor in certain circumstances. Imagine a customer requesting that a vendor lower their security controls to facilitate specific functional requirements. In such cases, a vendor probably wants to avoid accepting liability if something goes wrong.

As a customer, you should keep your options for litigation open fully. After all, you want to be able to take legal action if necessary. Agreeing to overly restrictive terms can pan out negatively for your organization if a judge dismisses a potential case due to the litigation clause in your contract.

At the same time, pick a favorable jurisdiction for your organization. For example, if you operate in multiple countries, you may only have legal insurance in some of them, and you may have a legal team in each of these countries. In such cases, it may be beneficial to pick a jurisdiction you understand well, have legal insurance, or have favorable laws for customers.

Assurance

Aside from the right to audit, your organization may require other assurance forms. For example, your organization may need products that comply with common assurance standards or certification levels. If your organization has such specific needs (this is often the case for governmental agencies) it can be beneficial to include such requirements as part of the contract.

It is common to use assurance requirements to terminate a contract if insufficient assurance is achieved. For example, if your company pays to use a service with an HSM compliant with FIPS 140-3 level 2, but the new HSM the company uses does not meet the standard's requirements, you may want to be able to terminate the contract.

Compliance

As mentioned previously, compliance is often a hot topic in a contract. A customer may be required by law or regulation to comply with certain standards or requirements. Whenever this is the case, the customer is accountable for the compliance, even when it shifts responsibilities to a vendor.

For example, if the GDPR regulates your organization, it remains your responsibility to comply with it, even when storing your data at a cloud provider. While your company is accountable, you should clearly define what laws and regulations the vendor is responsible for compliance within the contract.

After all, you cannot hold a vendor responsible for not being compliant with laws and regulations that apply to your organization (but not theirs directly). Therefore, you must define such cases in a compliance clause in the contract.

Using such clauses to establish a right to terminate the contract (or a fine) is also wise if compliance is not maintained. After all, a vendor that is not compliant can have significant repercussions for your organization.

EXAM TIP: Clearly define compliance requirements and establish a right to terminate or to fine if the vendor cannot prove compliance.

REAL-LIFE TIP: Write compliance clauses so that the vendor must prove compliance rather than requiring the customer to evaluate compliance.

Access to cloud data

As we covered earlier, access to cloud data is essential to a contract. Upon contract termination, a vendor may take your data hostage to prevent you from terminating the contract or simply out of spite. At the same time, access to cloud data goes beyond situations like termination.

For example, your organization may be one of many parties that are provided access to your data. In countries like the US, local laws and regulations may have provisions that allow government agencies to access your data for investigations that play a role in national security.

Similarly, your data may be sold to other parties by the vendor to earn money. This is especially common in free-to-use software. Your organization should carefully consider who your data may be shared with and in which fashion.

For example, your company may be right about sharing data with law enforcement agencies but may need to be more comfortable selling customer data for profit. Alternatively, your company may be all right with selling customer data, but only if the customer's privacy is protected or consent is provided.

Even more than in on-premises computing, cloud computing requires that you carefully and fully define who should have access to your data, in which situation, and under what circumstances. Otherwise, your company may face some unpleasant surprises when your data is suddenly confiscated (or disclosed) as part of a legal investigation.

Cyber risk insurance

We all know that security controls can always be flawed. A data breach or hack can happen to companies that pay much attention to security. Unfortunately, parties in this world can breach virtually any kind of system.

Your organization may use cyber risk insurance to alleviate some of the risks of operating in the digital (cloud) domain. Such policies cover some of the damages sustained by data breaches or hacks. They may even include coverage for the recovery of systems and implementing new security controls to prevent future hacks.

As you know, your company may be able to start litigation against a vendor in case a cyber incident occurs. If your contract allows legal action, your organization, in the worst case, may sue the vendor for extensive damages. Unfortunately, suing a vendor does not mean you will be compensated for your losses. Sometimes, the vendor may be unable to pay the damages a judge awards. Especially if your organization is large and you are using a vendor that is small of scale, it becomes unlikely that they will be able to cover damages to your organization.

Luckily, cyber risk insurance can help us reduce the risk that the vendor will be unable to pay damages if something goes wrong. We can do so by requiring the vendor to obtain legal insurance as a condition of the contract. This can be especially useful if your organization uses the vendor as a strategic partner. Of course, you should clearly define the terms of coverage that you require.

After all, some cyber risk insurances will only cover damages to the party itself but will not pay out any legal claims from customers. Similarly, some cyber risk insurances may have limited or capped coverage on damages. At the same time, your company should be prepared that if something goes wrong, multiple customers may be affected (especially in the cloud), which means that cyber risk insurance is not likely only to be used to cover damages claimed by your organization.

Your organization should determine if it requires cyber risk insurance and which terms would be acceptable to your organization. It is wise to factor in how many customers the organization has, its financial viability, and what a data breach or hack would cause in damages to your organization.

EXAM TIP: Cyber risk insurance is an example of risk transference. Likely, cyber risk insurance does not fully transfer all risk. Your organization may need other compensating controls.

Supply-chain management

As with much else, the ISO has designed a standardized framework for supply chain management. The ISO 27036:2021 standard contains valuable guidelines for the security of an IT supply chain and specific guidelines for the protection of cloud services.

The standard outlines controls like ownership, compliance, SoD, least privilege, and chain of custody. Additionally, the ISO 27036 provides a lifecycle for suppliers. The lifecycle consists of six steps, as shown:

Initiate	Need	Procure
Operate	Review	Terminate

Table 21.4: The supplier lifecycle as stated in the ISO 27036

Conclusion

Engaging in partnerships with other organizations like CSPs can create tremendous value for your organization. As with anything, partnerships also come with challenges and risks. If your organization aims to have successful partnerships with its vendors, it should include using service-level agreements to define what level of service must be provided by the vendor. Ensure that these SLAs are clear, concise, measurable, and, above all, enforceable.

Aside from SLAs, your organization may want to use master service agreements to govern long-lasting partnerships with multiple contracts. An MSA can define terms that should be carried out over multiple contracts. An MSA can make it easier for partners to engage in new contracts without always having to redefine all terms.

In addition to an MSA, your organization may need to use **statements of work (SoWs)** that represent the work a vendor should execute. By defining clear SoWs, both organizations can gain an in-depth understanding of the timelines and costs involved.

Every partnership should be formalized using a contract regardless of SLAs, MSAs, and SoWs. Whenever your organization drafts a contract, it must include standard components like the right to audit, definitions, metrics, litigation, termination, assurance, compliance, access to cloud data, and cyber risk insurance.

Including the above factors in a contract will allow your company to communicate its expectations with the vendor, which increases the chances of a successful partnership. At the same time, these terms protect your organization from adverse effects in case a partnership does not develop as expected.

By ensuring litigation, termination, and cyber risk insurance, your organization can significantly increase its ability to make a vendor accountable for not satisfying the terms of a contract. These terms are vital, especially in situations where a data breach or hack may result in significant damage to your organization. While everyone hopes partnerships work out as intended, the reality is that often they do not.

Throughout the book, you have learned much about supply management. It is essential to realize that the ISO has created a standard for managing supplier relations that can offer a great framework for managing partnerships within your organization. ISO 27036, defines controls that your organization should verify when it engages in a partnership with a vendor, as well as a lifecycle that allows your organization to manage its supplier relationships more effectively.

By combining best practices from ISO 27036, SLAs, MSAs, SoWs, and well-defined contracts, you will be able to protect your contract from many adverse consequences of poorly defined partnerships.

In the next chapter, duties of a CCSP will be discussed. You will learn more about what is expected of a (prospective) CCSP. Including abiding by the ISC2 code of ethics, the process for certification, and what is needed to maintain your certification after passing the exam will be explained.

Learning goals

This chapter addresses the following CCSP exam outline learning goals:

Domain 6: Legal, risk, and compliance

> Understand outsourcing and cloud contract design

Join our book's Discord space

Join the book's Discord Workspace for Latest updates, Offers, Tech happenings around the world, New Release and Sessions with the Authors:

https://discord.bpbonline.com

CHAPTER 22
Duties of a CCSP

Introduction

Becoming a Certified Cloud Security Professional can seem like a daunting task. You will need to study and take a challenging exam, but it does not stop there. To become a CCSP, you must join the **International Information System Security Certification Consortium** or **ISC2**. Aside from becoming a member, you must apply to be certified as a CCSP. The certification process verifies that a candidate has sufficient experience to become a CCSP. If you need more experience, you may still become an associate of ISC2. The coming chapter will examine the ISC2 code of ethics, the certification process, and your duties as a CCSP once you certify.

Structure

This chapter covers the following topics:

- ISC2 code of ethics
- Certification requirements
- How to certify
- Endorsement
- Evidence

- Maintaining certification (CPEs and AMF)

- Local chapters

- Cloud community

Objectives

By the end of this chapter, you will understand the ISC2 code of ethics. At the same time, you will be able to understand the requirements needed to certify as a CCSP. After reading the chapter, you will also be well-informed once you apply for your certification. You will be able to identify which options you have for endorsement and what evidence you should provide for the certification process. Lastly, you will understand how you can maintain your CCSP certification over time and what value local chapters and the cloud community can have for you.

ISC2 code of ethics

During your exam, you may be asked questions about the ISC2 code of ethics. This code of ethics is a collection of four canons to which every ISC2 member adheres. Adherence to this code is essential to remain in *good standing* with ISC2 and the industry. Failure to comply with the code of ethics can damage your reputation, customers, and even the cybersecurity and cloud industry.

Let us look at the four canons below:

- Protect society, the common good, necessary public trust and confidence, and the infrastructure.

- Act honorably, honestly, justly, responsibly, and legally.

- Provide diligent and competent service to principals.

- Advance and protect the profession.

Now that you have been able to read the canons, let us examine them in more detail.

The first canon states that an ISC2 member must always protect society and the common good. In practice, you should use your (cybersecurity) skills for good purposes. Use your cybersecurity skills to protect data, infrastructure, and organizations better rather than breaching them illegally.

The second canon dictates the type of behavior an ISC2 member should show. An example could be using responsible disclosure to inform a company of ineffective security controls (when discovered legally). ISC2 wants you to be their ambassador and expects you to act like it. If you have an option to use your cybersecurity skills in a questionable situation, you should refrain from doing so.

Our industry, unfortunately, encounters many people who pose as experts but are not. The third canon reminds you to provide competent and diligent service to principles. Giving sound advice based on facts, figures, and experience would be best. Try to advise on matters you thoroughly understand, as it could compromise your customers if you do not.

The last canon states that you should protect and advance the profession. Advocate for security in your surroundings, but also help build a positive image of security. Using your security powers for evil makes all cybersecurity experts look bad.

EXAM TIP: For any ISC2 exam, you should memorize and adhere to all code of ethics canons.

Once you become a member of ISC2, you must ensure you adhere to the code of ethics canons. A written complaint can be filed against (or by) you through an affidavit. The ISC2 ethics committee reviews these complaints and will make a recommendation to the organization's board. The board may then decide if they take disciplinary action against the accused. In the worst case, the board may decide you are no longer eligible to carry ISC2 certifications.

More information about the code of ethics and the complaints procedure can be found on the ISC2 website **https://isc2.org/ethics**.

How to certify

To certify for any ISC2 certification, you must first pass the related exam. On your exam day, you will receive the provisional outcome of your exam. Once the exam results have been confirmed, you will also receive an e-mail from ISC2.

If you passed, you should (if you still need to do so) create an account on **https://isc2.org**. The account is required to apply for your certification and can be used for various purposes, such as training, maintaining your certification, and communicating with the security community.

Once you have created your account, visit **https://isc2.org/endorsement** to start a certification application. It is important to note that you should apply within nine months of your exam date to be eligible. During the application, you must prove that you meet the certifying requirements. After that, you must find another ISC2-certified professional to endorse your application. If you do not know any ISC2-certified professionals who can attest to your experience, you may ask ISC2 to endorse you.

ISC2 will now process your application in the received order. This means you must wait for all other pending applications filed ahead of you. These applications may include other certifications than you are applying for.

ISC2 randomly audits applications and may ask you to provide further clarification, attestations, or other evidence to approve your application. Once you receive confirmation from ISC2 that your application has been approved, you must pay your **Annual**

Maintenance Fee (AMF). It is important to note that you only pay the AMF once yearly, regardless of the number of ISC2 certifications you have. So, if you already have ISC2 certifications and have paid your AMF, you may not be required to pay the AMF after approval of your application.

Certification requirements

At the time of writing, anybody wanting to certify as CCSP must have a minimum of five years of cumulative, full-time experience in IT. Three years of those five must be in information security, and one year must be in one or more of the six domains of the CCSP exam outline.

If you have a university degree (bachelor's or master's) in computer science, IT, or a related field, you can request a waiver of 1 year of experience. Similarly, you can do so if you hold a CSA CCSK certification. If you already are a CISSP, the experience requirement is met automatically.

If you do not have the required experience, you can become an associate of ISC2. An associate has six years to obtain the necessary five years of experience.

For details, please visit: **https://www.isc2.org/certifications/ccsp/ccsp-experience-requirements.**

Endorsement

As mentioned in the previous sections, to become a CCSP, you must get an endorsement from either ISC2 directly or from another ISC2-certified professional in good standing. An endorser must attest that your experience is correctly reflected in your application. To enter someone as an endorser, you must provide the endorser's ISC2 member number.

Evidence

As part of your application, you must provide evidence of your experience. Evidence is usually a statement from someone attesting to your experience (preferably a manager). However, it can also include copies of degrees and certifications. The more evidence you provide, the lower the chance auditors require more information to rule on your application if it is subjected to an audit.

Please adhere to the ISC2 code of ethics during your application and honestly represent your experience.

Maintaining certification

As with most professional certifications, your CCSP certifications require maintenance. If you meet the maintenance requirements, ISC2 does not need you to retake the exam.

Firstly, ISC2 requires you to pay your yearly AMF. Please do so to avoid revocation of your certification or may put you in poor standing with ISC2. Secondly, you must ensure you keep up to date with the developments in the industry.

ISC2 verifies your efforts by requiring you to submit **Continuing Professional Education (CPE)** credits. You must collect 90 CPEs through a three-year certification cycle. After three years, the counter resets, and you must gather more CPEs. Splitting your CPEs over the three-year cycle is advisable to balance the amount of CPE you must collect.

How CPEs can be collected is very extensive and specific. It is advisable to consult the ISC2 CPE handbook to determine how to earn CPEs and how they can be used to maintain your certification. Please find the link to the CPE handbook in the section further reading.

Local chapters

Once you join ISC2, you can also join a local chapter of ISC2 (it is available in your region). These local chapters have many opportunities to connect with other professionals, follow training, and earn CPEs. It is highly advisable to seek out your local chapter and become an active member.

At the time of writing, there are 150 chapters spanning 50 countries, with more than 38000 members worldwide. You can use **https://www.isc2.org/chapters** to find your local chapter.

Cloud community

Aside from joining the online ISC2 community and participating in your local chapter, you could benefit from joining other cloud communities. For example, the Cloud Security Alliance has an active and professional community. As a CCSP, it will be helpful for you to seek out others in the community.

Conclusion

The CCSP exam is the first step in the journey of a prospective CCSP. Following your exam, you must go through the certification application process, which includes evidence, endorsement, and stringent requirements. Ensure you provide solid evidence and identify an ISC2 professional in good standing who can endorse your application. Keep in mind that your application may be audited.

Once your application is approved, you must pay your AMF. As a CCSP or associate of ISC2, you must follow the ISC2 code of ethics canons. Please do so to ensure you get your certification. Aside from behaving ethically, you must maintain your certificate by paying your recurring AMF and submitting your required 90 CPEs for every three-year certification cycle. Please ensure you split the CPE workload over the three-year process to avoid situations where you may need more time to obtain all CPEs.

Once you become a CCSP or associate of ISC2, you should find your local ISC2 chapter and join it. Your local chapter will provide training, speaking engagements, learning opportunities, and CPE opportunities. Aside from your local branch, identify other cloud communities, such as the Cloud Security Alliance. Engaging with the security community will help you become a more well-rounded security professional.

In the next chapter, you will learn valuable tips and tricks to apply during your exam.

Learning goals

This chapter addresses the following CCSP exam outline learning goals:

ISC2 code of ethics

Further reading

1. CPE handbook - **https://www.isc2.org/-/media/Project/ISC2/Main/Media/documents/members/CPE-Handbook-2023.pdf?rev=3170b1b54f974a83a9570c5ef-6cf5061&hash=6101F8D84478D248172CE36FB44E17ED**

Join our book's Discord space

Join the book's Discord Workspace for Latest updates, Offers, Tech happenings around the world, New Release and Sessions with the Authors:

https://discord.bpbonline.com

CHAPTER 23
Exam Tips

Introduction

As you know, to become a CCSP, you must pass the ISC2 CCSP exam. Throughout the coming chapter, you will be informed about how the exam is conducted. You will also be provided with useful tips and tricks for the exam. How to prepare for the exam and interpret exam questions will help you be more effective at the exam.

Aside from details about the exam, we will also look at the scheduling process, the testing centers in which you must take the exam, and how you could schedule your exam.

Structure

This chapter covers the following topics:

- Exam scheduling
- Testing center
- Exam contents and requirements
- Question types
- Keywords
- Breaks

Objectives

After reading this chapter, you will know how to effectively prepare for the ISC2 CCSP exam. You will know how to schedule the exam and where the exam is conducted. At the same time, you will know how the exam is built up and how you should approach questions during the exam. This chapter will also allow you to identify essential keywords in exam questions to help you pick the correct answers.

Exam scheduling

The **Pearson Vue** company facilitates every ISC2 exam. Pearson Vue is an international (and esteemed) testing center provider. To register for any ISC2 exam, you must have an ISC2 account. So, if you already hold an ISC2 credential or have registered in the past, you should use your existing account with ISC2. If you do not have an account, you should go ahead and create one before starting the registration process.

Once you have created an account, visit **https://www.isc2.org/register-for-exam** to start the exam registration process. Use the **Register for Exam** button to begin the registration process, as shown:

After you've decided which ISC2 certification you're going to earn, it's time to register for your exam. The process is simple:

- Click on the Register for Exam button below.

- If you are already an ISC2 Member or ISC2 Candidate, you will be prompted to log in. If you do not already have an ISC2 account, you will need to create one.

- Complete the ISC2 Exam Account Information form.
  IMPORTANT: You must enter your information exactly as it appears on the identification (ID) you will present at the test center. If it is not an exact match, you will not be able to take your test and you will not be reimbursed for any fees paid.

- Once your form is submitted you will be redirected to the Pearson VUE website where you will be able to schedule your certification exam at a testing center most convenient for you.

Figure 23.1: Exam registration page

Once, you click this button, you will be prompted to sign in with your ISC2 credentials. After you authenticate, you will be asked to provide details like your contact information and address. Please ensure your information is correct. Using an incorrect address will result in your documents being delivered to the wrong address.

After you have completed your profile and verified your information, you may use the view exams button with the Pearson Vue portal to select the ISC2 exam you want to take.

Select the exam and pick one of the languages most suitable for you. The CCSP exam is offered in simplified Chinese, English, German, Japanese, Korean, and Modern Spanish.

Once you have selected your exam and language of choice, you will be asked to consent to various policies, including an NDA, Reschedule policy, cancellation policy, and an ISC2 admission policy.

After this, you must pick an exam location. Pearson Vue will suggest locations close to you. Please keep in mind that different testing centers have different test availability. Once you have selected a testing site and date/time, you will be asked to pay the exam fee. The fee for the CCSP exam is currently 550 EUR or 599 USD. Prices may vary in your locality. After paying your exam fee, the exam is confirmed.

Testing center

As mentioned, ISC2 exams are administered at Pearson Vue testing locations. There are some important factors to consider before leaving for the testing center.

- You must bring two valid forms of ID to the test location.

- You must also provide a palm vein scan (in some countries).

- You must provide your signature.

- You may not bring personal belongings into the testing area during the exam. You will have to store those in a locker provided by Pearson Vue.

- You must consent to a photograph being taken before the exam.

Once you enter the testing facility, you will be asked to sign the attendance form, have your photo taken, and provide any additional (biometric) information required in your region. After check-in, you will be provided a locker key and must store all personal belongings. At this point, you can still use the restroom before starting the exam.

Once you register a **Test Administrator** (**TA**) to start your exam, you may not take any personal belongings into the testing area. You must also respect the concentration of other test takers, so please be quiet.

Remember that the other candidates in your testing area may take different exams. The **Test Administrators** (**TAs**) also need to learn the contents of your exam. Instead, they are here to assist with testing infrastructure, such as your computer and testing software.

Once you enter the testing area, the TA will provide you with note-taking equipment, sign you into the testing computer, and start your exam. Please raise your hand if you have any questions about the testing software or the computer. Once you have completed the exam, please raise your hand as well. A TA will end your test and guide you out of the testing area.

At no point in time should you converse with any other test taker. Nor should you attempt to view other test taker's screens. Any of such actions may disqualify your exam attempt.

Exam contents and requirements

Now that you know the exam scheduling and the exam day process. Let us look at the CCSP exam. The CCSP exam consists of 150 multiple-choice questions. Of these 150 questions, 25 are trial questions. Meaning they do not influence your exam result. You will not be notified which questions are trail questions, so you should approach each as a real exam question.

At the time of writing, the CCSP exam is entirely linear. This means your exam will conclude after all 150 questions have been answered. During the exam, you cannot return to previously answered questions. This means that once you confirm your answer to a question, it is final and cannot be changed.

At the time of writing, the CCSP exam is four (4) hours long. This means you have 240 minutes to answer 150 questions. This means you have an average of 96 seconds per question. The speed with which you answer the questions does not influence your score.

It is important to note that the CCSP exam requires you to score 700 out of 1000 points. However, this measure should be seen as something other than a percentage. Different questions have varying values based on their difficulty. You must answer fewer questions correctly in an exam with many difficult questions to reach 700 points than in an exam with many lower-difficulty questions.

Each CCSP exam comprises different questions than the next, which means that even exams taken simultaneously feature different questions. Every exam is dynamically built out of the questions database, so each exam's passing grade is calculated differently.

As a rule of thumb, if you complete at least 85% of the questions in your practice exams correctly, you should be able to obtain a 700 score.

EXAM TIP: You will receive your exam results directly after completing the exam.

If you have passed the exam, you will receive a notice of provisionally passing the exam right after completing it. If you fail the exam, you will receive a notice showing your score per domain. That way, you can focus your study efforts on the domains you may not have mastered quite enough.

REAL-LIFE TIP: Do not be afraid to fail an exam. If you do not pass the first time, use the experience to prepare for your next attempt.

After you provisionally pass the exam, your exam by be subject to psychometric analysis or other audits. Once these are completed or waived, you will receive an e-mail from ISC2 confirming your exam result. For more details about the process after the exam, please review **https://www.isc2.org/exams/after-your-exam.**

Question types

As mentioned previously, the CCSP exam consists of only multiple-choice questions. You will not encounter questions that require you to formulate a complete answer. However, the CCSP exam does evaluate skills in addition to knowledge. Many exam questions may refer to a scenario or rely (to some extent) on the job experience in addition to domain knowledge.

The questions of the CCSP exam are randomly ordered and relate to the six domains of the CCSP exam outline. The random order means that you will encounter questions from each domain at random and not ordered by domain. Only some parts have the same number of questions. Each domain will contribute to the total possible score of the exam in the amounts shown:

Domains	Weight
1. Cloud Concepts, Architecture and Design	17%
2. Cloud Data Security	20%
3. Cloud Platform and Infrastructure Security	17%
4. Cloud Application Security	17%
5. Cloud Security Operations	16%
6. Legal, Risk and Compliance	13%
Total:	100%

Figure 23.2: ISC2 CCSP examination weights as shown in the CCSP exam outline 2022

Keywords

As mentioned, ISC2 tests your knowledge and your skills. The CCSP exam is not an exam that can be passed with memorization alone. ISC2 will include questions that test your ability to memorize important security concepts, but more often, it will evaluate your ability to apply the correct actions or principles.

For example, exam questions may be formulated like below:

Customer A deals with high fluctuations in website utilization. Which of the principles of cloud computing is most relevant to solving this problem:

- On-demand self-service
- Rapid elasticity

- Broad access

- Measured service

In the sample above, you have a question with an important keyword. The question asks about the most relevant principle, meaning there is more than one correct answer in the list. Throughout the exam, you will experience many questions with keywords like most, least, best, or worst. There may also be other keywords like governmental, compliance, cost-effective, and so on. Ensure you identify these keywords before answering a question, as they often help you identify the correct answer to a question.

Breaks

It may be helpful to note that ISC2 allows you to take breaks during your exam. If you need a break, raise your hand to inform the TA and wait for them to come over to you. Knowing that any breaks you take do not stop the exam time is essential. Meaning you will lose exam time by taking a break. During a break, you cannot leave the building or access any of your belongings.

Conclusion

The CCSP exam is an extensive exam that includes 150 questions and takes up to four (4) hours. You can schedule your exam through your ISC2 account at a Pearson Vue testing center. On your exam day, you should bring two valid identification documents, be prepared to be photographed, submit to a palm vein scan (for some locations), and supply your signature.

You will be asked multiple-choice questions in a linear format during the exam. If you need to know the answer, guess because you cannot return to previously answered questions. You can take breaks during the exam, but the break time will be deducted from your allotted exam time.

The exam questions are randomized for every test, but the number of points you can score per domain is aligned with the ISC2 exam outline. You will require a weighted score of 700/1000 points. Exams with more complex questions will need fewer total correct answers to pass than exams with more straightforward questions.

Once you have concluded your exam, you will be provided with the result by a TA immediately. If you have passed, you will receive a letter indicating you provisionally passed the exam. If you fail, you will receive an overview of your performance in each domain.

Good luck with your CCSP exam, and we hope to welcome you to the ISC2 and CCSP community soon.

CHAPTER 24
Exam Questions

Introduction

One vital part of preparing for the CCSP exam is practicing answering exam questions. The CCSP exam has a specific way of writing questions, which is essential to understand. The exams use a variety of keywords that can guide you to the correct answers.

It is important to note that every CCSP exam is unique, meaning this exam cannot be passed merely by memorizing questions and answers. Use these exam questions to test your knowledge and skills.

You will find practice exams and a self-assessment in this chapter. The answer keys for each are included at the end of the exam. Remember to aim for an 85% score to achieve a 700/1000 on the CCSP exam.

May the odds ever be in your favor!

Structure

This chapter covers the following topics:

- Quick self-assessment
- Self-assessment answer key

- Practice exam

- Practice exam answer key

Quick self-assessment

1. **What are the three aspects of data or systems that cybersecurity controls protect?**

    a. Confidentiality, integrity, and accessibility

    b. Integrity, availability, compliance

    c. Confidentiality, assurance, integrity

    d. None of the above

2. **Which method of expressing risks is easiest to understand for senior management?**

    a. Numerative

    b. Quantitative

    c. Qualitative

    d. Seniority

3. **What is the starting point for an organization to determine which systems should be protected and to what extent?**

    a. Risk management

    b. Pentest

    c. Vulnerability scanning

    d. Business impact analysis

4. **Which of the following is the most essential component in enabling single sign-on?**

    a. SAML

    b. OIDC

    c. Identity federation

    d. SOAP

5. **Which of the following is not a characteristic of cloud computing?**

    a. Broad access

    b. Strong security

    c. On-demand self-service

    d. Rapid elasticity

6. **What is the biggest threat to legal and regulatory compliance in a cloud environment?**

    a. Contradicting laws and regulations

    b. Limited security features

    c. Poor physical security

    d. Lack of auditability

7. **What is the difference between a network access control list (NACL) and a security group (SG)?**

    a. A NACL can conduct layer 7 inspection.

    b. An SG is configured to deny by default

    c. An SG can only be applied to subnets only

    d. All the above

8. **What is the best way to evaluate a cloud service provider's technical security controls effectiveness?**

    a. ISO 27001 audit

    b. SOC 2 type 2 report

    c. SOC 2 type 1 report

    d. SOC 3 report

9. **If your organization is likely to experience a fire in its datacenter every 2 years, and the fire would destroy 40% of the 5.000.000 USD datacenter, what is the annualized loss expectation of this risk?**

    a. USD

    b. 2.000.000 USD

    c. 10.000.000 USD

    d. 750.000 USD

10. **Which cloud service model has the highest level of responsibility for the cloud service consumer?**

    a. PaaS

    b. SaaS

    c. XaaS

    d. IaaS

11. **What is the difference between hashing and encryption?**

    a. Encryption is more secure than hashing

    b. Hashing is more secure than encryption

    c. Hashing is not reversible

    d. Hashing requires smaller key lengths than encryption

12. **Which type of data is best suited to be stored in a relational database?**

    a. Structured data

    b. Unstructured data

    c. Semi-structured data

    d. Information

13. **An organization is working on its disaster recovery plan. They determine which type of failover would be best as part of their plan. The company has a Maximum Tolerable Downtime of one day. Which failover model is best for this organization:**

    a. Cold site

    b. Shared site

    c. Hot site

    d. Warm site

14. **Your organization has decided to implement a threat modeling program. Which is not a threat modeling approach?**

    a. STRIDE

    b. PASTA

    c. OWASP

    d. All the above

15. **Your organization has employees who work from all over the world. Since your company heavily relies on cloud-based services your organization is looking for a way to secure access to your cloud services uniformly. What is the best approach to secure cloud access?**

    a. MFA

    b. SSO

    c. CASB

    d. VPN

16. Your organization wants to enable full-disk encryption for your laptops and phones. Where should the key material used to encrypt/decrypt the storage device ideally be stored?

    a. HSM

    b. SSD

    c. HDD

    d. TPM

17. Your organization is being attacked using ransomware. The attackers were able to exfiltrate important company data. The organization wants to identify the attackers and attempt to undertake legal steps. What is essential for forensic data collection?

    a. Retrieving data using a write-blocker

    b. Evidence management

    c. Chain of custody

    d. All of the above

18. An organization deploys applications to its Cloud environment. Unfortunately, many releases result in service disruptions because dependencies between services are overlooked. What process needs to be improved within the organization?

    a. Agile development

    b. Change management

    c. Penetration testing

    d. Secure software development life cycle

19. Your organization has a mature security program and a well-trained staff. Recently, your organization has been facing attacks from an unknown actor using a new kind of malware. What could your organization do to get more insight into the attacker?

    a. Deploy a honeypot

    b. Add a new firewall

    c. Implement **Security Orchestration and Automated Response (SOAR)**

    d. Conduct a **Business Impact Analysis (BIA)**

20. **Your organization is picking a new cloud service provider. In the past, your organization has been fined because one of your suppliers handled your data non-compliantly. What should your organization include in its contract with the new supplier to monitor compliance?**

   a. SLAs

   b. PHI

   c. PII

   d. Right to audit

Self-assessment answer key

1. D. The three components of the CIA-triad are Confidentiality, Integrity, and Availability

2. B. Quantitative risk measurement can be used to express risks in terms of costs. Costs are easily understood by senior management. Qualitative measurement often needs to be more specific. Numerative and seniority are ways to express risks.

3. D. A Business Impact Analysis (BIA) determines which processes, systems, and applications are crucial to an organization's operations. The criticality of a process, system, application, or data determines how much a system should be protected.

4. C. Identity federation centrally stores identities and makes them available to various systems and applications. SAML and OIDC are protocols for connecting systems and applications to an identity provider. SOAP is a communication protocol for web services.

5. B. Strong security is not a characteristic of Cloud computing. However, strong security can be achieved in Cloud environments. Broad access, on-demand self-service, and rapid elasticity are all characteristics of Cloud computing.

6. A. In a Cloud environment, your organization can easily be exposed to contradicting laws and regulations. In some cases, complying with the laws and regulations in one jurisdiction automatically makes you not compliant in another. The Cloud has extensive security features for physical security, and auditability can be achieved through well-defined contracts.

7. B. A SG is configured to deny all traffic by default, while a NACL allows all traffic by default. A NACL does not conduct layer seven inspection; it functions as a stateless firewall. SGs can be applied to a subnet and even network interfaces.

8. B. A SOC 2 TYPE 2 audit report evaluates the effectiveness of security controls over time. The SOC 3 report is a summary of other SOC reports that contain

limited data. SOC 1 reports only pertain to financial applications and systems. ISO 27001 audits pertain to the ISMS of an organization.

9. A. Annualized Loss Expectancy is calculated by multiplying the Annualized Rate of Occurrence with the Single Loss Expectancy. The Single Loss expectancy is calculated by multiplying the asset value (5.000.000 USD) with the exposure factor (0.40) = 2.000.000. The Annualized rate of occurrence is calculated by dividing one by the period in years in which the risk is likely to occur = ½. SLE * ARO = 2.000.000 USD * 0.5 = 1.000.000 USD.

10. D. IaaS or Infrastructure as a Service requires the CSC to take on the most responsibility. PaaS puts more responsibility on the service provider than IaaS, and SaaS puts more responsibility on the service provider than PaaS. XaaS is not an official service model.

11. A. Encryption is reversible, while hashing is not. Encryption and hashing are not more or less secure than each other; they are used for different purposes. Hashing does not use encryption keys.

12. B. Structured data is best stored in relational databases as it allows it to be queried. Semi-structured data is better stored in non-relational databases, while unstructured data is most suitable for object or file storage.

13. C. A hot site failover is the only model that could prevent an MTD of two days from being exceeded. Warm, cold, and shared sites would take too long to become operational.

14. C. The open worldwide application security project is a non-profit foundation that works on improving security for software applications. PASTA and STRIDE are threat modeling approaches.

15. C. A **cloud access security broker (CASB)** can secure access to multiple cloud service provider platforms regardless of the user's origin. MFA and SSO are important controls that can be applied through a CASB. A VPN can be used to regulate cloud access better but would require other security measures and relies on tunneling traffic through a (cloud) data center.

16. D. A **Trusted Platform Module (TPM)** can securely store certificates and key material on a local device. Storing this data in an HSM would make it possible to encrypt/decrypt the device with access to the HSM. Storing encryption keys on an HDD or SSD is an insecure approach that can sometimes prevent users from accessing their devices.

17. D. To be admissible you must manage evidence properly and maintain a chain of custody. Using write-blockers during forensics is essential to maintain the integrity of evidence.

18. B. During change management, you must investigate what other systems and applications your change may affect. Because the deployments disrupt other applications (unexpectedly) the company needs to conduct proper change management practices.

19. Your organization should deploy a honeypot. The team is well-trained, and the security program is mature. A honeypot can provide valuable information about the attackers, allowing your organization to analyze how the new malware works. Deploying a new firewall will not provide new information as the malware still needs to be discovered. SOAR is used to automate security response, while a BIA does not make sense in this context.

20. D. The right to audit allows your organization to evaluate your supplier's compliance with applicable laws and regulations. While SLAs can help define targets for the vendor to meet, they are only sufficient with the ability to audit. PII and PHI are types of data.

Practice exam

1. **Which party is not involved role in the cloud reference architecture?**

    a. Cloud service provider

    b. Cloud service consumer

    c. Cloud service broker

    d. Cloud service market

2. **An organization chooses to migrate its environment to a cloud service provider. Which cloud characteristic has an essential impact on security in a public cloud environment?**

    a. Multi-tenancy

    b. Rapid elasticity

    c. Measured service

    d. Scalability

3. **SkyNet is a defense contracting company. It handles highly classified governmental data, specifically military data. Which type of cloud is most secure for SkyNet?**

    a. Public cloud

    b. Hybrid cloud

    c. Private cloud

    d. Community cloud

4. **Broad access is an essential characteristic of cloud computing. What is the most important to limit the security impact of broad access?**

   a. Access control

   b. Firewalls

   c. IDS/IPS

   d. SSO

5. **Your organization has moved its on-premises virtual desktop environment to the cloud. Due to limited time and capacity, your organization cannot perform major work on your environment after moving it to the cloud. Which service model would fit the organization best:**

   a. Lift and shift the setting to IaaS

   b. Refactor the environment to PaaS

   c. Migrate to a SaaS tool

   d. None of the above

6. **Your organization uses an IaaS platform to run its hypervisor platform. Which party is responsible for the security of the hypervisors in use?**

   a. The CSP

   b. The CSC

   c. Both the CSP and CSC.

   d. Neither

7. **A University has a cloud environment that is shared with other universities. The universities also allow each other to use their on-premises supercomputers for scientific calculations. The on-premises environments are connected to the cloud environment using a VPN. Which combination of cloud deployment models is used by the university?**

   a. Private multi-cloud

   b. Hybrid community cloud

   c. Hybrid community multi-cloud

   d. Community multi-cloud

8. **The well-architected framework provides readers with:**

   a. Security best practices

   b. Ways to operate their cloud environment cost-effectively

   c. Architectures to achieve scalability

   d. All of the above

9. **You are likely to share data with another party whenever you use cloud services. The ability to take this data and move it to another provider is called?**

   a. Data portability

   b. Data moveability

   c. Data Interoperability

   d. Vendor move-out

10. **Which cloud service model has the highest level of responsibility for the cloud service provider?**

    a. IaaS

    b. SaaS

    c. PaaS

    d. XDR

11. **What could an organization gain from leveraging Cloud design patterns?**

    a. Save costs

    b. Better security

    c. Scalability

    d. All of the above

12. **The FIPS 140-2/140-3 provides requirements for hardware security modules and Trusted Platform Modules. To which companies do the FIPS 140-2/140-3 apply?**

    a. European governments

    b. Multinationals

    c. Non-profit organization

    d. None of the above

13. **Who regulates the Payment Card Industry – Data Security Standard (PCI-DDS)?**

    a. US Federal government

    b. The industry itself

    c. The EU

    d. Data protection agency

14. An organization is working on securing the virtual machines in the cloud. What is the most important operating system security control they should implement?

    a. NIPS

    b. Security baselines

    c. Anti-virus

    d. NIDS

15. An organization has calculated that implementing a security control to protect company laptops costs 1.500.000. The annualized loss expectancy is 100.000. Is the control implementation likely to result in a positive return on investment (ROI)?

    a. Yes, if the laptops last more than 15 years

    b. Yes, if the laptops last more than three years

    c. No

    d. Yes, the ROI is always positive

16. What are the stages of the cloud data life cycle?

    a. create, store, use, share, archive, destroy

    b. share, update, archive, destroy

    c. destroy, sell, create, use, archive,

    d. create, store, use, share, archive, sell

17. An organization is attempting to create insight in the ways data traverses its environment. Which of the options below provides this inside?

    a. BIA

    b. EA

    c. DFD

    d. XDR

18. A data center is confronted with a sudden power outage. Unfortunately, the data center's backup power did not kick on in time, and one of the Uninterruptible Power Supplies (UPS) also failed. Which storage type is likely erased?

    a. Tape storage

    b. Ephemeral storage

    c. HDD storage

    d. SSD storage

19. An organization has recently migrated to the cloud. It now stores data in its on-premises environment and at the cloud provider. In the cloud the data is distributed over multiple availability zones. What is this concept called?

    a. Data flow

    b. Data redundancy

    c. Data dispersion

    d. Data backup

20. An organization must discard Solid State Drives (SSDs) from its data center. Which is not a valid way to erase the data on the drives?

    a. Cryptographic erasure

    b. Degaussing

    c. Shredding

    d. Melting

21. Your organization needs fast write speeds for your virtual machines. But you also store archived data. What storage solution would be the best combination of cost and speed for the archived data?

    a. HDDs

    b. SSDs

    c. NVMe SSDs

    d. Tape

22. You are trying to send an e-mail to a customer. It is essential that the customer can verify you sent the e-mail and that no one can read the contents of the e-mail other than the recipient. Which type of encryption should you apply?

    a. Encrypt the message with the recipient's public and your private key

    b. Encrypt with the recipient's public key

    c. Encrypt with your public key

    d. Encrypt the message with the recipient's private key and your public key

23. An organization uses symmetrical encryption to allow employees to send messages to each other using a SaaS messaging tool. How many keys do you need to create if you want 50 employees to communicate with every other employee using symmetrical encryption?

    a. 1500

    b. 1125

    c. 50

    d. 100

24. An organization stores user information in its PaaS database. As part of this information, the organization stores user passwords. What should the organization do to store the password securely?

    a. Hiding + tokenization

    b. Hashing + salting

    c. Encryption + salting

    d. Hashing + encryption

25. An organization uses many different storage solutions. Recently, it has been noticed that employees accidentally send classified information outside of the organization through e-mails. The organization fears it may be fined if the data is in the wrong hands. What will help the organization prevent information leaking through e-mail?

    a. DLP

    b. Anti-virus

    c. IDS

    d. IPS

26. An organization collects IP addresses as part of its analytics process. The GDPR regulates the organization and wants to determine how it can easily reduce the privacy impact on its users. What should the company do?

    a. Tokenize IP addresses

    b. Encrypt IP addresses

    c. Delete all IP addresses

    d. Ask for user permission

27. An organization has created a data classification policy and determined how it should be protected. What should the organization do next to secure its data?

    a. Apply encryption

    b. Train employees

    c. Data labeling

    d. Archive data

28. An organization has a SaaS application stores user information in a PaaS database. The database is non-relational and has at-rest encryption. What type of data is likely stored in this database?

a. Structured data

b. Unstructured data

c. Confidential data

d. Semi-structured data

29. **A video streaming service wants to protect its copyrighted material from downloading illegally. What is the practice of protecting digital intellectual property called?**

a. Digital rights management

b. Copyright management

c. Trademark management

d. Digital information management

30. **A large webshop has been informed a legal hold has been placed on their order history. Can existing customers still change their orders?**

a. No, the order history must be preserved

b. Yes, legal holds do not apply to order data

c. Yes, legal holds only applies to data created after the hold

d. Yes, legal holds do not affect webshops

31. **Whenever your organization stores certificates on key material in the Cloud, which appliance allows you to store this information securely?**

a. HSM

b. TPM

c. Database

d. SSD

32. **Whenever an organization decides to collect data, it should create policies for:**

a. Data deletion

b. Data archival

c. Data retention

d. All of the above

33. **What is the most critical security concept to prevent customers from being able to access each other's data in a public cloud environment?**

    a. Access control

    b. Environment separation

    c. Tenant partitioning

    d. Authorization

34. **An organization provides cloud services to a variety of customers. Recently, they have purchased new type-1 hypervisors to virtualize customer environments. Who is responsible for securing the hardware used to virtualize these environments?**

    a. The CSP

    b. The CSC

    c. CSP and CSC

    d. Cloud auditor

35. **An organization is choosing a location to build two new data centers. Which factors should the organization not consider?**

    a. Distance between data centers

    b. Availability of multiple power providers

    c. Political environment

    d. All the above

36. **Which physical access control is most suitable for preventing tailgating a high security data center?**

    a. Turn stile

    b. Security guard

    c. Man trap

    d. Intrusion detector

37. **A CSP is experiencing a heatwave, and the air conditioning in the data center can no longer cool the data center sufficiently. The air in the data center has become hot and dry. What is the biggest threat to the CSP's servers?**

    a. Moisture

    b. Static electricity

    c. Fire

    d. Theft

38. **A CSP is experiencing issues with power interruptions. What is the most effective measure the CSP can take to limit the impact of the interruptions?**

    a. Contract a second power company

    b. Install UPSes

    c. Install back-up generators

    d. Turn-off servers

39. **Which of the following is not a risk treatment option?**

    a. Risk termination

    b. Risk avoidance

    c. Risk mitigation

    d. Risk transference

40. **An organization has decided that it does not have enough internal capacity to secure its web servers properly. As a result, the organization has decided to host their website on a PaaS solution at a CSP. What type of risk treatment is this example?**

    a. Risk mitigation

    b. Risk avoidance

    c. Risk transference

    d. Risk acceptance

41. **Which of the following are essential building blocks of a cloud environment?**

    a. Storage

    b. RAM

    c. Processors

    d. All the above

42. **A company uses a SaaS application as part of its critical business processes. If the SaaS application goes down it may not be able to continue its operations. How would you express this risk?**

    a. Risk = likelihood * impact

    b. Risk = vulnerability * threat

    c. Risk = threat * impact

    d. Risk = vulnerability * impact

43. An organization has posted warning signs, spotlights, and security guards. Which property do these controls have in common?

    a. They prevent

    b. They correct

    c. They deter

    d. They detect

44. The amount of data lost after an incident or disaster is expressed as.

    a. MTD

    b. RTO

    c. RPO

    d. Downtime

45. Which form of BC/DR testing is the most suitable for an organization that cannot afford the impact of BC/DR testing?

    a. Full simulation test

    b. Failover test

    c. Tabletop exercise

    d. Pentest

46. Which of the following provides information about vulnerabilities in web applications only?

    a. OWASP Top 10

    b. CVE

    c. SANS Top 25

    d. CVSS

47. Which of the following are good ways to ensure secure software development?

    a. Code review

    b. Code signing

    c. Static code analysis

    d. All the above

48. An organization operates in a new and evolving market. It is essential that the organization can quickly release software and pivot their priorities. Which development methodology is not suitable for the company?

    a. Agile

    b. Waterfall

    c. KANBAN

    d. SCRUM

49. An organization is implementing a secure software development lifecycle. At which stage of the lifecycle should the company start its security efforts?

    a. Design

    b. Requirements

    c. Testing

    d. Maintenance

50. A company is working on threat modeling a software application. It has already identified threats related to tampering, information disclosure, elevation of privilege, and repudiation. Which attack types should the organization investigate if it models threats using the STRIDE methodology:

    a. Smurfing and data disclosure

    b. Spoofing and data destruction

    c. Sniffing and denial of service

    d. Spoofing and denial of service

51. A hacker can steal the session token of an administrator. The session token is used to access the cloud portal to conduct malicious activity. What type of attack is this?

    a. Spoofing

    b. Repudiation

    c. Denial of service

    d. Elevation of privilege

52. A software development team includes various testing forms within their software development lifecycle. The engineers have written code to test the functionality of specific software functions. What is this type of testing called?

    a. Penetration testing

    b. Integration testing

    c. Unit testing

    d. Functional testing

53. An organization is trying to increase the security of its private Cloud environment. It already uses vulnerability scanning and code review. Which additional test would provide the most extensive information to the organization?

    a. White box testing

    b. Gray box testing

    c. Black box testing

    d. None of the above

54. An organization has a set of old APIs running in their on-premises environment. To integrate with other organizations, they must create REST APIs to make their services accessible to their partners. Which Cloud technology could be used to satisfy this requirement?

    a. Load balancing

    b. API management

    c. **Cloud access security broker (CASB)**

    d. Firewalling

55. Which form of security testing includes testing a running application?

    a. **Static Application Security Testing (SAST)**

    b. **Dynamic Application Security Testing (DAST)**

    c. Unit testing

    d. Code review

56. The process of adding a signature to code as part of the code commit process is called:

    a. Code verification

    b. Code validation

    c. Code signing

    d. Code signatures

57. An organization is looking to use open-source software in their environment. Because everyone can read open-source software, can any organization use it safely?

    a. Yes, open-source software can be protected better because the code is public

    b. No, open-source software is always unsafe because hackers can read the code

c. Yes, open-source software uses a community to develop, meaning open-source code is developed securely.

d. No, open-source software should be verified for security like any other software.

58. **An organization has a cloud environment with several different web applications. The organization wants to protect its applications against attacks like SQLi and XSS. Which security measure would be best suited for the job?**

a. Stateful firewall

b. Stateless firewall

c. Web application firewall

d. Network access control list

59. **An organization uses a variety of SaaS applications. Employees have been complaining that they must log in to each application with a different username and password. Which technologies are needed to address this issue?**

a. SAML and OIDC

b. SAML and SSO

c. Federation and SSO

d. IdP and AD

60. **Multi-factor authentication increases security by requiring a user to authenticate using multiple factors or methods. Which of the following is different from the factors that you can use?**

a. Something you are

b. Something you have

c. Something you know

d. None of the above

61. **A user must provide a password and PIN code when logging into a corporate application. Does MFA protect the application?**

a. No, MFA requires three factors,

b. No, MFA requires multiple factors that are not the same

c. Yes, two different factors have been provided

d. No, MFA requires using a password and an SMS

62. An organization has a database that contains valuable corporate information. The organization fears it cannot track who accesses or uses the database. What measure should the organization implement?

    a. Encryption

    b. IDS

    c. IPS

    d. DAM

63. A SOC employee was able to isolate a malware executable. She wants to investigate how the malware behaves. What should she do to test the malware securely?

    a. Sandboxing

    b. Jailbreaking

    c. Hyper scaling

    d. Isolating

64. An organization develops infrastructure as code, during the development process the developers add passwords to the code. What would be the best place to store these passwords?

    a. Password vault

    b. Text file

    c. Code repository

    d. Secrets manager

65. A security company builds hardware security modules. The HSM the company builds is resistant to tampering and erases data once tampering is detected. Which level of the FIPS 140-2 is the HSM likely to be built for?

    a. Level Two

    b. Level Three

    c. Level Four

    d. Level One

66. An organization is trying to virtualize some of its workloads. Currently, it has type-1 and type-2 hypervisors. The company has asked you for advice on the most secure and cost-effective solution for virtualization. What hypervisor is the least secure?

a. VMWare

b. Type 2 hypervisor

c. Type 1 hypervisor

d. Virtual box

67. **Your organization is a cloud service provider, and you are working on implementing security controls for your virtualization services. What attack allows an attacker to attack the hypervisor from the virtual machine?**

a. Side-channel attack

b. VM escape

c. Hyperjacking

d. VM injection

68. **What is the third layer of the OSI model?**

a. Data link

b. Transport

c. Application

d. Network

69. **An organization wants to ensure its cloud services remain available even when the CSP's data center goes offline. How can the organization achieve this in the most manageable and cost-effective way?**

a. Replicate services across availability zones

b. Replicate services across regions

c. Replicate data within an availability zone

d. Replicate data to an on-premises data center.

70. **An organization has a vNet in the cloud environment. The vNet contains applications and services that need to be available to users. What is the most secure way to allow users to access them?**

a. Open the vNet to direct internet access

b. Use a bastion host

c. Implement a firewall

d. Use a VPN

71. **To achieve a zero-trust architecture, security controls should be focused on?**

    a. Endpoints

    b. Networks

    c. Laptops

    d. Applications

72. **A serverless application must connect to an external service. The serverless application attempts to connect to the external service using it's domain name. However, the application seems to connect to the wrong application. What attack could be taking place?**

    a. Denial of service

    b. IP spoofing

    c. MAC Spoofing

    d. DNS Spoofing

73. **An organization wants to implement security baselines. They have asked to advice on how they should create these baselines. What is the most secure method you can suggest?**

    a. Use industry baselines like CIS benchmarks

    b. Use customer baselines based on the organization

    c. Develop a brand new baseline

    d. None of the above

74. **Your organization is experiencing a huge uptick in traffic to one of your IaaS systems. Which of the following would be an effective measure to prevent denial of service?**

    a. Vertical scaling

    b. Horizontal scaling

    c. Rate limiting

    d. All the above

75. **Your organization is looking to deploy new applications and infrastructure to the cloud. It is essential to your organization that deployments are frequent and secure. Deployments should not cause downtime. Which technology has the most significant impact on limiting downtime during deployments?**

    a. Blue-green deployments

    b. Continuous integration/ continuous deployment

    c. Infrastructure as code

    d. Agile

76. A virtual machine in your vNet is reporting high CPU utilization. The VM runs applications that cannot easily be replicated across other VMs. What is the best way to scale the VM?

    a. Horizontal scaling

    b. Vertical scaling

    c. Automatic scaling

    d. Diagonal scaling

77. Your organization runs various IaaS, PaaS, and SaaS applications in the cloud. The applications all generate logs that your organization monitors. What tool/system could help your organization automatically identify security incidents across these services?

    a. SIEM

    b. SOAR

    c. SOC

    d. None of the above

78. You work for a small organization with 50 employees. The organization has recently been hacked. An external agency has advised the creation of a Security Operations Center. Your manager has asked you for advice on how to set one up. What would be the most suitable approach?

    a. Hire and train security analysts and man a SOC during work hours

    b. Hira and train security analysts and man a SOC 24/7

    c. Contract an external agency to run a SOC during work hours

    d. Contract an external agency to run a SOC 24/7

79. An organization is looking to build a set of processes to manage changes, continuity, problems, and other important processes. What standard or framework can help the organization?

    a. ISO 27001

    b. ISO 27701

    c. ITIL

    d. Well-architected framework

80. An organization has been hacked. They have contracted you to investigate what data the attackers may have breached. Which of the following is essential to retain the integrity of evidence?

a. Turn off all computer

b. Disconnect all computers from their networks

c. Use a write-blocker to read storage devices

d. All the above

81. **Your organization has been attacked. You have been notified by the attacker that data has been breached and is now in their possession. Which parties should you include in your communication plans?**

   a. Regulators

   b. Customers

   c. Vendors

   d. All the above

82. **You work for a cyber forensics organization. They have asked you to conduct live forensics on a server. When you arrive at the customer, the machine if powered off. What kind of forensics can you perform?**

   a. Static forensics

   b. Live forensics

   c. Offline forensics

   d. None of the above

83. **The process of automatically responding to cyber incidents is called?**

   a. DLP

   b. SIEM

   c. AI/ML

   d. SOAR

84. **What are the steps for incident response according to NIST?**

   a. Detect, containment & eradication, destroy, and post-incident activity

   b. Preparation, detection & analysis, containment & eradication & recovery, and post-incident activity.

   c. Preparation, containment, analysis, eradication & recovery, and post-incident activity

   d. None of the above

85. An organization operates in both the EU and the US. They store data about EU citizens and transfer that data to the US. How can the organization ensure their data transfers comply with the GDPR?

    a. Adhering to the EU-US privacy shield

    b. Adhering to the EU-US data privacy framework

    c. Adhering to safe harbor

    d. Adhering to HIPAA

86. Your organization operates in the United States. Which federal data privacy laws must your organization adhere to?

    a. GLBA

    b. US PATRIOT ACT

    c. HITECH ACT

    d. None of the above

87. Which of the following data object is not PII?

    a. IP address

    b. First and last name

    c. Job title

    d. Home address

88. Which of the following is not part of the generally accepted privacy principles?

    a. Disclosure to third parties

    b. Choice and consent

    c. Monitoring and enforcement

    d. Unlimited access

89. An organization must undergo an audit to prove compliance to a local law. Your manager has asked to advise her on the best audit type. Your company has a CSP that has agreed to the right to audit.

    a. Internal audit

    b. External audit

    c. Penetration test

    d. Vulnerability scan

90. Your organization is trying to find an easy way to secure your cloud environment. Your environment is a multi-cloud that uses many cloud native technologies. What information/standard/list can your organization use to identify comprehensive controls to apply across your environment?

    a. CSA CCM

    b. CSA STAR

    c. ISO 27001

    d. ISO 27701

91. Your organization has created a new corporate strategy. As part of the strategy, your organization is looking to improve its security. Your manager has asked you to determine a roadmap to reach the desired improvement. What do you do next?

    a. Perform a Business Impact Analysis

    b. Perform a gap analysis

    c. Perform a differential investigation

    d. Perform a penetration test

92. You work for a SaaS provider that builds patient portals for hospitals outside of the US. Which of the following regulations apply to your organization?

    a. HIPAA

    b. SOX

    c. HITECH

    d. None of the above

93. Your organization has a contract with a cloud service provider. The contract outlines the level of service you can expect from the CSP. What is the term used to describe these levels?

    a. KPI

    b. SOW

    c. SLA

    d. MSA

94. Which of the following is a measure that indicates key risks within an organization?

    a. KPI

    b. KRI

    c. OLA

    d. SLA

95. The process of standardization laws across various jurisdictions is called?

    a. Equal law

    b. Law standardization

    c. Harmonization of law

    d. Safe harbor agreements

96. An organization has decided to purchase a SaaS system. It has transferred employee information to the system. Which role does the CSP have with regards to data?

    a. Data owner

    b. Data controller

    c. Data processor

    d. Data subject

97. Your organization is rolling out a new tool to collect data about customers. The data will be used to make automated decisions about providing loans. What is your organization required to do by the GDPR?

    a. Stop collecting data

    b. Conduct a BIA

    c. Conduct a (D)PIA

    d. Conduct a pentest

98. A customer asks a cloud service provider if they can provide access to the log files on their underlying infrastructure. Why is the CSP unlikely to comply?

    a. Hardware log files may contain data about other customers

    b. CSPs never comply with audits

    c. The CSP does not have logs for its infrastructure

    d. The CSP only shares logs with larger customers

99. An organization is in the process of determining which risk profile is suitable for it. What do you call the amount of risk a company is willing to take?

    a. Risk rule

    b. Risk appetite

    c. Risk allowance

    d. Risk score

100. **Recently, you have started working for an organization that handles top-secret government data. The company wants to benefit from cloud computing. What type of cloud would you recommend they use?**

 a. Multi-cloud

 b. Private cloud

 c. Public cloud

 d. None of the above

101. **Which of the following is not part of the ISC2 code of ethics?**

 a. Act honorably, honestly, justly, responsibly, and legally

 b. Provide cheap and competent service to principals

 c. Advance and protect the profession

 d. Protection society, the common good, necessary public trust and confidence, and the infrastructure

102. **What is an example of a cloud service broker?**

 a. A company that auctions servers

 b. A company that offers help with purchasing and configuring cloud services

 c. A cloud auditor

 d. A cloud service provider

103. **An organization manufactures leather car seats. Which threat actor is least likely to threaten that organization?**

 a. Criminal organizations

 b. Hacktivists

 c. State actors

 d. Script kiddies

104. **Your organization has stored data in the cloud and is concerned with data remanence. How should it destroy data in the cloud?**

 a. Overwriting

 b. Degaussing

 c. Melting

 d. Cryptographic erasure

105. **Which of the following is not an important factor to consider when choosing a CSP?**

    a. Interoperability

    b. Portability

    c. Privacy

    d. Operating system

106. **Your organization has started collecting data as part of their cloud data life cycle. What is the next step in the lifecycle?**

    a. Store

    b. Process

    c. Archive

    d. Unknown, not every life cycle contains every step

107. **A CSP has developed procedures to erase storage devices. It has contracted an organization to perform the data destruction on its behalf. What should the CSP require?**

    a. Certificate of destruction

    b. For the destroyed device to be returned

    c. A video of the destruction process

    d. A destruction test report

108. **An organization uses a variety of SaaS applications and an e-mail server to communicate internally. The organization wants to ensure that it can prevent credit card numbers from being sent by e-mail to external agencies. What tooling should the company implement?**

    a. IDS

    b. DLP

    c. IPS

    d. Encryption

109. **An organization wants to build a data protection program for their cloud environment. What is the first step it should take?**

    a. Label data

    b. Map data

    c. Classify data

    d. Collect data

110. An organization has established a special method for producing microchips. The company is highly concerned that other organizations may steal its ideas. What should the company do to protect their method without disclosing it?

    a. Treat it like a trade secret

    b. Register a trademark

    c. Register a copyright

    d. Register a patent

111. An organization has built a datacenter, as part of the physicals security of the datacenter it should take which of the following actions?

    a. Build 30ft fences

    b. Place no windows on the ground floor

    c. Hire mercenaries to protect the compound

    d. Place guard dogs around the DC

112. Your organization has discovered that it runs vulnerable software in its IaaS environment. Your manager has asked you to perform a risk assessment. Which factors should you consider to calculate the risk?

    a. Impact and criticality

    b. Criticality and probability

    c. Probability and impact

    d. Impact and threat

113. Your organization needs help with the availability of one of your applications. As a solution, your company has scaled the application horizontally. What should your organization implement to benefit from horizontal scaling?

    a. Reverse proxy

    b. Forward proxy

    c. Firewall

    d. Load balancing

114. Your organization has created a virtual network where many of its cloud services are placed. Your organization needs to connect this virtual network to its on-premises network. Which of the following are valid ways to do so?

    a. Use a direct connection

    b. Use a VPN

    c. Only B

    d. Both A & B

115. Your organization has implemented a Network-based Incident Detection System (NIDS). Which of the following limits the detection capabilities of this tool?

    a. Encryption

    b. Processor speed

    c. Storage size

    d. Data obfuscation

116. Your organization needs to be able to release software frequently. Due to security concerns, the company wants to limit developers' access to the production environment. What should your company implement?

    a. High availability

    b. CI/CD

    c. Agile

    d. Security testing

117. What is the name of the process that aims to determine software vulnerabilities by analyzing the way it is build?

    a. Vulnerability scanning

    b. Penetration testing

    c. SCA

    d. IAST

118. Which of the following is an architecture often used for JSON communication between web applications?

    a. REST

    b. SOAP

    c. APIM

    d. XML

119. Your organization is setting up a connection between various service providers using web-based APIs. What should your organization implement to ensure data confidentiality during transit?

    a. TLS 1.2 or higher

    b. SSL 3.0 or higher

    c. AES128

    d. SHA3

120. **A foreign non-profit organization operates within the US. Does Sarbanes Oxley regulate it?**

   a. Yes, it is a foreign company

   b. Yes, it wholly-owned

   c. No, it is not a US company

   d. No, it is not publicly traded

Practice exam answer key

1. D. Cloud Service Market is not an actor in the Cloud reference architecture.

2. A. Multi-tenancy means that multiple customers share a single environment. Logical isolation is essential to separate these environments and ensure the environments and their data remain confidential.

3. C. A private cloud environment is dedicated to an organization. Meaning it does not share its infrastructure with other tenants. Hence, private clouds can offer better security than other forms of cloud computing, especially when the private cloud environment implements organization-specific controls.

4. A. Broad access means your cloud environment can be accessed from virtually anywhere. It is essential to implement access control (in various ways) to ensure that only authenticated users can access your environment. Firewalls, IDS/IPS, and SSO can all play a role in your access control program.

5. A. Lift and shift to IaaS allows your organization to move your current environment to the cloud with the least changes needed.

6. C. The CSP is responsible for securing the hypervisor for the IaaS environment, and the CSC is responsible for the hypervisor's security inside the virtual environment.

7. B. The university has an environment comprising on-premises computing connected to the cloud and a shared public cloud, making the deployment model a hybrid community cloud.

8. D. The AWS well-architected framework consists of six pillars: security, cost optimization, and performance efficiency.

9. A. Data portability is the ability of an organization to move its data to another provider. Data interoperability is exchanging data with other applications and systems in a standard format. Vendor move-out and data moveability are made-up terms.

10. B. The SaaS service model has the highest responsibility for the CSP. XDR is not a cloud service model.

11. D. All the mentioned factors are benefits of using cloud design patterns, as these patterns are optimized designs that help organizations become scalable and secure while saving costs.

12. D. The FIPS applies to US governmental organizations and subcontractors.

13. B. PCI-DSS is an example of an automated standard. Companies within the payment card industry itself conduct enforcement.

14. C. Implementing security baselines is the most important security control you can implement for OS security. It creates a good starting point to implement additional security controls like patching and anti-virus.

15. A. The ALE is 100.000, meaning it would take 15 years of losses to equal the security control investment. Based on the ALE, the control would only provide a positive ROI if the laptops lasted more than 15 years.

16. A. The cloud data lifecycle consists of creating, storing, using, sharing, archiving, and destroying data.

17. C. A data flow diagram provides insight into how data traverses an environment or application. An enterprise architecture pertains to much more than data flows and does not offer the necessary detail. XDR and BIA are not the right tools for the job.

18. B. Ephemeral storage is erased once power is taken from the storage device. A common example of ephemeral storage is **random access memory (RAM)**.

19. C. Data dispersion is spreading data across providers, availability zones, or regions to lower the chance of data loss.

20. B. Degaussing is only effective on magnetic storage devices like tapes and **hard disk drives (HDDs)**.

21. A. HDDs are the most cost-effective storage solution for archived data (in the answer list). SSDs (in any form) are faster and more expensive. While archiving data on tape makes data retrieval slow.

22. A. Encrypting the message with the recipient's public key achieves confidentiality, while encrypting the message with your private key achieves non-repudiation.

23. B. You can calculate the number of symmetrical keys needed through the following formula $N*(N-1)/2 = number\ of\ keys$ needed.

24. B. Hashing is the best method to store passwords as it cannot be reversed. Salting improves the security of the stored passwords as it makes it more difficult to enumerate the input used to create a hash.

25. A. DLP tools can detect the disclosure of classified information through e-mail.

26. A. Tokenizing IP addresses allows the analytics process to continue (as the relations between data are maintained), but it removes the traceability to a user.

27. C. Data labeling should be undertaken after data classifications have been established. Data labeling allows an organization to identify which classification a specific data item belongs to and, hence, allows the organization to pick the correct controls.

28. D. Non-relational databases are best used to store semi-structured data.

29. A. DRM is the practice of protecting digital intellectual property. Trademarks and copyrights are some of the approaches one can take to do so.

30. A. Legal holds prevent an organization from modifying or deleting any data that has been placed in a legal hold. The applicability of legal holds is not affected by a company being web-based

31. A. Cloud service providers use HSMs to store customer keys and certificates.

32. D. Data retention, deletion, and archival policies are all important to organizations that collect data.

33. C. Tenant portioning is essential to ensure shared infrastructure cannot be used to access other tenants' data. Access control and authorization are part of tenant partitioning.

34. A. The CSP is responsible for hypervisor security (unless the customer runs the hypervisor on top of the virtualized environment provided by the CSP).

35. D. Data centers should have multiple power providers available; they should be built in geographically dispersed locations, and the political environment may influence the region's stability or the viability of a data center.

36. C. A man trap prevents tailgating by requiring that one person enters an enclosed area alone before opening the door to the room to be accessed.

37. B. Dry air can result in static electricity discharges, damaging electrical equipment like servers.

38. B. Contracting multiple power suppliers can be helpful, but oftentimes, they may rely on the same power grid. Interruptions are temporary; using a UPS can prevent systems from losing power for a short time. Back-up generators will not work immediately and are more effective for outages with a long duration.

39. A. Risk termination is not one of the risk treatment options.

40. C. The organization transfers the risks associated with hosting webservers to the CSP by using a PaaS offering to host its website.

41. A. Processors and RAM are part of the compute and storage building blocks. But are not building blocks on their own.

42. A. Risk is expressed as likelihood * impact.

43. C. Spotlights, signs, and security guards are all forms of deterring controls.

44. C. The recovery point objective represents the data lost after an incident occurs. For example, if backups are made daily, the RPO is a maximum of one day. However, if the data is backed-up weekly, the RPO can be a maximum of seven days. If data loss would impact your organization, you should implement controls to lower the RPO.

45. C. Tabletop exercises have limited impact on an organization.

46. A. The OWASP top 10 provides an overview of top vulnerabilities in web applications. The SANS top 25 applies to software applications in general. CVE and CVSS are related to describing and rating a vulnerability.

47. D. Code review, static code analysis, and code signing are all controls used in secure software development

48. B. Waterfall development does not allow for quick and frequent software releases. Due to the nature of the methodology, it is also more difficult to pivot in priorities.

49. B. Secure efforts should start in the requirements-gathering phase. Without gathering security requirements, it will be difficult to include security throughout the lifecycle successfully.

50. D. STRIDE stands for spoofing, tampering, repudiation, information disclosure, denial of service, and elevation of privilege.

51. A. Assuming another user's identity is an example of a spoofing attack.

52. C. Testing a specific function of a codebase is called **unit testing**.

53. A. White box testing provides the most extensive information, including reviewing the application code and testing using credentials.

54. B. API management can be used to expose services to external partners easily. API management allows you to convert REST to SOAP or SOAP to REST.

55. B. Dynamic application security testing is conducted on live or running applications.

56. C. Code signing is adding a signature to verify the commit's author.

57. D. Open-source software can be more secure than closed-source software. However, you must determine if the development community has sufficient security expertise. Attackers can also use open-source software contributions for nefarious purposes. This means you should always verify the security of open-source software.

58. C. A WAF can perform layer seven inspection, meaning it can evaluate the contents of a request and detect attacks like SQLi and XSS.

59. C. You need to use identity federation in combination with single sign-on technologies to let the employees log in with a single set of credentials to the different applications.

60. D. Something you have, something you are, and something you know are all factors that can be used in MFA.

61. B. MFA requires using multiple factors of a different kind. A password and a PIN code are both factors that you know. Meaning the application is not protected by MFA.

62. D. **Database activity monitoring (DAM)** will provide insight into who accesses and uses the database.

63. A. Sandboxing refers to running something in a safe and secure environment isolated from other parts of your environment.

64. D. Secrets management is the ideal place to store credentials that need to be loaded into code.

65. C. Tamper resistance and data erasure are FIPs 140-2 level four requirements.

66. B. Type 2 hypervisors are generally less secure than type-1 hypervisors because they run on top of a non-virtualization specific operating system.

67. B. VM escape attacks allow an attacker to interact with the hypervisor from a virtual machine.

68. D. The OSI model comprises the physical, datalink, network, transport, session, presentation, and application layers.

69. A. Replicating services across availability zones will allow your services to remain available if a CSP data center is unreachable. Replicating data across regions can also achieve this, but managing it is more challenging.

70. B. Using a bastion host allows an organization to limit traffic to its applications and services to the bastion host only. The bastion can then be secured effectively. Opening the vNet to the internet would increase the attack service, and using a VPN does not provide hardening of the hosts that connect to the services.

71. A. In a zero trust architecture, security controls should focus on the endpoint as the network should be considered as compromised. Encrypted communication also makes network security controls less effective.

72. D. DNS spoofing allows an attacker to fake the IP address associated with a domain name. Resulting in its victims connecting to the wrong IP address when connecting using the domain name.

73. A. Industry baselines like the CIS benchmarks are tested extensively. Building your baselines will likely result in overlooking certain applications and configurations. Additionally, it creates more maintenance work for your organization.

74. D. Vertical scaling (increasing VM resources), horizontal scaling (creating more VMs), and rate limiting are all good tools to prevent DoS.

75. A. Blue-green deployments deploy new applications and infrastructure to a new instance. Once the instance is up and running, traffic is switched from the old instance to the new one. After that, the old instance is shut down. That way, there is no downtime during deployments.

76. B. Vertical scaling is the best option for applications that cannot easily be replicated across VMs, as vertical scaling increases the capacity of a VM. At the same time, horizontal scaling creates more instances. Diagonal scaling does not exist.

77. A. An SIEM can centrally store, analyze, and correlate log files from different services to identify security incidents automatically.

78. D. Hiring and training professionals to work in a SOC is expensive and complicated. Small organizations may be better off contracting a SOC service from an external provider. Attackers do not care about work hours; your SOC should be operational 24/7.

79. D. ISO 27001 pertains to ISMS, ISO 27701 pertains to privacy, and the well-architected framework pertains to AWS.

80. C. Using a write blocker prevents data on storage devices from being altered, hence maintaining the integrity of evidence. Turning off the computer or disconnecting them from their networks can result in losing evidence.

81. D. Your organization should plan to communicate with vendors, customers, partners, regulators, and other stakeholders in the case of a breach.

82. A. Live forensics can only be conducted on equipment not powered off. Offline forensics is not a correct naming for static analysis.

83. D. Security orchestration and automated response is an approach to automatically respond to cyber incidents. SOAR might use AI and ML.

84. B. NIST defines the incident response process as, preparation, detection & analysis, containment & eradication & recovery, and post-incident activity.

85. B. The EU-US data privacy framework is a new framework with data protection requirements that ensures your organization can comply with GDPR while allowing for data transfer from the EU to the US.

86. D. The US does not have a federal data privacy act.

87. C. A job title is not considered **personal identifiable information (PII)**.

88. D. Unlimited access is not part of the generally accepted privacy principles. Rather the principle is called **access**.

89. B. An external auditor is likely more impartial than an internal auditor. External auditing is more reliable for proving compliance to other organizations.

90. A. The CSA CCM contains a set of controls that can be applied across different cloud environments. The CCM is a great starting point for determining which cloud controls your organization should implement.

91. B. A gap analysis determines the difference between the current and a desired state.

92. D. HIPAA and HITECH only apply within the US, while SOX applies to financial institutions.

93. C. Service levels are expressed as **service-level agreements** or **SLAs**. MSAs are comprehensive agreements that may govern multiple contracts. KPIs can be used to measure SLAs. At the same time, a SOW describes what work will be conducted by a vendor.

94. B. A **KRI** or **key risk indicator** is a measure that indicates important risks within an organization.

95. C. Harmonization of law is the practice of standardizing legal requirements across jurisdictions.

96. C. The CSP is the data processor, while the cloud service consumer is the data owner. The employees are data subjects.

97. A Data privacy impact assessment is required for data processing efforts that lead to automated decision-making.

98. A. Resource pooling means the hardware is shared between tenants. Sharing log files from infrastructure would reveal data about other customers and may be unlawful.

99. B. Risk appetite is the amount of risk an organization is willing to take.

100. B. A private cloud is not shared with other tenants. Hence, it can provide a higher level of security suitable for storing data with high classifications.

101. B. The principle mentioned is incorrect and should be *provide diligent and competent service to principals*.

102. B. A cloud service partner is an organization that offers cloud computing services to end customers. For example, a partner may offer to set up and maintain a public cloud environment for you.

103. C. hacktivists may target the company for the use of leather. Script kiddies target large numbers of companies without purpose, and criminal organizations may target the company for monetary gain. State actors have the least cause to attack the organization.

104. D. Cryptographic erasure is the only secure way of erasing data in the Cloud as you may not have direct access to the underlying storage devices.

105. D. CSPs offer virtualization that allows for the usage meant different OSes. For many cloud services you will never even know which OS they run on.

106. D. The cloud data lifecycle is not a fully iterative process. It may skip certain phases or return to them at a later point.

107. A. Any company should obtain a certificate of destruction when contracting external organizations for data destruction.

108. B. Data loss prevention technology can scan contents and warn users when sharing confidential information.

109. C. Data classification is essential to ensure your organization takes fitting data protection measures.

110. A. If your organization wants your special methods or approaches to remain confidential. It should treat it like a trade secret. While trade secrets have no legal protection, they limit exposure and copying by other organizations. Patents, copyrights, and trademarks may have to be registered publicly.

111. B. All other measures are excessive for basic data center security. Avoiding window placement on the main floor, however will make it more difficult to break into the data center.

112. C. Risk is expressed by probability * impact

113. D. Load balancing allows your organization to distribute load across multiple application instances.

114. D. VPNs and direct connections are both valid ways of connecting an on-premises environment to a cloud environment.

115. A. Data encryption makes it more difficult for network-based security applications to detect attacks as it would be required to decrypt traffic before inspection. Decryption is CPU intensive and may lead to some performance degradation.

116. B. CI/CD allows companies to deploy new software frequently on-demand without requiring developers to have direct access to production environments.

117. C. SCA is the process of analyzing software composition to determine its security.

118. A. REST is a communication architecture often used to communicate using JSON messages.

119. A. TLS 1.2 (or higher) can be used for secure encryption during transit.

120. D. SOX only applies to publicly traded companies. SOX does apply to foreign companies if they are publicly traded and do business in the US.

Index

Printed in Great Britain
by Amazon

38269625R00284